Atlanta

Here's what the critics say about Frommer's:

"Amazingly easy to use. Very portable, very complete."
                                        —*Booklist*

♦

"The only mainstream guide to list specific prices. The Walter Cronkite of guidebooks—with all that implies"
                                        —*Travel & Leisure*

♦

"Complete, concise, and filled with useful information."
                                        —*New York Daily News*

♦

"Hotel information is close to encyclopedic."
                                        —*Des Moines Sunday Register*

Other Great Guides for Your Trip:

Frommer's Carolinas & Georgia

Frommer's Portable Charleston & Savannah

Frommer's USA

Frommer's®

6th Edition

Atlanta

by Mary Lee

MACMILLAN • USA

ABOUT THE AUTHOR

Mary Lee, former features editor of the *Atlanta Journal-Constitution,* has spent most of her career as a newspaper reporter or editor. A firsthand witness of Atlanta's phenomenal growth, she's lived in or near the city since 1972. She has written for *Atlanta* magazine; was an assignment editor for *Seven Days in Dekalb,* a coffee-table book about a major metro Atlanta county; and was an associate editor for *The Prevailing South,* a book of essays on Southern life and politics.

MACMILLAN TRAVEL USA

A Pearson Education Macmillan Company
1633 Broadway
New York, NY 10019

Find us online at **www.frommers.com**

ISBN 0-02-862752-0
ISSN 1047-7888

Editor: Leslie Wiggins
Production Editor: Robyn Burnett
Photo Editor: Richard Fox
Design by Michele Laseau
Staff cartographers: John Decamillis and Roberta Stockwell
Front cover photo: Raffaele DeGennaro
Page Creation by John Bitter, Jerry Cole, Toi Davis, Natalie Evans, and Angel Perez

SPECIAL SALES

Bulk purchases (10+ copies) of Frommer's and selected Macmillan travel guides are available to corporations, organizations, mail-order catalogs, institutions, and charities at special discounts, and can be customized to suit individual needs. For more information write to Special Sales, Macmillan General Reference, 1633 Broadway, New York, NY 10019.

Manufactured in the United States of America

Contents

List of Maps

AN INVITATION TO THE READER

In researching this book, we discovered many wonderful places—hotels, restaurants, shops, and more. We're sure you'll find others. Please tell us about them, so we can share the information with your fellow travelers in upcoming editions. If you were disappointed with a recommendation, we'd love to know that, too. Please write to:

Mary Lee
Frommer's Atlanta, 6th Edition
Macmillan Travel
1633 Broadway
New York, NY 10019

AN ADDITIONAL NOTE

Please be advised that travel information is subject to change at any time—and this is especially true of prices. We therefore suggest that you write or call ahead for confirmation when making your travel plans. The authors, editors, and publisher cannot be held responsible for the experiences of readers while traveling. Your safety is important to us, however, so we encourage you to stay alert and be aware of your surroundings. Keep a close eye on cameras, purses, and wallets, all favorite targets of thieves and pickpockets.

WHAT THE SYMBOLS MEAN

✪ Frommer's Favorites

Our favorite places and experiences—outstanding for quality, value, or both.

The following abbreviations are used for credit cards:

AE	American Express	EC	Eurocard
CB	Carte Blanche	JCB	Japan Credit Bank
DC	Diners Club	MC	MasterCard
DISC	Discover	V	Visa
ER	EnRoute		

FIND FROMMER'S ONLINE

Arthur Frommer's **Budget Travel Guide** (**www.frommers.com**) offers more than 6,000 pages of up-to-the-minute travel information—including the latest bargains and candid, personal articles updated daily by Arthur Frommer himself. No other Web site offers such comprehensive and timely coverage of the world of travel.

Introducing Atlanta

Most visitors come to Atlanta looking for the Old South stereotypes—white-columned mansions surrounded by magnolias and owned by slow-moving folks with accents as thick as molasses. What they find is a lot more cosmopolitan and a heck of a lot more interesting.

When Gen. William Sherman burned Atlanta to the ground in 1864, the city rose from those bitter ashes and hasn't looked back since. Instead, it has spent the last 135 years or so building what's been described as the Capital of the New South and the Next Great International City. Atlanta's heritage may be Southern, but the current dynamic is brashly Sunbelt, and now it's economic vitality that drives the city's engines.

Atlanta is and always has been a city on the move. Longtime mayor William B. Hartsfield called it the city "too busy to hate," and the spirit of Atlanta is one of working together to get the job done. It is the city of Martin Luther King, Jr., father of one of the country's most important social revolutions, and of Ted Turner, who brought the world a revolution of another sort. The dramatic downtown skyline, with its gleaming skyscrapers, is testimony to Atlanta's inability to sit still—even for a minute. And its role as host for the Centennial Olympic Games in 1996 (it had already hosted Super Bowl XXVIII in 1994 and the Democratic National Convention in 1988) has finally convinced the rest of the world that Atlanta is a force to be reckoned with—and a great place to visit.

Consistently ranked as one of the best cities in the world in which to do business, Atlanta is headquarters for hundreds of corporations, including Coca-Cola, Delta Air Lines, UPS, Holiday Inn, Georgia-Pacific, Home Depot, and BellSouth and Cox Communications. A major convention city and a crossroads where three interstate highways converge, it's home to the country's second busiest airport and is the shopping capital of the Southeast. Although the city limits are only 131 square miles, the metro area is vast and sprawling. With 3.5 million in population and still counting, there seems to be no limit to its growth.

But commerce and development are not the only things that characterize this bustling metropolis. Its success is due in no small part to its quality of life, which is hard to beat. Atlanta is often called the City of Trees, and anyone who's ever strolled its streets when the

The Atlanta Region

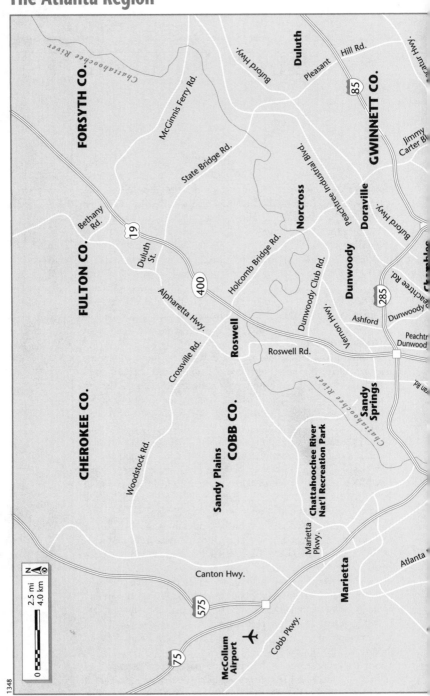

dogwoods and azaleas are in bloom knows that it has a small-town side with dozens of lush and beautiful neighborhoods and parks. A temperate climate makes it a magnet for anyone who enjoys the outdoors, and its Southern roots ensure a pleasant mix of graciousness and hospitality. As Atlanta has grown in stature, it has attracted residents from across the continent and around the world, further enriching the city's social fabric. You'll still hear gentle Southern accents here, but at least half of Atlanta's citizens were born outside the South. Those transplants, though, find themselves bending to the local customs, saying "please" and "ma'am" and holding doors open for each other.

When H. L. Mencken came south earlier in the century, he branded Atlanta a cultural wasteland. He should visit now. There are major art, science, nature, and archaeology museums, a vibrant theater community, an outstanding symphony, a well-regarded ballet company, opera, blues, jazz, Broadway musicals, a presidential library, Confederate and African-American heritage sights, and dozens of art galleries. Add to that entertainment attractions such as Georgia's Stone Mountain Park, a regional theme park, a botanical garden, and major league sports teams, and you have the makings of a lively and sophisticated city. The culinary spectrum ranges from grits and biscuits to caviar and sushi. Sure, you can still feast on fried chicken and barbecue, but Atlanta also serves up Thai, Ethiopian, and Russian cuisine.

So if you're looking for hoop skirts and plantations, it's best to just curl up with a copy of *Gone With the Wind.* But if you want to visit a vibrant, energetic city that's rich in heritage, culture, entertainment, and commerce, come have a look at Atlanta.

1 Frommer's Favorite Atlanta Experiences

- **A Step Back in Time at the Atlanta History Center.** A re-created farm (with original buildings from the 1840s) shows how rural Southern folks really lived before the Civil War. The kids can run off some steam on the walking trails after they take in the exhibits, which include hands-on discovery areas at the history museum. A great look at the rich tapestry of Atlanta's past and present.
- **Martin Luther King, Jr., Center for Nonviolent Social Change.** It's an inspiring experience to visit this living memorial to a true American hero, where you'll see lots of King memorabilia and a video display on his life and works. Especially moving is Freedom Plaza, where Dr. King is buried. The tomb is inscribed with his words: "Free at Last. Free at Last. Thank God Almighty I'm Free at Last."
- **A Day at the Ball Park.** Pack up the kids and take them out to the old ball game. Since the Braves won the World Series in 1995, baseball has become one of the hottest tickets in town. Even if there isn't a game scheduled, you can take a tour

Impressions

We're going to ride these buses desegregated in Atlanta, Georgia, or we're going to ride a chariot in heaven or push a wheelbarrow in hell.
—Rev. William Holmes Borders, civil rights leader (1957)

Atlanta is like Los Angeles was before it went bad.
—Jane Fonda, activist (1996)

of Turner Field, which was completed in 1996 and served as the Olympic Stadium for the Centennial Olympic Games before it was converted to a baseball park.

- **A Trek Through Virginia-Highland.** Atlanta's version of Soho, this trendy neighborhood is full of coffee bars, galleries, cafes, and funky little shops. It all makes for a pleasant stroll on a sunny afternoon.

- **A Frolic in the Fountain.** The biggest attraction at Centennial Olympic Park is the Fountain of Rings, where young and old can get delightfully soaked on warm days. The fountain is a simple but ingenious design on the plaza floor that consists of 251 water jets in the shape of the five Olympic rings. Take a deep breath and zip in and around the 12-foot water bursts or just sit and watch the timed light and sound effects show, when the air bursts send the water 35 to 40 feet into the air.

- **A Shopping Spree at Lenox Square.** The largest mall in the Southeast is a mecca for upscale shoppers looking for the very latest trends. It's hard to visit every store, even if you spend the whole day, but many visitors think it's a worthy goal. Great people-watching, too.

- **A High-Tech Day at SciTrek.** This see-and-do museum of science and technology is an interactive adventure that will fascinate anyone over the age of 3.

- **A Breath of Fresh Air in Piedmont Park.** Atlanta's favorite public park is fun and funky and a terrific place to watch the world go past. Take your in-line skates or pack a lunch and find a shady spot for a picnic.

- **Bargain Hunting at the Lakewood Antiques Market.** Crammed with everything from precious antiques to objets-de-junque, this huge once-a-month flea market is not to be missed if you're lucky enough to be in town on the right weekend.

- **A Chastain Park Amphitheatre Concert.** Big-name entertainers perform under the stars, and everyone brings elaborate picnic fare, complete with tablecloth and a candelabra for the picnic table. Even the entertainers seem dazzled by the setting.

- **A Morning at the Market.** Atlanta is home to two gigantic indoor farmers markets, both jammed with locals who are shopping in earnest and visitors who are having a hard time keeping their eyes from bugging out. Choose from the DeKalb Farmers Market, which has an international flavor, and Harry's, which is a little more upscale. Each has loads of gourmet goodies to take home or consume on the spot.

- **A Stroll Around Oakland Cemetery.** This 88-acre cemetery is a peaceful place, and its Victorian graves are of aesthetic, historic, and symbolic interest. The guided tour is recommended. Bring a picnic lunch.

- **A Tour of the Fox Theatre.** This Moorish-Egyptian palace exemplifies the glamorous movie-theater architecture of the 1920s, complete with onion domes, minarets, and a twinkling starlit sky over the auditorium.

- **A Tour of the World of Coca-Cola.** Atlanta is Coke's hometown, so it's only fitting that there's a monument here to the world's most renowned beverage. There's a replica of a 1930s soda fountain, a gigantic collection of memorabilia, interactive exhibits, and Club Coca-Cola, where you can sample all the beverages Coke has to offer, including many not marketed in the United States. It sounds pretty commercial, but it's all fascinating.

- **Georgia's Stone Mountain Park.** Spend a leisurely day seeing the sights, including lunch or Sunday brunch at the Evergreen Conference Center and

Atlanta's Olympic Moment

When Atlanta first bid for the Centennial Olympic Games, it was itching to prove that it was a world-class city that could put on a first-class international event. Unfortunately, the splendor of the Games was dimmed by the bombing in Centennial Olympic Park, which resulted in two deaths and scores of injuries.

Before the bombing, Atlanta was well on its way to hosting a heck of a party. The 1996 Games were the largest Olympic undertaking in history, with 11,000 athletes from 197 nations participating, and 8.5 million tickets sold—more than in Seoul and Barcelona combined. Journalists may have griped and the International Olympic Committee may have grumbled, but spectators partied in the streets and reveled in Atlanta's Southern hospitality.

The Games began with a spectacular opening ceremony, complete with a surprise appearance by the world's most famous Olympian, Muhammad Ali, who lit the Olympic torch. The citizens of Atlanta breathed a collective sigh of relief. Then, the first few days were a little rough: The weather was steamy, the computer information system was finicky, and good old American capitalism ran rampant. IOC officials complained about the street vendors hawking their wares, and the media lambasted the overwhelming corporate commercialism.

The spectators didn't seem to notice, though, as they were treated to fantastic sporting events in sparkling new venues. The airport was running like a Swiss watch, the rapid transit system recovered from its rocky start, and even the weather began to cooperate. The centerpiece of the Games became Centennial Olympic Park, where hundreds of tourists gathered day and night to celebrate, to bargain for pins (an Olympic sport in itself), and to become part of history. Parents brought their children to frolic in the Olympic fountain, and the park soon became everybody's favorite venue; you didn't even need a ticket to get in.

Yet, amid all the euphoria and pageantry, nerves were on edge; the Games began in the wake of the crash of TWA Flight 800 off Long Island, and

Resort. You can also choose from an array of activities—golf, tennis, swimming, biking, hiking, boating, and more.

- **Afternoon Tea at the Ritz-Carlton Buckhead.** It's served in the lovely mahogany-paneled lobby lounge, where an oak-log fire crackles in the hearth and a classical pianist provides soothing background music. Fresh-baked scones with fruit preserves and Devonshire cream, finger sandwiches, and English tea bread and tarts accompany pots of your favorite tea.
- **Time Travel at Fernbank Museum of Natural History.** Travel back 15 billion years and experience the "Big Bang" that heralded the formation of the universe. The museum's stunning architecture is notable. IMAX films here, too.

2 The City Today

The 1960s saw the beginning of downtown development with the rise of the million-square-foot Merchandise Mart, designed by an innovative young Atlanta architect named John Portman. It became the nucleus for the nationally renowned Peachtree Center complex. Portman's futuristic design for the downtown Hyatt Regency (1967) introduced a towering atrium-lobby concept that at the time was speculation was swirling that the jet was downed by a terrorist's bomb. Despite unprecedented levels of security in Atlanta, a pipe bomb was planted in Centennial Olympic Park. The explosion on July 27, 1996, caused two deaths and injured 111, and in an instant the glitches of the days before were overshadowed by a larger drama.

The park was closed, and for a few hours the future of the Atlanta Games seemed to be in jeopardy. Ultimately, organizers, volunteers, spectators, and athletes resolved that the Games should continue—that the Olympics should not bow to terrorism. The Games went on, and three days later Centennial Olympic Park, the symbolic heart of the Olympics, was reopened and reclaimed by even larger crowds.

As with any Olympics, the athletes took center stage—from swimmer Michelle Smith, the first Irish woman to win gold, to Fatuma Roba of Ethiopia, the first African woman ever to win a field event. For Americans, the images are dramatic and plentiful: golden-shoed Michael Johnson running 200 meters in record time; swimmer Amy Van Dyken's amazement at winning the gold; Kerri Strug's courageous vault on a badly sprained ankle; Carl Lewis's fourth victory in the long-jump; Dan O'Brien's comeback to win the decathlon; and the giddy celebrations of the women's soccer, basketball, and softball teams.

It's hard to say what Atlanta will be remembered for a decade from now. Each Olympics is marked by spellbinding performances on the playing field, and the Centennial Olympic Games had more than its share. The bombing will certainly be a lasting image, one that left Atlanta short of its promise to deliver the greatest Olympic Games in history. But along with that memory will surely come that of a city with a spirit too buoyant and determined to let anything stand in its way.

considered to be quite revolutionary. Today, Peachtree Center—a 14-city-block "pedestrian village"—comprises three Portman-designed megahotels, the Atlanta Market Center (including the International Sports/Atlanta Apparel Mart, the Atlanta Merchandise Mart, and the Atlanta Gift Mart), 200,000 square feet of retail space, many restaurants, and six massive office towers. Its various elements are connected by covered walkways and bridges.

MARTA rapid-transit trains began running in 1979, and today most of Atlanta is accessible by bus or subway.

In 1980, a revitalized black neighborhood called Sweet Auburn became a National Historic District, its 10 blocks of notable sites including Martin Luther King, Jr.'s boyhood home, his crypt, the church where he preached, a museum, and the Martin Luther King, Jr., Center for Nonviolent Social Change. It is probably *the* major black history attraction in the country, and in the last several years, it has undergone a major revitalization and restoration.

Media mogul Ted Turner inaugurated CNN here in 1980, following with Superstation TBS, Headline News, and TNT. The High Museum of Art opened its doors in 1983. And in 1989, Underground Atlanta, a retail/restaurant/entertainment complex with a historical theme, garnered national attention.

In the 1990s Atlanta continues to soar, with projects like the $214-million, 70,500-seat Georgia Dome, which attracts major sporting and entertainment events, including the Super Bowl in 2000 and basketball's Final Four in 2002 and 2007.

The city went all out in its preparations for the 1996 Olympic Games with new parks, hotels, and sports venues. In the center of downtown is the newly renovated Woodruff Park, which was spruced up to the tune of $5 million. The Olympic Village, erected just north of the central business district, now provides housing for Georgia State University students. South of the Olympic Village and stretching to CNN Center is the 21-acre Centennial Olympic Park—a major gathering place during the Olympics, with its dramatic Olympic Ring fountain, lawns, and gardens. Reopened in 1998, it regularly hosts concerts, street festivals and other cultural events and anchors the city's efforts to revitalize commercial and residential development in a once-neglected corner of downtown. The Olympic Stadium, the site of the opening and closing ceremonies as well as the track and field events, has been reincarnated as Turner Field, home of the Atlanta Braves baseball team.

Since the Olympics, Atlantans have had a little time to think about their future and how to shape it. They've always been an optimistic bunch, but the recent breakneck development, much of it connected with the Olympics, has many local citizens wondering if they have gotten too much of a good thing. The price for hosting the Olympics was high. The city was literally turned inside out for years, and commuters had to put up with vicious traffic jams as streets and highways were torn apart and massive construction projects disrupted the rhythm of everyday life.

Atlanta has had big-city problems like crime, urban blight, and clogged freeways for some time now. But the overall quality of life has been high. Now it's as if the monumental Olympics project has brought the consequences of further expansion sharply into focus. Currently the spotlight is not on growth and how to encourage it, but on growth and how to manage it. Of great concern is traffic—horrendous by any standards—and the accompanying decline in air quality. There's still enormous development in the suburbs, but everyone is rethinking the role the automobile plays and there's much discussion of how to improve public transportation and make the metro area more pedestrian-friendly. Of great significance is the recent development in downtown. For years, city leaders have tried to encourage central city living, and it's finally beginning to take hold as developers are remaking old buildings into attractive apartments and lofts. The mark of a great city is an attractive and vital downtown area where people live as well as work, and Atlanta finally appears to be headed in that direction.

Perhaps the new introspection means that a brash young city is reaching maturity. Whatever the future holds for Atlanta, its heritage is one of working together, and that's one thing that's unlikely to change.

3 History 101

Dateline

- 1782 Explorers discover Cherokee village of Standing Peachtree.

continues

It is most fitting that Atlanta in the 1990s is an international gateway and transportation hub. The city was conceived as a rail crossroads for travel north, south, east, and west, and its role as a strategic junction has always figured largely in its destiny. It all began with a peach tree.

THE STANDING PEACHTREE

Today, just about everything in Atlanta is called "Peachtree" something, but the first Peachtree reference dates back to 1782 when explorers discovered a Cherokee village on the Chattahoochee River called Standing Peachtree. Since peach trees are not native to the region, some historians maintain the village was actually named for a towering "pitch" tree (a resinous pine). Nevertheless, the Indian village became the location of Fort Peachtree, a tiny frontier outpost, during the War of 1812; a Peachtree Road connecting Fort Peachtree to Fort Daniel (in Gwinnett County) was completed by 1813.

In 1826, surveyors first suggested this area of Georgia as a practical spot for a railroad connecting the state with northern markets. This was not yet the heyday of railroads, and the report was more or less ignored for a decade. But in 1837, the state legislature approved an act establishing the Western & Atlantic Railroad here. Today a marker known as Zero Milepost in Underground Atlanta marks the W & A Railroad site around which a city grew. The new town was unimaginatively dubbed "Terminus." But future governor Alexander H. Stephens, visiting what was still dense forest in 1839, predicted that "a magnificent inland city will at no distant date be built here."

THE TRAIL OF TEARS

One aspect of the city's inception, however, was far from "magnificent." In the early 1800s, most of Georgia was still Native American territory. White settlers coveted the Cherokee and Creek lands they needed to expedite the railroad and further expand their settlements. To keep the peace, native leaders throughout the 1820s signed numerous treaties ceding millions of acres. They adopted a democratic form of government similar to the white man's, complete with a constitution and supreme court; erected schools and shops; built farms; and accepted Christianity. But the white frontierspeople cared little whether the Native Americans adapted—they wanted them to leave.

With President Andrew Jackson's support, Congress passed a bill in 1830 forcing all Southern tribes to move to lands hundreds of miles away on the other side of the Mississippi River. When the U.S. Supreme Court ruled against the order,

- **1820s** Cherokee and Creek leaders cede millions of acres to white settlers in hopes of keeping peace.
- **1837** The town, newly named Terminus, is selected as site of railroad terminus connecting Georgia with the Tennessee River. The same year, 17,000 Native Americans are forced to march westward on a "Trail of Tears."
- **1843** Terminus is renamed Marthasville.
- **1845** The first locomotive chugs into town; the city is renamed Atlanta.
- **1851** Georgia secedes from the Union, the Civil War begins, and Atlanta becomes a major Confederate supply depot and medical center.
- **1864** Union forces under Gen. William Tecumseh Sherman burn Atlanta.
- **1865** Civil War ends.
- **1877** Atlanta becomes the capital of Georgia.
- **1886** Newspaper editor Henry Grady inspires readers with vision of a "New South." John S. Pemberton introduces Coca-Cola.
- **1900** Atlanta University professor W. E. B. Du Bois founds the NAACP.
- **1904** Piedmont Park designed.
- **1917** Fire destroys 73 square blocks of the city.
- **1929** Atlanta's first airport opens; Delta Air Lines takes to the skies and becomes Atlanta's home carrier.
- **1936** Margaret Mitchell's blockbuster novel, *Gone With the Wind,* is published.
- **1939** The movie version of *Gone With the Wind* premiers in Atlanta.

continues

- 1952 The city of Atlanta incorporates surrounding areas, increasing its population by 100,000 and its size from 37 to 118 square miles.
- 1960 Sit-ins and boycotts protesting segregation begin. The million-square-foot Merchandise Mart is erected.
- 1961 Ivan Allen, Jr., defeats segregationist Lester Maddox in mayoral election. Atlanta's public schools and the Georgia Institute of Technology are peacefully desegregated.
- 1964 Atlanta native Martin Luther King, Jr., wins Nobel Peace Prize.
- 1965 106 civic and cultural leaders die in plane crash at Orly Airport in Paris; Atlanta Fulton County Stadium is built.
- 1966 Baseball's Braves move from Milwaukee and the Falcons become a new NFL expansion team. The Beatles perform in Atlanta.
- 1968 Martin Luther King, Jr., is assassinated in Memphis.
- 1974 Atlanta's first black mayor, Maynard Jackson, is inaugurated. Atlanta Brave Hank Aaron hits his record-breaking 715th home run.
- 1976 Georgian Jimmy Carter elected president. Georgia World Congress Center, the nation's largest single-floor exhibit space, is completed.
- 1979 MARTA rapid-transit train system opens.
- 1980 New Hartsfield International Airport dedicated.
- 1983 Martin Luther King, Jr.'s birthday becomes national holiday.
- 1988 Atlanta hosts Democratic National Convention.
- 1989 Underground Atlanta opens with great fanfare.

continues

Jackson ignored the ruling and backed the Georgia settlers. In 1832, the state gave away Cherokee farms in a land lottery; the white settlers assumed control over the land at gunpoint. The issue culminated in 1837, when 17,000 Native Americans were rounded up by federal soldiers, herded into camps, and forced on a cruel westward march called the "Trail of Tears." Some 4,000 died on the 800-mile journey to Oklahoma, and even those who survived suffered bitterly from cold, hunger, and disease.

Terminus and its surroundings were now firmly in the hands of the white settlers.

A CITY GROWS

Terminus soon began its evolution from a sleepy rural hamlet to a thriving city, a meeting point of major rail lines. In 1843, the town was renamed Marthasville, for ex-governor Wilson Lumpkin's daughter Martha. No one in Marthasville took note in 1844 when a 23-year-old army lieutenant, William Tecumseh Sherman, was stationed for two months in their area, but the knowledge he gained of local geography would vitally affect the city's history two decades later. The first locomotive, the *Kentucky,* chugged into town in 1845, and shortly thereafter the name Marthasville was deemed too provincial for a burgeoning metropolis. J. Edgar Thomson, the railroad's chief engineer, suggested Atlanta (a feminized form of Atlantic).

In 1848, the newly incorporated city held its first mayoral election, an event marked by dozens of street brawls. Moses W. Formwalt, a maker of stills and member of the Free and Rowdy Party, was elected over temperance candidate John Norcross. But if Atlanta was a bit of a wild frontier town, it also had civic pride. An 1849 newspaper overstated things poetically:

> *Atlanta, the greatest spot in all the nation, The greatest place for legislation, Or any other occupation The very center of creation.*

STORM CLOUDS GATHER: ANTEBELLUM ATLANTA

By the middle of the 19th century, the 31-state nation was in the throes of a westward expansion, and the institution of slavery was a major issue of the day. In his 1858 debate with Stephen Douglas, Abraham Lincoln declared, "This government cannot endure permanently half slave and half free." A year later it was obvious that only a war would resolve the issue. In 1861 (a year that began dramatically in Atlanta—with an earthquake), Georgia legislators voted for secession and joined the Confederacy.

In peacetime, the railroads had fashioned Atlanta into a center of commerce. In wartime, this transportation hub would emerge as a major Confederate military post and supply center—the vital link between Confederate forces in Tennessee and Virginia. Federal forces early on saw the city's destruction as essential to Northern victory.

On a lighter note, Atlanta made the following ridiculous bid to become the capital of the Confederacy: "The city has good railroad connections, is free from yellow fever, and can supply the most wholesome foods and, as for 'goobers,' an indispensable article for a Southern legislator, we have them all the time." The lure of plentiful peanuts not withstanding, the Confederacy chose Richmond, Virginia, as its capital.

- **1992** Atlanta completes the new 70,500-seat Georgia Dome.
- **1994** Atlanta hosts Super Bowl XXVIII at the Georgia Dome.
- **1995** On their third try, the Atlanta Braves win the World Series.
- **1996** Atlanta completes the 85,000-seat Olympic Stadium and hosts the Centennial Olympic Games.
- **1997** Atlanta reopens Olympic Stadium as the new Turner Field, home of the Atlanta Braves baseball team.
- **1998** A renovated Centennial Olympic Park opens as a major city gathering spot and a lasting legacy of the Centennial Olympic Games.

A CITY BURNS

Atlanta was not only a major Southern supply depot, it was also the medical center of the Confederacy. Throughout the city, buildings were hastily converted into makeshift hospitals and clinics, and trains pulled into town daily to disgorge sick and wounded soldiers. By 1862, close to 4,000 soldiers were convalescing here, and the medical crisis was further aggravated by a smallpox epidemic.

That same year, Union spy James J. Andrews and a group of Northern soldiers disguised as civilians seized a locomotive called the *General,* with the aim of blocking supply lines by destroying tracks and bridges behind them. A wild train chase ensued, and the raiders were caught and punished (most, including Andrews, were executed). The episode came to be known as the "Great Locomotive Chase," one of the stirring stories of the Civil War and the subject of two subsequent movies. The *General* is today on view at the Big Shanty Museum in Kennesaw.

The locomotive chase was an Atlanta victory, but the Northern desire to destroy the Confederacy's supply link remained intact. In 1864, Gen. Ulysses S. Grant ordered Major Gen. William T. Sherman to "move against Johnston's army to break it up, and get into the interior of the enemy's country as far as you can, inflicting all the damage you can against their resources."

Georgians had great faith that the able and experienced Gen. Joseph E. Johnston, whom they called "Old Joe," would repel the Yankees. As Sherman's Georgia campaign got under way, an overly optimistic editorial in the *Intelligencer* scoffed at the notion of Federal conquest, claiming "we have no fear of the results, for General Johnston and his great and invincible satellites are working out the problem of battle and victory at the great chess board at the front." Johnston himself was not as sanguine. Sherman had 100,000 men to his 60,000, and the Union troops were better armed.

By July, Sherman was forcing the Confederate troops back, and Atlanta's fall seemed a foregone conclusion; Johnston informed Confederate President Jefferson Davis that he was outnumbered almost two to one and was in a defensive position. His candid assessment was not appreciated, and Davis removed him from command, replacing him with the pugnacious 32-year-old Gen. John Bell Hood. The

Impressions

No one goes anywhere without passing through Atlanta.
—Francis C. Lawley, *London Times* reporter (1861)

I want to say to General Sherman, who is an able man . . . though some people think he is kind of careless about fire, that from the ashes he left us in 1864 we have raised a brave and beautiful city; that we have caught the sunshine in our homes and built therein not one ignoble prejudice or memory.
—Henry Grady, *Atlanta Constitution* editor (1886)

change of leadership only further demoralized the ranks, and Sherman openly rejoiced when he heard the news.

Some disgruntled Confederate soldiers deserted. Hood abandoned the defensive tactics of Johnston, aggressively assaulting his opponent. His policy cost thousands of troops and gained nothing. In the Battle of Peachtree Creek on July 20, 1864, Union casualties totaled 1,710; Confederate, 4,796. Throughout the summer, the city suffered a full-scale artillery assault. More than 8,000 Confederates perished in the Battle of Atlanta on July 22, while Union deaths totaled just 3,722. And after hours of fierce fighting on July 28, the Confederates had lost another 5,000 men; the Federals, 600. The Yankees further paralyzed the city by ripping up train rails, heating them over huge bonfires, and twisting them around trees into useless spirals of mangled iron that came to be known as "Sherman's neckties." The most devastating bombardment came on August 9—"that red day . . . when all the fires of hell, and all the thunders of the universe, seemed to be blazing and roaring over Atlanta."

By September 1, when Hood's troops pulled out of the area, first setting fire to vast stores of ammunition (and anything else that might benefit the Yankees), the town was in turmoil: Its roads were crowded with evacuees, and its hospitals, hotels, and private residences were flooded with wounded men. Crime and looting were rife, and food was almost unavailable; the price of a ham-and-eggs breakfast with coffee soared to $25. Rooftops were ripped off houses and buildings, there were huge craters in the streets, and many civilians were dead. The railroads were in Sherman's hands.

On September 2, Mayor James M. Calhoun, carrying a white flag to the nearest Federal unit, officially surrendered the city. The U.S. Army entered and occupied Atlanta, raising the Stars and Stripes at city hall for the first time in four years. Claiming he needed the city for military purposes, Sherman ordered all residents to evacuate. Atlantans piled their household goods on wagons and, abandoning their homes and businesses, became refugees. Before departing Atlanta in November, Union troops leveled railroad facilities and burned the city, leaving it a wasteland—defunct as a military center and practically uninhabitable. The Yankees marched out of the city to the strains of "The Battle Hymn of the Republic."

In January 1865, there was $1.64 in the treasury, the railroad system was destroyed, and most of the city was burned to the ground.

A CITY REBUILDS

Slowly, exiled citizens began to trickle back into Atlanta. Confederate money was worthless. At the inauguration of his second term in 1865, Lincoln pledged "malice toward none, charity for all"—but after his assassination later that year, this policy was replaced with one of harsh Republican vengeance. It wasn't until 1876 that Federal troops were withdrawn and Atlanta was freed from military occupation.

Still, the city was making a remarkable recovery. Like the ever-resilient Scarlett O'Hara ("It takes more than Yankees or a burning to keep me down"), Atlanta rolled up its sleeves and began rebuilding. A Northern newspaper reported, "From all this ruin and devastation a new city is springing up . . . the streets are alive from morning till night with drays and carts and hand-barrows and wagons . . . with loads of lumber and loads of brick."

In postwar years, Atlanta was filled with carpetbaggers and adventurers hoping to turn a quick buck, and with them came gambling houses, brothels, and saloons. But the city also boasted hundreds of new stores and businesses, churches, schools, banks, hotels, theaters, and a new newspaper, the *Atlanta Constitution*. Blacks chartered Atlanta University in 1867, today the world's largest predominantly black institution of higher learning. Moreover, the railroads were operative once again. Newspaper editor Henry Grady inspired readers with his vision of an industrialized and culturally advanced "New South." He was Atlanta's biggest civic booster. A new constitution in 1877 made Atlanta the permanent capital of the state of Georgia. Two years later, General Sherman visited the city he had destroyed and was welcomed with a ball and, lest he get any funny ideas, a grand military review.

In 1886, a new headache cure was introduced to the city—a syrup made from the cocoa leaf and the kola nut, which would eventually become the world's most renowned beverage, Coca-Cola. Atlanta adopted the symbol of a phoenix rising from the ashes for its official seal in 1888 and, the following year, dedicated the gold-domed state capitol and opened a zoo in Grant Park. Piedmont Park was built in 1904 as the site of the Cotton States and International Exposition—a $2.5-million world's fair–like extravaganza with entertainments ranging from Buffalo Bill and His Wild West Show to international villages. Former slave Booker T. Washington gave a landmark address, and John Philip Sousa composed the "King Cotton March" to mark the event.

THE TWENTIETH CENTURY

At the turn of the century, Atlanta's population was 90,000, a figure that more than doubled two decades later. Though a massive fire destroyed almost 2,000 buildings in 1917, the city was on a course of rapid growth. In 1929, Atlanta opened its first airport on the site of today's Hartsfield International, presaging the growth of a major air-travel industry. The same year, Delta Air Lines took to the skies and became Atlanta's home carrier.

Margaret Mitchell's blockbuster Civil War epic *Gone With the Wind*, which went on to become the world's second-best-selling book (after the Bible) and the basis for the biggest-grossing picture of all time, was published in 1936. Louis B. Mayer turned down a chance to make the film version for MGM, because "no Civil War picture ever made a nickel."

A more dire legacy of the Civil War and the institution of slavery was racial strife, and the early years of the 20th century were marked by violent race riots. Atlanta University professor W. E. B. Du Bois founded the NAACP in 1900. In 1939, black cast members were unable to attend the glamorous premiere of *Gone With the Wind* because the theater was segregated. And as late as 1960, segregation in Atlanta (as everywhere in the South) was still firmly entrenched and backed by state law. Unlike much of the South, though, the city has, for the most part, adopted a progressive attitude regarding race relations. Even before the civil rights movement there were black advancements—the hiring of black police officers, the election of a black to the Atlanta Board of Education, the desegregation of a public golf course in 1955, and, in 1959, the desegregation of public transit. Mayor Bill Hartsfield (who held office for almost three decades) called Atlanta "a city too busy to hate." And his successor, Mayor Ivan Allen, Jr., called on Atlantans to face race problems "and seek the answers in an atmosphere of decency and dignity."

Atlanta peacefully desegregated its public schools and the Georgia Institute of Technology in 1961. Atlanta native Dr. Martin Luther King, Jr., headquartered his Southern Christian Leadership Conference here and made Ebenezer Baptist Church, which he co-pastored with his father, a hub of the civil rights movement. In 1974, Atlanta inaugurated its first black mayor, Maynard Jackson, and, following a term by another black mayor, Andrew Young, Jackson was reelected.

In 1966, Atlanta went major league when the Braves and the Falcons came to town. Atlantans went wild in 1974 when Hank Aaron broke Babe Ruth's home-run record here.

4 Famous Atlantans

Henry Louis "Hank" Aaron (b. 1934)   An outfielder with the Milwaukee (later Atlanta) Braves, Aaron broke Babe Ruth's record in 1974 with his 715th home run, in Atlanta–Fulton County Stadium. He remained cool and dignified in the face of the media frenzy surrounding his pursuit of the record, despite receiving countless death threats and bags of hate mail from bigots who felt that Ruth's achievement should never be surpassed by a black man. He retired in 1976 with 755 homers.

Henry W. Grady (1850–89)   Managing editor of the *Atlanta Constitution,* Grady preached post–Civil War reconciliation, and he worked passionately to draw Northern capital and diversified industry to the agrarian South. His name is synonymous with the phrase "The New South."

Joel Chandler Harris (1848–1908)   Called "Georgia's Aesop," he created Uncle Remus, the wise black raconteur of children's fables. His tales of Br'er Rabbit and Br'er Fox were the basis for Disney's delightful animated feature *Song of the South.*

Elton John (b. 1947)   The career of this ever-popular singer-songwriter soared after his stirring tribute to Princess Diana at her funeral. He maintains an apartment in a Peachtree Road high-rise in Buckhead and can be seen around the neighborhood when he's in town.

Robert Tyre "Bobby" Jones (1902–71)   Golf's only Grand Slam winner, he was the founder of the Masters Tournament. Jones has been called the world's greatest golfer; he retired from the game in 1930 but his record remains unsurpassed. He also held academic degrees in engineering, law, and English literature.

Martin Luther King, Jr. (1929–68)   Civil rights leader, minister, orator, and Nobel Peace Prize winner, King preached Gandhi's doctrine of passive resistance.

Margaret Mitchell (1900–49)   Author of the definitive Southern blockbuster novel, *Gone With the Wind.* Originally a journalist, Mitchell began writing "the book" in 1926 when a severe ankle injury forced her to give up reporting. *GWTW* is, next to the Bible, the world's best-selling book.

John C. Portman (b. 1924)   Architect/developer who revolutionized hotel design in the United States with his lofty atrium-lobby concept and almost single-handedly designed Atlanta's skyline in the 1960s. He has been called "Atlanta's one-man urban-renewal program."

Impressions

It stinks, I don't know why I bother with it, but I've got to have something to do with my time.

—Margaret Mitchell, author of *Gone With the Wind*

Gone With the Wind is very possibly the greatest American novel.

—*Publishers Weekly*

Robert Edward "Ted" Turner III (b. 1938)   Dubbed "the mouth of the South," America's most dynamic media mogul, Ted Turner, created 24-hour cable news networks CNN and Headline News, along with entertainment networks Superstation TBS and TNT. Turner is vice chairman of Time-Warner Inc. and owns a portion of MGM and the Atlanta Braves and Atlanta Hawks; his high-profile wife is activist and former actress Jane Fonda.

Alfred Uhry (b. 1936)   One of the winningest present-day playwrights (an Oscar, a Tony, and a Pulitzer Prize), Uhry, who was born and reared in Atlanta and spent much of his adult life here, has since moved away from the city. But he still has Atlanta on his mind. Many of his plays, the most notable of which are "Driving Miss Daisy" and "The Last Night of Ballyhoo," take place in Atlanta. As a student at Druid Hills High School in the mid-1950s, Uhry had early scripts produced there, including one about rural life that was upstaged by a boisterous live chicken.

Robert W. Woodruff (1889–1985)   Coca-Cola Company president, philanthropist, and leading Atlanta citizen for over half a century. He put Coca-Cola on the map worldwide; promoted civil rights; and gave over $400 million to Atlanta educational, artistic, civil, and medical projects such as Emory University, the Woodruff Arts Center, and the High Museum.

2

Planning a Trip to Atlanta

In the pages that follow, you'll find everything you need to know to handle the practical details of planning your trip in advance—airlines, a calendar of events, visitor information, and more.

1 Visitor Information

As soon as you know you're going to Atlanta, write or call the **Atlanta Convention & Visitors Bureau (ACVB)**, 233 Peachtree St. NE, Suite 2000, Atlanta, GA 30303 (☎ **404/222-6688**). They'll send you a copy of *Atlanta Now* (a visitors' guide), a book of discount coupons, a *Metro Atlanta Map and Attractions Guide*, and a two-month calendar of events; they can also advise you on anything from Atlanta's hotel and restaurant scene to the best tour packages available. You can call weekdays between 8:30am and 5:30pm or visit the ACVB Web site at www.acvb.com.

2 Money

Finding a place to withdraw money is not very difficult in Atlanta: Automated teller machines (ATMs) are located at virtually every bank in the city, and credit cards are widely accepted (but watch out for smaller restaurants that only accept cash). Traveler's checks, however, are less necessary because Atlanta has 24-hour ATMs linked to a national network that most likely includes your bank at home. **Cirrus** (☎ **800/424-7787** or 800/4CIRRUS) and **PLUS** (☎ **800/843-7587**) are the two most popular networks; check the back of your ATM card to see which network your bank belongs to. The 800 numbers will give you specific locations of ATMs where you can withdraw money while on vacation.

Still, if you feel you need the security of traveler's checks and don't mind the hassle of showing identification every time you want to cash a check, you can get them at almost any bank. U.S.-dollar traveler's checks are also widely accepted for goods and services, and they can be exchanged at banks and check-issuing offices. **American Express** offers checks in denominations of $10, $20, $50, $100, $500, and $1,000. You'll pay a service charge ranging from 1 to 4%, though AAA members can obtain checks without a fee at most AAA offices. You can also get American Express traveler's checks over the phone by calling ☎ **800/221-7282;** Amex gold and platinum cardholders who call this number are exempt from the 1% fee.

What Things Cost in Atlanta	U.S. $
Taxi from airport to downtown, for one person	$18
Shuttle bus from airport to downtown	$10
MARTA bus or rail fare	$1.50
Double at the Ritz-Carlton, Buckhead (very expensive)	$175–$320
Double at Homewood Suites (expensive)	$125–$185
Double at the Comfort Inn downtown (moderate)	$79–$179
Double at Cheshire Motor Inn (inexpensive)	$62–$68
Three-course dinner at the City Grill, including wine, tax, and tip (very expensive)	$45 and up
Three-course dinner at Babette's Cafe, including wine, tax, and tip (expensive)	$35 and up
Three-course dinner at Indigo Coastal Grill, including wine, tax, and tip (moderate)	$25 and up
Three-course dinner at Pasta Vino, including wine, tax, and tip (inexpensive)	$15 and up
Theater ticket at the Alliance	$17–$36

Visa also offers traveler's checks, available at Citibank locations across the country and at several other banks. The service charge ranges between 1.5 and 2%; checks come in denominations of $20, $50, $100, $500, and $1,000. **MasterCard** also offers traveler's checks. Call ☎ **800/223-9920** for a location near you.

See the "Money" section in chapter 3 for currency and other information that will be useful to visitors from other countries.)

3 When to Go

Although there is no high season for tourism here, Atlanta is a major convention and trade show destination. Before choosing travel dates, it's wise to ask the ACVB or your travel agent what major events will be taking place in Atlanta when you plan to visit. Large conventions can mean an increase in hotel prices and longer waits at popular restaurants.

Spring and autumn are long seasons, and in terms of natural beauty and moderate temperatures, they're ideal times to visit. April, when the dogwoods and azaleas put on a brilliant, colorful display, is especially lovely, but May and October are excellent months here, too.

If you come during July and August, when Atlanta begins to get a little steamy, you may find that some hotels offer summer discounts, and almost all offer reduced rates during the Christmas holiday season.

THE WEATHER
Atlanta's climate is mostly temperate year-round. The city enjoys four distinct seasons, but the variations are less extreme than elsewhere.

It does get cold here in winter. The mercury dips below freezing—usually at night—an average of 50 days a year, and at least once a year there's a snowfall or an ice storm. (Northern transplants think it's pretty hilarious the way an inch or two of snow can paralyze the city.) But for the most part, winter days are mild, and it's often possible to enjoy the parks and even the outdoor restaurants in the middle of January or February.

Don't let the average daytime temperatures for July, August, and early September fool you. Summers can be hot and humid, with daytime highs reaching into the 90s, although the really stifling spells usually last just a few days at a time. Annual rainfall is about 48 inches, and the wettest months are December through April, and July.

Atlanta's Average Daytime Temperature & Rainfall

	Jan	Feb	Mar	Apr	May	June	July	Aug	Sept	Oct	Nov	Dec
Temp. °F	45	46	52	60	69	77	79	79	73	63	52	43
Rainfall (in.)	4.4	4.5	5.3	4.4	3.1	3.8	4.7	3.6	3.2	2.4	2.9	4.3

ATLANTA CALENDAR OF EVENTS

Note: Some events, such as the Georgia Renaissance Festival and the Georgia Shakespeare Festival, begin in one month and continue for several months thereafter. These are listed in the month of inception. So do look back a few months prior to your visit for ongoing events. The ACVB's Web site also offers a terrific calendar of events.

January

- **Martin Luther King Week.** This is a major happening, comprising more than 30 events. It begins with an interfaith service and includes plays, musical tributes, seminars, films, a parade down Peachtree Street to Auburn Avenue, and speeches by notables (including Coretta Scott King). There are also concerts by major performers (in past years Stevie Wonder and the Neville Brothers, among others). For details, contact the **King Center** (☎ **404/526-8900**). Second week of the month.

- **Atlanta Garden and Patio Show.** This 4-day event at the Galleria Centre in Cobb County showcases products and services for home gardens and patios. There are several landscaped gardens to tantalize you, and everything from birdfeeders and plants to statuary and how-to books. Admission is $8 for adults, $3 for children 6–12, under 6 free. For details, call ☎ **770/998-9800.** Usually at the end of the month.

- **Cathedral Antiques Show.** For 4 days, 30 to 35 dealers of high-quality antiques display their wares at the Cathedral of St. Philip, 2744 Peachtree Rd. The merchandise ranges from 18th- and 19th-century furnishings to vintage jewelry and Oriental rugs. Admission is $8 per day. On the first day of the show, there's a tour of homes and mansions in Buckhead for an additional fee. For details, call ☎ **404/365-1000.** Last week in January.

February

- ✪ **Southeastern Flower Show.** One of the South's premier gardening events takes place indoors at City Hall East (640 North Ave.) for 5 days. It offers 3 acres of stunning landscapes and gardens displaying both flowers and vegetables. Garden-related products are sold, and there are photography exhibitions, events for children, and demonstrations of gardening techniques. Admission is $12 for adults, with discounts for seniors and children. For information, call ☎ **404/888-5638.** Mid-month.

March
- **High Museum Atlanta Wine Auction.** Events begin with a gala champagne reception and formal dinner on Friday night. On Saturday, you can discuss wines with prominent winemakers and sample premium wines and gourmet fare prepared by Atlanta's finest chefs. The event culminates with the auctioning off of great wines, fabulous trips, wine dinners, and artwork. Admission to the gala is $250. Tickets for the vintner's reception auction are $200 per couple, $100 per person. Tickets are by invitation only. To be added to the invitation list, call **404/733-4424** as far in advance as possible. Last weekend of the month.
- **Atlanta Home Show.** This huge 4-day event at the Georgia World Congress Center emphasizes home improvement, remodeling, and interior design. There are usually more than 1,000 booths representing the latest in home and garden products and services. Admission is $8 for adults, $7 for senior citizens, $2 for children 7–12, under 6 free. Call ☎ **770/998-9800** for details. At the end of the month.

April
○ **Atlanta Dogwood Festival.** Held in Piedmont Park, this huge festival includes concerts, food booths, kite-flying contests, children's activities, a juried arts and crafts show, canine Frisbee championships, and Earth Day presentations by environmental groups. Particularly exciting is the display of hot-air balloons. For details, call ☎ **404/329-0501.** Three days in mid-April.
- **Easter Sunrise Services.** Held at the top and the base of Georgia's Stone Mountain at 6am. Park gates open at 4am and the skylift begins operation at 5am. For details, call ☎ **770/498-5690.**
- **Lasershow.** This sight-and-sound spectacular of laser lights and fireworks, held at Stone Mountain Park, is choreographed to popular, patriotic, country, and classical music. Admission is free, but you must pay for a parking permit to the park. For details, call ☎ **770/498-5690.** It begins on April weekends (Friday, Saturday, and Sunday nights at 9pm). From early May through Labor Day, Lasershow can be seen nightly at 9:30pm, and then it resumes its Friday through Saturday schedule through October.
- **Inman Park Spring Festival.** This Atlanta suburb is noted for its gorgeous turn-of-the-century Victorian mansions and Craftsman-style cottages. Activities include a tour of homes, live entertainment (theater, jazz bands, cloggers, Irish music, country music, and more), an arts-and-crafts festival/flea market, a parade, and food vendors. Tickets to the tour of homes are $10 in advance, $12 the day of the tour. All other events are free. For more information, call ☎ **770/242-4895.** Last weekend in April.
○ **Georgia Renaissance Festival Spring Celebration.** This re-creation of a 16th-century English county fair (held in Fairburn—8 miles south of the airport on I-85, Exit 12) in a 30-acre "village" features a juried crafts show with over 100 craftspeople (many of them demonstrating 16th-century skills); continuous entertainment on 12 stages (there are more than 100 shows each day); period foods; a birds of prey show; and a cast of costumed characters including jousting knights, jugglers, storytellers, giant stilt-walkers, minstrels, magicians, and choral groups. King Henry VIII and one of his wives oversee the festivities. Admission is $12.95 for adults, $11 for senior citizens, $5.75 for ages 6–12, 5 and under free. For details, call ☎ **770/964-8575.** On eight weekends, from the next to last Saturday in April through the first Sunday in June (plus Memorial Day).

- **Black College Spring Break** (also called Freaknik). The city plays host to tens of thousands of college students who come to Atlanta for one last party before final exams. (Unfortunately, most of them bring their cars and cruise around town looking for fun, which causes massive traffic jams in Buckhead, Midtown, and downtown.) A weekend near the end of April.

May

- **Gardens for Connoisseurs Tour.** If you're a gardening buff this is an excellent tour, allowing you a peek into 11 outstanding private gardens. Tickets, which benefit the Atlanta Botanical Garden, are $20 for the entire tour, $5 per garden. For details, call ☎ **404/876-5859.** Weekend of Mother's Day.

- ✪ **Music Midtown—An Atlanta Festival.** This terrific festival takes place in Midtown. Events—beginning Friday night—include dozens of concerts on seven stages (many of them big-name performers such as the Indigo Girls, Etta James, Al Green, Joan Baez, and blues artist Buddy Guy), a Southeastern artists' market, and 40 food booths from regional restaurants. There are kids' activities, too, from live performances to hands-on activities. Admission is $20 for 1 day, $30 for all 3 days; free for children under 10 accompanied by an adult. You may buy tickets at the gate, but they're also available through TicketMaster at ☎ **404/249-6400.** Call ☎ **770-MIDTOWN** or contact www.musicmidtown.com for locations and more information. Usually at the beginning of May.

- ✪ **Decatur Arts Festival and Garden Tour.** This 3-day event features an art show on the south lawn of the Old Courthouse in Decatur, various juried shows nearby, a garden tour, mimes, jugglers, puppet shows, clowns, children's art activities, great food, and performances by music, dance, and theater groups. The literary arts are celebrated with storytelling, readings, and book signings. Events are free, except for the garden tour, which is $10 for eight gardens. For details, call ☎ **404/371-8386.** Memorial Day weekend.

- **A Taste of the South.** This happening at Stone Mountain Park has music, dance, regional foods (everything from collard greens to grits to a BBQ cook-off), arts, crafts demonstrations, music, and more. For details, call ☎ **770/498-5690.** Four days, including Memorial Day weekend.

- **Atlanta Jazz Festival.** Free ongoing concerts in Piedmont Park. The afternoon begins with local performers and goes on to major stars by evening—for example, Wynton Marsalis, Nancy Wilson, Shirley Horn, Cyrus Chestnut, Max Roach, and Sonny Rollins. Take MARTA to the Midtown station and arrive early to get a good space. Some years, there's also a concert (admission is charged) featuring major jazz artists at the Chastain Park Amphitheatre at Powers Ferry Road and Stella Drive. For details call the **Festival Hotline** at ☎ **404/817-6851** or the city's **Bureau of Cultural Affairs** at ☎ **404/817-6815** www.bcaatlanta. org. Memorial Day weekend.

- **Atlanta Film & Video Festival.** The IMAGE Film/Video Center, 75 Bennett St. NW (and other Atlanta theaters), features more than 150 films and videos by some of the country's most important independent media artists. Admission is $7.50 per film, with discounts available for students and seniors. Call ☎ **404/352-4225** for details. Eight days in May or June.

- **Kingfest.** Held annually between mid-May and mid-June, Kingfest features music, theatrical performances, a kids' day, and many other events. For more information, call the Martin Luther King, Jr., Center for Nonviolent Social Change at ☎ **404/524-1956.**

June

✪ **Georgia Shakespeare Festival.** Five productions are held mid-June through December on the campus of Oglethorpe University, 4484 Peachtree Rd., in an intimate 510-seat theater. Before the summer performances, audiences enjoy farcical vignettes on the lawn. Everyone brings a pre-performance picnic or arranges in advance to purchase it on the premises. The company, made up of Actors Equity pros for the most part, offers both traditional and innovative Shakespearean productions as well as other classics. Picnic grounds open an hour and a half before summer performances, and the pre-show begins 1 hour before curtain time. There are both matinees and evening performances. Admission is $18 to $24 for adults, $3 less for seniors and students. Call for tickets as far in advance as possible, especially for weekend performances. For information about tickets or picnic lunches, call ☎ **404/264-0020.**

• **Stone Mountain Village Annual Arts & Crafts Festival.** This family-oriented festival has something for everyone. More than 125 Southeastern craftspeople display their wares in a juried show, and entertainment (cloggers, clowns, country music, and more) is offered continually in the Village. There are food booths and lots of activities for kids. Admission is $1 for adults, free for children under 12. For details, call ☎ **770/879-4971.** Father's Day weekend.

• **Atlanta Pride Celebration.** There are events all month long, but most of them take place in Piedmont Park on the last weekend of the month. They include musical entertainment, an artists' market, and a parade from a downtown site (selected annually) to the park. For details, call ☎ **888/ATL-PRIDE.**

July

• **Asian Cultural Experience.** The Atlanta Botanical Garden celebrates Asian culture with demonstrations of crafts, musical performances, children's activities, an art show, and dancing, among other things. Admission is included with Garden admission price. For details, call ☎ **404/876-5859.** A weekend in early July.

• **Independence Day.** If you're willing to get up early on July 4, you can start the day's celebrations by watching 50,000 runners take part in the **Peachtree Road Race,** a 10K run down Peachtree Road from Lenox Square to Piedmont Park. For details, call ☎ **404/231-9064.**

Independence Day is celebrated at Georgia's Stone Mountain Park's 3-day **Fantastic Fourth Celebrations**—a star-spangled festival of free concerts, sports competitions, patriotic music, clogging, choreographed fireworks displays, and laser shows. For details, call ☎ **770/498-5690.**

An old-fashioned **Fourth of July Parade,** complete with floats, bands, baton twirlers, cloggers and barbecue, also takes place in Stone Mountain Village, from Mountain Street at the foot of the west gate of Stone Mountain Park along Main Street through the Village shop area. The stores are open, and there's free watermelon for everyone. The parade begins at 10am, preceded by a 5K run at 7am. There are fireworks in the Village at night. For details, call ☎ **770/879-4971.**

About 100,000 people gather every July 4th at Underground Atlanta for a multicultural celebration featuring live entertainment from a variety of cultural backgrounds. Call ☎ **404/523-2311** for details.

• **South's Largest Children's Festival.** This month-long event at Stone Mountain Park, in cooperation with Nickelodeon, The Cartoon Network, and LEGO, to name a few, incorporate live entertainment, interactive displays such as climbing walls, LEGO building, and other attractions. The sandcastle building event, sponsored by the Guinness Book of World Records, usually yields a record-breaker. Call ☎ **770/498-5690** for details and admission prices. Usually begins Fourth of July weekend.

✪ **National Black Arts Festival.** More than 150 events (most of them free) take place throughout the city. Billed as "a celebration of the arts of the African Diaspora," it features concerts (including big names like Abbey Lincoln and Wynton Marsalis), theater, film, dance, storytelling, poetry readings, performance art, art and folk-art exhibitions, children's activities, and African puppet shows, and that's not the half of it. For details call ☎ **404/730-7315.** A 7- to 10-day affair (even-numbered years only) in late July and early August.

August

✪ **Folk Fest.** One of the Southeast's most interesting art shows, highlighting self-taught American and international artists. More than 70 galleries and art centers are represented, showing a great variety of paintings, pottery, wood carvings, quilting, and much more. Folk Fest takes place at the North Atlanta Trade Center in suburban Gwinnett County, about 20 minutes up I-85 North at Indian Trail Road (Exit 38). Admission Friday night (for the show's opening, when you can meet many of the artists) is $15, but your ticket is good for the entire weekend. Admission Saturday and Sunday is $6; parking is free. For information, call ☎ **770/932-1000.** Third weekend in August.

September

• **Montreux Atlanta Music Festival.** Jazz, blues, gospel, reggae, and zydeco music performed in Centennial Olympic Park and Piedmont Park. Both regional and internationally known artists perform. All events are free. Call the **Festival Hotline** at ☎ **404/817-6851** or the city's **Bureau of Cultural Affairs** at ☎ **404/817-6815.** www.bcaatlanta.org. A 4-day affair (including Labor Day).

• **Art in the Park.** This Labor Day weekend art show on the historic square in Marietta, just northwest of Atlanta, offers fine art by more than 120 artists, plus food and antiques. Free. Call ☎ **770/429-1115** for details.

• **Yellow Daisy Festival.** Georgia's Stone Mountain Park hosts a vast outdoor arts-and-crafts show (more than 400 exhibitors) with musical entertainment, a flower show, great food, storytellers, and puppetry. About 175,000 people attend each year. For details, call ☎ **770/498-5690.** Early September.

• **Atlanta Home Show.** This 4-day event at the Cobb Galleria Centre is the smaller autumn version of the home show held in the spring at the Georgia World Congress Center. It emphasizes products and services for home improvement, remodeling, and interior design. Admission is $8 for adults, $7 for senior citizens, $2 for children 7–12, under 6 free. Call ☎ **770/998-9800** for details. At the end of September or the beginning of October.

October

• **American Association of University Women's Annual Book Fair.** At this 4-day event in Lenox Square mall, the AAUW collects and categorizes over 75,000 used books each year for the fair. All are in good condition, some are valuable, and prices are low. Proceeds go to scholarships for women. Admission is free. Hours are 10am to 9:30pm. Call ☎ **404/355-1861** for details. Held in early October.

• **Miller Lite Chili Cook-off.** At Georgia's Stone Mountain Park, you can sample hundreds of varieties of chili, Brunswick stew, and cornbread. Entertainment varies each year but will likely include cloggers, country music, jalapeño-eating contests, and other folksy fun. For details, call ☎ **770/498-5690.** Cost is $7 and Stone Mountain Park parking fee. A weekend day early in the month.

- **Annual Scottish Festival and Highland Games.** This gathering of the clans at Stone Mountain comprises 3 days of military tattoos, Highland dancers, pipe and drum concerts, Scottish harping and fiddling, sword dancing, reels, lilts, and athletic events such as the hammer throw and caber toss. For details and admission charges, call ☎ **770/498-5690.** Mid-month.
- **Georgia Renaissance Fall Festival.** This 16th-century fair is the autumn complement to the spring celebration described above (see April listing for details). All of its offerings are the same, but since it's in October, a haunted house is added to the attractions and stores are geared up for holiday shopping. Admission is $12.95 for adults, $11 for senior citizens, $5.75 for ages 6–12, 5 and under free. For details, call ☎ **770/964-8575.** Five weekends in October and early November.
- **Sunday in the Park at Oakland Cemetery.** On an annually selected October Sunday this graveyard party features storytellers, historians, guided tours, a hat contest, a turn-of-the-century concert, and Victorian boutiques. Admission is free. For a small charge, you can reserve a picnic lunch. Call ☎ **404/688-2107** for details.

November

- **Veterans Day Parade.** Atlanta mounts an impressive version of this parade each year, with floats, drill teams, marching bands, clowns, color guards, and more. The parade begins at 11am at Sixteenth Street and Peachtree Street in Midtown and proceeds south to Tenth Street. For details, call ☎ **770/452-8387.** November 11.
- **Holiday Celebrations.** Things kick off with an array of events at Stone Mountain Park from the day after Thanksgiving through December 31. A "tree of lights" atop the mountain is visible from miles away; the park's roads offer a stunning display of lights, animated scenes, music, and traditional decorations; and activities include visits with Santa, carriage rides, holiday sing-along train rides, a special laser show, and lots of entertainment. For details, call ☎ **770/498-5690.**
- **Stone Mountain Village Candlelight Shopping.** Every Thursday and Friday night until 9pm, beginning the Thursday before Thanksgiving and continuing to Christmas, this charming shopping village is candlelit, and visitors are lured into decorated shops by the aroma of mulling cider. A jolly St. Nick, strolling carolers, gaily lighted trees, and carriage rides are part of the fun. No admission. Call ☎ **770/879-4971** for details.
- **Lighting of the Great Tree.** A 70-foot pine is decorated with 500 ornaments the size of basketballs, 50 flashing strobe lights, and thousands of tiny twinkly lights, and is topped by a 7-foot star. There are choirs and choruses singing Christmas carols. It all takes place at Underground Atlanta at Peachtree Fountains, across from Five Points MARTA station. Arrive early via MARTA; traffic comes to a standstill as tens of thousands converge to view the spectacle. Festivities start at 7pm, with the lighting at 8pm. For details, call **Rich's Department Store,** which has sponsored the event for decades, at ☎ **770/913-5551.** Thanksgiving night.

December

- **Christmas at Callanwolde.** Noted interior and floral designers decorate the Callanwolde Fine Arts Center, 980 Briarcliff Rd. NE, and shops (sweets, toys, pottery, garden, etc.) are set up in different rooms. Activities also include concerts on a 3,752-pipe Aeolian organ, children's breakfasts with Santa, caroling and hymn singing, and other entertainment. Admission at the door is $10 adults,

$8 seniors, $6 children 4 to 12, free for children 3 and under. For details, call ☎ **404/872-5338.** Usually held for 2 weeks in late November or early December.

- **Country Christmas.** The Atlanta Botanical Garden is beautifully decorated, and highlights of the afternoon include carolers, bell ringers, children's theater, entertainers, chestnuts roasting on an open fire, pony rides, cranberry and popcorn stringing, and strolling mimes, musicians, and magicians. Christmas crafts like wreath making are demonstrated, and you can shop for handcrafted gifts and homemade baked goods. Admission is free. For details and to inquire about off-site parking and shuttle buses, call ☎ **404/876-5859.** The first Sunday in December.

✪ **Egleston Children's Christmas Parade and Festival of Trees.** Both of these events raise money for Egleston Children's Hospital. The parade is a major to-do with award-winning bands, lavish holiday-themed floats, helium-balloon comic characters, and, of course, Santa Claus. The parade kicks off the 9-day Festival of Trees at the Georgia World Congress Center, for which Atlanta artists, interior designers, florists, and corporations innovatively decorate and donate trees, wreaths, and Christmas vignettes that are exhibited and auctioned off. The festival also features musical performances, children's activities, an antique carousel, a train ride, a roller coaster, ice-skating demonstrations, and heritage displays from 30 countries. Admission to the festival is $8 for adults, $5 for seniors and children 2 to 12, under 2 free. For details, call ☎ **404/264-9348.** The parade begins at 10:30am the first Saturday in December; the festival follows.

- **Peach Bowl Game.** Held annually at the Georgia Dome. Tickets are hard to come by; reserve well in advance. Call ☎ **404/223-9200** for information. Sometime between Christmas and New Year's (occasionally in early January).

- **New Year's Eve.** The Big Peach that rings in Atlanta's New Year is dropped at the stroke of midnight from the 138-foot light tower at Underground Atlanta. But festivities begin earlier (about 8pm) with live music for dancing in the streets, a pyrotechnic display and laser show, balloons, and usually a marching band. Call ☎ **404/523-2311** for details.

4 Insurance

There are three kinds of travel insurance: trip-cancellation insurance, medical, and lost luggage. Trip-cancellation insurance is only a good idea if you have paid a large portion of your vacation expenses up front—say, purchasing a package tour or a cruise. It doesn't make sense if you've just bought a regular plane ticket.

Your existing health insurance should cover you if you get sick while on vacation (though if you belong to an HMO, you should check to see whether you are fully covered when away from home). And your homeowner's insurance should cover stolen luggage if you have off-premises theft. Check your existing policies before you buy any additional coverage. The airlines are responsible for $1,250 on domestic flights if they lose your luggage; if you plan to carry anything more valuable than that, keep it in your carry-on bag.

Among the reputable issuers of travel insurance are:

Access America, 6600 W. Broad St., Richmond, VA 23230 (☎ **800/284-8300**)

Mutual of Omaha, Mutual of Omaha Plaza, Omaha, NE 68175 (☎**800/228-9792**)

Travel Guard International, 1145 Clark St., Stevens Point, WI 54481 (☎**800/826-1300**)

Factoid

If you own your own car, chances are that you're covered under your existing policy for both collision and liability. However, if you don't already have car insurance, you may want to take the extra insurance coverage offered by rental companies. If you can rent with certain types of credit cards, you may be automatically covered for collision (but *not* liability). Ask your credit card issuer before assuming anything.

Travel Insured International, Inc., P.O. Box 280568, East Hartford, CT 06128 (☎ **800/243-3174**)

5 Tips for Travelers with Special Needs

A free newspaper called *Creative Loafing,* available at over 3,000 locations around town (hotels, restaurants, shops, MARTA stations, etc.), lists numerous events each issue and has special sections for "Gay and Lesbian Activities" and "Singles." For a free copy prior to your visit, call ☎ **800/950-5623.**

FOR TRAVELERS WITH DISABILITIES

Before planning your trip to Atlanta, send for a copy of *The Atlanta Accessibility Guide,* available from the Shepherd Center, a nationally renowned Atlanta hospital specializing in the treatment of spinal cord injuries and diseases. The 62-page guide rates the accessibility of local museums, parks, restaurants, hotels, theaters, sports venues, and other popular tourist stops. Accessibility is rated in several categories, including rest rooms, parking, main entrance, and telephone. The booklet also lists services and information of interest to travelers with disabilities. For a free copy, contact the **Noble Learning Resource Center, Shepherd Center,** 2020 Peachtree Rd. NW, Atlanta, GA 30309 (☎ **404/350-7473**). The guide is also available at www.shepherd.org.

  Accessible Journeys (☎ **800/TINGLES** or 610/521-0339) and **Flying Wheels Travel** (☎ **800/535-6790** or 507/451-5005) offer tours for people with physical disabilities. The **Guided Tour Inc.** (☎ **215/782-1370**) has tours for people with physical or mental disabilities, people with visual impairments, and the elderly.

  A publisher called **Twin Peaks Press,** Box 129, Vancouver, WA 98666 (☎ **360/694-2462**), specializes in books for people with disabilities. Write for their *Disability Bookshop Catalog,* enclosing $4.

  Mobility International USA, P.O. Box 10767, Eugene, OR 97440 (☎ **503/343-1284**), offers accessibility information and has many interesting travel programs for travelers with disabilities. They also publish a quarterly newsletter called *Over the Rainbow* ($15 per year to subscribe). Accessibility information is also available from the **Travel Information Service** (☎ **215/456-9600**) and the **Society for the Advancement of Travel for the Handicapped** (SATH), 347 Fifth Ave., Suite 610, New York, NY 10016 (☎ **212/447-7284**).

Factoid

If you're looking for a travel agent that offers tours or can plan trips for travelers with disabilities, check www.access-able.com. You'll also find relay and voice numbers for hotels, airlines, and car-rental companies on this user-friendly site, as well as links to accessible accommodations, attractions, transportation, and tours; local medical resources and equipment repairers; and much more.

Avis (☎ 800/331-1212)and **Hertz** (☎ 800/654-3131) now offer hand-controlled care for disabled drivers. The number of hand-controlled cars may be limited, so be sure to book in advance.

Amtrak (☎ 800/USA-RAIL) provides redcap service, wheelchair assistance, and special seats at most major stations with 72 hours' notice. People with disabilities are also entitled to a 25% discount on one-way regular coach fares. Disabled children ages 2 to 15 can also get a 50% discount on already discounted one-way disabled adult fares. Documentation from a doctor or an ID card proving your disability is required. For an additional charge, Amtrak also offers wheelchair-accessible sleeping accommodations on long-distance trains, and service dogs are permissible and travel free of charge. Write for a free booklet called *Amtrak's America* from Amtrak Distribution Center, P.O. Box 7717, Itasca, IL 60143, which has a section detailing services for passengers with disabilities.

Greyhound (☎ 800/752-4841) allows a disabled person to travel with a companion for a single fare and, if you call 48 hours in advance, they will arrange help along the way.

FOR GAY & LESBIAN TRAVELERS

Atlanta has a large gay community and you can access it via a free magazine called *Etcetera Magazine,* like *Creative Loafing* (see above), available in front of MARTA stops and in some shops, bars, and restaurants. It lists current events, clubs, restaurants, entertainment, and establishments of interest to gay men and lesbians. If you'd like a copy in advance of your trip, send $2 for a current issue to 151 Renaissance Pkwy., Atlanta, GA 30308. Or, when you arrive, call ☎ 404/888-0063 to find out where you can pick up an issue near your hotel. You can also call that number for information on gay resources in town ("We call ourselves the gay 411," says an *Etcetera* representative). *Etcetera's* Web site is www.etcmag.com.

Another free gay publication is *Southern Voice.* Call ☎ 404/876-1819 for a free issue, a distribution point near your hotel, or additional information on gay resources in Atlanta.

FOR SENIORS

Always carry some form of photo ID so that you can take advantage of discounts wherever they're offered. And it never hurts to ask.

If you haven't already done so, consider joining the **American Association of Retired Persons** (AARP), 601 E St. NW, Washington, DC 20049 (☎ 202/434-2277). Annual membership costs $8 per person or per couple. You must be at least 50 to join. Membership entitles you to many discounts. Write to Purchase Privilege Program, AARP Fulfillment, 601 E St. NW, Washington, DC 20049, to receive AARP's Purchase Privilege brochure—a free list of hotels, motels, and car-rental firms nationwide that offer discounts to AARP members.

Elderhostel is a national organization that offers low-priced educational programs for people over 55 (your nonspouse companion must be at least 50). Programs are generally a week long, and prices average about $325 per person, including room, board, and classes. For information on programs in Atlanta, call or write Elderhostel headquarters, 75 Federal St., Boston, MA 02110-1941 (☎ 617/426-7788) and ask for a free U.S. catalog.

Amtrak (☎ 800/USA-RAIL) offers a 15% discount off the lowest available coach fare (with certain travel restrictions) to people 62 or over.

Greyhound also offers discounted fares for senior citizens. Call your local Greyhound office for details.

6 Getting There

BY PLANE

Hartsfield Atlanta International Airport, 10 miles south of downtown, is the world's largest and second-busiest passenger airport and transfer hub, accommodating 68 million passengers a year. It serves 186 U.S. cities with nonstop service.

Delta Air Lines (☎ **800/221-1212** or www.delta-air.com for reservations and flight information), which is based at Hartsfield, is the major carrier to Atlanta, connecting it to pretty much the entire country as well as 62 countries internationally. It carries 80% of the air passengers who come into Atlanta and serves 355 international cities.

Other major carriers include **America West** (☎ 800/235-9292; www.americawest.com), **American** (☎ 800/433-7300; www.americanair.com), **British Airways** (☎ 800/247-9297; www.british-airways.com), **Continental** (☎ 800/732-6887; www.flycontinental.com), **Japan Airlines** (☎ 800/525-3663; www.jal.com), **Kiwi** (☎ 800/538-5494; www.jetkiwi.com), **KLM** (☎ 800/374-7747; www.nwa.com), **Lufthansa** (☎ 800/645-3880; www.lufthansa-usa.com), **Northwest** (☎ 800/225-2525; www.nwa.com), **SABENA** (☎ 800/955-2000; www.sabina.com), **Swissair** (☎ 800/221-4750; www.swissair.com), **TWA** (☎ 800/221-2000; www.twa.com), **United** (☎ 800/241-6522; www.ual.com), **USAirways** (☎ 800/428-4322; www.usairways.com).

Generally, the least expensive fares (except for specially promoted discount fares announced in newspaper travel sections) are advance-purchase fares that involve certain restrictions. For example, in addition to paying for your ticket 3 to 21 days in advance of your trip, you may have to leave or return on certain days, stay a maximum or minimum number of days, and so on. Advance-purchase fares are often nonrefundable. Nonetheless, the restrictions are usually within the framework of normal vacation plans. The further in advance you reserve, the better your options, since sometimes there are a limited number of seats sold at discounted rates.

When you reserve, be sure to inquire about money-saving packages that include hotel accommodations, car rentals, tours, and other like expenses, with your airfare.

BY CAR

Three major interstate highways (I-20, I-75, and I-85) converge near the center of downtown Atlanta.

Below is a list of approximate mileages from other major cities in the region:

Birmingham, AL: 148
Charleston, SC: 320
Charlotte, NC: 240
Jacksonville, FL: 346
Louisville, KY: 417
Nashville, TN: 244

Flying for Less

Passengers within the same airplane cabin are rarely paying the same fare for their seats. Check with these companies to see what fares they're offering: Council Travel (☎ **800/226-8624**); STA Travel (☎ **800/781-4040**); Travel Bargins (☎ **800/AIR/FARE**); 1-800-FLY-CHEAP.

CyberDeals for Net Surfers

It's possible to get some great deals on airfare, hotels, and car rentals via the Internet. So go grab your mouse and start surfing before you make your reservations—you could save a bundle on your trip. The Web sites we've highlighted below are worth checking out, especially since all services are free (but don't forget that time is money when you're on line).

Microsoft Expedia (www.expedia.com)   The best part of this multi-purpose travel site is the "Fare Tracker": You fill out a form on the screen indicating that you're interested in cheap flights to Atlanta from your hometown, and, once a week, they'll e-mail you the best airfare deals. The site's "Travel Agent" will steer you to bargains on hotels and car rentals, and you can book everything, including flights, right on line. This site is even useful once you're booked: Before you go, log on to Expedia for oodles of up-to-date travel information, including weather reports and foreign exchange rates.

Preview Travel (www.reservations.com and www.vacations.com)   Another useful travel site, "Reservations.com" has a "Best Fare Finder," which will search the Apollo computer reservations system for the three lowest fares for any route on any days of the year. Say you want to go from Chicago to Atlanta and back between December 6th and 13th: Just fill out the form on the screen with times, dates, and destinations, and within minutes, Preview will show you the best deals. If you find an airfare you like, you can book your ticket right on line—you can even reserve hotels and car rentals on this site. If you're in the pre-planning stage, head to Preview's "Vacations.com" site, where you can check out the latest package deals by clicking on "Hot Deals."

Travelocity (www.travelocity.com)   This is one of the best travel sites out there. In addition to its "Personal Fare Watcher," which notifies you via e-mail of the lowest airfares for up to five different destinations, Travelocity will track the three lowest fares for any routes on any dates in minutes. You can book a flight right then and there, and if you need a rental car or hotel, Travelocity will find you the best deal via the SABRE computer reservations system (a huge database used by travel agents worldwide). Click on "Last Minute Deals" for the latest travel bargains, including a link to "H.O.T. Coupons" (**www.hotcoupons.com**), where you can print out electronic coupons for travel in the U.S. and Canada.

New Orleans, LA: 473
Norfolk, VA: 555
Orlando, FL: 441
Savannah, GA: 252
Tampa, FL: 458

BY TRAIN

Amtrak operates the *Crescent* daily between Atlanta and New York, with stops in Washington, D.C., Philadelphia, and other intermediate points. Three times a week, the *Crescent* also goes beyond Atlanta to many points south, terminating in New Orleans. And other Amtrak trains connect with most of the country. To find out if your city connects via rail with Atlanta, call ☎ **800/USA-RAIL.**

Trip.Com (www.thetrip.com)   This site is really geared toward the business traveler, but vacationers-to-be can also use Trip.Com's valuable fare-finding engine, which will e-mail you every week with the best city-to-city airfare deals on your selected route or routes.

Discount Tickets (www.discount-tickets.com)   Operated by the ETN (European Travel Network), this site offers discounts on airfares, accommodations, car rentals, and tours. It deals in flights between the U.S. and other countries, not domestic U.S. flights, so it's most useful for travelers coming to Atlanta from abroad.

E-Savers Programs   Several major airlines offer a free e-mail service known as **E-Savers,** via which they'll send you their best bargain airfares on a weekly basis. Here's how it works: Once a week (usually Wednesday), subscribers receive a list of discounted flights to and from various destinations, both international and domestic. Now here's the catch: These fares are only available if you leave the very next Saturday (or sometimes Friday night) and return on the following Monday or Tuesday. It's really a service for the spontaneously inclined and travelers looking for a quick getaway. But the fares are cheap, so it's worth taking a look. If you have a preference for certain airlines (in other words, the ones you fly most frequently), sign up with them first. Another caveat: You'll get frequent-flier miles if you purchase one of these fares, but you can't use miles to buy the ticket.

Here's a list of airlines and their Web sites, where you can not only get on the e-mailing lists, but also book flights directly:

- **American Airlines:** www.americanair.com
- **Continental Airlines:** www.flycontinental.com
- **Delta Air Lines:** www.delta-air.com
- **TWA:** www.twa.com
- **Northwest Airlines:** www.nwa.com
- **US Airways:** www.usairways.com

Epicurious Travel (travel.epicurious.com), another good travel site, allows you to sign up for all of these airline e-mail lists at once.

—Jeanette Foster

Like the airlines, **Amtrak** offers several discount fares, and though not all are based on advance purchase, you may increase your options by reserving early. At this writing, **full round-trip coach fares and discount fares** are as follows between Atlanta and these cities.

	Full Fare	Discount Fare
Boston–Atlanta	$368	$202
Chicago–Atlanta	$504	$252
Los Angeles–Atlanta	$1004	$554
Miami–Atlanta	$670	$350
New Orleans–Atlanta	$156	$78
New York–Atlanta	$328	$180

Call **Amtrak's Great American Vacations** (☎ **800/321-8684**) to inquire about money-saving packages that include hotel accommodation and attraction tickets with your train fare. **Amtrak** trains arrive in Atlanta at 1688 Peachtree St., just off I-85. From this very central location, you can take a taxi to your hotel or to the nearest MARTA station (Arts Center). For information, call **800/USA-RAIL** or 404/881-3060.

BY BUS

Greyhound buses (☎ **800/231-2222** or 404/584-1728 for reservations and information) connect the entire country with Atlanta. The new bus terminal, which opened in January 1996, is located at 232 Forsyth St. It's right at the Garnett Street MARTA station, one stop south of Five Points, the main MARTA station downtown. Taxis are available, but it's convenient and inexpensive to take MARTA into the central city.

The fare structure on buses is complex and not always based on distance traveled. The good news is that when you call Greyhound, they'll always give you the lowest-fare options. Once again, advance-purchase fares booked 3 to 21 days prior to travel represent big savings.

For Foreign Visitors

3

This chapter will provide some specifics about getting to the United States as economically and effortlessly as possible, plus some helpful information about how things are done in Atlanta—from mailing a postcard to making a long-distance call.

As soon as you know you're going to Atlanta, contact the **Atlanta Convention & Visitors Bureau** (ACVB), 233 Peachtree St. NE, Suite 2000, Atlanta, GA 30303 (☎ **404/222-6688**). At press time, the ACVB had plans in the works for an international visitors' guide to be printed in several languages.

1 Preparing for Your Trip

ENTRY REQUIREMENTS
DOCUMENT REGULATIONS

Immigration laws are a hot political issue in the United States these days, and the following requirements may have changed by the time you plan your trip. Check at any U.S. embassy or consulate for current information and requirements.

Canadian citizens may enter the U.S. without visas; they need only proof of residence.

The U.S. State Department has a Visa Waiver Pilot Program allowing citizens of certain countries to enter the United States without a visa for stays of up to 90 days. At press time these included Andorra, Austria, Belgium, Brunei, Denmark, Finland, France, Germany, Iceland, Ireland, Italy, Japan, Liechtenstein, Luxembourg, Monaco, the Netherlands, New Zealand, Norway, San Marino, Spain, Sweden, Switzerland, and the United Kingdom. Citizens of these countries need only a valid passport and a round-trip air or cruise ticket in their possession upon arrival.

Note that citizens of these visa-exempt countries who first enter the United States may then visit Mexico, Canada, Bermuda, and/or the Caribbean islands and then re-enter the United States, by any mode of transportation, without needing a visa. Further information is available from any U.S. embassy or consulate.

Citizens of all other countries, including Australia, must have two documents:

- a valid passport, with an expiration date at least six months later than the scheduled end of the visit to the U.S.; and

• a tourist visa, available without charge from the nearest U.S. consulate. To obtain a visa, the traveler must submit a completed application form (either in person or by mail) with a 1½-inch square photo and demonstrate binding ties to a residence abroad.

Usually you can obtain a visa at once or within 24 hours, but it may take longer during the summer rush from June to August. If you cannot go in person, contact the nearest U.S. embassy or consulate for directions on applying by mail. Your travel agent or airline office may also be able to provide you with visa applications and instructions. The U.S. consulate or embassy that issues your visa will determine whether you will be issued a multiple- or single-entry visa and any restrictions regarding the length of your stay.

MEDICAL REQUIREMENTS

No inoculations are needed to enter the United States unless you are coming from, or have stopped over in, areas known to be suffering from epidemics, particularly cholera or yellow fever.

If you have a disease requiring treatment with medications containing narcotics or drugs requiring a syringe, carry a valid signed prescription from your physician to allay any suspicions that you are smuggling drugs.

CUSTOMS REQUIREMENTS

Every adult visitor may bring in free of duty: 1 liter of wine or hard liquor; 200 cigarettes or 100 cigars (but no cigars from Cuba) or 3 pounds of smoking tobacco; $100 worth of gifts. These exemptions are offered to travelers who spend at least 72 hours in the United States and who have not claimed them within the preceding 6 months. It is altogether forbidden to bring into the country foodstuffs (particularly cheese, fruit, cooked meats, and canned goods) and plants (vegetables, seeds, tropical plants, and so on). Foreign tourists may bring in or take out up to $10,000 in U.S. or foreign currency with no formalities; larger sums must be declared to Customs upon entering or leaving.

INSURANCE

Unlike Canada and Europe, there is no national health system in the United States, and the cost of medical care here is extremely high. For this reason, we strongly advise every traveler to secure health insurance coverage before setting out. You may want to take out a comprehensive travel policy that covers sickness or injury costs (medical, surgical, and hospital) as well as loss or theft of your baggage, trip-cancellation costs, guarantee of bail in case you are arrested, and costs of accident, repatriation, or death.

Packages such as "Europe Assistance Worldwide Services" in Europe are sold by automobile clubs and travel agencies at attractive rates. **Travel Assistance International** (TAI) (☎ **800/821-2828** or 202/347-2025) is the agent for Europe Assistance Worldwide Services, Inc., so holders of this company's policies can contact TAI for assistance while in the United States.

Canadians should check with their provincial health scheme offices or call **HealthCanada** (☎ **613/957-3025**) to find out the extent of their coverage and what documentation and receipts they must take home in case they are treated in the United States.

MONEY

The foreign-exchange bureaus so common in Europe are rare even at airports in the United States and are nonexistent outside major cities. Try to avoid having to change foreign money, or traveler's checks denominated in other than U.S. dollars, at a small-town bank, or even a branch in a big city. In fact, leave any currency other than U.S. dollars at home—it may prove more nuisance to you than it's worth.

CURRENCY

The U.S. monetary system has a decimal base: 1 American dollar ($1) = 100 cents (100¢).

Dollar bills commonly come in $1 ("a buck"), $5, $10, $20, $50, and $100 denominations (the last two are not welcome when paying for small purchases and are not accepted in taxis or at subway ticket booths). There are also $2 bills (seldom encountered).

There are six denominations of coins: 1¢ (one cent or "penny"), 5¢ (five cents or "a nickel"), 10¢ (ten cents or "a dime"), 25¢ (twenty-five cents or "a quarter"), 50¢ (fifty cents or "a half dollar"), and the rare $1 piece.

TRAVELER'S CHECKS

Traveler's checks *denominated in U.S. dollars* are readily accepted at most hotels, motels, restaurants, and large stores. But the best place to change traveler's checks is at a bank. Do not bring traveler's checks denominated in other currencies.

CREDIT CARDS & ATMS

The method of payment most widely used is the credit card. Cards commonly used in the United States include Visa (BarclayCard in Britain), MasterCard (EuroCard in Europe, Access in Britain, Chargex in Canada), American Express, Diners Club, Discover, and Carte Blanche. You can save yourself trouble by using plastic rather than cash or traveler's checks in most hotels, motels, restaurants, and retail stores (a growing number of food and liquor stores now accept credit cards): There are, however, a handful of stores and restaurants that do not take credit or charge cards, so be sure to ask in advance. Most businesses display a sticker near their entrance to let you know which cards they accept. (*Note:* Often businesses require a minimum purchase price, usually around $10, to use a credit or charge card.)

You must have a credit card to rent a car, and many hotels require a credit-card imprint as a deposit against expenses. It can also be used as proof of identity (often carrying more weight than a passport), or as a "cash card," enabling you to draw money from banks that accept them.

It's also easy to find automated teller machines (ATMs) in Atlanta. Most accept Visa, MasterCard, and American Express, as well as ATM cards from other U.S. banks. Expect to be charged up to $3 per transaction if you're not using your own bank's ATM.

MONEYGRAMS   If the proverbial poop hits the fan, you can also have someone wire money to you very quickly via Western Union. There are several offices in Atlanta; call ☎ **800/325-6000** for the one nearest you.

SAFETY
GENERAL

While tourist areas are generally safe, crime is on the increase everywhere, and U.S. urban areas tend to be less safe than those in Europe or Japan. Visitors should always stay alert. This is particularly true of large U.S. cities. Ask the tourist office if you're in doubt about which neighborhoods are safe. Avoid deserted areas, especially at night.

Remember also that hotels are open to the public, and in a large hotel, security may not be able to screen everyone entering. Always lock your room door—don't assume that once inside your hotel you are automatically safe and no longer need to be aware of your surroundings.

DRIVING

Safety while driving is particularly important. Question your rental agency about personal safety, or ask for a brochure of traveler safety tips when you pick up your car. Obtain written directions, or a map with the route marked in red, from the agency showing how to get to your destination. And, if possible, arrive and depart during daylight hours.

Recently, more and more crime has involved cars and drivers. If you drive off a highway into a doubtful neighborhood, leave the area as quickly as possible. If you have an accident, even on the highway, stay in your car with the doors locked until you assess the situation or until the police arrive. If you are bumped from behind on the street or are involved in a minor accident with no injuries and the situation appears to be suspicious, motion to the other driver to follow you. *Never* get out of your car in such situations. Go directly to the nearest police precinct, well-lighted service station, or all-night store.

If you see someone on the road who indicates a need for help, do *not* stop. Take note of the location, drive on to a well-lighted area, and telephone the police by dialing **911.**

Park in well-lighted, well-traveled areas if possible. Always keep your car doors locked, whether attended or unattended. Look around you before you get out of your car, and never leave any packages or valuables in sight. If someone attempts to rob you or steal your car, do *not* try to resist the thief/carjacker—report the incident to the police department immediately.

2 Getting to the U.S.

Travelers from overseas can take advantage of the APEX (Advance Purchase Excursion) fares offered by all the major U.S. and European carriers.

Flying to Atlanta from 62 European cities, **Delta** offers daily nonstop flights from London, Manchester, Paris, Frankfurt, Zurich, Dublin, Shannon, and Madrid. **British Airways** (☎ **0345/222111** in the U.K.) flies daily from London. **KLM** has direct service daily from Amsterdam (☎ **020/4747-747**).

For Canadian travelers, **Air Canada** provides daily nonstop service to Atlanta from Toronto (☎ **800/268-7240**).

Some large American airlines (for example, TWA, American Airlines, Northwest, United, and Delta) offer travelers on their transatlantic or transpacific flights special discount tickets under the name **Visit USA,** allowing travel between any U.S. destinations at minimum rates. They are not on sale in the United States, and must, therefore, be purchased before you leave your foreign point of departure. This system is the best, easiest, and fastest way to see the United States at low cost. You should obtain information well in advance from your travel agent or the office of the airline concerned, since the conditions attached to these discount tickets can be changed without advance notice.

The visitor arriving by air, no matter what the port of entry, should cultivate patience and resignation before setting foot on U.S. soil. Getting through Immigration control may take as long as 2 hours on some days, especially summer weekends. Add the time it takes to clear Customs and you'll see that you should make very generous allowances for delay in planning connections between international and domestic flights—an average of 2 to 3 hours at least.

In contrast, travelers arriving by car or by rail from Canada will find border-crossing formalities streamlined to the vanishing point. And air travelers from Canada, Bermuda, and some places in the Caribbean can sometimes go through Customs and Immigration at the point of departure, which is much quicker and less painful.

For further information about travel to Atlanta, see "Getting There" in chapter 2.

3 Getting Around the U.S.

BY CAR Car culture reigns supreme in America, and driving will give you the freedom to make—and alter—your own itinerary. It also offers the possibility of visiting some of the off-the-beaten path locations, places that cannot be reached easily by public transportation. For information on renting cars in the United States, see "Orientation," in chapter 4, and "Automobile Organizations" and "Automobile Rentals" in "Fast Facts: For the Foreign Traveler," below.

Please note that in the United States we drive on the **right side of the road** as in Europe, not on the left side as in the United Kingdom, Australia, and New Zealand.

BY TRAIN International visitors can buy a **USA Railpass,** good for 15 or 30 days of unlimited travel on Amtrak. The pass is available through many foreign travel agents. (With a foreign passport, you can also buy passes at some Amtrak offices in the United States, including locations in San Francisco, Los Angeles, Chicago, New York, Miami, Boston, and Washington, D.C.) The prices are based on a zone system: eastern, central, and western. In 1998, a 15-day pass for the eastern third of the United States cost $205 off-peak, $250 peak; a 30-day pass cost $255 off-peak, $310 peak. A national pass, good for travel throughout the entire country, is also available. In 1998, the 15-day national pass was $285 off-peak, $425 peak; a 30-day pass was $375 off-peak, $535 peak. The peak seasons are from June 1 to September 7. Reservations are generally required and should be made for each part of your trip as early as possible.

Visitors should be aware of the limitations of long-distance rail travel in the United States. With a few notable exceptions (for instance, the Northeast Corridor line between Boston and Washington, D.C.), service is rarely up to European standards: delays are common, routes are limited and often infrequently served, and fares are rarely significantly lower than discount airfares. Thus, cross-country train travel should be approached with caution.

BY BUS Although ticket prices for short bus trips between cities are often the most economical form of public transit, at this writing, bus passes are priced slightly higher than similar train passes. **Greyhound** (☎ **800/231-2222**), the sole nationwide bus line, offers a **New Ameripass** for unlimited travel anywhere on its system. In 1998, prices for a 7-day pass started at $199; 15 days at $299; 30 days at $409; and 60 days at $599. Senior citizen discounts are available. Bus travel in the United States can be both slow and uncomfortable, so this option is not for everyone.

Travel Tip

Don't mix up the toll-free *800, 888,* or *877* area codes with numbers in area codes *700* or *900,* which are usually attached to chat lines, phone sex, and the like, all charging oodles per minute.

FAST FACTS: For the Foreign Traveler

Automobile Organizations   Auto clubs will supply maps, suggested routes, guidebooks, accident and bail-bond insurance, and emergency road service. The major auto club in the United States, with 983 offices nationwide, is the **American Automobile Association (AAA).** Members of some foreign auto clubs have reciprocal arrangements with AAA and enjoy its services at no charge. If you belong to an auto club, inquire about AAA reciprocity before you leave. AAA can provide you with an **International Driving Permit** validating your foreign license. You may be able to join AAA even if you are not a member of a reciprocal club. To inquire, call ☎ **800/222-4357.** In addition, some automobile rental agencies now provide these services, so you should inquire about their availability when you rent your car.

Automobile Rentals   To rent a car you need a major credit card. A valid driver's license is required, and you usually need to be at least 25. Some companies do rent to younger people but add a daily surcharge. Be sure to return your car with the same amount of gas you started out with; rental companies charge excessive prices for gasoline. All of the major national car-rental companies are represented in Atlanta. **Atlanta Rent-A-Car** (☎ **404/763-1160**), a local company, offers particularly low prices.

Business Hours   Offices are usually open Monday through Friday from 9am to 5pm. Banks are open Monday through Friday from 9am to 3 or 4pm, and sometimes on Saturday morning. Hundreds of **automated teller machines (ATM)** located throughout Atlanta offer 24-hour withdrawal with international ATM cards. Post offices are usually open Monday through Friday from 8:30am to 5pm, and on Saturday from 8:30am to noon. Shops are generally open from 10am to 5 or 6pm. Those in malls tend to stay open late, until about 9pm Monday through Saturday and until 5 or 6pm on Sunday. Museum days and hours of operation vary.

Climate   See "When to Go" in chapter 2.

Currency   See "Preparing for Your Trip," earlier in this chapter.

Currency Exchange   You will find currency exchange services in major airports with international service. Elsewhere, they may be quite difficult to come by. A reliable choice is **Thomas Cook Currency Services, Inc.,** which has been in business since 1841 and offers a wide range of services. They also sell commission-free foreign and U.S. traveler's checks, drafts, and wire transfers; they also do check collections (including Eurochecks). Their rates are competitive and service is excellent. In Atlanta, there are three Thomas Cook foreign exchange offices (☎ **800/287-7362**) at Hartsfield Atlanta International Airport. Each is open 7 days a week, but the hours vary.

Currency exchange is also available at the **American Express** office at 3384 Peachtree Rd. (☎ **404/262-7561**) in Buckhead.

Drinking Laws   See "Liquor Laws" in "Fast Facts: Atlanta," chapter 4.

Electricity   The United States uses **110–120 volts, 60 cycles,** compared to 220–240 volts, 50 cycles, as in most of Europe. In addition to a 100-volt converter, small appliances of non-American manufacture, such as hair dryers or shavers, will require a plug adapter, with two flat, parallel pins.

Embassies & Consulates   All embassies are located in Washington, D.C.; some consulates are located in major cities, and most nations have a mission to the United Nations in New York City. Foreign visitors can obtain telephone numbers for their embassies and consulates by calling **"Information"** in Washington, D.C. (☎ **202/555-1212**).

Nations with official consulates in Atlanta include: **Canadian Consulate General,** 1175 Peachtree St., 100 Colony Sq., Suite 1700, Atlanta, GA 30361 (☎ **404/532-2000**); **Consulate of France,** 285 Peachtree Center Ave., Suite 2800, Atlanta, GA 30303 (☎ **404/522-4226**); **Consulate General of the Federal Republic of Germany,** Marquis Two Tower, Suite 901, 285 Peachtree Center Ave. NE, Atlanta, GA 30303 (☎ **404/659-4760**); **British Consulate General,** 245 Peachtree Center Ave., Marquis One Tower, Suite 2700, Atlanta, GA 30303 (☎ **404/524-5856**); **Consulate General of the Republic of Korea,** 229 Peachtree St., Suite 500, Atlanta, GA 30303 (☎ **404/522-1611**); **Consulate General of Brazil,** 229 Peachtree St., Suite 2306, Atlanta GA 30303 (☎ **404/521-0061**); and **Consulate General of Japan,** 100 Colony Sq., Suite 2000, Atlanta, GA 30361 (☎ **404/892-2700**). For complete information, contact the **Atlanta Chamber of Commerce,** International Department, P.O. Box 1740, Atlanta, GA 30301 (☎ **404/586-8470**).

Emergencies   In all major cities (including Atlanta), you can call the police, an ambulance, or the fire department through the single emergency telephone number **911.** Another useful way of reporting an emergency is to call the telephone-company operator by dialing **0.**

See also listing for the **Travelers Aid Society of Metropolitan Atlanta** in chapter 4 under "Visitor Information."

Gasoline (Petrol)   One U.S. gallon equals 3.75 liters, while 1.2 U.S. gallons equals 1 imperial gallon. You'll notice there are several grades (and price levels) of gasoline available at most gas stations. And you'll also notice that their names change from company to company. The unleaded ones with the highest octane are the most expensive (most rental cars take the least expensive "regular" unleaded). Leaded gas is the least expensive but only older cars can take this, so check if you're not sure.

Holidays   On the following legal national holidays, banks, government offices, post offices, and many stores, restaurants, and museums are closed:

January 1 (New Year's Day)

Third Monday in January (Martin Luther King Day)

Third Monday in February (Presidents' Day, Washington's Birthday)

Last Monday in May (Memorial Day)

July 4 (Independence Day)

First Monday in September (Labor Day)

Second Monday in October (Columbus Day)

November 11 (Veterans Day/Armistice Day)

Last Thursday in November (Thanksgiving Day)

December 25 (Christmas)

Finally, the Tuesday following the first Monday in November is Election Day and is a legal holiday in presidential-election years.

Languages   Major hotels may have multilingual employees. Unless your language is very obscure, they can usually supply a translator on request.

Legal Aid   The foreign tourist, unless positively identified as a member of the Mafia or of a drug ring, will probably never become involved with the American legal system. If you are pulled over for a minor infraction (for example, of the highway code, such as speeding), never attempt to pay the fine directly to a police officer; you may wind up arrested on the much more serious charge of attempted bribery. Pay fines by mail, or directly into the hands of the clerk of the court. If accused of a more serious offense, it's wise to say and do nothing before consulting a lawyer. Under U.S. law, an arrested person is allowed one telephone call to a party of his or her choice. Call your embassy or consulate.

Mail   If you want your mail to follow you on your vacation and you aren't sure of your address, your mail can be sent to you, in your name, ᶜ/o General Delivery at the main post office of the city or region where you expect to be. The addressee must pick it up in person and produce proof of identity (driver's license, credit card, passport, etc.).

Generally found at intersections, mailboxes are blue and carry the inscription **U.S. MAIL.** If your mail is addressed to a U.S. destination, don't forget to add the five-figure postal code, or ZIP (Zone Improvement Plan) Code, after the two-letter abbreviation of the state to which the mail is addressed (GA for Georgia, FL for Florida, NY for New York, and so on).

Domestic postage rates are **20¢** for a postcard and **33¢** for a letter. Air mail postcards and letters to Canada both cost **46¢** for the first half ounce; those to other countries cost **60¢** for the first half ounce.

Newspapers & Magazines   With a few exceptions, such as the *New York Times, USA Today,* the *Wall Street Journal,* and the *Christian Science Monitor,* daily newspapers in the United States are local, not national.

There are also numerous weekly news magazines, such as *Newsweek, Time,* and *U.S. News & World Report,* as well as specialized periodicals, such as the monthly magazines devoted to a single city. In Atlanta, the major daily is the *Atlanta Journal-Constitution.* The city magazine is called *Atlanta.* Also informative is *Creative Loafing,* a free publication you'll see in stores, restaurants, and other places around town.

The air-mail editions of foreign newspapers and magazines are on sale only belatedly, and only at airports and international bookstores in the largest cities.

Radio & Television   Audiovisual media, with four coast-to-coast networks— **ABC, CBS, NBC,** and **FOX**—plus the **Public Broadcasting System (PBS)** and the cable news network **CNN,** play a major part in American life. In the big cities, televiewers have a choice of about a dozen channels (including the UHF channels), most of them transmitting 24 hours a day, without counting the pay-TV channels showing recent movies or sports events. In smaller communities, the choice may be limited to four TV channels (there are 1,200 in the entire country), and a half-dozen local radio stations (there are 6,500 in all), each broadcasting a particular kind of music—classical, country, jazz, pop, or gospel—punctuated by news broadcasts and frequent commercials.

Safety   See "Safety" in "Preparing for Your Trip," earlier in this chapter.

Taxes   In the United States there is no VAT (Value-Added Tax) or other indirect tax at a national level. Every state, and each city in it, has the right to levy its own local tax on all purchases, including hotel and restaurant checks, airline tickets, and so on. In Atlanta, hotel tax is 14%. That includes room tax (7%) and sales tax (7%).

Telephone & Fax   The telephone system in the United States is run by private corporations, so rates, especially for long-distance service, can vary widely—even on calls made from public telephones. AT&T, Sprint, and MCI are dependable long-distance companies that offer reliable, competitive rates. **Local calls** in Atlanta are **35¢.** When making a local phone call in the metro area, it's necessary to dial the area code first, even if you are calling a number within the same area code. (Note that almost all calls to phone numbers in area codes 800, 888, and 877 are toll-free.)

Generally, hotel surcharges on long-distance and local calls are astronomical. You are usually better off using a public pay telephone, which you will find clearly marked in most public buildings and private establishments, as well as on the street. Outside metropolitan areas, public telephones are more difficult to find. Stores and gas stations are your best bet.

Most long-distance and international calls can be dialed directly from any phone. For calls to Canada and other parts of the United States, dial 1 followed by the area code and the seven-digit number. For international calls, dial 011 followed by the country code, city code, and telephone number of the person you wish to call.

For reverse-charge or collect calls, and for person-to-person calls, dial 0 (zero, *not* the letter "O") followed by the area code and number you want; an operator will then come on the line, and you should specify that you are calling collect, or person-to-person, or both. If your operator-assisted call is international, ask for the overseas operator.

For local directory assistance ("information"), dial 411; for long-distance information, dial 1, then the appropriate area code and 555-1212.

You'll find **fax facilities** widely available. They can be found in most hotels and many other establishments. Try Mailboxes Etc. or any photocopying shop.

Telephone Directory   There are two kinds of telephone directories available to you. The general directory is the so-called **White Pages,** in which private and business subscribers are listed in alphabetical order. The inside front cover lists the emergency numbers for police, fire, and ambulance, and other vital numbers (like the Coast Guard, poison-control center, crime-victims hotline, and so on). The first few pages are devoted to community-service numbers, including a guide to long-distance and international calling, complete with country codes and area codes.

The second directory, printed on yellow paper (hence its name, **Yellow Pages**), lists all local services, businesses, and industries by type of activity, with an index at the back. The listings cover not only such obvious items as automobile repairs by make of car, or drugstores (pharmacies), often by geographical location, but also restaurants by type of cuisine and geographical location, bookstores by special subject and/or language, places of worship by religious denomination, and other information that you might not readily find another way. The Yellow Pages also include city plans or detailed area maps, often showing postal ZIP Codes and public transportation routes.

Time   The United States is divided into four time zones (six, if Alaska and Hawaii are included). From east to west, these are: eastern standard time (EST), central standard time (CST), mountain standard time (MST), Pacific standard time (PST), Alaska standard time (AST), and Hawaii standard time (HST). Always keep changing time zones in mind if you are traveling (or even telephoning) long distances in the United States. For example, noon in New York

City (EST) is 11am in Chicago (CST), 10am in Denver (MST), 9am in Los Angeles (PST), 8am in Anchorage (AST), and 7am in Honolulu (HST).

Atlanta observes eastern standard time.

"Daylight saving time" is in effect from the last Sunday in April through the last Saturday in October (actually, the change is made at 2am on Sunday) except in Arizona, Hawaii, part of Indiana, and Puerto Rico. Daylight saving time moves the clock 1 hour ahead of standard time.

Tipping This is part of the American way of life, on the principle that you must expect to pay for any service you get. Here are some rules of thumb:

Bartenders: 10–15%

Bellhops: at least 50¢ per piece; $2–$3 for a lot of baggage

Cab drivers: 15% of the fare

Cafeterias, fast-food restaurants: no tip

Chambermaids: $1 a day

Checkroom attendants (restaurants, theaters): $1 per garment

Cinemas, movies, theaters: no tip

Doormen (hotels or restaurants): not obligatory

Gas-station attendants: no tip

Hairdressers: 15–20%

Redcaps (airport and railroad station): at least 50¢ per piece, $2–$3 for a lot of baggage

Restaurants, nightclubs: 15–20% of the check

Sleeping-car porters: $2–$3 per night to your attendant

Valet parking attendants: $1

Toilets Foreign visitors often complain that public toilets are hard to find in most U.S. cities. True, there are none on the streets, but the visitor can usually find one in a bar, restaurant, hotel, museum, department store, or service station—and it will probably be clean (although the last-mentioned sometimes leaves much to be desired). The cleanliness of toilets at railroad stations and bus depots may be more open to question, and some public places are equipped with pay toilets, which require you to insert one or more coins into a slot on the door before it will open.

THE AMERICAN SYSTEM OF MEASUREMENTS

Length

1 inch (in.)			=	2.54cm			
1 foot (ft.)	=	12 in.	=	30.48cm	=	.305m	
1 yard (yd.)	=	3 ft.			=	.915m	
1 mile	=	5,280 ft.				=	1.609km

To convert miles to kilometers, multiply the number of miles by 1.61 (for example, 50 mi. × 1.61 = 80.5km). Note that this conversion can be used to convert speeds from miles per hour (m.p.h.) to kilometers per hour (kmph).

To convert kilometers to miles, multiply the number of kilometers by .62 (example, 25km × .62 = 15.5 mi.). Note that this same conversion can be used to convert speeds from kilometers per hour to miles per hour.

Capacity

1 fluid ounce (fl. oz.)			=	.03 liter	
1 pint (pt.)	=	16 fl. oz.	=	.47 liter	
1 quart (qt.)	=	2 pints	=	.94 liter	
1 gallon (gal.)	=	4 quarts	=	3.79 liters	=	.83 Imperial gal.

To convert U.S. gallons to liters, multiply the number of gallons by 3.79 (example, 12 gal. × 3.79 = 45.48 liters).

To convert liters to U.S. gallons, multiply the number of liters by .26 (example, 50 liters × .26 = 13 U.S. gal.).

To convert U.S. gallons to Imperial gallons, multiply the number of U.S. gallons by .83 (example, 12 U.S. gal. × .83 = 9.96 Imperial gal.).

To convert Imperial gallons to U.S. gallons, multiply the number of Imperial gallons by 1.2 (example, 8 Imperial gal. × 1.2 = 9.6 U.S. gal.).

Weight

1 ounce (oz.)			=	28.35g			
1 pound (lb.)	=	16 oz.	=	453.6g	=	.45kg	
1 ton	=	2,000 lb.	=		907kg	=	.91 metric ton

To convert pounds to kilograms, multiply the number of pounds by .45 (example, 90 lb. × .45 = 40.5kg).

To convert kilograms to pounds, multiply the number of kilos by 2.2 (example, 75kg × 2.2 = 165 lb.).

Area

1 acre			=	.41 ha		
1 square mile	=	640 acres	=	2.59 ha	=	2.6 sq. km

To convert acres to hectares, multiply the number of acres by .41 (example, 40 acres × .41 = 16.4ha).

To convert hectares to acres, multiply the number of hectares by 2.47 (example, 20ha × 2.47 = 49.4 acres).

To convert square miles to square kilometers, multiply the number of square miles by 2.6 (example, 80 sq. mi × 2.6 = 208 sq. km).

To convert square kilometers to square miles, multiply the number of square kilometers by .39 (example, 150 sq. km × .39 = 58.5 sq. mi.).

Temperature

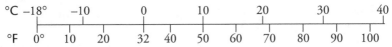

To convert degrees Fahrenheit to degrees Celsius, subtract 32 from °F, multiply by 5, then divide by 9 (example, 85°F – 32 × 5/9 = 29.4°C).

To convert degrees Celsius to degrees Fahrenheit, multiply °C by 9, divide by 5, and add 32 (example, 20°C × 9/5 + 32 = 68°F).

4 Getting to Know Atlanta

The Atlanta metropolitan area is quite large and sprawling, but the city itself is compact, only 131 square miles. Most of the areas popular with visitors are inside the city limits.

1 Orientation

ARRIVING

Despite its size, **Hartsfield Atlanta International Airport** is well planned and easy to get around in, with six concourses, dozens of restaurants and retail shops, facilities for the handicapped, car rental desks, and banking and currency-exchange facilities. Some travelers, however, are bound to be confused by all the concourses, terminals, and trains. If you need help, look for one of the 10 **Hartsfield Host desks.** Friendly volunteers wearing red shirts staff the desks and will help you with anything from finding your gate to choosing the appropriate ground transportation to locating the lost and found.

The airport has its own Web site, **www.atlanta-airport.com,** where you can check the status of flights for most major airlines, find maps showing how to get to and from the airport, check traffic conditions of the interstates leading to Hartsfield, and find a list of emergency contacts and concessionaires. There's also an array of airport facts. For example, there are more than 26,000 parking spaces—still not nearly enough.

The following major car-rental companies are, of course, represented at the airport, and they are reachable via toll-free numbers. These include: **Avis** (☎ 800/331-1212), **Alamo** (☎ 800/327-9633), **Budget** (☎ 800/527-0700), **Dollar** (☎ 800/800-4000), **Hertz** (☎ 800/654-3131), and **Thrifty** (☎ 800/367-2277).

Atlanta Rent-A-Car (☎ 770/448-6066), a local independently owned company, has been serving Atlanta for over 18 years. This company also has a desk at the airport, and their rates are lower than most. They stock a full range of compact and mid-size cars, and they offer friendly, competent service. They have 18 metro locations—including one close to the airport—and provide free courtesy pickup anywhere in metro Atlanta. Currently, Atlanta Rent-A-Car's compacts begin at $19.99 a day with 100 free miles, 24¢ for each additional mile; $8.88 a day and 29¢ a mile with no free miles. The same car costs $99.95 a week with 500 free miles, 24¢ for each additional mile. The inexpensive compacts are available on a first-come, first-served basis. You can reserve a mid-size car in advance, but get a compact if one is available.

GETTING DOWNTOWN FROM THE AIRPORT

Hartsfield Atlanta International Airport is just 10 miles south of downtown, and there are several options for getting from the airport to your hotel. The cheapest, if your luggage is manageable, is to take Atlanta's subway (MARTA), which has a stop right in the airport. The fare is just $1.50. Almost all major downtown and Buckhead hotels are close to MARTA rail stations. It should take you about 20 minutes to reach downtown, 35 minutes to reach Buckhead.

A taxi from the airport to a downtown hotel costs $18 for one passenger, $10 each for two or more, $8 each for three. The ride should take about half an hour. To midtown hotels, the fare is $22 for one passenger, $25 for two or more; to Buckhead hotels, the fare is $28 for one passenger, $30 for two or more.

Atlanta Airport Shuttle Vans (☎ **800/842-2770** or 404/524-3400) operate between the airport and most downtown, Midtown, and Buckhead hotels. They depart from the Delta baggage claim/ground transportation area in the South Terminal. Reservations from the airport are not necessary, and you can catch one about every 15 minutes, in either direction, from 7am to 11pm 7 days a week. To downtown and midtown locations, the cost is $10 one-way, $17 round-trip; children under 5 ride free. To Buckhead locations and the Emory University area in Decatur, the cost is $15 one-way, $24 round-trip, free for children under 5. It's a well-organized system, with clearly marked destinations and helpful attendants on hand. Call **Atlanta Airport Northside Shuttle Vans,** a division of the same company, at ☎ **800/277-1165** or 404/768-7600, for information about transport to northside suburban locations. Door-to-door service to the Marietta and Roswell suburbs is available with 24-hour notice. When you leave Atlanta, check with your hotel desk about departure times; for some hotels, reservations are required a day in advance.

If you're renting a car at the airport, it's easy to drive to your hotel. The airport is located off I-85, which merges with I-75 as you head toward downtown. I-285, known as the Perimeter because it rings the city, is also accessible from the airport.

VISITOR INFORMATION

For information about hotels, restaurants, and attractions, contact the **Atlanta Convention & Visitors Bureau (ACVB),** 233 Peachtree St. NE, Suite 2000, Atlanta, GA 30303 (☎ **404/222-6688**), www.acvb.com. Call or write in advance to obtain a copy of *Atlanta Now* (the official visitors' guide), a *Metro Atlanta Attractions Guide,* a map, a book of discounts, and a 2-month calendar of events. You can call weekdays between 8:30am and 5:30pm.

In town, you can visit ACVB information centers at:

Underground Atlanta, 65 Upper Alabama St. (☎ **404/222-6688**). Open Monday to Saturday 10am to 6pm, Sunday noon to 6pm, this is the most comprehensive of all the ACVB centers. In addition to information about attractions, dining, shopping, and city tours, highlights at the Underground location include:

• An interactive exhibit on the city's cultural organizations. Visitors can access information on museums, plays, events, and concerts. The exhibit displays a photo, written description, and map for each subject or organization.

• AtlantTIX!, a ticket booth where visitors can purchase day-of-show half-price tickets to theater, dance events, and other live performances throughout the metro area. Opened in the summer of 1998, this is the first half-price ticket booth in the South.

- A display about Hartsfield Atlanta International Airport that includes a real Delta Air Lines cockpit connected by a live feed to the airport control tower.
- An exhibit on how to travel around the city, which includes a MARTA rail car.
- A film about Atlanta, shown in a new high-definition theater.
- Exhibits highlighting Atlanta's history, neighborhoods, and sports teams.
- City tour departures. **Gray Line** of Atlanta runs daily sightseeing tours out of the Underground center. No reservations necessary. Call **404/767-0594** for information.

Lenox Square, 3393 Peachtree Rd. Open Tuesday to Saturday 11am to 5pm, Sunday noon to 5:30pm. No phone.

Hartsfield-Atlanta International Airport, near the car-rental booths between the north and south baggage claim areas. Open Monday to Friday 9am to 9pm, Saturday 9am to 6pm, Sunday 12:30 to 6pm. No phone.

Georgia World Congress Center, 285 International Blvd. Operates only during GWCC conventions. No phone.

The **Travelers Aid Society of Metropolitan Atlanta** is a private nonprofit agency providing help to travelers in difficulty. This might include assisting stranded travelers, providing crisis counseling, straightening out ticket mix-ups, or helping travelers with special needs.

Travelers Aid has an office at the airport (☎ **404/766-4511**), which is open Monday to Friday. Because the office is staffed by volunteers, the hours are irregular. Travelers in need of assistance who find that location closed should call the office at 828 W. Peachtree St., Suite 320 (☎ **404/817-7070**), open Monday to Friday 8:30am to 5pm.

CITY LAYOUT

Atlanta is girded by a beltway called I-285, usually referred to as **the Perimeter.** As a tourist, you'll be spending most of your time within the confines of the Perimeter. Two interstate highways (I-75 and I-85) converge just above the airport and proceed north, forking off just northwest of Piedmont Park: I-75 goes northwest, I-85 northeast. A fourth interstate highway just below the downtown area, I-20, is an east–west artery that cuts all the way through Georgia and Atlanta, connecting South Carolina with Alabama. Georgia Highway 400 is a toll road connecting I-85 with the suburbs to the north. Cost is 50¢.

There's a joke that all directions here begin with "Go to Peachtree... ." That's because there are a few dozen Peachtrees—Peachtree Street, Lane, Road, Avenue, Circle, Drive, Plaza, and Way, not to mention West Peachtree Street, Peachtree Memorial Drive, Peachtree Battle Avenue, Peachtree Valley Road, etc., etc., etc. So be sure to emphasize which Peachtree you're looking for when you ask for directions. **Peachtree Street** (which becomes **Peachtree Road** above Midtown and **Peachtree Industrial Boulevard** above Buckhead) is the backbone of Atlanta and its major north–south artery. It's possible, though time-consuming, to start out on Peachtree Street and travel all the way from downtown to beyond the Perimeter. Another main north–south thoroughfare is **Piedmont Avenue.** Peachtree is a two-way street, while Piedmont has two-way traffic above Fourteenth Street, but south-to-north only below Fourteenth Street. Major east–west streets include Memorial Drive, North Avenue, Ponce de Leon Avenue, Fourteenth Street, and, in Buckhead, East and West Paces Ferry Drives.

Because Atlanta just grew (and grew and grew) and wasn't planned out on a grid system, getting around the city by car can be confusing and frustrating, even for people who live here. Streets are often one-way downtown, or they change names, or they're cut off by the interstate or the Chattahoochee River. Be sure to have a good map in hand if you are driving or if you venture much off the beaten path, and make sure your directions are clear. But if you do get lost, Atlantans—who are very friendly—are always eager to help visitors find their way.

NEIGHBORHOODS IN BRIEF

You can't really get the feel of a city until you understand the characteristics of its neighborhoods. Here's a brief rundown of Atlanta's diverse districts.

Downtown   Atlanta's financial and business hub, this area of sleek skyscrapers includes the Peachtree Center hotel/convention center/trade mart/office-tower complex. Here, too: Underground Atlanta, a mix of shops, restaurants, and nightclubs fronted by a 138-foot light tower; the mammoth Georgia World Congress Center, one of the largest meeting and exhibition halls in the nation; the 71,500-seat Georgia Dome, home of the Atlanta Falcons and site of Super Bowl XXVIII; CNN Center; Georgia-Pacific Center, housing the downtown branch of the High Museum of Art; Georgia State University; the golden-domed, century-old State Capitol, a major landmark; the new 21-acre Centennial Olympic Park, the city's newest gathering place; Woodruff Park; and the SciTrek Museum.

Just south of downtown is Turner Field, home of the Atlanta Braves. In its previous incarnation it was the 85,000-seat Olympic Stadium but was retrofitted as a baseball field and reopened in 1997. Also in the general area are Oakland Cemetery (it's mentioned in *Gone With the Wind,* and Margaret Mitchell is one of the many notables buried here) and Grant Park, with the Atlanta Zoo and Cyclorama.

Unlike some big cities, Atlanta doesn't have a large population living in the downtown area, although it looks as if that is beginning to change. Currently downtown consists primarily of businesses, hotels, restaurants, and sports venues, and it doesn't possess the round-the-clock big city excitement that can be found in New York City, for example. People are beginning to move into newly renovated lofts and other buildings, but there's still not a lot of activity in the central city after business hours. For that reason, it's wisest for visitors to stick to the hotel district, the sports venues, and Underground Atlanta, where most of the nighttime goings-on take place.

Sweet Auburn   This traditionally black neighborhood, also called the **Martin Luther King, Jr., Historic District,** is just below downtown's central area. Under the auspices of the National Park Service, it was designated a park in 1980 to honor King, whose boyhood home, crypt, and church are located here. In spite of the yoke of segregation, affluent black businesspeople and professionals flourished here from the early part of the 20th century through the 1950s. Today it's one of Atlanta's major sightseeing draws.

Midtown   Though its boundaries have never been definitively decided, Midtown basically encompasses the area north of downtown from about Ponce de Leon Avenue to I-85. It includes Piedmont Park, the central city's major recreation area; the Woodruff Arts Center, home of the Atlanta Symphony Orchestra, the Alliance Theatre, and the High Museum of Art; the famed Fox Theatre, a 1920s Moorish-motif movie palace; the Atlanta Botanical Garden; Ansley Park, a 230-acre residential greenbelt area, designed at the turn of the century by Frederick Law Olmsted; and Colony Square, an office/hotel/retail complex. AT&T, IBM, Bank of America, and BellSouth maintain corporate offices in Midtown.

Buckhead   Named for an 1838 tavern called the Buck's Head, this is Atlanta's silk-stocking district—one of America's most beautiful and affluent communities. It begins about 6 miles north of downtown, just above I-85. Here you'll find tree-shaded residential areas of magnificent mansions surrounded by verdant acreage, as well as many smaller middle-class homes, shops, and boutiques (including Lenox Square and Phipps Plaza, two exclusive shopping malls), superb restaurants, and first-class hotels. On weekends, the bars and clubs in the center of Buckhead attract crowds of revelers. Buckhead is also a burgeoning business area, with most of the high-rise office buildings concentrated near Peachtree and Lenox roads. Its major sightseeing attraction is the Atlanta History Center, centered on a Palladian villa designed by noted architect Phillip Schutze and surrounded by 32 woodland acres. The Greek Revival Governor's Mansion is also in Buckhead.

Virginia-Highland   Every major American city has a district that claims kinship (however slight) with New York's Greenwich Village. In Atlanta it's the Virginia-Highland section, so named for its central avenues, northeast of downtown. Here you'll find ethnic restaurants, antique shops, bookstores, sidewalk cafes, art galleries, lively bars and bistros, and browsable shops selling everything from gourmet gadgets and woodworking tools to ecologically correct clothing. The surrounding area is full of tree-lined streets with charming little cottages, many of them recently renovated.

Little Five Points   Just below Virginia-Highland—and a funkier offshoot of it—Little Five Points offers a more offbeat ambience, attracting young and old members of the tie-dyed and pierced set. It is also the location of the Jimmy Carter Library/Carter Presidential Center, which opened in 1986 to house the correspondence and memorabilia of this Georgia-born president. Many Victorian homes make for an architecturally interesting stroll. The neighborhood is centered at the junction of Euclid and Moreland avenues.

Decatur   Founded in 1823 by Commodore Stephen Decatur, a dashing naval hero of the War of 1812 who died in a duel, this charming suburb centers on an old courthouse square. About a 15-minute drive east from downtown, Decatur is the scene of numerous annual events, festivals, and concerts, and it houses the sprawling DeKalb Farmers Market, an international food market that must be seen to be believed. Like Virginia-Highland and Little Five Points, Decatur weaves a splash of color and texture into Atlanta's tapestry of neighborhoods.

2 Getting Around

If you're here for a few days, you'll get a pretty good feel for the layout of the city. Just remember that the main drag is **Peachtree Street** (becoming Peachtree Road to the north), and use it to get your bearings.

BY PUBLIC TRANSPORTATION

The **Metropolitan Atlanta Rapid Transit Authority (MARTA)** operates a rail (subway) and bus network, making it possible, though not always convenient, to reach just about any part of town by public transportation. While the system is fairly extensive within the city limits, outside the city (except for areas of DeKalb,

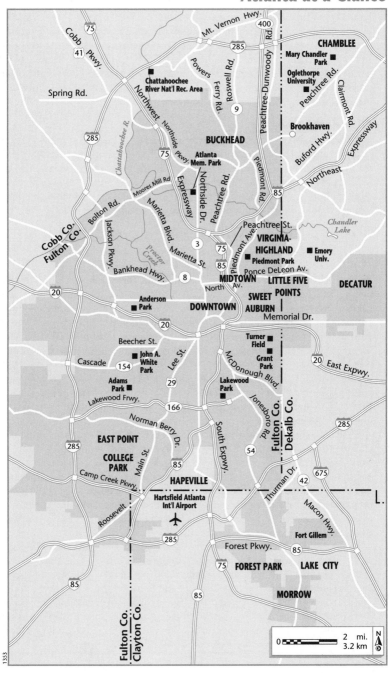

47

Fulton, and Clayton counties) the service is quite limited. Even in some areas served by bus and rail lines, it's sometimes necessary to walk a bit to a station or stop.

Cobb County, a suburban metro county that includes the city of Marietta, operates a bus system separate from MARTA. **Cobb Community Transit (CCT)** has five local routes and express routes that operate between Cobb and MARTA stations in Buckhead, Midtown, and downtown. Call ☎ **770/427-4444** for information.

MARTA RAPID RAIL

MARTA's rapid-rail (subway) service began in 1979. The stations are clean and modern, the service reliable. Although MARTA has a good safety record, there is the perception here—as in any big city—that subway travel is less than safe. MARTA moves half a million people every day, and regular riders seem to have more confidence in the security of the trains and stations than do infrequent riders. Visitors should find the subway most pleasant during the day and during early evening hours when usage is heavy.

The major problem with MARTA is that not enough parts of the city are served by rail, which is much faster than travel by bus. Eventually, this will be a 60-mile, 45-station system, but currently the rail system extends 39 miles and includes 36 stations. There are **two lines:** south–north trains (**orange lines** on the MARTA maps) travel between the airport and Doraville and Dunwoody; east–west trains (**blue** on the maps) travel between Indian Creek (east of Decatur) and Hamilton E. Holmes. They intersect at **Five Points Station** in downtown Atlanta, where you can transfer to another train for free. Scheduled to open in December 2000 are Sandy Springs and North Springs, two new stations on the north line that parallels Georgia Highway 400.

Fare is **$1.50** for any ride, payable in exact change, tokens, or TransCards. Tokens, available at the stations, cost $10 for 8. A weekly **TransCard,** available at Ride Stores—in the Five Points, airport, Lenox, or Lindbergh stations—is good for unlimited bus and rail travel for 1 week and costs $11.

MARTA trains generally arrive and depart every 8 to 10 minutes during operating hours: Monday to Saturday from 5am to 1am, Sunday and holidays from 6am to 12:30am. Free transfers are available between bus and rail when you board a bus or enter a rail station. Parking is free but limited at all rail stations, with the exception of those downtown and in Midtown, where there is no parking. If you wish to park overnight, you must use long-term secured parking, available at the Dunwoody, Medical Center, Lenox, Brookhaven and Lindbergh stations. Cost is $3 per day.

For MARTA schedule and route information, call **404/848-4711** Monday to Friday from 6am to 1am, Saturday and Sunday from 8am to 1am. Printed schedules are available from racks at Five Points and several other stations; instructions are in English, French, Japanese, German, and Spanish.

All stations and rail cars are fully accessible to disabled passengers. There are also special MARTA vans outfitted for easy boarding and for securing wheelchairs. The vans provide door-to-door service for $3 each way; advance notice is required. For information regarding van services, call ☎ **404/848-5389.**

BUSES

It's possible, but not always efficient, to get anywhere within the city limits by bus. The routes will deliver you to most major attractions and sightseeing stops, but travel can be slow and buses infrequent. MARTA buses operate on a 1,550-mile network of 150 routes, and the fare system is the same as described above for rail service. To find out what bus to take, call ☎ **404/848-4711** for route information (same hours as above). Drivers do not carry change; you must have **exact change** ($1.50), a token, a valid transfer, or a TransCard. Special shuttle buses operate from downtown in conjunction with major stadium sports events and conventions; call the above number for details.

BY CAR

It's possible to reach most major Atlanta sites by transit system (MARTA), but a car is preferable, with a few caveats.

Parking isn't usually a problem—though it can be expensive and difficult downtown during conventions and sporting events—but traffic often is. (There's even a column in the local newspaper devoted to traffic information and difficulties.) Rush hours—roughly 7 to 9am and 4:30 to 6:30pm—can be vicious, especially when traveling into town in the morning or out of town in the afternoon on any of the interstates. Besides the commuter traffic, there are travelers passing through Atlanta on their way to points north, south, east, and west. Atlanta drivers are generally courteous, but they tend to travel at breakneck speeds well above the posted limit, so it's wise to avoid the interstates—especially I-285, which supports a lot of truck traffic—during peak hours.

BY TAXI

Atlanta is not New York. It's not possible to step outside and hail a cab. There are always cabs outside the airport, major hotels, Underground Atlanta, and most MARTA stations, except those downtown. If a cab is not waiting at your MARTA rail stop, use the white assistance phone in the station and MARTA will call one for you.

Taxi fares are a bit complicated in Atlanta. In the Downtown Convention Zone (bounded by Boulevard, Fourteenth Street, Northside Drive, and the stadium), you pay a flat rate of $5 for one or two passengers, $2 for each additional rider. That's fine if you're going from one end of this extensive zone to the other; unfortunately, though, you pay the same if you only go 1 block.

There's also a flat rate for rides between downtown and the airport: $18 for one passenger, $10 each for two or more, $8 each for three or more. Between the airport and midtown, the rate is $22 for one passenger, $25 for two or more. Between the airport and Buckhead, the rate is $28 for one, $30 for two or more. Within the Buckhead zone during special events, there's a flat rate of $5 for one person, $2 for each additional person.

Outside these specified zones, Atlanta cabs charge a $1.50 drop when you get in, 20¢ for each additional ⅛ mile for the first passenger, and a flat rate of $1 for each additional passenger, adult or child. Waiting time is $12 per hour.

There are many taxi companies in town. If you need to call for a taxi, try **Yellow Cabs** (☎ **404/521-0200**), **Checker Cabs** (☎ **404/351-1111**), **Classic Taxi** (☎ **404/438-1040**), or **Buckhead Safety Cab** (☎ **404/233-1152**). All accept cash and some accept credit cards.

If you have a complaint about taxi service, call ☎ **404/658-7600.**

FAST FACTS: Atlanta

Airport   See "Getting There" in chapter 2.

American Express   The Buckhead office across from the Swissôtel near Lenox Square provides travel services and currency exchange (☎ **404/262-7561**).

Area Codes   In metro Atlanta, you must dial the area code (404, 770 or 678) and the seven-digit telephone number, even if you are calling a number within the same area code. It is not necessary to dial "1" before the area code when calling between communities within the Atlanta local calling area that have different area codes.

Baby-sitters   Most hotels will arrange baby-sitters for you. If yours doesn't, a highly recommended service is **A Friend of the Family** (☎ 770/643-3000), which has been in business 15 years. All of their sitters are carefully screened, bonded, and at least 21 years of age. On request, they can send someone who is also trained in CPR and first aid. You can interview the sitter in advance on the phone or in person. The rate is $8 to $10 per hour, with a 4-hour minimum, plus an agency fee of $20 per day. The agency fee must be paid by credit card; the sitters prefer cash to out-of-state checks. Sitters will charge $10 per hour in a downtown hotel where they must pay to park. Advance notice of 24 hours is appreciated but not required. A Friend of the Family also provides pet care and companions for adults. Office hours are Monday to Friday 7am to 10pm and Saturday 8am to 10pm, but someone is on call 7am to 10pm, 7 days a week.

Buses   See "Getting Around," earlier in this chapter.

Car Rentals   See "Orientation," earlier in this chapter.

Climate   See "When to Go," in chapter 2.

Concierge Service   A Friend of the Family (see "Baby-sitters," above) offers a complete concierge service, running just about any personal errand imaginable. That might include buying tickets to local events, shopping, airport pickup, elderly escort, and so forth. Call ☎ 770/643-3000 for fee schedule and more information.

Dentists   The **Georgia Dental Association of Atlanta** (☎ 404/636-7553) offers a free referral service. They'll refer you to a dentist close to your hotel, or if need be, one who can accommodate special needs (for example, a dentist who does cosmetic work, offers home visits or senior-citizen discounts, speaks a foreign language, keeps emergency hours, or otherwise specializes). The service cannot match patients with dentists who offer services through specific insurance companies. Hours of operation are weekdays from 8:30am to 5pm. At other times, inquire at your hotel desk.

Doctors   The **Medical Association of Atlanta** (☎ 404/881-1714), with more than 2,000 member physicians in town, runs a free referral service for every kind of medical specialty and subspecialty. Hours are Monday to Friday, 9am to noon.

Piedmont Hospital in Buckhead also operates a free referral service (☎ 404/605-3556); all of its doctors are on the Piedmont Hospital staff and most have their offices close by. Some speak foreign languages. The service is open weekdays from 9am to 5pm; at other times, inquire at your hotel desk.

Promina Health Systems, a well-respected local consortium of physicians, hospitals, and clinics, operates its own referral service Monday to Friday, 8am to 5pm (☎ 404/541-1111).

Drugstores   See "Pharmacies," below.

Emergencies   To report a fire, summon the police, or procure an ambulance, simply dial **911.** See also the listing for the **Travelers Aid Society of Metropolitan Atlanta** in "Visitor Information," earlier in this chapter.

Eyeglass Repair   Lenscrafters, which has one location in the Lenox Square mall (☎ **404/239-0784**) and another in the Around Lenox Shopping Center (south of Lenox Square, just behind Neiman-Marcus; ☎ **404/262-2020**), offers 1-hour service on contacts and eyeglasses (including bifocals and trifocals), stocks a gigantic selection of frames (from designer to economy), provides on-premises eye examinations by independent doctors of optometry, maintains a complete contact-lens center, and gives discounts to senior citizens and college students. Check your phone book for other locations.

Hospitals/Emergency Rooms   Piedmont Hospital, 1968 Peachtree Rd., just above Collier Road (☎ **404/605-3297**), offers 24-hour full emergency-room service.

Information   See "Visitor Information" earlier in this chapter.

Liquor Laws   No alcohol is served at bars, restaurants, or nightclubs between 2:55am and 12:30pm Sunday. Alcoholic beverages are not sold on Sunday in liquor stores, convenience stores, or grocery stores. The drinking age is 21.

Maps   See "City Layout," earlier in this chapter.

Newspapers/Magazines   The major newspaper in town is the *Atlanta Journal-Constitution.* Its "Preview" section, published every Friday, and the "Leisure" section, published on Saturday, highlight movies, plays, festivals, live music, gallery openings, and other happenings for the weekend and the week ahead. The Preview section also includes restaurant reviews. You'll also find it helpful to pick up a current issue of *Atlanta* magazine when you're in town. And keep an eye out for *Creative Loafing,* an offbeat free publication available in shops, restaurants, and on the street; it offers much interesting information, including excellent restaurant reviews.

Pharmacies (Late-Night)   Drug Emporium, 2625 Piedmont Rd. in Buckhead, about 1 mile south of Peachtree Road (☎ **404/233-1048**), is open 24 hours and offers full pharmaceutical services.

Poison Center   Call ☎ **404/616-9000.**

Police   Call ☎ **911** in an emergency. Call ☎ **404/658-6600** for non-emergencies.

Road Conditions   Call ☎ **404/656-5267** for information about delays due to road construction.

Salons   To some of us, a gifted hairdresser can be the most essential of services. Carey Carter and Mitchell Barnes of **Carter/Barnes Hair Artisans,** on the upper level of Phipps Plaza shopping mall (☎ **404/233-0047**), are among the best and best-known stylists in Atlanta (for men and women). Their work is often featured in well-regarded fashion magazines, and they regularly make the lists of top national salons. Their shop is in Buckhead, but their clients come from all over the Southeast and other points around the country. The salon is quite large, relaxed, and friendly, and it's almost always possible to get an appointment on short notice with one of the several stylists. Besides haircuts, color, and perms, there's also a full complement of salon and spa services—facials, manicures/pedicures, waxing, massage, extensive skin care, deep therapy for hands and feet, and full days of beauty services. Particularly fun (and valuable) is a makeup lesson with one of the makeup artists.

Two more excellent salons that are conveniently located and that serve both men and women include **Scott Cole Salon,** 2859 Piedmont Rd. NW

(☎ **404/237-4970**); and **Van Michael Salon,** 39 West Paces Ferry Rd. (☎ **404/237-4664**). In addition to the regular salon, Van Michael has a **New Talents** salon next door where you can get a lower-priced haircut ($19–$25) from a stylist in training.

Taxes   Sales tax in Atlanta is 7%. A total of 14% is paid by hotel and motel guests within the city of Atlanta and Fulton County. Of that tax, 7% is sales tax and 7% is room tax.

Taxis   Call Yellow Cabs (☎ **404/521-0200**), Checker Cabs (☎ **404/ 351-1111**), or Buckhead Safety Cab (☎ **404/233-1152**) in Buckhead.

Tickets   For tickets to almost all sports and performing arts events, call **TicketMaster** (☎ **404/249-6400**) to charge by phone. TicketMaster also has 110 locations throughout Georgia, including all Publix Supermarkets, where customers can purchase tickets in person, though they must be paid for in cash. To avoid the TicketMaster surcharge, it's often possible to purchase tickets at the box office. If you are staying in a large hotel, the concierge service often is able to obtain tickets to even the most popular events. Call ☎ **404/222-6688.**

Day-of-show half-price tickets are available at AtlanTIX! ticket booth at the Atlanta Convention and Visitors Bureau in Underground Atlanta. Customers can look over the showboard to see what plays and other live performances have tickets available that day, purchase a voucher for the show, and pick up the ticket at the show's box office before curtain time. Vouchers must be paid for in person; phone sales are not available. Call ☎ **404/222-6688** for more information.

Time   Call ☎ **770/455-7141** or ☎ **404/387-1666.** Atlanta is on eastern standard time.

Transit Info   To find out how to get from point A to point B via MARTA (bus and rail), dial ☎ **404/848-4711.**

Weather   Call ☎ **770/455-7141** or ☎ 404/387-1666.

Accommodations 5

As a major convention city, metro Atlanta is capable of accommodating vast numbers of visitors. It has nearly 70,000 rooms at 477 properties, including budget digs, bed-and-breakfast lodgings, and bastions of luxury. The choices listed below—offering good value in several different price brackets—are in the parts of the city frequented most by tourists. If you have trouble finding a spot at these places, look to the suburbs. Nearly every chain is represented, and if you have a car and you're near one of the major interstates, getting into the city should be relatively simple, especially if you avoid rush hour.

Many preferential rates are available only when you reserve via toll-free reservation numbers. These numbers are supplied in all applicable listings below.

Also inquire about reduced-price packages (they may include extras such as meals, parking, theater tickets, and golf fees) and reduced rates for senior citizens, families, and active-duty military personnel. Reservation agents don't usually volunteer this information, though; you should always take the initiative and ask about special packages.

Although 100% occupancy is a rarity in Atlanta, it is a major convention city; booking well in advance assures you a room in the hotel of your choice.

Though many of the hotels are quite full during the business week, they're usually not sold out on the weekend. Most of the major hotels that cater to business travelers, especially those downtown, offer reduced weekend tariffs. For example, the Four Seasons, one of the most elegant hotels in the city, offers weekend doubles at only $125 per night, based on availability.

And finally, keep in mind that a hotel makes zero dollars per night on an empty room. Though they don't exactly advertise it (for obvious reasons), most hotels are willing to bargain on rates rather than leave a room unoccupied. Haggling won't work when hotels are running close to 100% occupancy, but whenever a rate is quoted it's a good idea to ask, "Can I get a better deal?" If the reservations clerk can't help you, ask to speak to the desk captain. That doesn't mean you won't risk a snub or two, but those who persevere can sometimes save some money. An especially advantageous time to secure lower rates is late afternoon or early evening on the day of your arrival, when a hotel's likelihood of filling up with full-price bookings is remote.

RATES   Any extras included in the rates (for example, breakfast or other meals) are listed for each property. A 14% tax will be added onto your hotel or motel bill within the city of Atlanta and Fulton County (7% sales tax plus 7% room tax); the rates listed below do not include that tax.

Also keep in mind that the prices quoted are subject to change. They're rack rates, and if you ask about discounts and packages, or if you book through a travel agent, you can often do better than these posted rates. If you have a car, be sure to consider the price of parking in the hotel garage.

Note: You will spot rates in the above-listed categories higher than those quoted. Those are special-events rates; most of the year, they will not apply.

BED & BREAKFASTS   **Bed & Breakfast Atlanta,** 1608 Briarcliff Rd. NE (☎ **800/967-3224** or 404/875-0525; fax 404/875-8198; www. bedandbreakfastatlanta.com; E-mail: bnbinfo@mindspring.com), is a professional reservation service that has been carefully screening facilities in the Atlanta area since 1979. Their list comprises more than 100 homes and inns, all accommodations offering private baths. They include—among others—a turreted Queen Anne–style Victorian home with nine fireplaces near the Carter Library, a delightful honeymoon cottage with a Jacuzzi in "Miss Daisy's" Druid Hills, an elegant 1920s Tudor-style home in Buckhead, and a fully furnished garden cottage in Ansley Park. They even have kosher homes on their roster. All rates include continental breakfast, in many cases extended considerably beyond the usual pastry and coffee. Reserve as far in advance as possible for the greatest number of selections. Call during office hours, which are Monday to Friday from 9am to 5pm.

The rates run the gamut from $60 to $240 (the latter for a luxurious Buckhead guest cottage on a 4-acre estate that accommodates four people). Rates during special events may be higher. Weekly and monthly rates are available (in guesthouses and apartments) for long-term visitors. There's no fee. American Express, Diner's Club, MasterCard, and Visa are accepted.

1 Best Bets

- **Best for Business Travelers:** All the major downtown megahotels—which cater largely to a business and convention clientele—are fully equipped to meet your business needs. Of them all, the finest is the **Ritz-Carlton Atlanta** (181 Peachtree St. NE; ☎ **404/659-0400**), which combines a full business center and a can-do concierge with superb service.
- **Best for a Romantic Getaway:** The **Ansley Inn** (253 Fifteenth St. NE; ☎ **404/872-9000**), has charming antique-furnished rooms; step outside and you're in one of Atlanta's most beautifully landscaped neighborhoods, perfect for sunset strolls.
  If you prefer a hotel to a B&B, a stay at the **Ritz-Carlton Buckhead** (3434 Peachtree Rd.; ☎ **404/237-2700**) sets the stage for romance.
- **Best for Families:** The **Marriott Residence Inn Buckhead** (2960 Piedmont Rd. NE; ☎ **404/239-0677**) offers accommodations large enough to ensure privacy for all, plus fully equipped kitchens, washers and dryers, indoor and outdoor swimming pools, barbecue grills, and basketball, volleyball, and paddle tennis courts. Many rooms have fireplaces; prepare some popcorn in the microwave and enjoy a fun family evening before the fire.
- **Best Moderately Priced Hotel: Courtyard by Marriott** (Buckhead) (3332 Peachtree Rd. NE; ☎ **404/869-0818**) offers luxury in an excellent location.

Downtown, you can't beat the **Marriott Residence Inn Atlanta-Downtown** (134 Peachtree St. NW; ☎ **404/522-0950**).

- **Best Inexpensive Accommodations: Biltmore Suites** (30 Fifth St. NE; ☎ **404/874-0824**), an elegant property that is on the National Register of Historic Places, delivers a lot of luxury at low prices. Accommodations are in spacious, residentially furnished suites with 10-foot ceilings, hand-carved crown moldings, and French doors.
- **Best Location:** Buckhead is the loveliest part of town, and there's lots of exceptional nightlife, dining, and shopping. There are two MARTA stations (Buckhead and Lenox) where you can connect to other parts of the city, and any hotel within walking distance of either of those stations is a sure bet. A good example is the **J.W. Marriott** (3300 Lenox Rd. NE; ☎ **404/262-3344**), adjacent to upscale Lenox Square mall.
- **Best Service:** The **Ritz-Carlton Atlanta** and the **Ritz-Carlton Buckhead** (see addresses and telephone numbers above) are in a class by themselves. A close second (and gaining) is the **Four Seasons** (75 Fourteenth St.; (☎ **404/881-9898**).
- **Best Architectural Digest Interior:** The most exquisite interior is found at the **Gaslight Inn** (1001 St. Charles Ave.; ☎ **404/875-1001**), a bed-and-breakfast where the rooms might inspire you to redecorate your own home. Its location in charming Virginia-Highland is a plus for vacationers.
- **Best Trendy Hotel:** The **Swissôtel** (3391 Peachtree Rd. NE; ☎ **404/365-0065**), with its clean Euromodern style, is a favorite among visiting celebrities.
- **Best for Travelers with Disabilities:** The **Embassy Suites Hotel Buckhead** (3285 Peachtree Rd. NW; ☎ **800/362-2779**), which hosts the participants in the wheelchair event for the Peachtree Road Race, is fully accessible, with 10 suites completely equipped for disabled visitors. Two of the suites have roll-in showers. The hotel is also a block from the Buckhead MARTA station.
- **Best for Pets:** Some hotels can get downright snooty if you try to check in with your pooch, but not the lavish **Four Seasons Hotel** (see address and phone number above). Pets are welcome (just call ahead) and even get special treats to make them feel at home. The more modest **Cheshire Motor Inn,** 1865 Cheshire Bridge Rd. (☎ **800/827-9628** or 404/872-9628), also welcomes pets.

2 Downtown

Downtown hotels primarily cater to the business/convention traveler, but a tourist will also enjoy the services and facilities of these properties. In addition to the listings you'll find below, there are two new hotels, the Embassy Suites at Centennial Park and the Wyndham Atlanta Downtown. Both were still under construction at press time and only limited information was available.

VERY EXPENSIVE

Atlanta Hilton & Towers

255 Courtland St. (between Baker and Harris sts.), Atlanta, GA 30303. ☎ **800/HILTONS** or 404/659-2000. Fax 404/524-0111. www.hilton.com. 1,224 units. A/C TV TEL. Mon–Thurs $190–$245 double, Fri–Sun $99–$159 double, depending on the season. Tower rooms $255 double. Extra person $20. Children stay free in parents' room. AE, CB, DC, DISC, ER, JCB, MC, V. Valet parking $12; self-parking $8. MARTA: Peachtree Center.

One of Atlanta's top convention hotels—with 104,000 square feet of meeting and exhibit space—the Hilton is surprisingly upscale for a chain hotel. The rooms and bathrooms are very nice and quite large, and if you're going to stay in one of the downtown megahotels, this is a good choice. Renovated in 1996, the rooms offer coffeemakers and hair dryers, plus video checkout and account-review functions. Many rooms have minibars, and some of the suites have Murphy beds for extra guests.

Dining/Diversions: The Hilton's premier restaurant is the newly refurbished Nikolai's Roof, a 30th-floor dining room offering spectacular skyline vistas. Multi-course prix-fixe French and Russian dinners are the specialty, and it's wise to book well in advance. A Point of View, the bar adjacent to Nikolai's Roof, has live jazz on Wednesday nights. Trader Vic's, a South Seas–Polynesian restaurant found at numerous Hiltons, here offers its signature setting and potent rum drinks. The Garden Terrace, a pretty lobby-level eatery centered around a vast fountain, serves buffet meals at breakfast and lunch and Sunday champagne brunch. Adjoining it are the Cafe Express Deli (a 24-hour facility) and Le Café, the Hilton's casual dining facility. Finally, there's the Bogart-and-Bergman–themed Casablanca Bar, whose big-screen TV attracts a sports-minded crowd.

Amenities: Airport shuttle, outdoor pool/sundeck, fitness center, sauna, whirlpool, jogging track, four outdoor tennis courts, business center, room service, concierge, shops, and shoeshine stand.

Hyatt Regency Atlanta

265 Peachtree St. NE (between Baker and Harris sts.), Atlanta, GA 30303. ☎ **800/233-1234** or 404/577-1234. Fax 404/588-4137. www.hyatt.com. 1,322 units. A/C MINIBAR TV TEL. $225 double; Regency Club $260 double. Business Plan $240. Extra person $25. Children under 18 stay free in parents' room. Packages and promotional rates often available. AE, CB, DC, DISC, ER, JCB, MC, V. Parking $17 (valet only). MARTA: Peachtree Center.

One of the city's major convention hotels, the Hyatt was designed in 1967 by famed Atlanta architect John Portman. With its innovative 23-story atrium lobby, it created quite a stir and was the prototype not only for future downtown hotels in the city, but for hotel architectural design throughout the United States. The hotel connects to the Peachtree Center shopping mall through a covered walkway.

The Hyatt, which underwent a $35-million renovation in 1996, accommodates guests not only in this original building, but in two later additions—the 24-story International Tower and the 22-story Ivy Tower. Rooms throughout feature plush modern furnishings, and they are equipped with safes, irons, full-size ironing boards, and video checkout and account review. The comfortable bathrooms are equipped with hair dryers.

The main building's 22nd floor houses the Regency Club, and Business Plan rooms (equipped with personal work stations, in-room faxes, desk phones with computer jacks, and coffeemakers) are on the 21st floor. Business Plan guests get free local calls and other perks.

Dining/Diversions: The blue dome capping Polaris, the Hyatt's revolving rooftop restaurant, is a landmark on the city's skyline. Open for dinner, it features steak, seafood, and decadent desserts. You can enjoy the same spectacular views over cocktails in the adjoining lounge. Overlooking the lobby is the informal Kafe Köbenhavn, which offers buffets at all meals, as well as an à la carte coffee-shop menu. One level below the lobby is Avanzare, a charming Italian restaurant with an 1,800-gallon saltwater aquarium along one wall. Also in the lobby is Perks, a 24-hour cafe offering specialty coffee drinks, ice cream, chocolates, pastries, and other snacks. And the Parasol Bar is the large new lobby lounge, providing a spot for drinks before or after dinner.

Downtown Accommodations

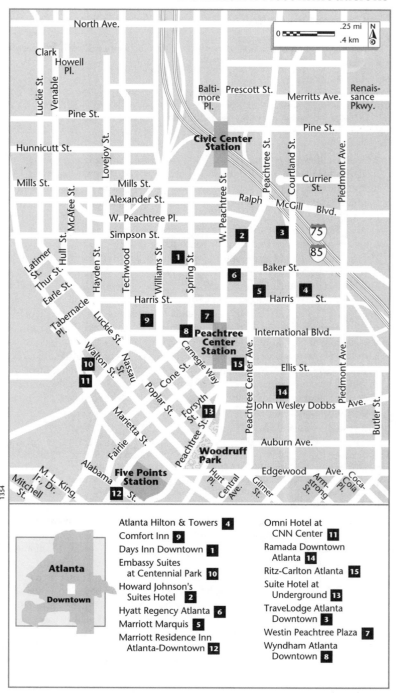

Atlanta Hilton & Towers **4**
Comfort Inn **9**
Days Inn Downtown **1**
Embassy Suites
  at Centennial Park **10**
Howard Johnson's
  Suites Hotel **2**
Hyatt Regency Atlanta **6**
Marriott Marquis **5**
Marriott Residence Inn
  Atlanta-Downtown **12**

Omni Hotel at
  CNN Center **11**
Ramada Downtown
  Atlanta **14**
Ritz-Carlton Atlanta **15**
Suite Hotel at
  Underground **13**
TraveLodge Atlanta
  Downtown **3**
Westin Peachtree Plaza **7**
Wyndham Atlanta
  Downtown **8**

57

Amenities: Large outdoor pool and whirlpool, courtesy car, children's programs, business center, room service, gift shop, Delta Air Lines desk, concierge, and multilingual staff. For $12 a day, guests may visit the full health club in Peachtree Center.

Marriott Marquis

265 Peachtree Center Ave. (between Baker and Harris sts.), Atlanta, GA 30303. ☎ **800/228-9290** or 404/521-0000. Fax 404/586-6299. www.marriott.com. 1,671 units. A/C TV TEL. $230–$260 double. Concierge level $230 double. Extra person $20. Children under 12 free. Packages available. AE, CB, DC, DISC, MC, V. Parking $17 (self or valet). MARTA: Peachtree Center.

A dramatic downtown landmark, the Marriott Marquis is a first-class megahotel designed by Atlanta's John Portman. Fronted by a vast fountain that looks like a flying saucer, it has a 50-story atrium lobby that is said to be the largest in the southeast. It's connected, via a covered walkway, to shops in the Peachtree Center mall.

The rooms, which were completely renovated in 1998, are nicely decorated and feel absolutely fresh and new. They're outfitted with coffeemakers, irons, and full-size ironing board, and some rooms have dataports. The spiffy bathrooms have hair dryers and upscale complimentary toilet articles.

Dining/Diversions: On the Garden Level, above the lobby, you'll find all the hotel's restaurants and lounges. Allie's American Grille, open for all meals, features light fare. The elegant Marquis Steakhouse seats diners amid a forest of ficus trees. There's a self-service Atrium Express that offers coffee, sandwiches, and pastries. Champions, with its big-screen TV, is a popular sports bar and grill. And up a brass-railed stairway, seemingly suspended in space, is the Grandstand Lounge.

Amenities: Airport shuttle, full fitness center, large swimming pool with adjoining whirlpool, concierge, 24-hour room service, *USA Today* delivered daily to your room, shops, unisex hairstylist, shoeshine stand, Delta Air Lines desk, conference and banquet facilities.

Omni Hotel at CNN Center

100 CNN Center (at Marietta St. and International Blvd.), Atlanta, GA 30335. ☎ **800/THE-OMNI** or 404/659-0000. E-mail: omnicnn@mindspring.com. 458 units. A/C MINIBAR TV TEL. $285 double, $775–$1,100 1-bedroom suite, $950–$1,100 2-bedroom suite. Children under 18 free in parents' room. Weekend packages start at $139 double when available. Prices are higher during special events. AE, CB, DC, DISC, ER, EC, JCB, MC, V. Parking $17 (valet only). MARTA: Omni/Dome.

The Omni is one of those megahotels that caters to the convention crowds, so it's not big on charm and personality, and it's also expensive. What it does have going for it is location—especially if you're attending a sporting event. It adjoins the Georgia World Congress Center, the Georgia Dome, and CNN Center; is across from Centennial Olympic Park; and will be connected to the Atlanta Arena (home of the NBA Atlanta Hawks and the NHL Thrashers) when that sports venue opens in 1999. The rooms, which are unusually large, underwent a much-needed renovation in 1997, although they're still rather impersonal. The public spaces will be refurbished in 1999. Many of the rooms have balconies that overlook the bustle of the CNN Center atrium; the rest have views of Centennial Olympic Park or the downtown skyline. There are three phones in each room (including one in the bathroom), and all rooms have dataports. The tile baths have hair dryers and makeup mirrors. Most of the suites, with their huge living/dining areas (with wet bar), can easily accommodate 35 to 45 people for receptions or parties. Eleven rooms have been modified for disabled visitors.

Dining/Diversions: Bugatti restaurant, which serves Northern Italian fare, used to be one of the fanciest restaurants downtown. It has lots more competition now, but it's still stylish and reliable. The American Cafe offers breakfast and lunch buffets as well as à la carte service in a casual garden setting in the CNN Center atrium. The Take Two lounge in the lobby features live piano entertainment in the evening.

Amenities: Business center, conference and banquet facilities, laundry service, car rental desk, concierge, beauty salon and some shops in CNN Center, room service 6am to 2am, secretarial services, privileges at nearby fitness center $12 a day.

✪ Ritz-Carlton Atlanta

181 Peachtree St. NE (at Ellis St.; main entrance on Ellis), Atlanta, GA 30303. ☎ **800/ 241-3333** or 404/659-0400. Fax 404/688-0400. 471 units. A/C MINIBAR TV TEL. Sun–Thurs $185–$229 double, Fri–Sat $139 per room. Club Level $325 double; $485–$1,200 suite. Extra person $25. AE, CB, DC, DISC, ER, MC, V. Parking $17 (valet only). MARTA: Peachtree Center.

Without a doubt, this is Atlanta's finest downtown hotel. With Persian rugs strewn on marble floors, silk-tapestried and African mahogany-paneled walls hung with a collection of 18th- and 19th-century paintings, and valuable antiques throughout its public areas, it's hard to believe that the Ritz was built as late as 1984. The impeccable service also harks back to another, more gracious era; you'll be cosseted as never before. Elegant rooms, many with bay windows, are furnished with beautiful mahogany pieces (some have four-poster beds). Amenities include terry robes, scales, and extra phones in the bath. All rooms were renovated at the end of 1998.

Dining/Diversions: The two eating establishments on the premises are among the best downtown Atlanta has to offer. The hotel's premier dining room is The Restaurant, an equestrian-themed setting with 19th-century, gilt-framed hunt paintings. Open for dinner only, it offers Asian-influenced French cuisine; a pianist entertains during dinner. Afterward, you might retreat to the adjoining Bar, where a jazz trio plays Wednesday to Saturday night until 11:30pm. The intimate Café, on the lobby level, is the hotel's informal dining room. An afternoon tea, complete with fresh-baked scones and watercress sandwiches, is served in the lobby lounge daily.

Amenities: Fitness center, business center, multilingual concierge staff, 24-hour room service, twice-daily maid service, nightly turndown, complimentary overnight shoeshine, your regional paper delivered to your door on request, evening pressing service, car rental, limousine, gift shop.

Westin Peachtree Plaza

210 Peachtree St. NW (at International Blvd.), Atlanta, GA 30303. ☎ **800/228-3000** or 404/659-1400. Fax 404/589-7424. www.westin.com. 1,068 units. A/C TV TEL. $295–$320 double; suites $350–$1,450. Extra person $20. Children under 18 free in parents' room. Inquire about packages. AE, CB, DC, DISC, ER, JCB, MC, V. Valet parking $18; self-parking $14. MARTA: Peachtree Center.

You wouldn't expect that a 73-story 1,000-room hotel could be described as cozy, but that adjective fits the Westin. The 300-square-foot rooms, which were undergoing renovations at press time, are both elegant and intimate, and floor-to-ceiling windows provide dramatic views of the city. In-room amenities include wall safes and irons with full-size ironing boards. There are hair dryers in each of the marble baths. The $35 million renovation was due to be completed at the end of 1999, so if you stay at the Westin before then, be sure to ask for a new room.

Dining/Diversions: The revolving Sun Dial Restaurant, on the 71st floor, offers sophisticated American fare and an impressive 360-degree view of the city-skyline. It also will be renovated–to the tune of $2.5 million. Its revolving bar, on the 73rd floor, is a good spot for cocktails and light fare; a jazz trio entertains there nightly.

The lobby-level Savannah Fish Company, with seating overlooking a splashing 100-foot horizontal waterfall, specializes in fresh seafood. The Café restaurant, located in the atrium lobby, serves buffet and à la carte breakfasts. The Tivoli Coffee Bar is open daily for coffee drinks and tea, sandwiches, and pastries. There's also the International Bar and the adjoining Sidewalk Café.

Amenities: Newly equipped health club, beautiful large pool (under a retractable skylight for year-round indoor/outdoor use), comprehensive business center, concierge, 24-hour room service, shopping gallery that connects with Macy's.

EXPENSIVE

Embassy Suites at Centennial Park
267 Marrietta St., Atlanta, GA 30303. ☎ **800/EMBASSY.**

This all-suites hotel will be the first new full-service hotel downtown when it opens its doors in mid-1999. Although details were not available at press time, plans call for 321 one-bedroom suites with rates from $130 to $200. The location is excellent, right on Centennial Olympic Park, with many of the suites overlooking the park.

✪ Suite Hotel Underground Atlanta
54 Peachtree St. SW, Atlanta, GA 30303. ☎ **404/223-5555.** Fax 404/223-0467. 156 units. $145–$210. (Higher rate applies for suite with Jacuzzi.) Weekend rates can be as low as $89 double when available. Children under 16 stay free in parents' suite. Packages available. AE, CB, DC, DISC, JCB, MC, V. Self-parking $8. MARTA: Five Points.

If huge, convention-oriented hotels turn you off, this place may be just the thing. One of the best-kept secrets in downtown, it's elegant and understated, and attracts a clientele that prefers the intimacy of a European hotel. Each suite has a small living room, a separate bedroom, and a marble bathroom, some with Jacuzzis. The living area has a wet bar and refrigerator, and the entire suite is elegantly appointed with solid cherry furniture and modern prints. There are two televisions (one with Spectravision) and three phones, including one in the bathroom. Many of the rooms have views of the downtown skyline. All were renovated in 1998.

This 16-story hotel was originally a 1918 office building to which 10 stories were added in 1990. It's on the top level of Underground Atlanta and convenient to all the shops and restaurants that attraction has to offer. It's within walking distance of the downtown business area and close to the main MARTA station, where all the lines converge, making it easy to travel to Midtown, Buckhead, and the airport.

Dining/Diversions: The Dining Room specializes in basic American fare. It serves a buffet breakfast and dinner, and also has a cozy bar.

Amenities: Room service 7am to 10am and 5pm to 11pm, valet, limited business center, access to nearby Peachtree Health Center for $15.

Wyndham Atlanta Downtown
160 Spring St., Atlanta, GA 30303. ☎ **800/WYNDHAM.**

This promises to be a luxury property by the time it opens in mid-1999. Renovators have spent upwards of $25 million to turn the old Best Western American Hotel into an upscale Wyndham with 312 rooms, including 26 suites. Rates will probably range from $99 (weekends) to $199.

MODERATE

Comfort Inn
101 International Blvd. (at Williams St.), Atlanta, GA 30303. ☎ **800/535-0707,** 800/228-5150, or 404/524-5555. Fax 404/221-0702. comfort@mindspring.com. 260 units. A/C

TV TEL. $79–$179 double. Rates may be higher—up to $250 a night—during major conventions or special events. Extra person $10. Children 18 and under stay free in parents' room. AE, CB, DC, DISC, MC, V. Self-parking $10, may be higher during special events. MARTA: Peachtree Center or Omni/Dome.

Comfort Inns are based on the theory that a low-cost hotel needn't be a no-frills hotel, and this 11-story property is a good example. It offers appealing rooms with oak furnishings, which were renovated in 1998. Each room has a desk, a table with two chairs (or sleeper sofa), and a hair dryer. It's adjacent to the Gift, Apparel, and Merchandise Marts, and it's two blocks from CNN Center and Centennial Olympic Park.

Bistro 101, the on-premises eatery, is rather charming, with tables amid potted ferns and copper cookware on the walls. Many seats overlook the pool. It offers typical American fare. In the Blind Zebra Bar, sporting events are aired on the TV.

There's also a nice-size outdoor pool/sundeck, concierge, room service during restaurant hours, a courtesy car (reserve in advance), a small business center, electric shoeshine machines on each floor, and a gift shop.

Days Inn Downtown

300 Spring St. (at Baker St.), Atlanta, GA 30308. ☎ **800/DAYS-INN** or 404/523-1144. Fax 404/577-8495. 262 units. A/C TV TEL. $99–$225 double (high end reflects major special events). Extra person $10. Children under 18 stay free in parents' room. Special weekend rates subject to availability. AE, DC, DISC, JCB, MC, V. Self-parking $9. MARTA: Peachtree Center.

This central Days Inn allows visitors to stay in the heart of the business district at a moderate cost. In-room amenities include safes and coffeemakers. A few rooms have refrigerators, and those on floors 3 to 10 have balconies. Although you don't get all the luxury-hotel frills here, accommodations are clean and fresh-looking; facilities are ample. Renovations to all the rooms were to be completed in 1999. A Wendy's restaurant adjoins the property. There's also a comfortable lounge in the hotel, open 5pm to midnight, where sporting events are aired. And the large outdoor pool is a plus.

Howard Johnson Suites

330 Peachtree St. NE (between Baker St. and Ralph McGill Blvd.), Atlanta, GA 30308. ☎ **800/362-5600** or 404/577-1980. Fax 404/688-3706. www.hojo.com. 94 units. A/C TV TEL. $149 double. Prices may be lower on weekends. Rates include deluxe continental breakfast. Children 16 and under stay free in parents' room. AE, CB, DC, DISC, MC, V. Self-parking $6.50 . MARTA: Peachtree Center or Civic Center.

Just a few blocks from the center of downtown, this newly refurbished hotel (1998) offers a lot for its price range. Rooms are large and nicely furnished, each equipped with a desk, a dataport, two armchairs or a sofa, and a compact kitchen that includes a sink, small refrigerator, coffeemaker, and microwave.

Complimentary extended continental breakfast is served each morning in a cozy room off the lobby; weather permitting, you might breakfast outdoors at patio tables. Room service is available from about a dozen area restaurants (you'll find a comprehensive menu in your room). There's a well-equipped exercise room, and *USA Today* is free in the lobby.

✪ Marriott Residence Inn Atlanta-Downtown

134 Peachtree St. NW (1 block north of Woodruff Park), Atlanta, GA 30303. ☎ **800/331-3131** or 404/522-0950. Fax 404/577-3235. www.marriott.com. A/C TV TEL. $129 double (1–4 nights), $119 double (5–11 nights), $109 double (12–29 nights), $89 (more than 30 nights). Rates include deluxe continental breakfast. Rates are higher during special events. Children under 18 stay free in parents' room. AE, DC, DISC, MC, V. Valet parking $14; self-parking $7.50. MARTA: Peachtree Center.

This is the best deal downtown. It's close to all the action, the accommodations are nicely appointed studios or suites, and it's incredibly inexpensive—especially for an extended stay. The rooms, most of which are more like small apartments, all have queen-size beds and full kitchens outfitted with all the necessary equipment, with the exception of some of the smaller studios, which have kitchenettes. The baths are equipped with hair dryers, the phones have dataports, there are coin-op washers and dryers, and there is same-day valet service. In addition to the complimentary breakfast, the hotel provides a light supper Monday, Tuesday, and Thursday, holds a cookout on Wednesday, and will even do your grocery shopping. What more could you ask? Oh, yes. You can even bring your pet (although the $100 nonrefundable fee is a little steep). And if the exercise room is too small for you, you can use the fitness center at the posh Marriott Marquis just a few blocks away. For a nice view of downtown, ask for one of the suites on the higher floors.

The building itself was constructed in 1928 and is listed on the National Register of Historic Places. Because it's an older building, the rooms are extremely quiet, and the high ceilings lend an added feeling of spaciousness. As you pass through the marble lobby, be sure to look up at the ceiling. It was painted by European artists when the building was new and has been restored to its original splendor.

Ramada Downtown Atlanta

70 John Wesley Dobbs Ave. NE (at Courtland St.), Atlanta, GA 30303. ☎ **800/2RAMADA** or 404/659-2660. Fax 404/524-5390. 223 units. A/C TV TEL. $69–$129 double; $189 1-bedroom suite; $214 2-bedroom suites. Extra person $10. Children under 18 stay free in parents' room. AE, CB, DC, DISC, MC, V. Free parking, subject to availability. MARTA: Peachtree Center.

An eight-story stucco building that forms a courtyard around its swimming pool, the Ramada was renovated in 1998. Rooms, 90% of them with balconies, are charmingly decorated with traditional cherrywood furniture. Because this is an older property, the rooms are a generous size; the bathrooms are clean but about what you'd expect for a chain. Hair dryers and coffeemakers are available on request. Some of the rooms have dataports.

The Courtland Café, a pretty garden-motif restaurant with an adjoining lounge, is open for all meals. There's also room service during restaurant hours, a medium-size outdoor pool, and a gift shop. For a $10 fee, guests can use the state-of-the-art Phoenix Health Club nearby.

INEXPENSIVE

TraveLodge Atlanta Downtown

311 Courtland St. NE (between Baker St. and Ralph McGill Blvd.), Atlanta, GA 30303. ☎ **800/578-7878** or 404/659-4545. Fax 404/659-5934. 71 units. A/C TV TEL. $64–$114 double. Rates include continental breakfast. Extra person $8. Children under 18 stay free in parents' room. AE, CB, DC, DISC, MC, V. Free parking. MARTA: Peachtree Center.

Operated by the Clark family since 1964, this small TraveLodge offers an inexpensive alternative in the heart of downtown. Its rooms, renovated in 1996, still look clean and fresh, with new furniture, carpet, drapes, and bedspreads. More king-size beds have been added, too. Each room is equipped with a safe, hair dryer, and coffeemaker; pay-per-view movies are available. Complimentary continental breakfast is served in the lobby each morning, and numerous restaurants are within walking distance. Free daily newspapers are another plus. Facilities include a nice-size outdoor pool, and TraveLodge guests can use the extensive facilities of the nearby Peachtree Center Athletic Club for $12 a day.

⊕ Family-Friendly Hotels

Four Seasons Hotel *(see p. 63)*   Kids enjoy a special program that includes cook- ies and milk on check-in, a book (*James and the Giant Peach)*, a toiletries box with baby shampoo and a rubber duck, chocolates at nightly turndown, board games, and children's movie videos and video games.

Marriott Residence Inn Buckhead *(see p. 82)*   This place not only has a swimming pool, but the accommodations come with fully equipped kitchens—a potential money-saver when you're traveling with your family. Rates here include breakfast, and there are barbecue grills and picnic tables on the premises. It's like having your own Atlanta apartment, with parking at your door. The property also contains basketball, volleyball, and paddle-tennis courts, and guests can rent movies at the front desk.

Stone Mountain Park Inn *(see p. 84)*   Located in Stone Mountain Park, this lovely inn is a perfect spot for families who want to take full advantage of the park's recreational opportunities. The inn itself has an outdoor pool, but in the park there are also fishing, boating, miniature golf, bicycle rental, hiking along wildlife trails, picnicking, and more.

Summerfield Suites Hotel Buckhead *(see p. 82)*   Suites hotels are almost always the most economical way to travel with a family, and this hotel is in an excellent location. An expanded continental breakfast is included in the rate, and there's also a fully equipped kitchen in each of the suites. There's a lovely pool on the premises, a barbecue grill on the patio, and VCRs in each room. A short walk down the street, there's a city park with a playground.

3 Midtown

Travelers interested in the cultural highlights will appreciate a hotel in Midtown, home to the Woodruff Arts Center, the High Museum of Art, the Fox Theatre, and the Margaret Mitchell House. Joggers and other outdoor enthusiasts will like the proximity to Piedmont Park and the Atlanta Botanical Garden.

VERY EXPENSIVE

✪ Four Seasons Hotel

75 Fourteenth St. (between Peachtree and West Peachtree sts.), Atlanta, GA 30309. ☎ **800/332-3442** or 404/881-9898. Fax 404/873-4692. 244 units. A/C MINIBAR TV TEL. $210 double; $450 suites; $1,500 presidential suite. Children under 18 stay free in parents' room. Excellent weekend cultural packages available. AE, MC, V. Valet parking $18. MARTA: Arts Center.

This elegant hotel is the one to choose if you're looking for luxurious surroundings in the heart of Atlanta's cultural area. Built in 1991 as the Grand Hotel Atlanta, and acquired in 1998 by Four Seasons, it immediately underwent a $65 million renovation.

Accommodations are lavish and sophisticated, with large windows, upholstered lounge chairs and sofas, and handsome wooden furnishings that lend a Beidermeir effect. All rooms are equipped with three phones (bedside, desk, and bath), modem lines, and safes. Gorgeous marble bathrooms contain scales, terry robes, hair dryers, upscale toiletries, and linen hand towels. Some have separate showers. Fourteen of the rooms have been modified to accommodate the disabled.

Midtown Accommodations

Ansley Inn **7**

Biltmore Suites **11**

Cheshire Motor Inn **1**

Comfort Inn Buckhead **2**

Days Inn Peachtree **12**

Fairfield Inn Midtown **3**

Gaslight Inn **15**

The Georgia Terrace **13**

Four Seasons Hotel **5**

Marriott Suites **4**

1355A

Marriott Residence Inn Midtown **8**
Shellmont Bed & Breakfast **10**
Sheraton Colony Square Hotel **6**
Woodruff Bed & Breakfast **14**
Wyndham Garden Hotel **9**

The public spaces are stunning; don't miss the massive Baccarat crystal chandelier (which originally graced a turn-of-the-century Paris hotel) that sparkles overhead in the lobby. Service, of course, is impeccable.

Dining/Diversions: At press time, both dining spaces and the bar were undergoing complete renovations, but plans call for a fine-dining restaurant serving regional American cuisine with an emphasis on boutique wines; a terrace restaurant in the three-story atrium that will serve light fare and afternoon tea; and an elegant bar serving classic cocktails.

Amenities: 24-hour room service, 24-hour concierge, extensive business center, complete health club with individual televisions at each cardiovascular exercise machine, large indoor pool, outdoor sundeck, whirlpool, steam, sauna, nightly bed turndown, newspaper with breakfast room service, complimentary shoeshine, complimentary round-trip transport by luxury car to downtown, Buckhead, the airport, and points within a 5-mile radius. Kids enjoy wonderful special gifts and treats. Pets are permitted and receive suitable treats also. A beauty salon with a full-service spa is planned for 1999.

EXPENSIVE

✪ Ansley Inn

253 Fifteenth St. NE (at Lafayette Dr., between Piedmont Ave. and Peachtree St.), Atlanta, GA 30309. ☎ **800/446-5416** or 404/872-9000. Fax 404/892-2318. www.ansleyinn.com. E-mail: reservations@ansleyinn.com. 22 units. A/C TV TEL. $109–$119 double for garden rooms; $129–$169 for rooms in the main house. Rates include full Southern breakfast. AE, DC, DISC, JCB, MC, V. Free parking. MARTA: Arts Center.

Occupying a 1907 yellow brick Tudor mansion, this former estate of department-store magnate George Muse is located in Ansley Park, one of the city's most beautiful and chic residential areas. Ancient magnolias and white oaks shade the inn's front lawn.

All the rooms are lovely, and the garden rooms behind the house have their own entrances. Choose one of those if privacy is important, but ask for one in the main house if you prefer the ambience of an elegant old mansion. Rooms have oak floors, some strewn with Oriental rugs, and are elegantly furnished with antique pieces and reproductions. Your accommodation might have a brass bed or an 18th-century mahogany four-poster, crystal lamps, or a cushioned window seat overlooking the park. Some rooms have lofty cathedral ceilings and working fireplaces, and all rooms feature wet bars, comfortable armchairs with ottomans, and full baths with whirlpool tubs. All have dataports and some have VCRs, rare for a B&B.

Breakfast, served in a dining room furnished with a long English Chippendale–style table and Empire sideboards, is quite lavish. Hors d'oeuvres are served in the handsomely furnished living room, which boasts an 8-foot ceramic tile fireplace. In addition, there's a concierge, room service from local restaurants, and the newspaper of your choice on request daily. Privileges are available at a nearby health club at no charge. Most important, the Ansley Inn's staff offers warm hospitality and gracious service.

The Georgian Terrace

659 Peachtree St. (just north of Ponce de Leon Ave.), Atlanta, GA 30308. ☎ **800/651-2316** or 404/897-1991. Fax 404/724-9116. www.grandheritage.com. 320 units. A/C TV TEL. $145 double (studio), $170 1-bedroom suite, $195 2-bedroom suite, $220 3-bedroom suite. Children 16 and under stay free in parents' room. Inquire about weekend rates and packages. Reduced rates for stays of more than 30 days. AE, CB, DC, DISC, MC, V. Valet parking $12. MARTA: North Avenue.

This place is a real steal and a slice of history as well. Listed on the National Register of Historic Places, the Georgian Terrace has seen its share of dignitaries and celebrities since it opened in 1911 as a luxury hotel. Clark Gable and Vivien Leigh stayed here in 1939 and attended the premier party of *Gone With the Wind.* The hotel closed in 1981 after years of neglect, reopened in 1991 as upscale apartments, and has been in the process of being converted back to a hotel since 1997. The marble floors, soaring columns, and dramatic French windows hark back to the opulence and grandeur of a bygone era, but the rooms themselves are thoroughly modern.

The apartments have been turned into studios and one-, two-, and three-bedroom suites, with kitchens and laundry facilities in the suites. All rooms have hair dryers and modem lines. Staying here is like having your own private apartment on Peachtree Street. It's excellent for extended stays (some of the suites even have dens) and convenient to all that Midtown has to offer. The Fox Theatre is right across the street. If you'd like a view of Stone Mountain, ask for a suite on the east side of the hotel. Breakfast is served in the original hotel lobby, and cocktails are served in the parlor.

Note: Although the suites have full-size kitchens, they lack pots and pans and have only enough dinnerware for two people. Additional accoutrements are available on request for a small fee. If you're staying 30 days or longer, a more complete package of kitchen equipment is complimentary. Also, most guests are inevitably puzzled about how to turn the shower on. If you can't figure it out, call the front desk.

Dining/Diversions: The hotel doesn't operate its own restaurant, but there are two excellent choices on the premises. Basta, specializing in rustic Italian cuisine and authentic brick-oven pizzas, serves dinner and lunch and is right downstairs. Alon's at the Terrace is a casual French cafe serving outstanding soups, sandwiches, salads, pastries, and cakes.

Amenities: Business center, concierge, room service, heated junior Olympic rooftop swimming pool, sundeck, fully equipped fitness center, children's amenities, room service 6am to 10:30pm, nightly turndown on request, twice-daily maid service on request, laundry service, daily newspaper, airport shuttle, limousine service (when available) within a 3-mile radius, conference and banquet rooms.

Marriott Suites

35 Fourteenth St. NE (between Peachtree and West Peachtree sts.), Atlanta, GA 30309. ☎ **800/228-9290** or 404/876-8888. Fax 404/876-7727. www.marriott.com. 254 suites. A/C TV TEL. $189 double. No extra-person charge. Discounted rates and packages may be available through the toll-free number. AE, CB, DC, DISC, MC, V. Valet parking $12; self-parking $10. MARTA: Arts Center.

This hospitable all-suite hotel is a perfect choice for culture buffs, but its proximity to MARTA makes it easy to get to the rest of the city's attractions, too. Each spacious suite, attractively decorated in a warm, homey style, offers a king-size bed, full living room with a convertible sofa, an extra phone on the desk (with voice mail), a wet bar/refrigerator, and a big console TV. Bedrooms are set off from living room areas by lace-curtained French doors. Each marble bath has a separate shower. Additional in-suite amenities are dataports, coffeemakers, hair dryers, and irons with full-size ironing boards.

Dining/Diversions: Off the palm court–style lobby, plant-filled Allie's American Grille serves lavish buffet breakfasts (everything from blintzes to Belgian waffles) and à la carte lunches and dinners featuring moderately priced American fare. There's a bar next door.

Amenities: Health club, connecting indoor and outdoor swimming pools, whirlpool, room service between 6 and 9:30am and 5:30 and 11pm, airport shuttle, *USA Today* delivered to your door each morning, coin-op washer/dryer, gift shop.

Sheraton Colony Square Hotel

188 Fourteenth St. NE (at Peachtree St.), Atlanta, GA 30361. ☎ **800/422-7895** or 404/892-6000. Fax 404/872-9192. 467 units. A/C TV TEL. Mon–Thurs $158–$185 double; Fri–Sun (subject to availability) $109 double, including free buffet breakfast. Colony Club concierge level $178–$205 double. Extra person $20. Children 18 and under stay free in parents' room. AE, CB, DC, DISC, MC, V. Valet parking $12; self-parking $8.50. MARTA: Arts Center.

This theatrically themed property is popular with entertainers playing at the Woodruff Arts Center just across the street. It was built in 1974 as an opulent anchor of the Colony Square complex (which includes a mini-mall of 20 shops and restaurants that offers conveniences such as a copy shop, shoe repair, a photo shop, clothing and shoe stores, a drugstore, a florist, and more). Colony Square has hosted Frank Sinatra and Linda Ronstadt, not to mention Presidents Reagan, Ford, Carter, Bush, and Clinton. For outdoor enthusiasts or those who like a daily run or walk outdoors, this hotel is a perfect choice. Piedmont Park is just a few blocks away, and the hotel borders the lovely Ansley Park neighborhood. Also nearby are the High Museum of Art and the Atlanta Botanical Garden.

Rooms, which were renovated in 1998, are plush and gorgeous. In-room amenities include electric shoe buffers, coffeemakers, iron and ironing board, and upscale toiletries, cosmetic mirrors, and hair dryers in the bathroom.

Dining/Diversions: The oak-columned 14th Street Bar & Grill serves American fare at all meals. Also here is the cozy lamplit Lobby Bar. There are other restaurants in the mall food court, including the Country Place (details in chapter 6).

Amenities: Concierge, room service 6:30am to 1am, airport shuttle, business services, nice-size outdoor pool, workout room.

Wyndham Garden Hotel

125 Tenth St. NE (just east of Peachtree St.), Atlanta, GA 30309. ☎ **800/996-3426** or 404/873-4800. Fax 404/870-1530. 191 units. A/C TV TEL. Sun–Thurs $141 executive king, $151 double, $161 junior suite; Fri–Sat $99 per room. Rates include full buffet breakfast. Extra person $10. Children 12 and under stay free in parents' room. AE, CB, DC, DISC, MC, V. Valet parking $12; self-parking $9.50. MARTA: Midtown.

An 11-story Georgia redbrick building, the Wyndham is close to many of the Midtown cultural attractions, including the Margaret Mitchell House and Museum. It's also convenient to Georgia Tech, and a favorite among visitors whose children are students there or who are attending Tech sporting events. It offers nicely appointed rooms, many with bay windows. Each has a comfy armchair, coffeemaker, dataport, ironing board, and iron. Some rooms have mini-bars. There are hair dryers and cosmetic mirrors in the bathroom. Suites feature separate sitting areas with sofas, extra TVs and phones, and refrigerators.

Dining/Diversions: The complimentary buffet breakfast is served in the art nouveau Juniper Street Café; at lunch there's also a buffet, as well as an à la carte menu at lunch and dinner. A lunchtime pasta bar is a unique feature. The adjoining Butler's bar and lounge specializes in premium wines by the glass.

Amenities: Large indoor pool, 7,000-square-foot fitness center offering Nautilus equipment, courtesy van within a 5-mile radius (that includes Buckhead and downtown), room service 5 to 11pm, comprehensive business services, complimentary *USA Today* at front desk.

MODERATE

Marriott Residence Inn Midtown

1041 W. Peachtree St. (at Eleventh St.), Atlanta, GA 30309. ☎ **800/331-3131** or 404/872-8885. Fax 404/872-8885, ext. 1805. 78 units. A/C TV TEL. $119 studio, $124 1-bedroom suite, $149 2-bedroom suite. Rates include continental breakfast. Rates are higher during special events, and are reduced off-season and for stays of more than 7 nights. AE, DC, DISC, MC, V. Free parking. MARTA: Midtown.

Staying here is like having your own apartment in Atlanta. Accommodations are studios or spacious suites with handsome oak or mahogany furnishings—mostly antique reproductions, such as Chippendale-style beds. Both bedrooms and living rooms have their own TVs and telephones, and kitchens are fully equipped. Most rooms have balconies with French doors. There's not a whole lot that's interesting to walk to, but you're not far from a MARTA station.

The inn provides hot tea and coffee all day in the lobby, and hot and cold hors d'oeuvres Monday to Thursday night from 5:30 to 7:30pm. Every Wednesday night there's a complimentary dinner. There's also a rooftop Jacuzzi, complimentary membership at the fitness center of the nearby Marriott Suites hotel, coin-op washers/dryers, complimentary grocery-shopping service, and free newspapers daily in lobby.

Shellmont Bed and Breakfast Lodge

821 Piedmont Ave. NE (at Sixth St.), Atlanta, GA 30308. ☎ **404/872-9290.** Fax 404/872-5379. 4 units, plus carriage house. A/C TV TEL. $120–$130 double in main house; $129–$170 double in carriage house. Extra person $20. Rates include full breakfast. Children 12 and under allowed in the carriage house only. AE, DC, DISC, MC, V. Free parking. MARTA: North Avenue or Midtown.

This charming two-story Victorian mansion looks, from the outside, like a Wedgwood fairy-tale house embellished with ribbons, bows, garlands, and shells. It has both a front porch and a small veranda out back with wicker rocking chairs overlooking a flower garden and fish pond. The building, which dates to 1891, is on the National Register of Historic Places, and is designated a landmark by the city. Innkeepers Ed and Debbie McCord have done a superb job of restoration, not only in repairing all functional aspects, but in meticulously researching original paint colors, stencil designs, woodwork, and period furnishings and reproducing them with 100% accuracy.

There's a cozy living room downstairs, and up the stairway (its landing graced by a five-paneled stained-glass window the McCords believe is an authentic Tiffany) are the four guest rooms. They have elegant queen-size beds (perhaps you'll have an Eastlake or a bed with a 6-foot oak headboard embellished with carved ribbons and bows), leaded-glass or bay windows, and Oriental rugs on pine floors. All have VCRs. The carriage house offers a master bedroom, full modern bath with steam bath shower, fully equipped kitchen, living room, and dressing area.

Breakfast consists of fresh-squeezed juice, fresh and dried fruits, an entree (perhaps Belgian waffles or frittatas), cereal, and tea or coffee. The McCords live on the premises and offer all the services of a hotel concierge, plus nightly bed turndown, and fruit and fresh flowers in your room daily.

Woodruff Bed & Breakfast Inn

223 Ponce de Leon Ave. NE (at Myrtle St.), Atlanta, GA 30308. ☎ **800/473-9449** or 404/875-9449. Fax 404/870-0042. E-mail: rsvp@mindspring.com. 12 units (8 with bathroom). A/C TV (on request) TEL. $79–$159 double; $149 for 2 rooms with a shared bath (for up to 4 people); $109–$159 for a 2-room Jacuzzi suite. Rates include full breakfast. AE, DISC, MC, V. Free parking. MARTA: North Avenue.

This B&B is not as convenient as some lodgings to most of the area's attractions, but it's a short cab ride away, and its interesting history and ambience may be worth the trade-off. The three-story white-brick Victorian house, built in 1906 by an Atlanta physician, went on to a more interesting incarnation in the 1950s, when Miss Bessie Woodruff bought the property and turned it into a house of ill repute. Officially, it was a licensed massage facility (the "girls" actually wore white nurses' uniforms), and some of Atlanta's most prominent politicians came by frequently to relieve the tensions of public office. Current owners Joan and Doug Jones not only honored Bessie by naming their bed-and-breakfast for her, but they've displayed light boards that were used to keep track of the rooms in use, framed photographs of Bessie (she was a beauty), and her old love letters.

The cozy, first-floor parlor is furnished with turn-of-the-century antiques and has a cable TV with a VCR. The rooms contain a mix of 19th- and early 20th-century English antiques, along with pieces you might categorize as "Grandma's house" furnishings. Your accommodation might have stained-glass or bay windows or French doors leading to a porch furnished with swings or rocking chairs. The house itself has a large front porch overlooking the oak-shaded lawn. You'll receive a free daily newspaper, and magazines and books are available. Guests in Jacuzzi suites enjoy complimentary flowers and champagne on arrival.

INEXPENSIVE

✪ Biltmore Suites

30 Fifth St. NE (at West Peachtree St.), Atlanta, GA 30308. ☎ **800/822-0824** or 404/874-0824. Fax 404/458-5384. 60 units. A/C TV TEL. $69–$99 studios and 1-bedroom suites (for 1 or 2 people); $89–$129 2-bedroom suites (for up to 4); $129–$189 2-bedroom suites with Jacuzzi; $299 tri-level penthouses. Rates include continental breakfast. AE, DC, DISC, MC, V. Parking $5. MARTA: North Avenue.

A majestic 10-story brick building with a white-columned facade, the Biltmore, with its rich and glamorous history, is a favorite among the traveling theater troupes playing at the nearby Fox. Built in 1924 (as a hotel-cum-luxury apartment complex) by Coca-Cola heir William Candler, in its heyday it played host to everyone from *GWTW* stars Vivien Leigh and Olivia de Havilland to Presidents Franklin Roosevelt and Dwight Eisenhower. Closed in 1982, its apartment section was refurbished as an all-suite hotel in 1986.

Suites offer fully equipped kitchens, dining areas, and (except in some studios) living rooms. You'll find 10-foot ceilings, hand-carved crown moldings, multipaned windows, brass bathroom fixtures, and French doors. All accommodations but studios feature extra TVs and phones in the living rooms, and the penthouse suites, as well as some two-bedroom suites, contain Jacuzzis. The tri-level penthouses are dramatic, but avoid them if steps are a problem. At press time, all rooms were due to be renovated. There is no hotel room service, but you can order from dozens of local restaurants.

Cheshire Motor Inn

1865 Cheshire Bridge Rd. NE (near the intersection of Piedmont Rd.), Atlanta, GA 30324. ☎ **800/827-9628** or 404/872-9628. 58 units. A/C TV TEL. $62–$68 double. Extra person $5. Children under 12 stay free in parents' room. Rates may be higher during special events. AE, DC, DISC, MC, V. Free parking. MARTA bus: 27 from Lindbergh Station, which is about a mile away.

This is the best kind of budget hotel, a small property run for decades by caring private owners who offer homelike hospitality and many personal touches. On attractively landscaped grounds, the Cheshire offers rooms (completely renovated in 1998) that are nothing fancy, but they are spacious and nicely kept. Many of the rooms have minibars, and half have pull-out sofas, making this an especially good choice for families on a budget. In the clean but basic bath, you'll find shampoo, a toothbrush, toothpaste, and a razor. This is one of the few centrally located hotels that allows pets. Another big plus is that a famous Atlanta restaurant, the Colonnade, is on the premises, serving authentic Southern food (see details in chapter 6). Free newspapers (*USA Today* and the *Atlanta Journal-Constitution*) and coffee and doughnuts are available in the lobby each morning. Cheshire Bridge Road is an odd mix of sleazy bars and second-hand furniture and antiques shops. Parts of the street are pretty weird, but the restaurant and motel are quite respectable.

Comfort Inn Buckhead

2115 Piedmont Rd. NE (between Lindbergh Dr. and Cheshire Bridge Rd.), Atlanta, GA 30324. ☎ **800/228-5150** or 404/876-4444. Fax 404/873-1007. 186 units. A/C TV TEL. $79 double; $120 suite (for 5–8 people). Rates may be higher during special events. Children 12 and under stay free in parents' room. AE, CB, DC, DISC, MC, V. Free parking. MARTA: Lindbergh (about three-fourths of a mile north; bus no. 31 stops at the door).

Poised on the border between Midtown and Buckhead, this Comfort Inn is not in the most attractive location. But rooms were renovated in 1998, the price is right, and it's not far from a MARTA station. The large rooms are furnished with king-size beds, desks, and recliners; suites offer full living rooms with pull-out sofa, microwave ovens, and refrigerators. Local calls are free, and there's no service charge for credit-card calls. A free copy of *USA Today* in your room is another plus. Doughnuts, juice, tea, and coffee are served in a pleasant room off the lobby each morning (coffee is available all day). There's also a small outdoor pool and sundeck.

Days Inn Peachtree

683 Peachtree St. (between Third St. and Ponce de Leon Ave.), Atlanta, GA 30308. ☎ **800/DAYS-INN** or 404/874-9200. Fax 404/873-4245. 140 units. A/C TV TEL. $79–$129 double; $125–$199 suite. Rates may be higher during conventions and special events. Rates include continental breakfast. Extra person $10. Children under 18 stay free in parents' room. Weekend rates and packages available via the toll-free number. Super Saver rate of $59 a night may be available if you reserve at least 30 days in advance. AE, DC, DISC, MC, V. Self-parking $6. MARTA: North Avenue.

You'll realize this Days Inn is not your average chain motel from the moment you enter its charming lobby with Persian rugs on Saltillo-tile floors and a brass chandelier suspended from a lofty mahogany ceiling. Built as a fancy boardinghouse in 1925, it's right across from the Fox Theatre, so it's a good choice if you're attending a performance there. All rooms were renovated in 1998 and are nicely fitted with traditional cherrywood furnishings; many have comfortable sofas or upholstered recliners. There are coffeemakers in each room, and the five suites feature small refrigerators, pull-out sofas, two bathrooms, and two televisions.

Bridgetown Grill, a good Caribbean restaurant (see chapter 6), is next door, and a Wendy's is on the premises. Complimentary wine and hors d'oeuvres are served at a cocktail party in the lobby every Thursday night; coffee is served in the lobby throughout the day. There's also a business center as well as coin-op washers/dryers. Although there is no exercise room on the premises, guests have access to the fitness center in the NationsBank office building down the street for a small fee.

Fairfield Inn Midtown

1470 Spring St. NW (at Nineteenth St.), Atlanta, GA 30309. ☎ **404/872-5821.** Fax 404/874-3602. 182 units. $59–$69 double. Rates include extended continental breakfast. A/C TV TEL. Children 12 and under are free. AE, CB, DC, DISC, MC, V. Free parking. MARTA: Arts Center.

This is not the most charming location in Atlanta, but the price is right, and a MARTA station, from which you can zip to the rest of the city, is 4 blocks away. The rooms are standard motel decor with queen-size beds and average bathrooms, but seven have small, well-equipped kitchens (sink, refrigerator, microwave). All rooms have desks and dataports for computer hookup. The outdoor pool with sundeck is a plus, as is the exercise room, which contains a treadmill, stair machine, exercise bike, and Nautilus machine. Services here include a coin-operated laundry, and a complimentary shuttle within a 2-mile radius 7am to 11pm. There's no room service, but takeout is delivered from local restaurants.

4 Buckhead

There's something for everyone in Buckhead—shoppers, gourmets, history buffs, business travelers, and those looking for lively nighttime entertainment. It's the optimum hotel location. A word about dining: You'll find listings here of the dining rooms and lounges of most of the major hotels. But it's mostly just to let you know what's convenient to you at your hotel. There are so many fine restaurants and nightspots in Buckhead, it's foolish to limit yourself to hotel fare. There are two notable exceptions—the Swissôtel and the Ritz-Carlton Buckhead, which have outstanding restaurants. You'll find them listed in chapter 6.

VERY EXPENSIVE

✪ Embassy Suites Hotel Buckhead

3285 Peachtree Rd. NW (1 block north of Piedmont Rd.), Atlanta, GA 30326. ☎ **800/ 362-2779** or 404/261-7733. Fax 404/262-0522. www.embassy-suites.com. 317 units. A/C TV TEL. Mon–Thurs $199 double. Weekend rates $139 double; $159 for up to 4 people in some suites. Rates may be higher during special events; lower during some holidays and in summer. Prices include full breakfast. Children under 18 stay free in parents' room. AE, CB, DC, DISC, ER, EC, MC, VISA. Valet parking $11; self-parking $8. MARTA: Buckhead.

This suites hotel stacks up well to other, more expensive hotels in the same area. A favorite with business travelers, the suite arrangement is also ideal for families, and the location can't be beat with Lenox Square, Phipps Plaza, and many fine restaurants within walking distance. The Buckhead MARTA station is less than a block away, so it's easy to connect quickly with other parts of the city and the airport.

Built in 1988, the property was renovated in 1996, and each elegantly appointed 800-square-foot, two-room suite has a queen-size fold-out sofa, two televisions, microwave, refrigerator, coffeemaker, sink, full-size ironing board, and iron. In addition to the bathroom with marble vanity and hair dryer, there is a sink in the separate bedroom. Although the entire hotel is accessible to the disabled (most of the participants in the wheelchair division of the Peachtree Road Race stay here), 10 of the suites are completely equipped for the handicapped; two have roll-in showers. Two popular bonuses: the complimentary cooked-to-order breakfast served in the atrium lobby and complimentary cocktails each afternoon. Because almost everyone takes breakfast in the lobby, room service is available 11am to 11pm only.

Amenities: Large pool with sundeck; small indoor pool; whirlpool, saunas, small exercise room; conference rooms; laundry and dry cleaning service, coin-operated laundry; concierge; newspaper delivery Monday to Friday; courtesy van anywhere within a 1-mile radius; pool table; Nintendo games in some suites; small gift shop and delicatessen with sandwiches to go.

Grand Hyatt Atlanta

3300 Peachtree Rd. (just east of Piedmont Rd.), Atlanta, GA 30305. ☎ **800-233-1234** or 404/365-8100. Fax 404/233-5686. www.hyatt.com. 439 units. A/C MINIBAR TV TEL. Mon–Thurs $230 double; Fri–Sun $159 double. Regency Club floor $265 double. Suites $450–$2,200. Extra person $25. Children under 16 stay free in parents' room. AE, CB, DC, DISC, ER, JCB, MC, V. Valet parking $17; self-parking $12. MARTA: Buckhead.

The towering Grand Hyatt Atlanta offers a winning combination of 18th-century American architecture and Japanese attention to aesthetic detail. Formerly the Hotel Nikko, the Grand Hyatt has retained much Japanese flavor and sensibility. Its lobby overlooks a 9,000-square-foot garden with traditional plantings, rock forma-tions, and splashing waterfalls created by noted Kyoto landscape architects, and a collection of museum-quality Japanese art, spanning four centuries, is displayed throughout the hotel. Lenox Square and Phipps Plaza shopping malls are 2 blocks away.

Rooms, redone in 1998, are furnished in 18th-century mahogany reproductions, with crane-motif headboards, fresh orchids, and Japanese prints in black lacquer frames providing Eastern atmosphere. Every luxury is provided: three phones (bed-side, bath, and desk) with dataports, fax machine, terry robes, and bathrooms equipped with hair dryers, TV speakers, cosmetic mirrors, and scales. You'll even find an umbrella in your closet.

Dining/Diversions: Kamogawa, Atlanta's premier Japanese restaurant, offers an authentic dining experience (see chapter 6). The delightful Cassis, with soaring arched windows overlooking the Japanese garden, is also much acclaimed for its sophisticated cuisine; all meals are served here, including a Japanese breakfast and lavish Sunday brunch. The plush Lobby Lounge is the setting for lunch, dinner, and English-style afternoon teas as well as nightly entertainment.

Amenities: 24-hour room service, 24-hour concierge, baby-sitting, toys/activities for children, massage, airport shuttle, complimentary town car within a 2-mile radius of the hotel, complimentary overnight shoeshine, comprehensive business center, fully equipped fitness center (with TVs and VCRs on the exercise bikes, Life Trim equipment, stair machines, aerobics videos, steam, and sauna), a lovely out-door pool and sundeck.

✪ J.W. Marriott Hotel Lenox

3300 Lenox Rd. NE (a few blocks east of Peachtree Rd. at East Paces Ferry Rd.), Atlanta, GA 30326. ☎ **800/228-9290** or 404/262-3344. Fax 404/262-8689. www.marriott.com/marriott/atljw. 371 units. A/C MINIBAR TV TEL. Mon–Thurs $194–$265 for up to 4 people; Fri–Sun $149–$189 per room. Club Level rooms $20 extra. Weekend packages available. AE, CB, DC, DISC, MC, V. Valet parking $13; self-parking $7. MARTA: Lenox.

This luxurious Marriott is a lovely property in an excellent location. Connected to the Lenox Square mall, adjacent to MARTA, and within walking distance of the posh Phipps Plaza mall and many good restaurants, it's popular with business trav-elers and shoppers alike. Rooms, renovated in 1996, are charmingly furnished with Chippendale-style mahogany pieces, and picture windows offer great views of Buckhead or the downtown skyline. Each room has a coffeemaker, three phones, and an iron and full-size ironing board. Lavish marble bathrooms are equipped with scales, terrycloth robes, and hair dryers.

Dining/Diversions: The Lenox Grille, a bistro-style restaurant, specializes in upscale American cuisine for breakfast, lunch, and dinner. The clubby Ottley's offers piano bar entertainment and light fare. Yet another plush setting for cocktails/light fare is the cozy Lobby Lounge, with comfortable sofas and armchairs in front of a fireplace.

Buckhead Accommodations

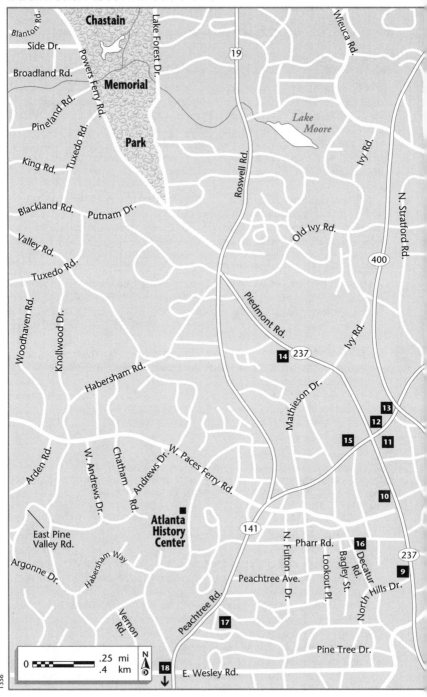

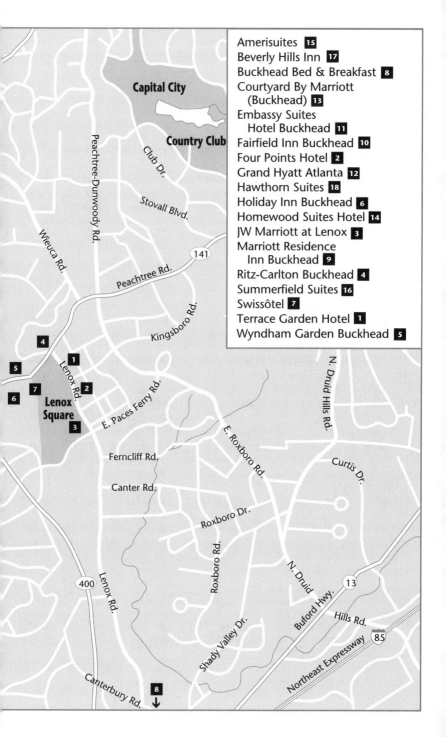

Amerisuites **15**
Beverly Hills Inn **17**
Buckhead Bed & Breakfast **8**
Courtyard By Marriott
  (Buckhead) **13**
Embassy Suites
  Hotel Buckhead **11**
Fairfield Inn Buckhead **10**
Four Points Hotel **2**
Grand Hyatt Atlanta **12**
Hawthorn Suites **18**
Holiday Inn Buckhead **6**
Homewood Suites Hotel **14**
JW Marriott at Lenox **3**
Marriott Residence
  Inn Buckhead **9**
Ritz-Carlton Buckhead **4**
Summerfield Suites **16**
Swissôtel **7**
Terrace Garden Hotel **1**
Wyndham Garden Buckhead **5**

Amenities: 24-hour room service, multilingual concierge staff, nightly bed turn-down, airport shuttle, one-hour dry cleaning, *USA Today* at your door each morning, large indoor pool in a setting patterned after a Roman bath, full health club with steam and sauna, car-rental desk, full business center, pastry shop.

✪ Ritz-Carlton Buckhead

3434 Peachtree Rd. NE (at Lenox Rd.), Atlanta, GA 30326. ☎ **800/241-3333** or 404/237-2700. Fax 404/239-0078. www.ritzcarlton.com. 553 units. A/C MINIBAR TV TEL. Mon–Thurs $223–$255 double, Club Floor $270–$320 double. Fri–Sun $155–$255 double, $175–$270 Club Floor. Rollaway bed $30. Children under 12 stay free in parents' room. Inquire about packages. AE, DC, DISC, JCB, MC, V. Valet parking $19; self-parking $8. MARTA: Buckhead or Lenox.

The Ritz-Carlton Buckhead is the Rolls Royce of Atlanta hotels. From the lobby to the public areas, which are graced with Regency and Georgian antiques and an out-standing collection of 18th- and 19th-century paintings and sculpture, every inch of this hotel bespeaks luxury. And the quality of service matches the sumptuous sur-roundings. The location is excellent—on the fringe of lovely neighborhoods, across the street from two upscale malls (Phipps Plaza and Lenox Square), and close to Buckhead's fine restaurants and nightspots. Many visiting celebrities, used to dis-creet elegance, choose to stay here. Even Atlantans, looking for a special getaway, check in on the weekends.

The rooms, all with large bay windows, are exquisitely decorated, with burled-walnut armoires, sofas or armchairs upholstered in raw silk, and 18th-century-reproduction beds. Luxurious baths contain the usual amenities you'd expect in a posh hotel. All rooms were due to be refurbished in 1999.

Dining/Diversions: The Dining Room at the Ritz-Carlton Buckhead, one of Atlanta's premier restaurants, is detailed in chapter 6. The Lobby Lounge, with mahogany-paneled walls and a glowing fire, is the setting for afternoon English-style teas. A classical pianist plays here from 2:30 to 4:30pm daily, jazz artists enter-tain evenings, and from 5 to 7:30pm, 11 different martinis are featured on a special drink menu. The Café, open all day, offers a continental menu and a lavish buffet brunch on Sunday. In the adjoining Café Bar, there's music for dancing Friday and Saturday nights. And Expresso's, with indoor seating as well as outdoor umbrella tables on a poplar-shaded courtyard, serves full breakfasts and deli lunch specials weekdays from 7am to 3pm.

Amenities: Full business center, swimming and fitness center, steam and sauna rooms, Jacuzzi, concierge, 24-hour room service, limousine on request, airport shuttle, shuttle when available to nearby malls, newspaper delivered to your door each morning, nightly bed turndown, currency exchange, one-hour pressing, on-premises seamstress, hair salon, personalized shopping, complimentary overnight shoeshine, gift shop.

✪ Swissôtel

3391 Peachtree Rd. NE (between Lenox and Piedmont rds.), Atlanta, GA 30326. ☎ **800/63-SWISS** or 404/365-0065. Fax 404/233-8786. www.swissotel.com. 382 units. A/C MINIBAR TV TEL. $265–285 double, Club Level $315 double. Extra person $25. Weekend rates available. Children under 16 stay free in parents' room. AE, DC, DISC, ER, JCB, MC, V. Valet parking $15. MARTA: Buckhead.

If the Ritz-Carlton is the Rolls Royce of Atlanta hotels, the Swissôtel is the Ferrari. Its fresh Euromodern design makes it a favorite among trendsetters visiting the city, and its excellent location—in the heart of Buckhead between Lenox Square and the Atlanta Financial Center—makes it a top choice among business travelers and serious shoppers.

Opened in 1991, the Zurich-based Swissôtel (it's owned by Swissair) added a new dimension to Atlanta's hotel scene. Its postmodern European architecture and interior spaces use Bauhaus elements, exemplified in a pristine white-tile exterior with a graceful piano curve. Original works by internationally known contemporary artists—Warhol, Rauschenberg, Chagall, Schnabel, Stella—grace public spaces. In fact, the hotel owns the second-largest private art collection in the Southeast, exceeded only by the High Museum of Art.

Rooms are sleekly furnished in Beidermeier-style bird's-eye maple pieces with black lacquer accents. The desks are leather-topped, and all rooms are equipped with terry robes, three phones, coffeemakers, irons, and full-size ironing boards. Marble baths offer cosmetic mirrors, TV speakers, hair dryers, and upscale biodegradable toiletries. Especially nice are corner king rooms (ask for one when you reserve). Renovations to all rooms will begin in 1999 and will be completed in the first quarter of 2000.

Dining: The superb Palm restaurant is described in chapter 6.

Amenities: A small but nicely equipped health club offers massage, exercise equipment, lap pool, sauna, steam room, and aerobics studio. Gift shop, unisex hair salon/spa, airline desk (Swissair), business center, concierge, 24-hour room service, complimentary shuttle to any destination in a 2-mile radius (including MARTA and the upscale Lenox Square and Phipps Plaza malls), multilingual staff, airport shuttle, daily newspaper delivery, complimentary shoeshine.

EXPENSIVE

Hawthorn Suites

2030 Peachtree Rd. NW (just north of Collier Rd.), Atlanta, GA 30309. ☎ **800/527-1133** or 404/352-3131. Fax 404/355-9902. www.hawthorn.com. 80 units. A/C TV TEL. $149 double; $99 weekends when available. Children under 18 stay free in parents' room. Rates include full buffet breakfast. AE, CB, DC, DISC, MC, V. Free parking. MARTA: Lindbergh or Arts Center. Bus no. 23 stops in front of the hotel.

Located at the southern reaches of Buckhead, this is a convenient spot for anyone visiting Piedmont Hospital or the Shepherd Center. And although it's not ground zero for most of what Buckhead has to offer, it's still close to many fine restaurants and shops, and a courtesy van will take you to anything within a 5-mile radius.

All the rooms are 600-square-foot one-room suites, remodeled and converted from corporate apartments in 1998. The suites are large, with queen-size beds, pull-out sofas and kitchens with full-size appliances, making them outstanding choices for an extended stay. There are two phones with dataports, a VCR, and Nintendo. Because it's an older building, all the suites are fairly quiet, and the bathrooms, though nothing special, are spacious and have hair dryers. Monday through Thursday you can enjoy hot hors d'oeuvres and complimentary beer and wine in the lobby.

Amenities: Business services, privileges at Shepherd Center fitness center for $5 fee, video library, large heated outdoor pool and sundeck, complimentary daily newspaper, room service delivery from neighboring restaurants 11am to 11pm, small conference center, coin-operated washers and dryers.

Holiday Inn Buckhead

3777 Peachtree Rd. NE (between Lenox and Piedmont rds.), Atlanta, GA 30326. ☎ **800/526-0247** or 404/264-1111. Fax 404/233-7061. 297 units. A/C TV TEL. $129–$159 double. Extra person $10. Children under 18 stay free in parents' room. AE, DC, DISC, ER, JCB, MC, V. Valet parking $10; self-parking $8. MARTA: Buckhead.

Conveniently located near the Lenox Square mall and MARTA, this 11-story Holiday Inn redecorated all of its rooms in 1996. The accommodations are a little more special than most Holiday Inns, equipped with hair dryers, coffeemakers, iron and ironing board, phones with computer jacks, plus Game Boy (your kids will be thrilled even if you're not). Most also have small refrigerators.

Dining: The Brentwood Café, a pretty dining room with a wall of windows, serves a buffet breakfast and à la carte American fare at lunch and dinner.

Amenities: There's also room service from 7am to 2pm and 5 to 10pm, an airport shuttle, free *USA Today* in the restaurant, complimentary van transport within 3 miles of the hotel, an outdoor pool and sundeck, coin-op washers and dryers, and a business center. Guests can use a nearby health club for $5.

Homewood Suites Hotel

3566 Piedmont Rd. (between Peachtree and Roswell rds.), Atlanta, GA 30305. ☎ **800/ 225-4566** or 404/365-0001. Fax 404/365-9888. 92 units. A/C TV TEL. $125 double for 1-bedroom suites; $185 double for 2-bedroom suites. Children under 18 stay free in parents' room. Rates include extended continental breakfast. Ask about special packages. AE, CB, DC, DISC, JCB, MC, V. Free parking. MARTA: Buckhead. Bus no. 59 stops in front of hotel.

This is a well-run suites hotel that's an excellent value and perfect for an extended business stay or a long weekend. The spacious one- and two-bedroom suites feel a lot like home with pull-out sofas and large kitchen areas that include the usual (full-size) appliances, plus coffeemakers, dishwashers, and toasters. There are two televisions, a VCR, and two telephones, most with dataports. The bathrooms are fairly standard, but they do have hair dryers. Some of the two-bedroom suites can easily sleep eight people. The hotel, which opened late in 1997, is set back from a busy street, so all the rooms are quiet, with the nicest ones overlooking the pool and patio. Although you won't be within walking distance of most of the Buckhead attractions or the MARTA station, there is a courtesy van to take you to anything within a 3-mile radius.

In addition to a complimentary deluxe continental breakfast, there is an evening social Monday to Thursday with complimentary beer, wine, and light snacks or meals. About once a week the social moves out to the patio for a cookout. If you're in the mood, you can even cook out yourself. There's no restaurant or room service, but delivery is available from several restaurants.

Amenities: Concierge, complimentary newspaper, business center, small heated outdoor pool with patio, small exercise room, video rental, small conference rooms, coin-operated washers and dryers, one room specially modified for the disabled.

Terrace Garden Inn

3405 Lenox Rd. NE (between Peachtree and East Paces Ferry rds.), Atlanta, GA 30326. ☎ **800/241-8260** or 404/261-9250. Fax 404/848-7391. 366 units. A/C TV TEL. $119–$195 double. Club level $150–$190 double. Extra person $20. Children under 18 stay free in parents' room. AE, DISC, MC, V. Parking $8. MARTA: Lenox.

This is a lovely hotel that offers abundant services and facilities plus a great location, close to MARTA, Lenox Square, Phipps Plaza, and many restaurants. It's not quite as fancy as other hotels in the area, but it's still very stylish and is an excellent value. Rooms, renovated in 1998, are furnished with French country and 18th-century-reproduction mahogany pieces (some have four-poster or brass beds). Several have balconies, and all offer extra phones in the bathroom, hair dryers, coffeemakers, and full-size ironing boards with irons. Phones are equipped with dataports. Rooms with king-size beds have plush armchairs with ottomans.

Dining: The two-level Café, which serves regional American cuisine, is garden-themed with flower-bedecked tables amid lots of leafy greenery. A window wall on the upper level overlooks the pool. There's also a cozy lounge with a vast stone-walled, copper-hooded fireplace.

Amenities: Health center, outdoor swimming pool with waterfalls, concierge, complimentary van within 3-mile radius, room service, free daily newspaper, Lufthansa/United Airlines desk, gift shop.

Wyndham Garden Hotel Buckhead

3340 Peachtree Rd. NE (between Lenox and Piedmont rds.), Atlanta, GA 30326. ☎ **800/WYNDHAM** or 404/231-1234. Fax 404/231-5236. www.wyndham.com. 221 units. A/C TV TEL. Sun–Thurs $152 double; Fri–Sat $99 double. Suites $169–$219. Extra person $10. Children under 14 stay free in parents' room. AE, CB, DC, DISC, JCB, MC, V. Free parking. MARTA: Buckhead.

Designed with the business traveler in mind, this is an equally good choice for the tourist. The comfortable guest rooms are outfitted with large desks and upholstered recliner chairs. Large king-bedded rooms are especially desirable. In-room amenities include coffeemakers, phones with 25-foot cords and computer jacks, voice mail in eight languages, and hair dryers. Buckhead's posh shopping malls and many fine restaurants are close by.

Dining/Diversions: The garden-themed, bi-level Savannah Room, with a wall of windows overlooking a brick patio, serves all meals. The menu features steak, seafood, pastas, pizzas, and quesadillas. Beauregard's is a handsome lounge.

Amenities: Room service 5 to 10pm, airport shuttle, complimentary *USA Today* and Atlanta paper at front desk, free courtesy van within a 2-mile radius. The front desk supplies free toothbrushes, toothpaste, razors, shaving cream, deodorant, and other amenities you may have neglected to pack. Guests enjoy free use of the adjacent Sports Life Fitness Center, offering a full complement of exercise equipment, massage, steam, sauna, aerobics classes, child care, basketball/racquetball courts, indoor track, and more.

MODERATE

Amerisuites

3242 Peachtree Rd. NE (at the intersection with Piedmont Rd.), Atlanta, GA 30305. ☎ **800/833-1516** or 404/869-6161. 172 units. A/C MINIBAR TV TEL. $129–$139 double; $99 weekends. Extra person $20. Children under 12 stay free in parents' room. Rates include extended continental breakfast. AE, DC, MC, V. Free parking. MARTA: Buckhead.

This is a new (1997), but rather plain-Jane, all-suites hotel in a good location. It's not the best buy in Buckhead, but it's still a nice room for the money. The typical suite is not a true suite with a separate bedroom, but more like a studio or efficiency with the "bedroom" set off from the rest of the room by a low wall. There's a pull-out couch, VCR, kitchenette with coffeemaker, mini-refrigerator, wet bar, and microwave. There are two phones and modem lines in some suites. The bathrooms are typical of most motels, but they do have hair dryers.

The hotel offers a complimentary shuttle within a 3-mile radius, free coffee in the lobby, a limited business center, and a small, heated outdoor pool. The exercise room is small, but guests enjoy free privileges at a nearby full-size health club.

Beverly Hills Inn

65 Sheridan Dr. NE (just off Peachtree Rd.), Atlanta, GA 30305. ☎ **800/331-8520** or 404/233-8520. Fax 404/233-8520, ext. 18. www.beverlyhillsinn.com. 18 units. A/C TV TEL. $90–$120 1-bedroom suite; $120–$240 2-bedroom suite accommodating up to 4 people. Extra person $7. Children under 12 stay free in parents' room. Rates include deluxe continental breakfast. Discounts available for stays of a week or more. AE, CB, DC, DISC, MC, V. Free parking. MARTA bus: no. 23 at the corner of Peachtree and Sheridan.

Housed in a 1920s former apartment building, with forest-green shutters and window awnings, this charming B&B is located on a tree-lined residential street. British owner/host Mit Amin offers warm hospitality to guests. This is a good spot for an extended stay, especially for families who prefer a neighborhood atmosphere to that of a commercial hotel. On the first floor is a cozy parlor/library where a decanter of port is available all day. (You'll find a half-bottle of burgundy in your room upon arrival.) Another library is downstairs in the sunny garden room, which has a skylit conservatory area filled with plants.

The spacious rooms are cheerful and attractive, decorated in a mix of antiques (many of them English pieces) and collectibles. Some have canopied beds. All are equipped with kitchenettes (the housekeeper does your dishes), and there's a private balcony through the French doors. Two supermarkets are within easy walking distance, should you want to cook in your room, but there are plenty of good restaurants close by. Daily newspapers and local phone calls are complimentary. There's no elevator, so if stairs are a problem, reserve one of the six rooms on the ground floor.

Guests also have access to a washer/dryer and a lounge with a copy machine, fax machine, and computer. Also included in your room's price are complimentary membership privileges at the nearby Buckhead Towne Club, a state-of-the-art facility offering two outdoor swimming pools, saunas, Jacuzzi, racquetball, and squash, as well as the usual exercise equipment.

Buckhead Bed & Breakfast Inn

70 Lenox Pointe NE (at the corner of Lenox Rd. and Sidney Marcus Blvd.), Atlanta, GA 30324. ☎ **888/224-8797** or 404/261-8284. Fax 404/237-9224. www.georgiabedandbreakfast. com. E-mail: bandb@mindspring.com. 18 units. A/C TV TEL. $85–$105 double. Rates include extended continental breakfast. AE, MC, V. Free parking. MARTA bus: no. 39 from Lindbergh Station, which is about a mile away.

Unlike most bed-and-breakfasts, which are nestled in leafy residential neighborhoods in historic old homes, this charming B&B is on the corner of a busy intersection in a new building surrounded by offices. Though not within walking distance to most of Buckhead's attractions and restaurants, it's still one of the best bargains in an otherwise pricey part of town.

Housed in a lovely columned building with two wide porches, the inn evokes the plantations of the Old South, even though it was built in 1996. Each of the rooms is unique in name and decor, but they're all tastefully decorated and feel a lot like home. Some have vaulted or 9-foot ceilings and others have dormers; you might have a sleigh bed, a four-poster, a Chippendale reproduction, or an old-fashioned iron bed. The loveliest accommodation is the Peachtree, a large room with two queen-size four-poster beds, a vaulted ceiling, and dormers. Each room has an elegant writing desk, telephone with separate modem lines, VCR, and hair dryer.

An extended continental breakfast—homemade breads, ham or sausage biscuits, fresh fruit, pastries, coffee, juice, tea—is served buffet-style in the tasteful and cheerful dining room, which sports Chippendale reproduction tables and chairs. There's a small, fully stocked bar with a wood-burning fireplace and comfortable Windsor chairs. It's open 24 hours a day; guests can fix their own drinks when the staff is not available. There's also an elevator, a rarity in most B&Bs.

Note: The inn has a strict no-smoking policy. You may smoke on the porches and balconies, but you will be assessed a hefty service charge if you smoke in your room.

Courtyard by Marriott (Buckhead)

3332 Peachtree Rd. NE (between Lenox and Piedmont rds.), Atlanta, GA 30326. ☎ **800/ 321-2211** or 404/869-0818. Fax 404/869-0939. www.impachotels.com. 181 units. A/C TV

TEL. $114–$124 double, $150 suites. Rates may be lower on weekends, higher during special events. Children under 18 stay free in parents' room. AE, CB, DC, DISC, JCB, MC, V. Free parking (self and valet). MARTA: Buckhead.

Not your typical Courtyard property, this lovely hotel provides excellent value in a prime location. It's a short walk to the Atlanta Financial Center, the Lenox Square and Phipps Plaza shopping malls, and the MARTA station, and it's close to everything Buckhead has to offer. Built in 1996, it's a full-service hotel that's a favorite among business travelers, but it's a good choice for tourists, too. The rooms, which were redone in 1998, are large and bright, with more amenities than you would expect for the price. The roomy suites—perfect for families in town for a few days—have a full-size pull-out couch, microwave oven, refrigerator, and wet bar. All rooms have generous desks with ergonomic chairs, modem lines, SEGA game systems, coffeemakers, irons with ironing boards, and hair dryers. Some of the rooms are equipped with whirlpool tubs—in the room, not in the bathroom. Ask for an end room, which is a little larger than the others. Eight of the rooms are equipped for travelers with disabilities.

Guests have access to a small heated indoor pool with outdoor courtyard/patio, a small exercise room, complimentary use of a nearby full-size health club, and a complimentary shuttle within a 1-mile radius. There are also conference rooms, a laundry service, room service 6 to 10pm, complimentary washers and dryers, and a complimentary newspaper Monday to Friday.

On the Marriott's first floor is the Atlanta Architects Grill and Bar, featuring standard American fare for breakfast, lunch, and dinner, as well as a nice breakfast buffet. The bar specializes in martinis. There are architects' drawings throughout, but don't miss the rendering of the opulent Atlanta mansion owned by heavyweight world champion boxer Evander Holyfield.

Fairfield Inn Buckhead

3092 Piedmont Rd. NE (between Peachtree and E. Paces Ferry rds.), Atlanta, GA 30326. ☎ **800/228-2800** or 404/846-0900. Fax 404/846-0900. 116 units. A/C TV TEL. $91–$109 double. Price includes expanded continental breakfast. Children under 18 stay free in parents' room. AE, CB, DC, DISC, MC, VISA. Free parking. MARTA: Lindbergh.

There's nothing fancy about the Fairfield Inn, except for its neighborhood. A stone's throw from several excellent restaurants and close to all that upscale Buckhead has to offer, this is an economical choice for business and leisure visitors who are more interested in location than luxury. Built in 1997, the large rooms are well-maintained and pleasant, with surprisingly high ceilings. The bathroom is fairly standard, but the vanity and sink are conveniently located outside the bathroom. The rooms near the elevators and ice machines can be a little noisy, so ask for one away from those locations. If you're in town for an extended stay, try to book one of the five suites, which have mini-fridges, microwaves, and wet bars. Added bonuses are free local phone calls, a small indoor pool, a whirlpool, free coffee in the lobby, and a complimentary continental breakfast in the breakfast room. There's also a coin-operated laundry, an overnight laundry, and dry-cleaning service.

Four Points Hotel Atlanta Buckhead

3387 Lenox Rd. NE (between Peachtree and East Paces Ferry rds.), Atlanta, GA 30326. ☎ **800/241-0200** or 404/261-5500. Fax 404/261-6140. 180 units. A/C TV TEL. $84–$135 double. Extra person $20. Rates include continental breakfast. Children under 18 stay free in parents' room. AE, CB, DC, MC, V. Free parking. MARTA: Lenox.

Considering all you get here, in a great location just across the street from Lenox Square mall and close to MARTA, the Four Points is a great bargain. Under the same ownership as the adjacent Terrace Garden Inn (details above), and sharing all of its facilities, the hotel offers charming motel-style rooms with 18th-century-reproduction mahogany furnishings. All the rooms were refurbished in 1996. Only one building has an elevator: If stairs are a problem, either request the building or ask for a first-floor room elsewhere.

Guests gather in a cozy restaurant with a working fireplace for complimentary cocktails and hors d'oeuvres Monday to Saturday from 5:30 to 6:30pm. In the summer there are occasionally free poolside cookouts/buffets with an open bar. There's an airport shuttle, complimentary newspaper, and valet service. There are also two large outdoor swimming pools, and guests can use the Terrace Garden fitness center next door at no charge.

Marriott Residence Inn Buckhead

2960 Piedmont Rd. NE (just south of Pharr Rd.), Atlanta, GA 30305. ☎ **800/331-3131** or 404/239-0677. Fax 404/262-9638. 136 suites. A/C TV TEL. $135 studio suites (for up to 3); $169 penthouse suite (for up to 6). Reductions are available for stays of 7 nights or longer. AE, DC, DISC, MC, V. Free parking. MARTA bus: no. 5 from Lindbergh Station; it stops at the corner of Pharr Rd. and Piedmont Rd., about half a block away.

This home-away-from-home was designed to meet the needs of travelers making extended visits, but it's great even if you're only spending a single night. It's like having your own apartment, with a private entrance and a large, fully equipped kitchen. It's in a good spot—near several excellent restaurants and not far from shopping and nightlife. Accommodations, which were redone in 1998, include comfortable living-room areas. About half the suites have working fireplaces, and during the winter logs are available from the front desk. The most luxurious accommodations are duplex penthouses with vaulted ceilings, full dining-room/office areas, two bathrooms, and living-room fireplaces.

The inn offers cocktail-hour parties on Monday, Tuesday, and Thursday from 5 to 7pm (free beer, wine, and hot and cold hors d'oeuvres); Wednesday a complimentary full barbecue or buffet dinner is served. There's free shuttle service within a 3-mile radius, complimentary grocery shopping, free daily newspapers in the lounge, outdoor pool and whirlpool, coin-op washers/dryers, outdoor barbecue grills, on-premises basketball/volleyball/paddle-tennis courts, and complimentary use of a well-equipped health club nearby (with every kind of workout equipment, a Junior Olympic indoor pool, an outdoor pool, jogging track, and tennis/racquetball/squash courts).

Summerfield Suites Hotel Buckhead

505 Pharr Rd. (about a block off Piedmont Rd.), Atlanta, GA 30305. ☎ **800/833-4353** or 404/262-7880. Fax 404/262-3734. 88 units. A/C TV TEL. $109–$159 1-bedroom suite (for up to 3); $129–$189 2-bedroom suite (for up to 5). (The higher rates apply during special events.) Weekend rates and summer packages available. AE, DISC, JCB, MC, V. Free valet parking. MARTA bus: no. 5 from Lindbergh Station; it stops at the corner of Pharr Rd. and Piedmont Rd., about a block away.

This is a good choice if you're looking for a great Buckhead location at less than the usual Buckhead price. It's within walking distance of several fine restaurants (Pricci is just across the street and the Atlanta Fish Market is a few blocks away) and close enough to Buckhead nightlife to be convenient, but far enough away for some peace and quiet. There's also good shopping in the area, and even though the hotel is on a commercial street, it feels a little residential because it's on the edge of a nice middle-class neighborhood. There's a park nearby, complete with tennis courts and a baseball diamond, where the kids can run off a little steam.

Accommodations include spacious one- or two-bedroom suites with queen-size beds, separate living rooms with VCRs, and fully equipped kitchens with full-size appliances. There is a separate vanity/dressing area with a sink outside the bathroom. Hair dryers are available on request. Several one-bedrooms are equipped for travelers with disabilities. The complimentary expanded continental breakfast is served buffet-style in a bright room next to the lobby and includes the usual fare (bagels, fruit, cereals, muffins) as well as one hot dish such as scrambled eggs or pancakes.

The hotel offers complimentary shuttle service within a 3-mile radius of the property and to Lindbergh MARTA station, as well as a medium-size outdoor pool (with BBQ grill and picnic area adjacent), Jacuzzi, small exercise room, convenience store/gift shop, and coin-op laundry.

5 Virginia-Highland

This is a marvelous choice for tourists—within easy walking distance of shops, galleries, and trendy restaurants. The only problem is that because it's mostly a residential area, there's precious little available.

✪ Gaslight Inn

1001 St. Charles Ave. (between Frederica St. and North Highland Ave.), Atlanta, GA 30306. ☎ **404/875-1001.** Fax 404/876-1001. www.gaslightinn.com. E-mail: innkeeper @gaslightinn.com. 6 units. A/C TV TEL. $85–$195 double. Higher rates apply to suites. Rates include extensive continental breakfast. AE, DISC, MC, V. Some parking spaces behind house; street parking is not usually a problem. MARTA bus: nos. 2 and 16 stop a block away.

Owner Jim Moss has turned this charming, Craftsman-style 1913 house into a delightful B&B, with exquisitely decorated rooms and public areas. As its name implies, much of the inn is lit by flickering gaslight fixtures, and there are working fireplaces throughout. There are two downstairs parlors, a small screened porch, and a comfortable den with cable TV, well-stocked bookcases, a baby grand piano, and a large selection of CDs and cassettes. Guests can breakfast on fruit, fresh-squeezed juice, muffins, and breads in the formal dining room, in a flower garden, or on the front porch furnished with antique wicker chairs and a swing.

The elegant English Suite—with a four-poster mahogany bed, a vast bathroom equipped with steambath and whirlpool, a working fireplace, and a private deck overlooking the garden—is perfect for a romantic getaway. The Ivy Cottage, a detached bungalow with a full kitchen (with washer/dryer) and living-room area, will remind you of Nantucket; it has a private balcony overlooking a garden. And the Rose Room, with its lace draperies, working fireplace, and mahogany four-poster bed hand-painted with roses, is another charmer. The other accommodations—some of them located in a 1904 house across the street—are equally lovely. On-premises facilities include a kitchen and laundry room.

6 Stone Mountain

Georgia's Stone Mountain Park, just 16 miles east of downtown Atlanta, is a recreation area with 3,200 acres of lakes and wooded parkland. It is, in itself, a major travel destination, visited by more than 6 million tourists annually. *Note:* There's a one-time $6 parking fee to enter the park.

EXPENSIVE

Evergreen Conference Resort

One Lakeview Dr., Stone Mountain Park, Stone Mountain, GA 30086. ☎ **800/722-1000** or 770/879-9900. Fax 770/413-9052. www.evergreenresort.com. 249 units. A/C TV TEL.

$119–$159 double; $189–$250 suites. Rates depend on view and season. Extra person $20. Children under 18 free in parents' room. Inquire about packages when you reserve. AE, CB, DC, DISC, ER, MC, V. Free parking.

Geared primarily to business groups, Evergreen is also a good choice for vacationing families who want to take advantage of all the activities in Stone Mountain Park. A turreted stucco lakefront "castle" nestled in a fragrant pine forest, it has large, luxuriously appointed rooms with balconies. Each room contains a hair dryer, coffeemakers, iron and full-size ironing board, and dataports on the telephones. For a small fee, you can rent a VCR.

Dining/Diversions: The Waterside Restaurant has wonderful lake, mountain, and treetop views. Buffets are offered at all meals, in addition to à la carte regional American fare. Even breakfast can get fancy here, with entrees such as quail eggs and sautéed quail with grits. Both Stonewall's, a window-walled lounge, and Vista, a wicker-furnished lobby lounge, overlook the pool.

Amenities: Complimentary *USA Today* at front desk, 24-hour room service, airport shuttle on request, concierge (who sells tickets to all park attractions), 17 tennis courts (two are lighted), two 18-hole championship golf courses, full business/meeting facilities, gift shop, fitness center, indoor swimming pool, large outdoor pool, whirlpools, kiddie pool, sundeck.

INEXPENSIVE

Stone Mountain Park Inn

Stone Mountain Park, Stone Mountain, GA 30086. ☎ **800/277-0007.** Fax 404/498-5691. 92 units. A/C TV TEL. $59–$125 for 1 or 2 people (rates vary seasonally). Children under 12 stay free in parents' room. Honeymoon package $130, including a bottle of champagne and breakfast. Golf and other packages available. AE, CB, DC, MC, V. Free parking.

This charming inn is housed in a two-story, white-colonnaded brick building that wraps around a central courtyard. Rooms are lovely, featuring Chippendale-reproduction furnishings, and most have large vanity/dressing room areas and spacious parlors. Honeymoon suites offer king-size, four-poster beds. Almost all accommodations have courtyard-facing balconies or patios with rocking chairs.

The inn's attractive dining room has picture windows with lovely views and balcony seating facing the mountain sculptures. All meals here are reasonably priced buffets featuring Southern fare, and there is limited room service during restaurant hours. There's a coin-op laundry on the premises, business service, and an outdoor pool/sundeck in a woodsy setting. Tickets for all park attractions are sold across the street.

A CAMPGROUND

Stone Mountain Park Campground

Stone Mountain Park, P.O. Box 778, Stone Mountain, GA 30086. ☎ **770/498-5710.** $17 for a tent site, $19 for site with water and electricity, $21 for full hookup. Rates cover 2 people; additional people pay $2 per night. Children 11 and under stay free. AE, DISC, MC, V.

A large campground with sections for pop-ups, RVs, and tents, this is a great place to stay. Nestled in the woods, the area has many sites overlooking the lake, especially in the tent section. All have barbecue grills, and picnic tables are scattered throughout. Public facilities include a dining pavilion, playgrounds, laundries, and showers. The park's beach is close by. Your pet is permitted; just keep it on a leash. This is a popular place, so be sure to call ahead. You may reserve a spot up to 90 days before you stay; all reservations must be made at least 2 weeks in advance.

7 Druid Hills/Emory University/Brookhaven

Though not a happening section of town in terms of restaurants or attractions, this area, east of Midtown and Buckhead, offers good value for your hotel dollar. And if you have a car, the properties listed below are only about a 10-minute drive from the center of things.

MODERATE

Courtyard by Marriott

1236 Executive Park Dr. (off North Druid Hills Rd.), Atlanta, GA 30329. ☎ **800/321-2211** or 404/728-0708. Fax 404/636-4019. 145 units. A/C MINIBAR TV TEL. Sun–Thurs $96–$109 double; Fri–Sat $89 double. Suites $106–$125 double. Children under 18 stay free in parents' room. Reduced rates offered for stays of 7 days or more. AE, CB, DC, DISC, MC, V. Free parking. MARTA bus: In front of the hotel.

This hotel is a little bit out of the tourist areas, but it's close to town and convenient to I-85. Popular with business travelers, this is a limited-service (no bellhops, though you can get a luggage cart), moderately priced lodging. But don't picture a Spartan, no-frills atmosphere. This property has pleasant rooms, all of which were remodeled in 1996. All accommodations here feature large desks, nice-size dressing-room areas, coffeemakers, and hair dryers. Suites—a good bet for families—have full pull-out sofas and extra phones and TVs. A lobby restaurant, with seating around a fireplace and overlooking a garden, serves breakfast and a limited menu at dinner. There's also a comfortable bar.

Airport shuttle service and limited room service are offered; there's an outdoor pool, indoor whirlpool, and poolside gazebo (nice for picnicking) for a little rest and relaxation; and guests also have access to an exercise room and coin-op washers/dryers.

Emory Inn

1641 Clifton Rd. NE (between Briarcliff and North Decatur rds.), Atlanta, GA 30329. ☎ **800/933-6679** or 404/712-6700. Fax 404/712-6701. 107 units. A/C TV TEL. Sun–Thurs $99–$109 per room, Fri–Sat $89. AE, CB, DC, DISC, MC, V. Free parking. MARTA bus: no. 6 Emory stops in front of the hotel.

The delightful hotel, owned by Emory University, is popular with visitors to Emory and the nearby Centers for Disease Control and Prevention. Rooms, furnished with early American–style knotty-pine pieces, are attractively decorated and equipped with coffeemakers, hair dryers, irons, and full-size ironing boards.

Emory Inn also offers a number of amenities: an airport shuttle on request, room service during restaurant hours, complimentary *USA Today* in the lobby, complimentary shuttle service to the Emory campus and hospital, coin-op washers/dryers, swimming pool/sundeck bordered by flower beds, and Jacuzzi. Guests also enjoy free use of a vast fitness complex on campus with an indoor pool, 12 lighted tennis courts, basketball, indoor track, racquetball, a full complement of Nautilus equipment, and much more.

The Emory Café, with bamboo and wicker garden furnishings, serves buffet and à la carte American/continental fare at all meals. There's also outdoor seating for dining or cocktails in a beautiful flower garden.

INEXPENSIVE

Baymont Inn

2535 Chantilly Dr. NE (just off Cheshire Bridge Rd.), Atlanta, GA 30324. ☎ **800/428-3438** or 404/321-0999. Fax 404/634-3384. 102 units. A/C TV TEL. $49.95–$59.95 double. Suites

$59.95–$65.95. Extra person $7. Children 18 and under stay free in parents' room. AE, CB, DC, DISC, MC, V. Free parking. MARTA bus: no. 47 stops at the corner weekdays.

Just off I-85 and not too far from Buckhead and downtown, this motel offers good value to price-conscious travelers. The rooms are nothing special, but they are clean and well-tended. In-room amenities include dressing areas, coffeemakers, VCRs, and pay movies. Ten larger rooms, called leisure suites, offer refrigerators, microwave ovens, hair dryers, and sofa beds. Coin-op washers and dryers are on the premises. There's no restaurant, but a sweet roll and juice are delivered to your room each morning. Local calls are free.

8 Airport

There are more than three dozen hotels near the airport, most of them well-known chains. It's often convenient to stay there, especially if you're flying out very early or in very late. Although most airport hotel guests are business travelers, it's not out of the question for leisure travelers to choose accommodations at the airport. Weekend rates there are often very low, and many of the hotels offer free shuttles to the Airport MARTA station, making it easy to reach other parts of the city. Buckhead, for instance, is about 35 minutes away by MARTA rail. The hotels listed below are two of the finest.

EXPENSIVE

Hilton Atlanta Airport and Towers

1031 Virginia Ave. (at I-85 Exit 19), Atlanta, GA 30354. ☎ **800/HILTONS** OR 404/767-9000. Fax 404/768-0185. www.hilton.com. 503 units. A/C MINIBAR TV TEL. $109–$189 double; suites $450–$550. Weekend packages $79–$89. Rates may be lower during summer, higher during special events. AE, CB, DC, DISC, ER, EC, JCB, MC, V. Valet parking $6; self-parking $4.

Mercifully, this airport hotel is out of the normal flight pattern. That, and its triple-paned windows, make it quieter than many hotels, especially the less expensive ones. (For the *very* quietest location, ask for a room with a city view.) The rooms, which were redone in 1996, are a good size with tasteful, contemporary decor. They're outfitted with king-size beds or two doubles, coffeemakers, and irons and ironing boards. Each phone has two lines and a dataport. The bathrooms, which have generous vanities, are equipped with hair dryers. For an excellent value, ask for one of the Executive Corner rooms, which are only $20 more than the standard rooms. They're twice as big, though, and are spacious enough to accommodate a sofa and two easy chairs in the sitting area. The bathrooms have separate showers and garden tubs. The suites, of course, are quite large and luxurious. Twenty-five of the standard rooms have been modified for guests with disabilities.

Dining/Diversions: The Hilton's premier restaurant is Andiamo, specializing in northern Italian cuisine; it's open for dinner only. Cafe Magnolia, serving American fare for breakfast, lunch, and dinner, also offers a buffet lunch Monday to Friday and a buffet breakfast daily. The Finish Line Sports Bar is open until 2am.

Amenities: 24-hour room service, 24-hour concierge, complimentary airport shuttle, extremely large and well-equipped fitness center for a $6 fee (aerobics classes, personal trainers, massage available), valet service, outdoor swimming pool with multi-level deck, small indoor heated pool with adjacent whirlpool, business center, conference and meeting rooms, lighted tennis court, gift shop, beauty salon/barber, free weekday newspaper, nightly turndown and twice-daily maid service on request.

Renaissance Atlanta Hotel-Concourse

One Hartsfield Center Parkway, Atlanta, GA 30354. ☎ **800/HOTELS-1** or 404/209-9999. Fax 404/209-8934. www.renaissancehotels.com. 387 units. A/C MINIBAR TV TEL. $135–$155 double; suites $425 and up. Weekend packages $79–$109. Rates may be higher during special events. AE, CB, DC, DISC, MC, V. Valet parking $6; self-parking free.

If you're an airplane buff, this is the ticket. Built on the site of the old airport terminal in 1992, the Renaissance is literally on the edge of the runway. Half the rooms, in fact, face the runway, so you can step out on your balcony and watch the planes take off and land; on the other side, the rooms have views of the downtown skyline. Sounds noisy, but the soundproofing is more than adequate, and back in your room you'd hardly know you were at the airport. The rooms themselves are luxuriously decorated, light, open, and quite large. They're equipped with coffeemakers, dataports, irons, and ironing boards; the oversized bathrooms have hair dryers. Twenty rooms have been specially modified for travelers with disabilities; 19 have roll-in showers.

Dining/Diversions: The Concorde Grille is open for breakfast, lunch, and dinner daily. A` la carte is available, but there's also a generous breakfast buffet daily and a lunch buffet Monday to Friday. The Concorde Bar, where a jazz combo plays most nights, has a great view of the runway.

Amenities: 24-hour room service, 24-hour concierge, complimentary airport shuttle, fully equipped fitness center with steam rooms and sauna, valet service, medium-size nicely landscaped outdoor pool, indoor heated lap pool with adjacent whirlpool, business center with secretarial services, conference and meeting rooms, small gift shop, free newspaper with wake-up call.

9 South of Town

Seren-Be Bed and Breakfast Farm

10950 Hutcheson Ferry Rd., Palmetto, GA 30268. ☎ **770/463-2610.** Fax 770/463-4472. www.serenbe.com. 4 units, 1 cottage. A/C. $145–$170 double; $180 2-bedroom cottage. Rates include full farm breakfast. No credit cards. Free parking. Call ahead for directions.

Thirty-two miles south of Atlanta—amid rolling meadows, horse pasture, verdant woodlands, and fields of sage—Steve and Marie Nygren have created a retreat on 284 acres of farmland. Here they offer warm Southern hospitality to visitors seeking a place to kick back and relax, a romantic getaway, or a family vacation that offers close encounters with farm animals. Visiting children are invited to pet the baby animals, milk cows, feed chickens, and otherwise participate in farm chores. Other activities include occasional hayrides, marshmallow roasts around a bonfire, fishing from a well-stocked lake, hiking along trails dotted with streams and waterfalls, moonlit canoe rides, and antiquing in the nearby town of Newnan.

A rustic recreation room with a working stone fireplace is comfortably furnished and equipped with games, books, puzzles, a TV, and videos. There are also many patios, porches, and gazebos where guests can gather or enjoy their privacy. Other facilities are a swimming pool with a water slide and hot tub, and a communal kitchen and barbecue grill. In the dining room, which has lovely views of the surrounding countryside, guests enjoy a hearty breakfast—perhaps cheese grits, baked ham, fresh eggs, fried green tomatoes, and biscuits.

The rooms—all with private bath, one with a Jacuzzi tub—are charming but unpretentious. Yours might have knotty-pine floors strewn with rag rugs, antique or white painted furnishings, a bed piled high with decorative pillows, or lace-curtained windows. The cottage has its own full kitchen, living room, front porch, and screened dining porch.

The Nygrens are Atlanta restaurant royalty: Steve, now retired, was the founder of the successful Peasant group (including Mick's, City Grill, and others), while Marie is the daughter of Margaret Lupo, who established Mary Mac's Tearoom, a local institution.

Dining 6

Not too many years ago, most of what was offered in Atlanta's restaurants was standard, fairly uninventive American fare or down-home Southern cooking. Eating out was hardly a culinary adventure, and the city's biggest contribution to gastronomy was Coca-Cola. But in the last decade or so the dining scene has exploded, and Atlanta has emerged as a sophisticated restaurant town. Many new places were opened to take advantage of Atlanta's Olympic moment, but even before that buildup, there was already an impressive array.

Innovative chefs, who once left Atlanta for the great food capitals, have brought their expertise and ideas to the New South. As a result there's now a little bit of everything available—from all around the world. You can munch on pierogies in East Atlanta, fragrant basil rolls in Virginia-Highland, or breast of capon in Buckhead. There's French as authentic as any you'll find on the Left Bank, and Italian that tastes like a direct import.

The Colonnade and Thelma's Kitchen, two bastions of tradition, still turn out some of the best Southern cooking you've ever put in your mouth, but the current trend in many kitchens is to take heirloom recipes and give them a contemporary twist. So pork chops might be stuffed with eggplant and andouille sausage, collard greens sautéed and seasoned with balsamic vinegar, and the comfy, familiar grits spiked with Stilton.

The audience for all these culinary concoctions is huge. Atlantans love to eat out, spending half their annual food budget on dining away from home. The debut of a new restaurant is more eagerly awaited than the opening of a new play, and Atlantans avidly peruse the local newspapers to find out about the hottest names in the food game. Competition is fierce because there's always something fresh and exciting on the horizon.

Dining out in Atlanta can be expensive, but it doesn't have to be. The highest concentration of restaurants is in Buckhead, where you'll also find most of the glitzy, special-occasion places that may call for coat and tie. Still, sprinkled around that part of town are a great number of less expensive, more casual bistros that will welcome you whether you're wearing black tie or blue jeans. Another hot spot is Virginia-Highland, which is more laid-back and offers everything from sumptuous seafood to bargain burgers. Don't be surprised—or discouraged—if you find that many of the following recommendations are in shopping malls or strip-malls: Some of Atlanta's finest restaurants rub shoulders with the local hardware store.

Reservations, where accepted, are always a good idea—in some places, they're imperative. Much to the consternation of regular restaurant patrons, a large number of popular spots don't take reservations, so you've got to get there early to arrive ahead of the crowds or go in off-peak hours to avoid the crowds.

1 Best Bets

- **Best Spot for a Romantic Dinner:** When the weather is balmy, there's no better spot than the tree-shaded terrace at **Horseradish Grill,** 4320 Powers Ferry Rd. (☎ **404/255-7277**). On chillier nights, ask for a table by the fireplace in the cozy house that is home to **Bacchanalia,** 3125 Piedmont Rd. NE (☎ **404/365-0410**).
- **Best Spot for a Business Lunch:** The power brokers head for **Bones,** 3130 Piedmont Rd. NE (☎ **404/237-2663**) in Buckhead, where the food is serious and the service is impeccable and unobtrusive.
- **Best Spot for a Celebration: The Dining Room** at the Ritz-Carlton, Buckhead, 3434 Peachtree Rd. NE (☎ **404/237-2700**), is Atlanta's premier dining venue; the cuisine and decor are equally exquisite.
- **Best Decor:** The rustic but classy **Canoe,** 4199 Paces Ferry Rd., in Vinings (☎ **404/432-2663**), is a fascinating mix of polished wood, old brick, and artistic metalwork, designed by the team from Johnson Studio, a local architecture and design firm.
- **Best View:** Even the ride to the **Horseradish Grill** (see "Best Spot for a Romantic Dinner" above) (☎ **404/255-7277**) is scenic. On the premises, windowed walls and a lushly planted patio overlook the woodlands and meadows of Chastain Park. A close runner-up is **Canoe** (see "Best Decor," above), which is perched on the side of the Chattahoochee River. Ask for a table on the large, canopied patio, surrounded by landscaped gardens, and watch the river go by.
- **Best Wine List:** At **The Dining Room,** the refined pleasure palace at the Ritz-Carlton, Buckhead (see "Best Spot for a Celebration," above), the culinary creations are complemented by a vast wine cellar.
- **Best Italian Cuisine: Veni, Vidi, Vici,** at 41 fourteenth St. (☎ **404/875-8424**), gets the vote for inspired rustic Italian cuisine.
- **Best Italian on a Budget: Pasta da Pulcinella,** 1027 Peachtree St. (☎ **404/892-6195**), serves gourmet pasta for next to nothing; and **Pasta Vino,** 2391 Peachtree Rd. NE (☎ **404/231-4946**), is a kid-friendly spot with dishes to please the whole family.
- **Best Pizza:** Go for the vegetarian special at **Athens Pizza House,** at 1341 Clairmont Rd. in Decatur (☎ **404/636-1100**), and in several other Atlanta locations; its chewy, yeasty crust is topped with tomatoes, peppers, onions, Greek olives, and a generous portion of feta cheese.
- **Best Seafood:** For best fresh seafood overall, the **Atlanta Fish Market,** 265 Pharr Rd. (☎ **404/262-3165**), is the ticket, with an enormous selection of superbly done dishes.
- **Best New Southern Cuisine:** The competition is stiff, but the **Horseradish Grill** (see "Best View," above) wins by a nose.
- **Best Traditional Southern Cuisine:** The tie goes to the **Colonnade,** 1879 Cheshire Bridge Rd. NE (☎ **404/874-5642**), keeper of the best heirloom

recipes; and **Thelma's Kitchen,** 764 Marietta St. NW (☎ **404/688-5855**), the premier soul food spot.

* **Best Southwestern Cuisine: Nava,** 3060 Peachtree Rd. (☎ **404/240-1984**), is a stunning restaurant with a kitchen under the auspices of a proven Southwestern star—Dallas's Kevin Rathbun.

* **Best Steakhouse:** There's quite a turf war going on in Atlanta, but **Bone's,** that powerhouse for powerbrokers, gets the vote (see "Best Place for a Business Lunch," above). A close second is **Chops,** 70 W. Paces Ferry Rd. (☎ **404/ 262-2675**).

* **Best Desserts:** Without a doubt, **Bacchanalia** (see "Best Spot for a Romantic Dinner," above) is the winner with its warm Valrhona chocolate cake with vanilla bean ice cream, a flourless confection with a sinful, gooey center. They tried to take it off the menu once, but the public outcry was too great. (Actually, anything at Bacchanalia deserves to be on the best dessert list.)

* **Best Fried Chicken:** There are lots of New Southern restaurants trying to invent newfangled ways to cook fried chicken. Well, they should just cut it out: If it ain't broke, don't fix it. And you should head to the **Colonnade** or **Thelma's Kitchen** (see "Best Traditional Southern Cuisine," above) for some of the best fried chicken you've ever tasted. These two establishments have been turning it out for years for a demanding local audience, and they know what they're doing.

* **Best Pastries:** The fresh pastries made by the **Buckhead Bread Co.,** 3070 Piedmont Rd. (☎ **404/240-1978**), are gorgeous and taste as good as they look. Have one with a cup of coffee or take a selection with you. You'll think you've been to the best patisserie Paris has to offer.

* **Best Brunch:** Drive over to **Canoe** (see "Best Decor," above) for excellent food (banana-stuffed French toast, decadent eggs Benedict) and a lovely setting. For something more informal, **Indigo Coastal Grill,** 1397 North Highland Ave. NE (☎ **404/876-0676**), is the way to go. You'll find melt-in-your-mouth biscuits, cornmeal blueberry pancakes, and crab cakes topped with poached egg and hollandaise.

* **Best Breakfast:** The fun and funky **Flying Biscuit Cafe,** 1655 McLendon Ave. (☎ **404/607-8888**), fulfills all the usual breakfast expectations (orange French toast, organic oatmeal pancakes, killer biscuits) but there's also a great selection of offbeat specialties. Best are Love Cakes—sautéed black bean and cornmeal cakes topped with salsa, onion, sour cream, and feta cheese.

* **Best Late-Night Dining:** You can eat food like Mom's around the clock at the **OK Cafe,** 1284 West Paces Ferry Rd. NW (☎ **404/233-2888**). Try the baked macaroni made with six cheeses. For something more sophisticated, head downtown to **Mumbo Jumbo Bar & Grill,** 89 Park Place NE (☎ **404/523-0330**); the folks there stay up *very* late.

* **Best People-Watching:** Famous beef-eaters—from Atlanta sports teams to celebs such as Liza Minnelli and Frank Sinatra—have flocked to **Morton's,** especially the Buckhead location at 3379 Peachtree Rd. (☎ **404/816-6535**), or **Bone's** (see "Best Steakhouse," above), which has seen the likes of Bob Hope, George Bush, and the Atlanta Braves. Many famous folks stay at the **Ritz-Carlton Buckhead** (see "Best Spot for a Celebration," above), so any of the restaurants or bars there are prime spots (Kevin Costner was spotted in the Lobby Lounge).

* **Best Afternoon Tea:** Fresh-baked scones with Devonshire cream, finger sandwiches, pastries, and tea are served every afternoon in the posh lobby lounge of

the **Ritz-Carlton Buckhead** (see "Best Spot for a Celebration," above), and in the mahogany-paneled Persian-carpeted lobby lounge of the **Ritz-Carlton Atlanta,** 181 Peachtree St. NE (☎ **404/659-0400**).

- **Best for Kids: Fratelli di Napoli,** 2102-B Tula St. NW (☎ **404/351-1533**), has a festive atmosphere kids will enjoy, and the huge platters of food—served family style—will please the most discriminating adults. Other kid-friendly venues include **Mick's** (several Atlanta locations), and **Pasta Vino** (see "Best Italian on a Budget," above).
- **Best Pre- and Post-theater Dining:** If you're attending a show at the Woodruff Arts Center—Atlanta's major performance facility—dine at **Veni, Vidi, Vici** (see "Best Italian Cuisine," above). If your destination is the Fox Theatre, the **Bridgetown Grill,** 689 Peachtree St. NW (☎ **404/873-5361**), is right across the street.

2 Restaurants by Cuisine

REGIONAL AMERICAN
City Grill (Downtown, *VE*)
Harvest (Virginia-Highland, *E*)

AMERICAN
Buckhead Diner (Buckhead, *M*)
Country Place (Midtown, *E*)
George's Restaurant and Bar
   (Virginia-Highland, *I*)
Gorin's (Midtown, *I*)
Houston's (Buckhead, *I*)
Mick's (Downtown, *I*)
Murphy's (Virginia-Highland, *M*)
OK Cafe (Buckhead, *I*)
Pano's & Paul's (Buckhead, *E*)
R. Thomas Deluxe Grill
   (Buckhead, *I*)
Swan Coach House
   (Buckhead, *I*)
Varsity (Downtown, *I*)

BURRITOS
Burrito Art (East Atlanta, *I*)

CAFE/BAKERY
Corner Cafe/Buckhead Bread
   Company (Buckhead, *M*)

CAJUN/CREOLE
French Quarter Food Shop
   (Midtown, *I*)

CARIBBEAN
Bridgetown Grill (Midtown, *M*)

CONTEMPORARY AMERICAN
Bacchanalia (Buckhead, *E*)
Canoe (Vinings, *E*)
Delectables (Downtown, *M*)
dish (Virginia-Highland, *E*)
Flying Biscuit Cafe (Little Five
   Points, *I*)
Mumbo Jumbo Bar & Grill
   (Downtown, *E*)
Terra Cotta (Virginia-Highland, *E*)
Tiburon Grille (Virginia-Highland,
   M)
Toulouse (Buckhead, *E*)

CONTEMPORARY SOUTHERN
Blue Ridge Grill (Buckhead, *E*)
Horseradish Grill (Buckhead, *E*)
Kudzu Café (Buckhead, *M*)
South City Kitchen (Midtown, *E*)

CONTINENTAL
103 West (Buckhead, *VE*)
Pano's & Paul's (Buckhead, *VE*)

COUNTRY FRENCH & ITALIAN
Floataway Cafe (Decatur, *E*)

CROSS-CULTURAL/FUSION
Luna Si (Buckhead, *M*)

Key to abbreviations: *I*=Inexpensive, *M*=Moderate, *E*=Expensive, *VE*=Very Expensive

ECLECTIC

Heaping Bowl and Brew (East Atlanta, *I*)

EUROPEAN PROVINCIAL

Babette's (Virginia-Highland, *E*)

FRENCH

Anis Cafe and Bistro (Buckhead, *M*)
Brasserie Le Coze (Buckhead, *E*)
Ciboulette (Midtown, *E*)
The Dining Room, at the Ritz-Carlton Buckhead (Buckhead, *VE*)
Riviera (Buckhead, *VE*)

GREEK

Athens Pizza (Decatur, *I*)

ICE CREAM

Gorin's (Midtown, *I*)

ITALIAN

Abruzzi Ristorante (Buckhead, *VE*)
Fratelli di Napoli (Buckhead, *M*)
Original Rocky's Brick Oven Italian Restaurant (Buckhead, *I*)
Pasta da Pulcinella (Midtown, *I*)
Pasta Vino (Buckhead, *I*)
Pricci (Buckhead, *E*)
Veni, Vidi, Vici (Midtown, *E*)

JAPANESE

Kamogawa, in the Hotel Nikko (Buckhead, *VE*)

MEDITERRANEAN

Anis Cafe and Bistro (Buckhead, *M*)
The Dining Room, at the Ritz-Carlton Buckhead (Buckhead, *VE*)

MODERN CLASSICAL

Seeger's (Buckhead, *VE*)

PIZZA

Athens Pizza (Decatur, *I*)
Bertucci's Brick Oven Pizzeria (Downtown, *I*)
Fellini's Pizza (Buckhead, *I*)
Original Rocky's Brick Oven Italian Restaurant (Buckhead, *I*)
Pasta Vino (Buckhead, *I*)

SEAFOOD

Atlanta Fish Market (Buckhead, *E*)
Bone's (Buckhead, *VE*)
The Cabin (Buckhead, *E*)
Chops and The Lobster Bar (Buckhead, *VE*)
Indigo Coastal Grill (Virginia-Highland, *M*)
Morton's of Chicago (Downtown, *VE*)
The Palm, in Swissôtel (Buckhead, *VE*)
Prime (Buckhead, *VE*)

SOUTHERN/REGIONAL

Beautiful Restaurant (Sweet Auburn, *I*)
Colonnade (Midtown, *I*)
Mary Mac's Tea Room (Midtown, *I*)
Thelma's Kitchen (Downtown, *I*)

SOUTHWESTERN

Nava (Buckhead, *E*)

SPANISH

La Fonda Latina (Buckhead, *I*)

STEAK

Bone's (Buckhead, *VE*)
The Cabin (Buckhead, *E*)
Chops and The Lobster Bar (Buckhead, *VE*)
Coohill's (Midtown, *E*)
Morton's of Chicago (Downtown, *VE*)
The Palm, in Swissôtel (Buckhead, *VE*)
Prime (Buckhead, *VE*)

SUSHI

Prime (Buckhead, *VE*)

TEXAS BARBECUE

Rib Ranch (Buckhead, *I*)

THAI

The Dining Room, at the Ritz-Carlton Buckhead (Buckhead, *VE*)
Surin of Thailand (Virginia-Highland, *E*)
Thai Chilli (Decatur, *M*)

3 Downtown

Your choices here range from the ultra-elegant City Grill to the world's largest drive-in.

VERY EXPENSIVE

City Grill

50 Hurt Plaza (at Edgewood Ave.). ☎ **404/524-2489.** Reservations recommended. Lunch items $7.50–$15; dinner main courses $17–$27. AE, CB, DC, MC, V. Mon–Fri 11:30am–2pm; Mon–Sat 6–10pm. Complimentary valet parking at dinner. MARTA: Peachtree Center or Five Points. REGIONAL AMERICAN.

One of Atlanta's most opulent restaurants, City Grill is a mecca for downtown power-lunchers and for couples celebrating a special occasion. Located in the lavishly refurbished Hurt Building, the two-level restaurant is entered through a marble-walled rotunda with a rosette-and-gold-leaf-adorned dome. Downstairs, murals of misty pastoral scenes adorn the walls, candelabra chandeliers glitter overhead, and floor-to-ceiling windows are framed by gold draperies. The setting is quite grand, but the service is more relaxed than you might expect.

Chef David Gross specializes in regional American fare with a few Southern overtones. A recent menu included starters such as lobster ravioli with mango-lemongrass sauce and a leek and potato soup with Smithfield ham and Blue Point oysters. Main courses included blue crab cakes with corn and spring onion cakes and a hefty, hickory-grilled veal chop with Tennessee whiskey sauce. City Grill's extensive cellar is stocked with more than 400 wines (most of them French and Californian) in all price ranges, with about 20 selections available by the glass.

Morton's of Chicago

303 Peachtree St. NE (entrance is on Peachtree Center Ave. just north of Baker St.). ☎ **404/577-4366.** Reservations required. Main courses $18.95–$29.95. AE, CB, DC, MC, V. Mon–Sat 5:30–11pm, Sun 5–10pm. Complimentary valet parking. MARTA: Peachtree Center. STEAK/SEAFOOD.

The Morton's chain of gourmet steakhouses was founded in 1978 by onetime *Playboy* executive vice-president Arnie Morton, and his restaurant empire has been as successful as his bunny business. A keynote of every Morton's is a star-studded clientele. Here the walls are lined with photos of famous beef-eaters, ranging from Liza Minnelli to Vice President Al Gore.

Few restaurants offer more in the way of solid comfort, and this one is full of business types out to impress clients. Much of the seating is in roomy horseshoe-shaped cream leather booths at lamp-lit tables. Servers roll up carts laden with several cuts of meat, a cooked chicken, and a frisky live lobster. What you see is what you get. Main course choices include prime Midwestern beefsteaks, chicken, lamb chops, Sicilian veal chop, whole baked Maine lobster, broiled swordfish béarnaise, and prime rib. Side orders such as hash browns or asparagus in hollandaise sauce are huge, so you can share. For dessert you'll need something light, perhaps one of the specialty soufflés. There is an extensive wine list. The bartenders here also know how to make a good, stiff drink.

Morton's has a second location in the Peachtree Lenox Building in Buckhead, 3379 Peachtree Rd., just south of Lenox Road (☎ **404/816-6535**); hours are the same as above.

EXPENSIVE

✪ Mumbo Jumbo Bar & Grill

89 Park Place NE (at Woodruff Park). ☎ **404/523-0330.** Fax 404/523-2908. Reservations recommended. Lunch items $8–$14; dinner main courses $16–$28. AE, DC, DISC, MC, V. Mon–Fri 11:30am–2:30pm and 5:30pm–around midnight. Valet parking for dinner only; parking in nearby garages. MARTA: Peachtree Center. CONTEMPORARY AMERICAN.

Since the day it opened, just before the Olympics, this energetic restaurant/bar/club has been the place downtown to see and be seen. It is fairly carpeted with beautiful people, from the classic old art-filled bar out front to the sleek supper-club-like restaurant in the back. Although it's a flashy place, it's definitely not a flash in the pan. The menu, designed by the revered Guenter Seeger of local Ritz-Carlton Buckhead fame, reflects the fact that, even though everyone is having a great time, they're also serious about the food. Chef Shaun Doty, former sous-chef at the Ritz, has worked closely with Seeger to create an eclectic array of dishes. They range from the rustic (risotto with Fontina, wild mushrooms, and prosciutto dust) to the regal (herb-crusted beef tenderloin with spring vegetables and mousseline). And there's a nod here and there to the South; Mumbo Gumbo, a spicy stew of shrimp, crayfish, sausage, and okra, is the signature starter. The wine list is as eclectic as the menu. (Order by the bottle if you can; wines by the glass are pricey.) And if you're looking for a sedate experience, try lunch or an early dinner. Things crank up later in the evening with the arrival of the trendiest customers, and the noise level in the restaurant can be uncomfortably high.

MODERATE

Delectables

113–117 Peachtree St. (at Woodruff Park). ☎ **404/681-2909.** Reservations accepted. Lunch items $5.25–$8.95; dinner main courses $11–$22 (most under $18). AE, MC, V. Mon–Sat 11:30am–2:30pm; Mon–Thurs 5:30–9:30pm, Fri–Sat 5:30–10pm. Paid valet parking. MARTA: Peachtree Center. CONTEMPORARY AMERICAN.

Delectables, an upscale lunch favorite for several years, was in the midst of big changes at press time—moving to more spacious digs and expanding its lunch-only menu to include dinner. If the past is any indication, the new venture should be a roaring success. The lunches, made from fresh, first-quality ingredients, were the best you could find: excellent sandwiches, salads, and soups at extremely reasonable prices. The new restaurant will include a small takeout shop, a bakery, a full bar and wine cellar, and a dining area on the second floor with a balcony overlooking Woodruff Park. Set in an old brick building, the atmosphere will be airy and loft-like. The menu is still to be determined, but the same high quality is expected. One early indication is the choice of a meat purveyor—the same company that supplies Chops, a pricey Buckhead steakhouse.

Delectables is a favorite of downtown office workers, but don't be discouraged if you see a line at lunch. Tables seem to turn over fairly quickly, so you won't have to wait long. (Or order takeout and people-watch in nearby Woodruff Park.)

INEXPENSIVE

Bertucci's Brick Oven Pizzeria

230 Peachtree St. NW (north of International Blvd., next to the Merchandise Mart). ☎ **404/ 525-2822.** Reservations for parties of six or more. Sandwiches and salads $4.50–$7.25; pastas $7.50–$10.95; pizzas $6.25–$13.45, depending on size and toppings. AE, DISC, MC, V. Mon–Thurs 11am–11pm, Fri–Sat 11am–midnight, Sun noon–11pm. Park in garage next door. MARTA: Peachtree Center. PIZZA/AMERICAN ITALIAN.

Bertucci's is a chain from Massachusetts, but this crew knows their pizzas, and Atlanta's all the better for it. Located in the heart of downtown, near two other big chains (Planet Hollywood and Hard Rock Cafe), Bertucci's draws a big lunch and takeout crowd from conventions and surrounding office towers. The ambience is energetic, colorful, and bold. The walls—purple, yellow, and mustard in hue—are adorned with murals of Old World streets. There are plenty of tables and cozy booths inside, but the sidewalk patio out front makes for good people-watching.

The pizzas here are exceptional, fired up in brick ovens to tender, yeasty perfection. The clam pizza is a favorite—topped with meaty clams, cheese, loads of garlic, and tomato chunks, and spiked with hot peppers. If you can't make up your mind, the quattro stagioni has four separate segments on one pizza: artichoke hearts, green peppers, mushrooms, and prosciutto. The pizza is what makes Bertucci's work, and if you stick with that (and bypass the pastas and desserts), you can't go wrong.

Note: Delivery to downtown hotels is available from this location. Check your phone book for other locations.

✪ Mick's

In Underground Atlanta (at the corner of Pryor and Alabama sts.). ☎ **404/525-2825.** www.micksfood.com. Reservations not accepted. Main courses $6.20–$16. AE, CB, DC, DISC, MC, V. Mon–Thurs 11am–10pm, Fri–Sat 11am–11pm, Sun noon–9pm. MARTA: Five Points. AMERICAN.

One of the best of the Underground restaurants is Mick's, a two-story, turn-of-the-century–themed restaurant in Humbug Square. It's fronted by a gaslit wraparound porch enclosed by black wrought-iron fencing, great for viewing indoor "street" action while sipping vodka-spiked pink lemonade. The main dining room, done up in Victorian saloon red and black, has whitewashed brick walls hung with Early American patchwork quilts. Upstairs is a cozy bar. There's also cafe seating on both levels, and the upper level is actually outdoors on a patio overlooking the fountain plaza.

Mick's is best known for solid casual fare from snacks to full meals, but the best bets are the hefty burgers or chicken grills, in various incarnations, accompanied by fries or pasta salad. Daily pasta specials and salads are also good, and the portions are generous. There's also a pretty good kids' menu, making this a favorite for families. Whatever you order, leave room for the rich, silky-smooth chocolate-cream pie topped with whipped cream, one of the best chocolate desserts in town.

Mick's has additional locations, including one in Midtown at 557 Peachtree St. (☎ **404/875-6425**), one near Peachtree Center at 229 Peachtree St. (☎ **404/ 688-6425**), one on the main level of Lenox Square mall (☎ **404/262-6425**), and one in Buckhead at 2110 Peachtree Rd. (☎ **404/351-6425**). Hours vary by location, but takeout is available at each.

✪ Thelma's Kitchen

768 Marietta St. NW (just north of Means St.). ☎ **404/688-5855.** Everything under $9. No credit cards. Mon–Fri 7:30am–4:30pm. Free parking out front and on neighboring streets; or take the no. 1 Howell Mill bus from downtown. TRADITIONAL SOUTHERN.

Tucked into a storefront across Marietta Street from Georgia Tech, Thelma's is not a fancy place, but it's where you want to come for a typical Southern meal (fast becoming an endangered species in this increasingly cosmopolitan city). There are plastic tablecloths on the tables, the plates are likely to be chipped, and the general ambience is that of a grade-school cafeteria. But, oh, the food. This is fried chicken as it was meant to be. Not mass-produced stuff that's more crust than bird, but big meaty pieces with just the right seasoning in the crispy skin. Chicken is the most popular dish, but there's also excellent country fried steak, barbecued ribs, fried fish,

Downtown Dining

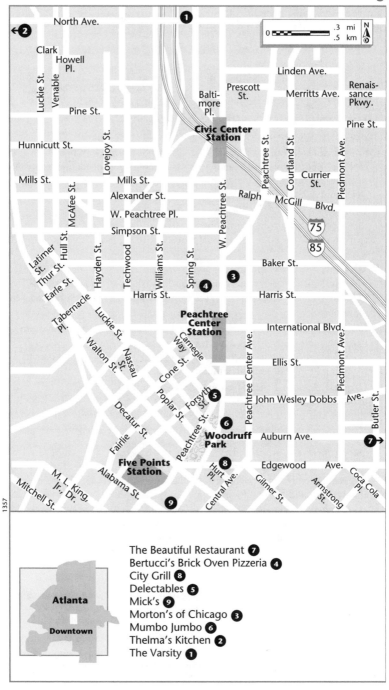

The Beautiful Restaurant **7**
Bertucci's Brick Oven Pizzeria **4**
City Grill **8**
Delectables **5**
Mick's **9**
Morton's of Chicago **3**
Mumbo Jumbo **6**
Thelma's Kitchen **2**
The Varsity **1**

ⓘ Family-Friendly Restaurants

The Varsity *(see p. 98)*   The greasy feasts of the world's largest drive-in restaurant are big kid-pleasers.

Gorin's *(see p. 104)*   This place offers the best kind of fast food—everything is homemade and fresh, prices are low, you can have quiche while the kids eat grilled cheese, and there are ice-cream sundaes for dessert.

Fellini's Pizza *(see p. 121)*   The New York–style pizza Fellini's serves is a treat that will please everyone, and it's available by the slice.

Fratelli di Napoli *(see p. 120)*   A big, bustling SoHo-like loft, Fratelli's bases its entire concept on feeding a family—it offers big platters of food that serve two or three. It's sophisticated enough to interest the adults and friendly enough to welcome the kids.

Houston's *(see p. 122)*   There are always lots of families in Houston's, where there's prime rib for the grown-ups, burgers for the kids, and reasonable prices that won't bust the budget. It's casual, but still a good place to take the family for a special occasion.

Mick's *(see p. 96)*   If you're looking for real sit-down meals in pleasant surroundings, the several locations of this local chain all serve the simple foods kids love at moderate prices. Even the teenagers will like the retro-hip soda shop atmosphere.

Pasta Vino *(see p. 123)*   Do kids like this place? One 3-year-old from the neighborhood insisted on having his birthday party here so he could have his favorite—a slice of white cheese pizza with pesto. There's plenty for parents too, including fresh veal, seafood, and excellent lasagna.

Original Rocky's Brick Oven Italian Restaurant *(see p. 123)*   OK, this is another pizza place, but there are lots of other dishes to choose from—for both children and grownups. And the kids get free gelato for dessert.

and Brunswick stew, as well as different daily specials. The typical meal of two pieces of white-meat fried chicken, two vegetables, and corn bread is $6.95; substitute barbecued ribs and the price goes all the way up to $7.95. On the high end are rib-eye steak and baked salmon for $9.

A fresh vegetable plate is a great alternative at $1.20 per veggie for the likes of collard greens, black-eyed peas, rutabagas, steamed carrots, or okra; others are available depending on the season. Sweet-potato soufflé or macaroni and cheese (a vegetable in the South) are $1.75 each. For dessert, try the peach fried pie or the banana pudding.

The Varsity

61 North Ave. (at Spring St.). ☎ **404/881-1706.** Fax 404/874-3989. Reservations not necessary. Everything under $5. No credit cards. Sun–Thurs 9am–11:30pm, Fri–Sat 9am–1:30pm. Closed Christmas. Free parking. MARTA: North Avenue. AMERICAN.

Atlanta grew up around the Varsity, the world's largest drive-in restaurant, opened in 1928 by Frank Gordy and today run by his daughter Nancy Simms. This fast-food mecca's greasy feasts are an essential element of the Atlanta experience. A 150-foot stainless-steel counter is the hub of the operation, behind which red-shirted cooks and counterpeople rush out thousands of orders. It's a constant chorus of "What'll ya have?" with customer responses translated into such esoteric orders as "walk a dog sideways, bag of rags" (a hot dog with onions on the side and potato chips). It takes 200 employees to process the ton of onions, 2,500 pounds of potatoes, 2 miles of hot dogs, and 300 gallons of chili consumed here by throngs of hungry customers each day. The Varsity's interior is Spartan, with seating in large, windowed rooms with Formica tables. Big TVs are always on.

Order up a slaw dog or a couple of chili burgers (they're only 2 ounces each), with fries, onion rings, and a frosted orange (it's a creamy frozen orange drink). Barbecued pork, homemade chicken salad, and deviled-egg sandwiches are other options. And since none of this is health food (though it's all fresh and made from scratch), don't resist the fried apple or peach pie à la mode for dessert.

4 Midtown

Many Midtown restaurants are a little less flashy than those in downtown or Buckhead, perhaps because they draw more locals than tourists. But to this rule, the first two listings are glamorous exceptions.

EXPENSIVE

✪ Ciboulette

1529 Piedmont Ave. NE (at Monroe Dr.). ☎ **404/874-7600.** Reservations recommended. Main courses $19–$29. AE, CB, DC, MC, V. Mon–Thurs 6–10pm, Fri–Sat 5:30–11pm. Ample free parking. MODERN FRENCH.

It's amazing how many good restaurants are in shopping centers in this city: Pano's and Paul's, Abruzzi, Brasserie Le Coze. So don't let Ciboulette's location put you off; it offers some of the city's most inventive French cuisine. The decor is posh and comfortable, with mirror-lined walls that make the room seem bigger than it is, and the open kitchen adds to the energy of the place. Although the dining room can be noisy, nobody in the casually chic crowd seems to mind. If you're looking for a good selection of French wines, you're in the right place; it's even possible to order half bottles of some.

The chef's five-course tasting menu ($58) is highly recommended, but you can put together a to-die-for meal on your own. The house specialties are fish and game, and there are always several well-chosen appetizer and entree specials on the menu, which changes monthly. The grilled Hudson Valley foie gras is pricey but divine; the crab cakes make a great start to any meal. If you're lucky, squab will be on the list, perhaps with a ragout of red cabbage and mushrooms. Top things off with the chocolate creme caramel or the warm apple tart. Ciboulette has gotten a lot of national press, so the person at the next table is just as likely to be from Seattle as Atlanta.

Coohill's

1100 Peachtree St. (at Twelfth St.). ☎ **404/724-0901.** www.coohill.com. Reservations recommended. Lunch items $6.25–$12.50; dinner main courses $11.95–$21.95. AE, CB, DC, MC, V. Mon–Fri 11:30am–2:30pm; Mon–Thurs 5:30–10pm, Fri–Sat 5:30–11pm. Complimentary validated parking in adjacent garage. MARTA: Midtown. STEAKS.

Toting an impressive resume ranging from a Michelin three-star restaurant in France to the chic Ma Maison in Los Angeles, chef Tom Coohill first became prominent here when he opened Ciboulette, his first Midtown gem. Now we have Coohill, an upscale steakhouse dedicated to conspicuous consumption. Sun-drenched by day (when it's inhabited by business types) and softly lit by night, this is a perfect spot for a pre-theater dinner.

As at most other steakhouses of the moment, the portions are huge—New York strip steaks from 16 to 21 ounces, 2- to 5-pound lobsters, generous all-lump crab

Dining in
Midtown, Virginia-Highland & Little Five Points

Babette's Cafe **20**
Coohill's **5**
Bridgetown Grill **10**
Ciboulette **2**
The Colonnade **1**
The Country Place **3**

dish **17**
Flying Biscuit Café **21**
French Quarter Food Shop **8**
George's Restaurant and Bar **14**
Gorin's **9**

1358A

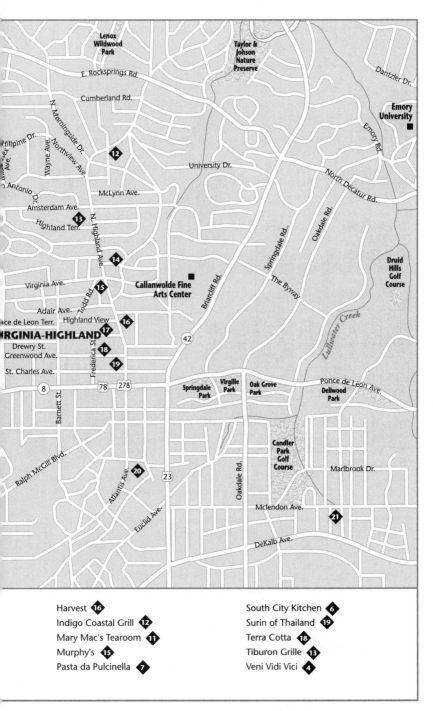

Harvest 16
Indigo Coastal Grill 12
Mary Mac's Tearoom 11
Murphy's 15
Pasta da Pulcinella 7

South City Kitchen 6
Surin of Thailand 19
Terra Cotta 18
Tiburon Grille 13
Veni Vidi Vici 4

cakes, martinis in glasses the size of hubcaps (well, almost). You get the picture. Some side dishes have Southern accents—fried okra, spoon bread, cheese grits good enough to convert skeptical Northerners. The wine list is first-rate, and the pastry chef offers great endings. The best is a chocolate cake with chocolate ganache and coconut.

Country Place

1197 Peachtree St. NE (at Fourteenth St., in the Colony Square complex). ☎ **404/ 881-0144.** Reservations recommended on weekends. Lunch and brunch items $6.95–$11.50; dinner main courses $14–$28. AE, CB, DC, DISC, MC, V. Mon–Fri 11:30am–2:30pm, Sun 11:30am–2:30pm; daily 5:30–10pm. Free validated parking in the Colony Square lot. MARTA: Arts Center. AMERICAN.

This low-key restaurant just across from the Woodruff Arts Center is a convenient choice for pre-theater dining and post-theater desserts and cocktails. A link in the local chain of Peasant restaurants, it has a reputation for good, if not outstanding, American fare. It's a pretty setting—bamboo chairs, banquettes, booths, trellises, lots of greenery—and the service is casual.

Dinner might begin with baked elephant garlic with marinated goat cheese, roasted plum tomatoes, and rounds of hickory-grilled French bread. A recent menu offered entrees of shrimp over pumpkin ravioli with goat cheese, and wood-fired rack of lamb with roasted acorn squash. This chain is known for its rich desserts, such as a brown-sugary six-nut pie, served warm with vanilla ice cream. At lunch there are salads, sandwiches, and burgers in addition to regular main courses. The wine list features many selections by the glass.

South City Kitchen

1144 Crescent Ave. (between Eleventh and Fourteenth sts.). ☎ **404/873-7358.** Reservations recommended after 6pm; reservations for 6 or more at lunch. Lunch items $6.95–$12.50; dinner main courses $7.25–$21.50. AE, MC, V. Sun–Thurs 11am–11pm, Fri–Sat 11am–midnight. Paid parking in nearby lots. MARTA: Arts Center or Midtown. CONTEMPORARY SOUTHERN.

Fronted by a brick patio lined with pear trees, South City Kitchen is set in a converted two-story house. It's a bright space with light filtering through large windows, and a bustling exhibition kitchen serves as a visual focus. There's a lot of meeting and greeting here, and the place can be a little loud, but the crowd of well-dressed young professionals (sometimes four and five deep at the small bar) seems to be energized by all of it. The patio is pleasant, more sedate, and a great people-watching spot.

The seasonally changing menu reflects widely varied Southern influences, and most of the dishes work, although a few are a little rich. If you're not in the mood for a full meal, this is a good destination. There are several options for light fare, and side dishes—such as the yummy cheese grits—can be ordered à la carte. (If you've never tried grits, this is a good time to take the plunge.) Entrees are likely to range from paella to pastas, or there might be barbecued swordfish served atop those cheese grits. A basket of fresh-baked buttermilk biscuits and corn muffins accompanies all main courses. The wine list includes small signature acquisitions, plus two dozen wines available by the glass.

✪ Veni, Vidi, Vici

41 Fourteenth St. (between West Peachtree and Spring sts.). ☎ **404/875-8424.** www. buckheadrestaurants.com. Reservations recommended. Lunch items $7.95–$15.75; dinner main courses $12.95–$22.50 (most under $17). AE, CB, DC, DISC, MC, V. Mon–Thurs 11am–11pm; Fri 11am–midnight; Sat 5pm–midnight; Sun 5–10pm. Complimentary valet parking. MARTA: Arts Center. AUTHENTIC ITALIAN.

This elegant theater-district restaurant manages to create an intimate feeling in a 5,000-square-foot space. Its cutting-edge design (handsome cherrywood wine cabinets, stenciled oak flooring, and sophisticated track lighting that replaces the glow of candles with a pinpoint splash of light on each table) is complemented by a bustling exhibition rotisserie kitchen. There's more seating on a covered terrace that overlooks the Midtown skyline and a lawn with traditional bocce ball courts. You'll want to dress up a little bit to fit in with the well-heeled crowd.

Chef Jamie Adams, who apprenticed for 4½ years in some of northern Italy's most acclaimed restaurants, specializes in antipasti, fresh handmade pastas, and meat or seafood from the wood-fired rotisserie and grill. It's easy to make a meal of the antipasti, but the pastas are all available as appetizers, so it's possible to squeeze one of those into the lineup, too. Especially good is the house specialty—linguine with plump baby clams in a white or spicy red sauce. There are also other traditional dishes such as risotto, osso buco, and veal scallopine. For dessert, there's a wonderful crostata of almond praline and chocolate ganache served with fresh cream and blackberries. The well-chosen wine list is almost 100% Italian.

MODERATE

Bridgetown Grill

689 Peachtree St. NE (just north of Ponce De Leon Ave.). ☎ **404/873-5361.** Reservations accepted for 6 or more. Lunch items $6.25–$14.95 (most under $10); dinner main courses $7.95–$14.95. AE, MC, V. Sun–Thurs 11am–11pm, Fri–Sat 11am–midnight. Dinner menu begins at 4pm. Paid parking across the street; first hour is free. MARTA: North Avenue. CARIBBEAN.

If you're going to a show at the Fox Theatre, this is a good place for dinner. It's right across the street, and if you alert your waiter, they'll whisk you in and out in time for the show. There's not much fancy about Bridgetown. It has a laid-back attitude and decor reminiscent of the tropics, with reggae music, Haitian folk art, and a pleasant covered open-air porch. The thing to order here is spicy jerk chicken, served three different ways: grilled in a sandwich; as a main dish served with raspberry-tamarind sauce (like all entrees, it comes with cucumber salad, black beans, and rice); or in a salad tossed with greens, cheese, and tropical fruit. Also worth trying are the guava barbecued ribs and the sautéed shrimp served with chipotle pepper sauce. There's a full bar, but the house specialty is a frozen "mangorita" made with mango nectar. Very beachy.

There's another, more casual Bridgetown Grill in Little Five Points at 1156 Euclid Ave. NE (between Moreland and Colquitt aves.), ☎ **404/653-0110.**

INEXPENSIVE

✪ Colonnade

1879 Cheshire Bridge Rd. NE (between Wellborne Dr. and Manchester St.). ☎ **404/874-5642.** Reservations not accepted. Lunch items $6–$9; dinner main courses $8–$14. No credit cards; personal checks accepted. Mon–Sat 11am–2:30pm; Mon–Thurs 5–9pm, Fri–Sat 5–10pm; Sun 11am–9pm. Free parking. SOUTHERN.

This Atlanta institution, established in 1927, offers authentic Southern specialties, without any newfangled twists. (Thank goodness.) It has an enormous local clientele of devoted regulars—many of whom look like they might enjoy a birthday greeting from Willard Scott any day—and some of the waitstaff have worked here for decades. The Colonnade is unpretentious but comfortable, with most of the seating at butcher-block tables in a large room. A cozy bar with a working fireplace is a nice place to sit if you have to wait for a table—and you probably will.

At lunch or dinner, you can order fresh turkey and dressing (they roast about a dozen a day), ham in redeye gravy, or roast leg of lamb, all served with a choice of two fresh vegetables (whipped potatoes, black-eyed peas, macaroni and cheese, sweet-potato soufflé, collard greens, fried okra, etc.). The fried chicken is some of the best in town—four huge pieces done the way Mama used to make it. The homemade yeast rolls will melt in your mouth. In addition to menu listings, there are economical blue-plate specials and fancier offerings ranging from Cornish game hen to frogs' legs. Fish is done exceptionally well. The portions are huge, and it's doubtful you'll have room for dessert.

✪ French Quarter Food Shop

923 Peachtree St. NE (just north of Eighth St.). ☎ **404/875-2489.** Fax 404/875-0101. Reservations not necessary. Po'boy sandwiches $6.95–$8.95; main courses $6.95–$15.95 (most under $10). AE, DC, DISC, MC, V. Mon–Thurs 11am–10pm, Fri–Sat 11am–11pm. Free parking in lot behind restaurant off Eighth Street. MARTA: Midtown. CAJUN.

This unpretentious little joint is 100% authentic; Cajun owners Tony and Missy Privat (they met in a Louisiana cooking school) grew up on this cuisine and know its every nuance.

Daily changing soups range from dark, rich, spicy gumbos, thickened with roux, to velvety oyster-andouille bisque. Cajun signature dishes—red beans and rice, po'boy and muffaletta sandwiches, crawfish étouffée, and jambalaya—reach their culinary apogee here, and plumply juicy, lightly battered fried oysters, served with rémoulade sauce, rice, beans, and Cajun fries, are memorable. For dessert, the pièce de résistance is nutmeg/cinnamon-flavored bread pudding. Studded with crushed pineapple, pecans, and raisins, it's smothered in fresh whipped cream and buttery bourbon sauce. The French Quarter serves wine and several unusual beers. A small shop sells Louisiana food products; there's also a deli case for to-go traffic.

Gorin's

620 Peachtree St. (between Ponce de Leon and North aves.). ☎ **404/874-0550.** Reservations not accepted. Everything under $5. AE, MC, V. Mon–Fri 9:30am–4pm; open until 8pm during Fox Theatre events. Sat–Sun noon–8pm only during Fox events. Parking difficult on street. MARTA: North Avenue. AMERICAN/ICE CREAM.

Gorin's homemade ice cream is Atlanta's answer to Häagen-Dazs. And Gorin's locations, which also serve food in an ice cream–parlor setting, are a great choice for casual meals with the kids. Not only is the ice cream homemade, sandwich meats and salads are also freshly prepared on the premises. Menu selections include a classic Reuben sandwich with Thousand Island dressing, ham and cheese with honey mustard on grilled egg bread, an almond chicken/pasta salad platter, and homemade soups. For dessert, go for the ice cream. Of the 200 flavors they make, 16 are available each day—from amaretto almond to peach cobbler. Light ice creams, frozen yogurts, and sherbets are also served, as are milk shakes, malts, ice-cream sodas, and sundaes. In nice weather you can indulge at tables on the front patio.

A few blocks from this location is Gorin's Diner, at 1170 Peachtree St., at fourteenth Street (☎ **404/892-2500**). Similar fare—but with a broader menu, including breakfast and items such as burgers grilled to order—is served here in a recreation of a classic American diner, complete with stainless-steel facade, gleaming neon, and checkerboard-tile floors. Open Monday to Friday 10am to 10:30pm; Saturday and Sunday 8am to 10pm. Check your phone book for other locations.

Mary Mac's Tea Room

224 Ponce de Leon Ave. NE (at Myrtle St.). ☎ **404/876-1800.** Limited reservations accepted. Lunch $6–$9, dinner $7–$10. AE, DC, DISC, MC, V. Mon–Sat 11:30am–8:30pm, Sun 11:30am–3pm. Free parking. MARTA: North Avenue. SOUTHERN.

Mary Mac's is a colorful Atlanta institution, a bastion of classic Southern cuisine that has been patronized by everyone from truck drivers to bank presidents. Jimmy Carter sometimes came by for lunch when he was governor. You'll find a glass of pencils on your table; check off menu items you desire (they change daily) and hand your selections to your server.

Among the famous entrées are fried chicken dredged in buttermilk and flour, country-style steak, and chicken pan pie topped with thick giblet gravy. All come with a choice of side dishes. You might select corn bread with pot likker (a broth made with chicken drippings and turnip greens), black-eyed peas, fried green tomatoes, whipped potatoes, steamed okra, macaroni and cheese, or sweet-potato soufflé. Fresh-from-the-oven corn and bran muffins and yeast rolls are served with lunches; at night there are hot cinnamon rolls, too. Desserts include peach cobbler and pound cake topped with strawberries and whipped cream. There's a full bar.

✪ Pasta da Pulcinella

1123 Peachtree Walk (off Peachtree near Eleventh St.). ☎ **404/892-6195.** Reservations not accepted. Main courses $4.95–$7.95. MC, V. Mon–Fri 11:30am–2pm; Mon–Thurs 5:30–10pm, Fri–Sat 5:30–11pm. Free parking in lot out back; paid parking farther down the street. REGIONAL ITALIAN.

This cheerful yellow dining room is pleasant enough and the wooden tables are candle-lit, but the emphasis is on the food, not the ambience, which is a little rough around the edges. Customers place their orders at the counter, then the dishes are brought to the table. And what dishes they are: each made from scratch on the premises and beautifully presented, with a surprising and innovative combination of flavors in each concoction.

For example, Pulcinella's take on cheese ravioli is *tortelli alla menta* from Tuscany, a round pasta stuffed with ricotta and parmesan, then spiked with mint. The most popular dish is *tortelli di mele*—plump round shapes filled with sweet Italian sausage, browned Granny Smith apples, and parmesan, then topped with browned butter and sage. There are three specials—pasta, risotto, ravioli—each day, and they may range all the way up to $12.95. The salads (mixed field greens or Caesar) are huge and as good as you'd find in a much more expensive restaurant. There are beer and a small selection of Italian wines that changes often. Pulcinella is near a number of theaters and is a perfect pre-theater stop if you care more about good food than fancy surroundings.

5 Buckhead

Buckhead contains most of Atlanta's posh dining choices.

VERY EXPENSIVE

Abruzzi Ristorante

2355 Peachtree Rd. NE (in the Peachtree Battle Shopping Center at Peachtree Battle Ave.). ☎ **404/261-8186.** Reservations recommended. Lunch items $11.75–$20; dinner main courses $13–$24.45. AE, DISC, MC, V. Mon–Fri 11:30am–2pm; Mon–Thurs 5:30–10pm; Fri–Sat 5:30–10:30pm. Ample free parking. ITALIAN.

Situated in an unlikely spot—a strip shopping center with a hardware store on one side and a five-and-dime on the other—is one of the city's finest Italian restaurants. It's upscale but hearty New York Italian both in ambience and cuisine. Owner Nico Petrucci himself is likely to greet you as a long-lost friend, and the rest of the staff will smother you with attention. You'll want to dress up and ask for one

Picnic Fare & Picnic Spots

There's plenty of opportunity to picnic in Atlanta (most of the year), and there are plenty of outdoor spots to spread your picnic blanket. Good bets include Piedmont Park in Midtown, Georgia's Stone Mountain Park, and Grant Park. And here are some places that can help you round up a great picnic lunch:

Alon's Bakery, 1394 N. Highland Ave. NE (☎ **404/872-6000**), and 659 Peachtree St. NE (☎ **404/724-0444**), has loads of delectable baked goods for a snack (some of the best pastries in town), and a variety of made-to-order sandwiches at reasonable prices. Try the garlic-roasted lamb or the Tuscany (goat cheese, arugula, roasted eggplant). The shop on Peachtree also has a selection of salads.

The BREADGARDEN, 549–5 Amsterdam Ave. (☎ **404/875-1166**), is tucked away on a little dead-end street, but it's worth seeking out, especially if you want to picnic in nearby Piedmont Park. This shop started out as a retail bread store, but it now serves up sandwiches on its incomparable freshly baked breads. You can design your own sandwich, but it's hard to come up with anything better than the Mediterranean vegetarian—goat cheese, roasted red peppers, tomatoes, Kalamata olives, eggplant, and olive spread on whole grain bread.

With two locations in Buckhead, the **Bread Market,** 1937 Peachtree Rd. NE (☎ **404/352-5252**), and 3167 Peachtree Rd. NE (☎ **404/816-8600**), has a variety of baked goods and breads, entree salads, and sandwiches. There are always special lunch sandwiches in addition to the usual combinations. Try the grilled shiitake and portabello mushroom with fresh mozzarella on Greek olive bread or the black pepper smoked turkey club.

Located adjacent to the Corner Cafe, the upscale **Buckhead Bread Company,** 3070 Piedmont Rd. (☎ **404/240-1978**), offers unusual sandwiches to go, as well as authentic French pastries that taste as good as they look. (The tiny fruit tarts are out of this world.)

Delectables, 115 Peachtree St. (☎ **404/681-2909**), located in the heart of downtown near **Five Points,** is a popular spot specializing in gourmet salads and sandwiches at lunch. Everything is fantastic, so order something to go and trot over to nearby Woodruff Park for some serious people-watching.

of the flower-decked banquettes—a perfect spot for a special occasion. It's also a great vantage point from which to watch all the goings-on in the main dining area.

Fresh pastas are a specialty, and all of them are excellent. If lobster fra diavolo is a special, don't pass it up. The Thursday night special is osso buco with saffron risotto. If you don't see exactly what you want on the menu, just ask. Special requests are seen as a challenge rather than an inconvenience. Entrees are large, so don't get so carried away that you have no room for dessert. Favorites are tiramisù and rich New York–style cheesecake, but there's plenty more to choose from on the dessert cart. The selection of Italian wines is one of the best in the city. If Abruzzi is too much for your budget, try Pasta Vino, an ultra-casual outpost run by Petrucci's son, Billy, in the same shopping center.

✪ Bone's

3130 Piedmont Rd. NE (a half-block below Peachtree Rd.). ☎ **404/237-2663.** Reservations essential. Lunch items $10.95–$34.95; dinner main courses $19.95–$34.95. AE, CB, DC,

Busy Buckhead folks call **The Easy Way Out,** 2449 Peachtree Rd. (☎ **404/ 262-9944**), when they just don't have time to pull together a picnic for a concert under the stars at Chastain Park. These folks can really rustle up a basket or box lunch—anything from Low Country shrimp salad to cold sliced tenderloin. The prices are upscale, but so is the food. If you give them a call a day ahead, you'll be more likely to get exactly what you crave.

Located in the heart of Buckhead, **EatZi's Market and Bakery,** 3221 Peachtree Rd. NE (just south of Piedmont Rd.) (☎ **404/237-2266**), boasts that it has more than 1,800 daily choices to take home. Hard to believe, but this is a huge store dedicated to takeout, with everything from bread and wine to main dishes and desserts.

Offshoots of the suburban Harry's Farmers Markets, **Harry's in a Hurry,** 1875 Peachtree Rd. NE at Collier Road (☎ **404/352-7800**), and 3804 Roswell Rd. (☎ **404/266-0800**), are ritzy little convenience stores offering excellent sandwiches, rotisserie rosemary chicken, ribs, and "briefcase lunches" (sandwich and salad combinations designed for on-the-go business folks, but suitable for a picnic).

Indigo Out-To-Go, 1397 North Highland Ave. NE (☎ **404/876-0676**), located next to the popular Indigo Coastal Grill in Virginia-Highland, is a small takeout shop with freshly made sandwiches and salads. There are also a few entrees (which change daily) from the restaurant next door, some of which would be appropriate picnic fare. Be sure to ask them to slip a piece of their signature key lime pie into the picnic basket.

Paris Market, 1833 Peachtree Rd. NE, at Palisades Road (☎ **404/ 351-4212**), is full of gourmet goodies, pastries, and wines, and proprietor Brigitte Barnes (a native of Paris) can help you put together a picnic lunch worthy of Luxembourg Garden. The homemade pâtés and imported raw-milk French cheeses are exceptional, but there are also baguette and croissant sandwiches, cold gourmet entrees, and salads. (The niçoise is authentic.) Don't leave without a homemade pastry, a creme caramel, or a little bag of Leonidas chocolates.

DISC, MC, V. Mon–Fri 11:30am–2:30pm; Sun–Thurs 5:30–10:30pm, Fri–Sat 5:30–11pm. Closed most major holidays. Complimentary valet parking. STEAK/SEAFOOD.

Atlanta's best and most famous steakhouse, Bone's is a top power-lunch venue for the expense-account crowd, who are provided with notepads and phones at the midday meal. As many deals as steaks are cut here. And the place is rich with celebrity lore. When Bob Hope dined here, everyone respected his privacy until he rose to leave; then the entire dining room gave him a standing ovation. And during his presidency, George Bush came in for dinner one night, booking six surrounding tables for Secret Service men (they ate, too). The setting is traditional masculine-clubby.

As well noted for its seafood as for its steaks and chops, Bone's flies Maine lobster in daily and serves fresh Gulf Coast crabmeat and shrimp. There is prime-aged, corn-fed Iowa beef, hand cut on the premises, always prepared exactly as ordered. Thick, juicy lamb chops are excellent alternatives to the beef. Similar entrees are available at lunch, along with salads, sandwiches, and soups.

The wine gallery at Bone's houses over 500 selections; international in scope, it highlights French and Californian wines. There are rich desserts like mountain-high pie—layers of chocolate chip, rum raisin, and vanilla ice cream on a crème-de-menthe-soaked brownie, topped with chocolate sauce and whipped cream.

Chops and The Lobster Bar

70 W. Paces Ferry Rd. (at Peachtree Rd.). ☎ **404/262-2675.** www.buckheadrestaurants. com. Reservations highly recommended. Lunch items $6.95–$14.95; dinner main courses $16.95–$35.50. AE, CB, DC, DISC, MC, V. Mon–Fri 11:30am–2:30pm; Mon–Thurs 5:30–11:30pm, Fri–Sat 5:30pm–midnight, Sun 5:30–10pm. The Lobster Bar is open only for dinner. Complimentary valet parking at West Paces Ferry entrance. STEAK/SEAFOOD.

Apparently this popular Atlanta steakhouse wasn't decadent enough. Now they've added the Lobster Bar downstairs to the mix. Steaks are the specialty at Chops, but lobster and seafood are available. Lobster is the main attraction in the Lobster Bar, but you can also order the steaks and chops from upstairs.

The steakhouse is an extremely elegant version of its clubby genre—definitely macho, but less so than its archrival, Bone's. Still, it's power dining at its best and much in demand, so reserve in advance. Trilevel seating is in comfortable upholstered armchairs or roomy banquettes. Meat entrees require a hefty wallet and a hearty appetite—witness a 22-ounce portion of lamb loin chops, a 3-pound porterhouse steak (for two), or a large serving of roast prime rib of beef au jus. There are traditional à la carte side dishes such as creamed spinach, jumbo asparagus hollandaise, cottage fries, or onion rings. A large selection of wines is available, and if you have room for dessert, the chocolate-chip butterscotch pie is noteworthy. At lunch, hefty sandwiches are options.

The elegant Art Deco Lobster Bar is reminiscent of the Oyster Bar at Grand Central Station. The menu is a blend of Chops' power steaks and seafood items, with new seafood additions. Lobster is prepared just about every way imaginable—lobster fingers, lobster cocktail, lobster oreganato, lobster bisque, lobster salad. You get the picture. The star of the menu, though, is the crab lobster entree, one or two Maine one-pounders prepared six different ways. For the purist there is good old live Maine lobster (3 to 9 pounds), steamed and cracked. And for those who don't like lobster (what are you doing here, anyway?) there's a wide variety of impeccably prepared fish, shrimp, crab, etc.

✪ The Dining Room

At the Ritz-Carlton Buckhead, 3434 Peachtree Rd. NE (at Lenox Rd.). ☎ **404/237-2700.** Reservations essential, and as far in advance as possible. Prix-fixe dinners $65 and $78. AE, CB, DC, MC, V. Mon–Sat 6:30–9:30pm. Complimentary valet parking. MARTA: Lenox or Buckhead. FRENCH MEDITERRANEAN/THAI.

For 11 years, The Dining Room was the domain of the nationally celebrated Guenter Seeger, and when he left to open his own restaurant, the hotel management launched an international search for a new chef. They came up with Joel Antunes, a Frenchman who has trained in Nice (under Paul Bocuse) and went on to win his own accolades in Lyon, London, and Thailand. His experience as chef of a restaurant in the Oriental Hotel in Bangkok shaped his style—and has given The Dining Room an exciting cuisine that successfully strikes the chords of both East and West. His American debut here has been stunning, and he's filled the shoes of a chef everyone thought was irreplaceable.

Antunes offers two tasting menus, a three-course and a five-course, but little *amuse-geules* throughout stretch the menus beyond the advertised number of courses. There is a selection of wines to accompany each course for $34. The menu changes nightly, but you might begin with the house specialty, a wonderful foie gras and artichoke terrine or a tomato sorbet with chilled tomato broth. The main course might be veal accompanied by artichoke risotto, chanterelles, and cherry tomatoes accented by lemongrass, or pheasant with roast pear and truffled polenta. Everything is sensational, and presentations are works of art. Desserts are often spiked with herbs and spices for wonderfully surprising combinations: chocolate and coriander cake, blueberry-date tart with honey-thyme ice cream. Service, of course, is impeccable, and the room is elegantly comfortable.

Kamogawa

In the Grand Hyatt, 3300 Peachtree Rd. (just east of Piedmont Rd.). ☎ **404/841-0314.** Reservations highly recommended, especially for tatami rooms. Lunch items $7.75–$19.50; dinner main courses $14–$28.50; prix-fixe lunch $7.50; prix-fixe dinner $22–$50; kaiseki dinner $70 and up. AE, CB, DC, JCB, MC, V. Daily 11:30am–2pm and 6–10:30pm. Complimentary valet parking. MARTA: Buckhead. JAPANESE.

Built by temple craftspeople from Kyoto, Kamogawa has an understated decor authentically reflective of traditional Japanese interior design. Its clean lines derive from simple materials—rice paper, bamboo, pale cedar paneling, and granite pathways. Large windows overlook a classic Japanese garden—a serene backdrop of waterfalls, carefully placed rocks and plants, and a teahouse structure meant for meditation.

When the cuisine is prepared and presented, every aesthetic element is considered, and dishes are accompanied by flowers and other adornments. A favorite entree is the bouillabaisse—Alaskan crab legs, salmon, Japanese pasta, chrysanthemum leaves, and vegetables, all gently cooked in a special miso bouillon. For those with a less adventurous palate, there's a simply grilled New York strip steak, with soy sauce and other Japanese seasonings. Always available is an à la carte selection of sushi and sashimi. Plum wines and sake are essential accompaniments, though your server can recommend appropriate French and California wines. A specialty here is the prix-fixe kaiseki dinner, a ceremonial meal with seven or eight courses selected by the chef.

103 West

103 W. Paces Ferry Rd. NW (off Peachtree Rd.). ☎ **404/233-5993.** www.buckheadrestaurants.com. Reservations recommended. Main courses $17.50–$34.50. AE, CB, DC, DISC, MC, V. Mon–Sat 6–11pm. Complimentary valet parking. CONTINENTAL.

Unrestrained Victorian opulence is the keynote of 103 West, from its porte-cochère entranceway lit by 19th-century coach lights to its posh interior with rose silk moiré wall coverings, Venetian sky-painted domes, and Aubusson tapestries. Walls are hung with gilt-framed mirrors and oil paintings, and arched windows are framed by heavy silk draperies. Old money from the neighborhood (the Governor's Mansion is just up the street) dines here often, and the cuisine, which seems to have been given a recent tweak, caters to traditional tastes.

The restaurant is known for its crab-cake appetizer, thick but light. The scallion-studded cakes are topped with sautéed shredded leeks and sit on a basil-flavored beurre blanc sauce. For entrees, you can't go wrong with the rosemary and garlic lamb chops or any of the fish dishes, but the star of the menu is the cold water lobster tail in a crisp batter with honey and Chinese mustard sauce. (Any item can be ordered broiled, sautéed, steamed, or poached, and without salt, butter, or sauces.) The dessert menu offers many temptations—a luscious hot soufflé Grand Marnier served with cold vanilla sauce, and a dark chocolate mousse with brandied cherries and White Russian ice cream. An extensive wine list offers over 600 wines, at least 50 of them available by the glass.

Buckhead Dining

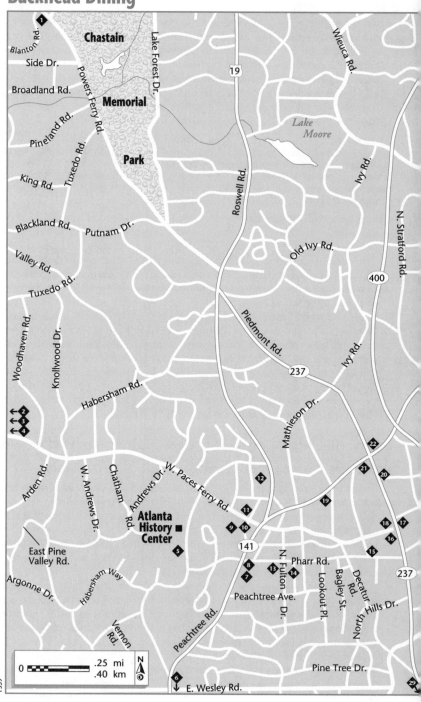

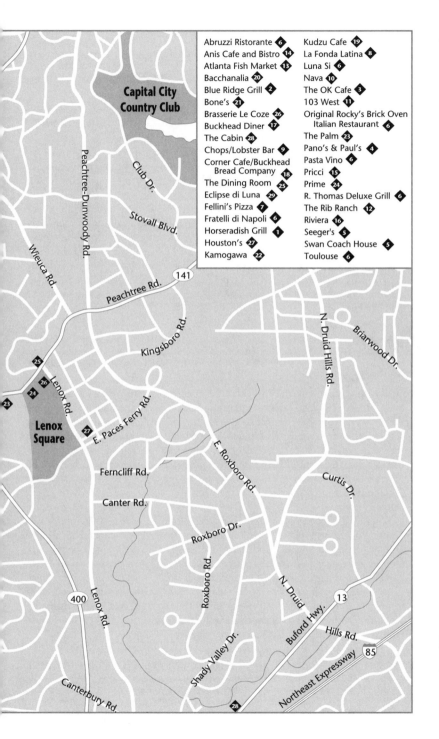

Abruzzi Ristorante **6**
Anis Cafe and Bistro **14**
Atlanta Fish Market **13**
Bacchanalia **20**
Blue Ridge Grill **2**
Bone's **21**
Brasserie Le Coze **26**
Buckhead Diner **17**
The Cabin **28**
Chops/Lobster Bar **9**
Corner Cafe/Buckhead Bread Company **18**
The Dining Room **25**
Eclipse di Luna **29**
Fellini's Pizza **7**
Fratelli di Napoli **6**
Horseradish Grill **1**
Houston's **27**
Kamogawa **22**

Kudzu Cafe **19**
La Fonda Latina **8**
Luna Si **6**
Nava **10**
The OK Cafe **3**
103 West **11**
Original Rocky's Brick Oven Italian Restaurant **6**
The Palm **23**
Pano's & Paul's **4**
Pasta Vino **6**
Pricci **15**
Prime **24**
R. Thomas Deluxe Grill **6**
The Rib Ranch **12**
Riviera **16**
Seeger's **5**
Swan Coach House **5**
Toulouse **6**

The Palm

In Swissôtel, 3391 Peachtree Rd. (between Lenox and Piedmont rds., just south of Lenox Square). ☎ **404/814-1955.** Reservations recommended. Lunch items $8.50–$14; dinner main courses $14–$27.50. AE, DC, MC, V. Daily 11:30am–11pm. Complimentary valet or free validated parking in the hotel garage. STEAKS/LOBSTER.

New York's legendary purveyor of juicy prime steaks and succulent outsized lobsters—established in 1926 and still run by its founding family—also has a branch in Atlanta, and it's a beauty. Glossy oak floors, soft lighting, a lofty pressed-tin ceiling, potted palms, and tables well spaced for power-lunch privacy create the classic Palm setting—a setting that would not be complete without the restaurant's signature "Wall of Fame," plastered with celebrity caricatures—from Frank Sinatra to famous locals Jane Fonda and Ted Turner.

The crowd is mostly from affluent Buckhead, folks looking for the kind of food served at Chops or Bone's (two premier steakhouses), but in a brasher, more boisterous setting. Food preparation is simple here (nothing drizzled or infused); the emphasis is on the freshest fish and seafood, the highest-quality cuts of meat—all served up in satisfying hungry-man portions. The strip steak is huge and divine, done exactly to order. But the most popular entree is the lobster, a hefty critter weighing from 3 to 5 pounds. Other excellent choices are fluffy jumbo lump crab cakes and linguine with garlicky white clam sauce.

✪ Pano's & Paul's

1232 W. Paces Ferry Rd. (at Northside Pkwy., in the West Paces Ferry Shopping Center). ☎ **404/261-3662.** www.buckheadrestaurants.com. Reservations essential. Main courses $16.75–$37.50. AE, CB, DC, DISC, MC, V. Mon–Sat 6–11pm. Free parking. AMERICAN/CONTINENTAL.

When Pano Karatassos and Paul Albrecht opened their deluxe dining emporium in 1979, they brought big-city sophistication to Atlanta's restaurant scene. Since then, they've continued to dazzle the public with culinary creations that have garnered countless awards. Well-heeled Atlanta business and society people consider the place a kind of posh private club. And very posh it is—velvet curtains, damask clothed tables, ornate gilt-framed mirrors, and antique chandeliers. (A bit reminicent of a bordello—but somehow it all works.) It's set in a strip shopping center, just down the sidewalk from the A&P, and it's still one of the most special places in town.

Everything is good—absolutely everything—and the service is smooth as silk. Dinner might begin with smoked salmon, accompanied by a potato pancake and minced onions, and continue with battered lobster tail with Chinese honey mustard, or a mixed grill of lamb loin chop, veal, and beef tenderloin medallions. In season, the soft-shell crabs, lightly battered and sautéed crisp, are a succulent treat. If you don't see what you want on the menu, just ask; the staff will make every effort to prepare something that will tempt you. Desserts are as lush as the surroundings—from a classic crème brûlée to Kahlúa-flavored ice-cream pie with Oreo crust, roasted pecans, and chocolate sauce. The wine list is excellent.

Prime

3393 Peachtree Rd. NE (upstairs at the main entrance to Lenox Square). ☎ **404/812-0555.** www.primeatlanta.com. Lunch items $6.95–$14.95; dinner main courses $14.95–$32.50. AE, DC, DISC, JCB, MC, V. Mon–Fri 11:30am–2:30pm and 5–10pm; Sat 11:30am–3pm and 5–11pm; Sun 3–9pm. Limited sushi menu daily 3–5pm. MARTA: Buckhead or Lenox. SUSHI, STEAKS, SEAFOOD.

Don't be put off by the fact that this restaurant is located in a shopping mall. For one thing, it's in Lenox Square, *the* shopping mall of the Southeast. And what better finish to a shopping spree than a martini and a steak (or sushi)? If you're going to indulge, you might as well go all the way. And this is an extremely indulgent place—a suave, very hip interior with food to match. It's a steakhouse, but it's bright and contemporary rather than dark and clubby. Do start with a martini. The French say hard liquor spoils the meal, but what the hell, this isn't France and several specialty martinis are available. The sushi is the freshest you can get, the steaks are sublime and huge, and the seafood is stylish. At lunch you'll find lighter entrees, sandwiches, and a divine (no mayo) lobster salad.

Riviera

519 E. Paces Ferry Rd. NE (1 block west of Piedmont Rd.). ☎ **404/262-7112.** www. rivierarestaurant.com. Reservations essential. Main courses $21–$28; 4-course prix fixe menu $35. AE, DC, MC, V. Mon–Thurs 6–10pm, Fri–Sat 5:30–11pm. Valet parking. FRENCH.

Set in an old house, this restaurant is a star in the constellation of fine Buckhead restaurants. It's casual and unassuming (although many of the patrons are not), with exposed beams, brightly colored walls, and French doors. The main dining room is not large, but there's additional seating in the cozy bar downstairs or out front on the patio.

The food is stunning, from the crusty rolls flecked with olive to the grand finale chocolate torte. There are quite a few appetizers and salads, and entrees include seafood, duck, lamb, veal, and beef. Start with the incredible lobster ravioli—a delicate striped pasta with enough lobster to make it an entree—or try the crab cake with mustard seed sauce. You can't go wrong with any of the seafood entrees, but the tuna au poivre with mushroom ravioli and red wine sauce is exceptional. The mustard-glazed grilled lamb chops are also outstanding. Everything is quite rich, but it would be a shame to miss dessert—especially the warm flourless chocolate torte topped with cappuccino ice cream.

✪ Seeger's

111 W. Paces Ferry Rd., (between Peachtree Rd. and East Andrews Dr.). ☎ **404/846-9779.** Reservations essential. 3-course menu $58, 4-course vegetarian menu $58, 5-course menu $75 (pairing wine $35 extra). AE, DC, MC, V. Mon–Sat 6–10pm. Self-parking only in lot off East Andrews Dr. MODERN CLASSICAL.

Dinner at Seeger's has been one of the most sought-after reservations in town since the doors opened late in 1997. And for good reason. It is the new domain of Guenter Seeger, the high priest of Atlanta cuisine, who worked his magic for 12 award-winning years at The Dining Room in Buckhead's Ritz-Carlton. Set in a converted cottage that has been transformed into pure space, this restaurant is as much about theater as it is about food. The setting is sleek yet simple, an uncluttered background for an elegant dinner, beautifully prepared and presented. Each prix-fixe meal is a series of little treasures from the kitchen: Parma ham and citrus confit, miso codfish with braised shiitakes and lemongrass, roasted Muscovite duck with Savoy cabbage and figs, sable with flambéed apples in Calvados. The wines are excellent, and the service, of course, is smooth as silk. If you sit downstairs, you have the added pleasure of glimpsing the master and his team creating in the kitchen. One small word of warning, however. Some hearty eaters, accustomed to the gargantuan portions in many American restaurants, have been known to go home, well, hungry. The courses here are decidedly more delicate. Think quality, not quantity, and you won't be disappointed.

EXPENSIVE

✪ Atlanta Fish Market

265 Pharr Rd. (between Peachtree Rd. and North Fulton Dr.). ☎ **404/262-3165.** www.buckheadrestaurants.com. Reservations recommended. Lunch sandwiches $7.95–$9.95; dinner main courses $12.50–$32.95 (most under $17). AE, CB, DC, DISC, ER, MC, V. Mon–Thurs 11am–11pm, Fri–Sat 11am–midnight, Sun 5–10pm. Complimentary valet parking. SEAFOOD.

It's hard to miss the place, and you really don't want to. It's a great mix of whimsy outside (there's a three-story copper fish standing on its tail out front) and serious seafood inside—some of the best you'll find anywhere. Like the Buckhead Diner (see below), the Atlanta Fish Market is simultaneously glitzy and informal. You'll want to dress up, but not too much; your best casual clothes will do. Housed in a brick building inspired by a 1920s Savannah train station, it has a dramatic interior with a soaring ceiling, plush leather booths, and distressed pine tables, and there's an enclosed porch that will make you feel as if you're at the beach.

The menu is vast, the seafood as fresh as it's possible to get. To some folks, seafood in the South means fried, and the fried dishes are okay, but the others are exceptional. There are several daily specials and a list of over a dozen fresh catch items that can be ordered charbroiled or steamed. The best regular item is the Hong Kong–style steamed fish, spiked with soy, ginger, and scallions. There are pasta dishes and salads, too. Desserts include chocolate toffee crunch pie drenched in caramel sauce and garnished with fresh fruit.

✪ Bacchanalia

3125 Piedmont Rd. NE (just south of Peachtree Rd.). ☎ **404/365-0410.** Reservations essential. 4-course prix-fixe menu $50; 6-course tasting menu $60 ($85–$95 for accompanying wines). AE, DC, MC, V. Tues–Thurs 6–9:30pm, Fri–Sat 6–10pm. Closed Christmas Eve to New Year's Eve and 2 weeks in summer. Free parking. CONTEMPORARY AMERICAN.

There should be more restaurants like Bacchanalia. Set in an old house on the edge of an in-town neighborhood, it offers the feeling of a California wine country cottage, pleasantly informal but sophisticated. Owner-chefs Anne Quatrano and Cliff Harrison, who consistently win reams of accolades (the restaurant was voted the city's best in 1998 by *Gourmet* magazine), are in the kitchen every night. The result is consistently high quality—cuisine that is dependable and exciting.

The prix-fixe menu lists five to seven entrees and always includes seafood and game. Though the menus change often, there are a few popular items that are always present: an appetizer of blue crab fritters with citrus, avocado, and Thai pepper essence, and a warm Valrhona chocolate cake with vanilla bean ice cream. This flourless concoction, the best chocolate dessert in the city, oozes a puddle of richness from its gooey middle. Don't share this with anyone. The American wine list is excellent and extensive, with many wines available by the glass. The place is small, seating about 50 in just four cozy rooms, so reservations can be hard to come by. Occasionally walk-ins get lucky. Dress up if you like, but you'll be welcome even if you're in blue jeans.

Blue Ridge Grill

1261 W. Paces Ferry Rd. (at Northside Pkwy. in the Paces Ferry Plaza Shopping Center). ☎ **404/233-5030.** Reservations recommended. Lunch and brunch items $7.95–$14.95; dinner main courses $14.95–$24.95. AE, DC, DISC, MC, V. Sun–Fri 11:30am–2:30pm; Sun–Thurs 5:30–10pm, Fri and Sat 5:30–11pm. Complimentary valet parking. CONTEMPORARY SOUTHERN.

The Blue Ridge Grill's inviting Adirondacks-style interior has the woodsy warmth of a national park lodge: stone pillars, weathered logs, and a soaring pine ceiling with massive heart pine beams salvaged from an old cotton mill. But this spot is as upscale as it is rustic, with gorgeous antiques, original artwork, and cozy leather booths. And though it could hardly be called stuffy, it's in the middle of the most affluent part of Atlanta, and caters to a crowd that likes to be taken care of.

The cuisine is unabashedly Southern, but with a sophisticated spin. An appetizer of hush puppies, for example, is stuffed with Savannah rock shrimp. An entree of iron-skillet trout sprinkled with crunchy roasted pecans is a great interpretation of a traditional mountain dish. Vegetables are served family style; especially good are the collards with pecan butter and the fresh corn pudding. For dessert, adjourn to the screened porch and try the sassafras ice cream float or the lemon buttermilk pie. Lunch fare includes sandwiches and blue-plate specials, and weekend brunch offers the likes of shrimp–andouille sausage hash with poached eggs and tomato hollandaise.

Note: Driving here along West Paces Ferry Road, remember you're looking for Northside Parkway—not Northside Drive, which you'll pass first.

Brasserie Le Coze

3393 Peachtree Rd. NE (in the Lenox Square mall). ☎ **404/266-1440.** Reservations recommended. Lunch items $8.50–$14.50; dinner main courses $13 (vegetarian plate)–$24. AE, DC, MC, V. Main dining room Mon–Thurs 11:30am–2:30pm, 5:30–10pm; Fri 11:30am–3pm, 5:30–11pm; Sat 11:30am–3:30pm, 5:30–11pm. Bar and cafe Mon–Thurs 11:30am–10pm; Fri–Sat 11:30am–11pm. Complimentary valet parking. TRADITIONAL FRENCH.

Mon Dieu. Is this Atlanta or the heart of St. Germain? Once inside Brasserie Le Coze, you'd swear you were in Paris rather than an outpost created by Maguy Le Coze and her late brother Gilbert, who built their reputations at Le Bernardin in New York. And this little bit of France lies in a shopping mall, no less. With small round tables and an abbreviated menu offering traditional French sandwiches, appetizers, and desserts, the restaurant's tiny mall-side cafe is the perfect spot to stop for a nibble of pâté when shopping gets you down. The bar just inside is grand and cosmopolitan, all dark wood and brass and soft lights. The bright, mirror-lined main dining room with its hand-painted tiles, posh banquettes, and staff in traditional vests and long aprons is straight from Paris. All this would mean nothing if the cuisine failed to match the ambience, but it doesn't. It is very French— disciplined and bold while maintaining the casual bistro style.

Settle in with a (huge) bowl of mussels in an aromatic broth or sip the creamy onion soup. A green salad and the crusty rolls would make this a full meal, but do go on to the incomparable herb-roasted chicken or the rosemary cod (available on Fridays). The extensive, exceptional wine list will not disappoint, nor will the desserts—certainly not the warm, gooey chocolate cake. When it's crowded, the dining room can be as loud as the Paris Metro, but who cares?

The Cabin

2678 Buford Hwy. NE (north of Lenox Rd.). ☎ **404/315-7676.** Reservations recommended. Lunch items $5.95–$8.95; dinner main courses $16.95–$23.95. AE, DC, DISC, MC, V. Mon–Fri 11:30am–2:30pm; Mon–Thurs 5:30–10pm, Fri–Sat 5:30–11pm. Complimentary valet parking at night. STEAK/SEAFOOD.

Located in a 70-year-old log cabin slightly off the regular Buckhead track is a little mountain hideaway offering up aged Midwestern beef and Southern-style seafood. Southern style in this case does not mean deep-fried, but interesting variations of regional favorites. High marks go to the salmon (the preparation changes daily) and

Horseradish Grill's Lemon Buttermilk Chess Pie

1½ cups sugar

1 tablespoon yellow cornmeal

1 tablespoon flour

¼ teaspoon salt

4 large eggs, room temperature

⅓ cup unsalted butter, melted and cooled

1 tablespoon finely grated lemon zest

⅓ cup lemon juice

½ cup buttermilk, room temperature

1 teaspoon vanilla

1 unbaked 9-inch pie shell

1 tablespoon confectioner's sugar

Whipped cream for garnish

- Preheat oven to 350 degrees.
- In a bowl, combine sugar, cornmeal, flour, and salt.
- In another bowl, beat eggs thoroughly. Add sugar mixture; mix well.
- Add melted butter, lemon zest and juice, buttermilk, and vanilla to egg mixture, mixing to blend thoroughly after each addition to prevent lumping.
- Pour the mixture into the unbaked pie shell; bake for 30 to 45 minutes or until the top is golden brown and custard is set.
- Remove pie to rack; cool completely.
- Sprinkle top with confectioner's sugar and garnish each serving with whipped cream.

an interpretation of a South Carolina low-country boil crammed with lobster, shrimp, clams, and mussels. The rack of lamb and the cowboy steak (a 22-ounce bone-in rib eye) are popular with the casually dressed Buckhead crowd that comes here in search of serious food. (I did find the horseradish-crusted grouper rather mediocre, though.)

The decor is Highlands cabin, complete with elk-antler chandeliers. The downstairs bar with its stacked stone fireplace is the more rustic of the two dining areas, and it's also where you'll find a selection of martinis, the specialty drink of the house. Even though the steaks and seafoods are the main attractions, the Southern-style vegetables are a real treat, especially the creamed fresh corn and the bourbon-spiked mashed sweet potatoes.

✪ **Horseradish Grill**

4320 Powers Ferry Rd. (at West Wieuca Rd.). ☎ **404/255-7277.** www.horseradishgrill.com. Reservations recommended. Lunch items $8.95–$15.95 (most items under $10); dinner main courses $15.95–$24.95. AE, CB, DC, DISC, MC, V. Mon–Fri 11:30am–3pm; Mon–Thurs 5:30–10pm, Fri–Sat 5–11pm; Sun 11am–3pm, 5–9pm. Complimentary valet parking. CONTEMPORARY SOUTHERN.

This restaurant had a previous incarnation as the Red Barn Inn, and it still retains some of the rustic atmosphere: barn wood walls, a raftered pine ceiling, and a massive stone fireplace. Big windows overlook the restaurant's organic garden on one side, Chastain Park on the other; patio seating is under ancient oaks. The view is lovely, whether you're inside or out, but pick the patio if you have a choice.

Chef Dave Berry, nominated as one of America's Rising Star Chefs by the James Beard House, emphasizes innovative but authentic Southern recipes, simply prepared. Ingredients are seasonal and of the region: no salmon or lobster, no tomatoes in winter, no turnip greens in summer. You can indulge yourself in his excellent specialties: spicy North Carolina barbecue on corncake, hickory-grilled mountain trout, or a Low Country seafood stew. The wine list is predominantly American, but there are international selections, too. Oatmeal spice cake is the not-to-be-missed dessert. At lunch there are sandwiches, small plates, and salads. The brunch menu is especially good. Try the cornmeal griddle cakes with blueberry syrup.

✪ Nava

3060 Peachtree Rd. (at West Paces Ferry Rd.). ☎ **404/240-1984.** www.buckheadrestaurants.com. Reservations recommended. Totopos $5–$9; lunch items $6.25–$15.50; dinner main courses $14.50–$25. AE, DC, DISC, MC, V. Mon–Fri 11am–3pm; Mon–Thurs 5:30–11pm, Fri–Sat 5:30pm–midnight, Sun 5:30–10pm. Complimentary valet parking. CONTEMPORARY SOUTHWESTERN.

Nava's trilevel earth-toned interior is gorgeous—the work of architect Bill Johnson, who is known for creating fabulous settings. There's a bundled spruce ceiling beamed with tree trunks; a kiva-style fireplace; a copper-hooded exhibition kitchen; and a rustic-elegant decor rich with Southwestern and Native American art. Chef Kevin Rathbun, formerly of Dallas, is a rising star on the national culinary scene who has garnered rave reviews, and his work at Nava is no exception.

Dinner might begin with mussels dry roasted in a hot iron skillet and served in spicy chipotle broth; or an excellent and unusual tortilla-crusted shrimp relleno. The spicy, corn-crusted sautéed filet of snapper is superb, as is the roasted pork tenderloin with tamarind-bean glaze. At lunch there are special entrees and sandwiches, and at either meal you can enjoy totopos (a Southwestern answer to tapas). For dessert, try the frozen tequila-passionfruit mousse. Nava's extensive wine list was composed to complement Southwestern dishes; there's also a large selection of tequilas, beers, and margaritas.

Pricci

500 Pharr Rd. (at Maple Dr.). ☎ **404/237-2941.** www.buckheadrestaurants.com. Reservations recommended. Pizzas and calzones $6.50–$8.50; lunch $8.25–$11.50; dinner $14.75–$21.50. AE, CB, DC, DISC, MC, V. Sun–Thurs 11am–11pm, Fri 11am–midnight, Sat 5pm–midnight, Sun 5–10pm. Complimentary valet parking. REGIONAL ITALIAN.

Pricci is strikingly glamorous, and so is the clientele—well-dressed young professionals who don't mind spending their allowances on a night on the town. Part of the drama comes from an exhibition kitchen where a team of white-hatted chefs are engaged in culinary frenzy around an oak-fired pizza oven. The interior is theatrical—art deco chrome and brass dividers, rich decorative woods, cozy banquettes, and a snazzy bar. The downside is the noise; it's hard to escape all the dining clatter.

Pricci's fare is the hearty cuisine of Italy's Tuscan, Ligurian, and Milanese regions: thin-crusted oak-fired pizzas; pastas such as butternut squash ravioli with arugula, sun-dried cherry tomatoes and smoked ricotta; osso buco with saffron risotto. The specialty of the house, which serves two, is an excellent whole roasted fish (selection changes daily) with grilled asparagus and risotto. Desserts are excellent, especially the chocolate tart with warm chocolate sauce and white chocolate sorbet. The lunch menu lists focaccia sandwiches, pastas, salads, pizzas, and calzones.

The award-winning wine list highlights every wine-producing region of Italy and features a good selection of grappas.

Toulouse

2293 Peachtree Rd. NE (south of Peachtree Battle Ave.). ☎ **404/351-9533.** Reservations recommended. Main courses $10–$20. AE, DC, MC, V. Sun–Thurs 6–10pm, Fri–Sat 6–11pm, Sun 11:30am–2pm. Free parking. CONTEMPORARY AMERICAN.

The name is French, and the cuisine is New American with influences from the south of France. Toulouse is tucked away behind a strip of shops along Peachtree; it's a little hard to spot, but you'll be glad you did. The mostly neighborhood crowd, attired in anything from blue jeans to black tie, likes to keep this place a secret, revealing it only to friends and special visitors. It's casual and charming, a spacious loft with a large wooden bar and an open kitchen in full view.

The menu changes monthly, perhaps more often depending on the whims of the chef. But you're likely to find some of the house specialties always available. A good bet is the plump roast chicken done to perfection in a wood-fired oven, accompanied by arugula bread salad. Another favorite is the braised lamb shank with a Kalamata olive–sweet pepper sauce and roasted vegetables. The excellent wine list has lots of good values.

MODERATE

Anis Cafe and Bistro

2974 Grandview Ave. (1 block south of Pharr Rd.). ☎ **404/233-9889.** Reservations suggested on weekends. Sandwiches and pastas $5.95–$9.95; main courses $9.95–$15.95; Sun brunch $5.95–$11.95. AE, DC, MC, V. Daily 11:30am–2:30pm; Sun–Thurs 6–10pm, Fri–Sat 6–10:30pm. FRENCH/MEDITERRANEAN.

In the midst of pricey Buckhead is an unpretentious little cafe serving up good food at the right price. Set in a converted cottage on a side street (and inexplicably surrounded by several hair salons), it's a perfect spot for a nice light meal or a Sunday brunch. The specialty is the Provençal version of healthy Mediterranean cuisine, and the atmosphere is reminiscent of that region, especially if you're lucky enough to snag a table on the tree-shaded brick patio. The key word here is *informal.* The service is sometimes maddeningly casual, and occasionally there are glitches in the kitchen. But if you relax and pretend you've been invited to a friend's house in the south of France, you won't be disappointed.

Starters include an authentic niçoise salad and warm focaccia toasts topped with tomatoes, mozzarella, and fresh basil. The pasta with lemon chicken and roasted eggplant is a great entree choice, but so are the grilled lamb chops spiked with fresh thyme. Brunch is a treat here, and features the likes of crêpes stuffed with prosciutto and spinach, homemade cheese ravioli, and fried eggs in a fresh tomato and basil coulis. There are also several specialty coffee drinks, including espresso over ice cream.

✪ Buckhead Diner

3073 Piedmont Rd. (at East Paces Ferry Rd.). ☎ **404/262-3336.** www.buckheadrestaurants.com. Reservations not accepted. Snacks, sandwiches, salads $5.25–$11.95; lunch items $7.95–$12.50; dinner main courses $13.50–$18.50. AE, CB, DC, DISC, MC, V. Mon–Sat 11am–midnight, Sun (including brunch) 10:30am–10pm. Complimentary valet parking. AMERICAN.

As sleek as a Thunderbird convertible, the exterior of this nouvelle diner glitters with neon tubing and chrome, and the posh interior conjures up images of the Orient Express. It's almost always crowded, so be prepared to wait at prime time; it's usually worth it—full of hustle and bustle and lots of fun.

A Buckhead Fish Tale

If you travel down Pharr Road in Buckhead, it's pretty hard not to notice that huge fish sculpture outside the Atlanta Fish Market, one of the city's finest seafood restaurants. The fish, which is perched on its swooped tail and appears to be about to leap over the restaurant, caused quite a commotion when it was first proposed. Although the restaurant was quite enthusiastic about its construction, many folks in the surrounding neighborhoods were not exactly hooked on the idea. Despite the protests, the project was approved, and the enormous creature, which resembles a cross between a salmon and a trout, was unveiled in late 1995. Here are some fish facts about a sculpture that, like it or not, is on its way to becoming an Atlanta landmark.

- The fish is about three stories high and weighs 50 tons.
- Measured from head to tail, it's 100 feet long, about the size of a large whale.
- It sports more than 600 copper scales, 3½ feet each, which are shiny now but will age to a patina over the years.
- Made of solid copper and steel, it is supported by a welded-iron infrastructure that is connected to a 35-foot-deep steel-and-concrete cason.
- Cost was in excess of $360,000.
- The fish is being considered for inclusion in the *Guinness Book of World Records* as the largest fish sculpture in the world.

Main courses are a mix of Mom and modern, some quite heavy on the fat grams and calories (but who's counting?). Long-time favorites include thick-cut grilled smoked pork chops with turnip greens, excellent cheese grits, and black-eyed pea salsa; veal and wild mushroom meat loaf with celery mashed potatoes; and a thick BLT made with grilled salmon. Many low-priced snacks—such as spicy shrimp dumplings or crispy Florida rock shrimp popsicles—make grazing fun here. If you order nothing else, be sure to get the homemade potato chips slathered with melted Maytag blue cheese. You will not be too embarrassed to lick the plate. Desserts are great, ranging from peach bread pudding with Southern Comfort–flavored cream to a to-die-for chocolate-chip crème brûlée.

✪ Corner Café and Buckhead Bread Company

3070 Piedmont Rd. (at East Paces Ferry Rd.). ☎ **404/240-1978.** www.buckheadrestaurants. com. Reservations not accepted. Lunch items $6.95–$12.50; brunch items $5.95–$9.50; dinner main courses $9.75–$14.95. AE, DC, DISC, MC, V. Corner Café Sun–Thurs 6:30am–10pm, Fri–Sat 6:30am–10pm. Buckhead Bread Company Mon–Fri 6:30am–8pm, Sat 8am–8pm, Sun 8am–6pm. Complimentary self and valet parking. CAFE CUISINE/BREADS & PASTRIES.

This spot is a combination of an upscale cafe and gourmet bakery. The cafe portion is more casual and relaxed than the Buckhead Diner, its glitzy cousin across the street, but the food is decidedly upscale. The menu is large and varied, with wonderful soups (potato leek with fried mashed potatoes) and hearty sandwiches (roasted rosemary lamb on onion focaccia). There are also interesting main-dish salads, and a variety of seafood (pan-seared salmon fillet and mashed potato sandwich) and meat entrees (roasted maple-glazed pork tenderloin).

About half the space is given over to a vast bakery (the Buckhead Bread Company) that displays about 30 varieties of fresh-baked breads each day—everything from focaccia flavored with fresh rosemary and basil to honeyed eight-grain loaves studded with roasted sunflower seeds. (The breads are used for the cafe sandwiches and are a major attraction.) The gorgeous pastries have a French pedigree and will transport you to the Left Bank. It's possible to get something to go or pick out a pastry and have it served to you in the cafe or on the small patio with a cup of specialty coffee.

Weekday breakfast includes fresh-roasted granola, cinnamon buns, bagels, muffins, croissants, and other traditional breakfast fare. The weekend brunch menu is fancier and includes a scrumptious pecan-apple French crepe and poached eggs with roasted corn grits, jalapeño cheese toast and avocado pico de gallo. The French toast, made with brioche, is very special.

Fratelli di Napoli

2101 Tula St. NW (in the Bennett St. complex behind Mick's restaurant). ☎ **404/351-1533.** www.fratelli.net. Reservations accepted for 6 or more. Main courses (which serve 2 or more) $10–$29. AE, DC, DISC, MC, V. Mon–Thurs 5–11pm, Fri–Sat 5pm–2am, Sun 4–10pm. Complimentary valet parking. ITALIAN AMERICAN.

Grab a plate and sit down at the family dinner table in this upbeat, energetic establishment. Housed in a former warehouse on an odd little street filled with antiques shops and galleries, the place feels like a sunny loft in the middle of Soho. It's noisy as the devil, so if that bothers you, ask for a table on the enclosed patio.

Service is friendly, traditional family style, with generous platters designed to serve two or three people. Many of the selections are available as half orders, but it's more fun to go for broke and share around the table. Takeout is available if you want to sneak back to the hotel and wolf down some chicken scarpiello on your own. The menu is as huge as the portions, and everyone in the family (kids included) will be able to find something they can't live without. Stellar specialties include tender-crisp calamari fritti, and Tony's chicken, a lightly breaded, sautéed chicken breast with fresh tomato and basil in a balsamic vinaigrette. The shrimp fra diavolo, sautéed with hot pepper and tomato sauce, is divine, especially when accompanied by hefty, chewy squares of focaccia. The desserts are forgettable, but who has room anyway? (P.S. There's no pizza, but there is a jazz trio every Friday and Saturday night 11pm to 2am.)

Kudzu Café

3215 Peachtree Rd. (at East Shadowlawn Ave.). ☎ **404/262-0661.** Limited reservations accepted. Lunch and brunch items $6.95–$16.95; dinner main courses $9.95–$21.95. AE, DC, DISC, MC, V. Sun–Thurs 11am–11pm, Fri–Sat 11am–midnight. Complimentary valet parking. CONTEMPORARY SOUTHERN.

Themed around a vine that flourishes in the South, the Kudzu Café has often been placed in the Top 10 by the *Atlanta Journal-Constitution*. And while that rating seems excessive—the cooking is often uneven and prices seem a little high for what you get—Kudzu Café does offer some fine interpretations of Southern fare in a casual setting. The decor is thoroughly contemporary with Southern roots—comfy booths, exposed brick, and ceiling fans.

If you have a hankering for fried green tomatoes, you'll find them done just right here, battered with cornmeal and lightly fried. Skip the crab cakes, but try the roast chicken basted with red pepper jelly or the grilled meat loaf with chunky tomato sauce. The vegetable plate is a great choice; you can order four dishes alone or two with dinner. Especially good are the grilled corn on the cob, sautéed turnip greens, and chunky red-skin mashed potatoes spiked with horseradish. For dessert, you'll swoon over the rich pecan pie, served warm, or the witty moon pie interpretation, with vanilla ice cream, peanuts, and hot fudge sauce. Kudzu is very kid friendly; one of the side orders is homemade jumbo saltines with peanut butter.

Luna Si

1931 Peachtree Rd. (near Collier Rd.). ☎ **404/355-5993.** Reservations recommended. Main courses $9–$21; four-course tasting menu $35. AE, MC, V. Mon–Thurs 5:30–10:30pm, Fri–Sat 5:30–11pm. Free parking on the street or in the lot out back. FUSION.

This small storefront restaurant is a favorite among locals in Buckhead. The interior, reminiscent of an artist's atelier, is draped with creamy fabric that softens the noise level and separates the tables. It's a great spot for a romantic dinner—without credit-card hangover.

The health-conscious menu, which changes monthly, is not extensive but is planned for variety and seasonal freshness. There are always several interesting pastas and risottos (including a ravioli of the day), and each can be prepared vegetarian-style. There is also a small selection of seafood and meat entrees; the most popular is a delectable ginger-crusted salmon, restored to the menu after disappointed regulars made a fuss. For good value try the chef's four-course tasting menu, a selection of creative off-menu dishes. The Spanish-style flan is a great house specialty, but the warm chocolate cake with vanilla ice cream (more like a soufflé) will make you swoon.

INEXPENSIVE

Eclipse di Luna

764 Miami Circle (all the way to the end of the street on the left). ☎ **404/846-0449.** Lunch soups, sandwiches, and pastas $3.50–$6.25; tapas at dinner $2.95 each. AE, DC, MC, V. Daily 11:30am–2:30m, 5:30pm–1am. Free parking. MARTA: Lindbergh. TAPAS.

Tucked away at the end of a street of shops and warehouses devoted to wholesale and retail decorative arts, this little restaurant is a popular lunch spot for designers and their clients. Lunch is cheap and good—especially the vegetarian sandwich with avocado, roasted peppers, and homemade mozzarella. You can get as much or as little to eat as you like at dinner, so it's a great choice if you're on a limited budget or don't have a huge appetite, or both. Each of the tapas is $2.95, and the list of 20 wines is $5.50 a glass no matter which one you order. How's that for uncomplicated? The menu includes everything from prawns to Spanish-style ribs to mussels braised in garlic and wine. The decor is rustic and the attitude laid-back, a welcome respite from the rest of bustling Buckhead. About the only thing to remind you of where you are is the MARTA train whizzing by just outside. On Fridays and Saturdays, there's live music, usually flamenco or jazz, from 8pm until closing.

Fellini's Pizza

2809 Peachtree Rd. (at Rumson Rd.). ☎ **404/266-0082.** $1.25–$2.65 for a slice; $8.50–$15 for a medium pie, with additional toppings $1–$1.50; $4.50–$5 for calzones. No credit cards. Mon–Sat 11:30am–2am, Sun noon–midnight. Free parking. PIZZA.

You won't get chèvre or cilantro on your pies here, but you will get traditional toppings like anchovies, Italian sausage, meatballs, pepperoni, fresh mushrooms, and onions piled on cheesy New York–style pies with thin, doughy crusts that exude the heavenly aroma of fresh-baked bread. Fellini's is a classic pizza joint, and a damn good one.

It's a wacky place, very atypical for Buckhead. Most of the seating is at tables on a large outdoor patio centered on a tiered fountain, with statues of angels, the god Pan, gargoyles, and King Tut here and there. Because it fronts on Peachtree Road, it's a great spot to sit and watch the city go by. When the heat is wilting, you can retreat to the funky, spare interior with red plastic booths and brightly painted overhead pipes and brick walls.

The pizzas, regular and thick-crusted Sicilian, are made with only the freshest ingredients. Other options include salads (not outstanding) and immense calzones stuffed with fillings like sausage and cheese. The beer is always ice cold.

There are several additional locations; the most convenient for visitors are at 422 Seminole Ave. in Little Five Points (☎ **404/525-2530**) and in Midtown at 909 Ponce de Leon Ave. (☎ **404/873-3088**).

Houston's

3321 Lenox Rd. (at East Paces Ferry Rd.). ☎ **404/237-7534.** Reservations not accepted; arrive off-peak hours. Burgers and salads $7–$9; main courses $10–$25. AE, MC, V. Sun–Thurs 11am–11pm, Fri–Sat 11am–midnight. Free parking. Complimentary valet parking only. MARTA: Lenox. AMERICAN.

Part of an Atlanta-based group with restaurants throughout the country, Houston's serves up lavish portions of fresh, first-quality fare. It's always packed with people who are looking for an exciting but informal spot, with service as snappy as the food. There's almost always a wait, but you won't mind spending time on the front patio or in the bar. If you're in a rush, eat at the bar during lunch. The patio, across from Lenox Square, is a terrific people-watching spot.

Thick, hickory-grilled burgers are a specialty, as are the tender, meaty ribs, served with a choice of side dishes: skillet beans, fries, coleslaw, or couscous. The same fixings come with barbecued chicken. A lighter main course is the salad of sliced grilled chicken, tossed with chopped greens and julienned tortilla strips in a honey-lime vinaigrette, garnished with a light peanut sauce. For dessert you can indulge in a huge, chewy brownie topped with vanilla ice cream and Kahlúa.

Check your phone book for other locations. There's another one in Buckhead at 2166 Peachtree Rd. (at Colonial Homes Drive in the Brookwood Square Shopping Center), ☎ **404/351-2442.**

La Fonda Latina

2813 Peachtree Rd. NE (between Rumson Rd. and Sheridan Dr.). ☎ **404/816-8311.** Main courses $5.50–$8.95. No credit cards. Sun–Thurs 11:30am–11pm, Fri–Sat 11:30am–midnight. Free parking in lot behind restaurant. SPANISH.

Funky and festive, La Fonda is brightly painted little hole-in-the-wall consisting of a small interior dining area with an open kitchen, a covered outdoor patio under a striped awning, and a canopied, open-air rooftop patio with seating in wooden booths amid lots of plants. Outdoor areas are heated in winter and cooled by large fans in summer.

The food is both fresh and refreshingly authentic. You might simply order up a bottle of vino blanco and a delicious ensalada mixta (tuna, black olives, lettuce, onions, and peppers in a classic vinaigrette you can soak up with Cuban bread). Grilled quesadillas layered with cheddar, Monterey Jack, sautéed shrimp, and tomato salsa come with yellow rice and black beans. The paella—yellow rice cooked with herbed baked chicken, calamari, shrimp, chorizo sausage, peppers, onions, and pimientos—is hearty and satisfying. Ditto the mesquite-grilled chicken served with rice and black beans, and the sandwiches on crusty Cuban bread (try one stuffed with roast pork, ham, Swiss cheese, mayo, mustard, and mojo sauce, served with rice and beans). There are flans for dessert.

Note: La Fonda has two other locations; the most convenient for visitors is in Little Five Points at 1150B Euclid Ave., off Colquitt Avenue (☎ **404/577-8317**).

OK Cafe

1284 W. Paces Ferry Rd. NW (at Northside Pkwy., in the West Paces Ferry Shopping Center). ☎ **404/233-2888.** Reservations not accepted. Burgers, salads, and sandwiches $5.25–$7.95; lunch $8.95–$10.50; dinner $9.95–$11.50. AE, DC, DISC, MC, V. Daily 24 hours (closed Mon 11pm–6am). Takeout 11am–9pm daily. Free parking. AMERICAN.

The specialties here are down-home classics in a classic setting of leather booths at old-style Formica tables, a jukebox stocked with oldies, and waiters in white diner uniforms. There's a witty sculpture of a money tree in the dining room—perhaps to pay homage to the moneyed crowd, which flocks here for updated comfort food. It's a good spot to bring the whole family, especially if you have kids who turn their noses up at anything more complex than mashed potatoes. And because it virtually never closes, it's perfect for serious late-night cravings.

The place is full of memories of Mom: really good blue-plate specials such as meat loaf, pot roast, and roast turkey with corn-bread dressing, all served with corn muffins and two side dishes—the best of which is a to-kill-for six-cheese macaroni. Sandwiches, burgers, salads, and thick, old-fashioned shakes are other options. It's also a great place for country-style breakfasts and brunches. Stop in for a three-egg omelet (with a filling of smoked turkey, leeks, and cheese) served with grits and homemade biscuits. Don't pass up the cheese grits. Takeout is available.

Original Rocky's Brick Oven Italian Restaurant

1770 Peachtree St. NE (at Twenty-sixth St.). ☎ **404/870-7625.** Reservations for 6 or more. Individual pizza $7.95; $14.95 thin-crust pie (serving 2–3 people); $17.95 thick-crust pie (serving 4); $9.95–$13.95 for pasta dishes. AE, DC, DISC, MC, V. Mon–Thurs 11:30am–10:30pm, Fri 11:30am–11pm, Sat 5:30–11pm, Sun 5:30–10pm. Free parking. ITALIAN/PIZZA.

Ex-Brooklynite Bob Russo (his father was Rocky) makes his own mozzarella fresh everyday, grows his own herbs and tomatoes, uses garlic lavishly, and bakes the pies in a wood-burning oven from Milan. Rocky's is candlelit at night, with seating in booths, at tables covered with red-and-white-checkered cloths, or on the screened patio.

The motto here is "Pizza for grown-ups, but we love kids," and there's plenty to please the whole family. The salad ingredients are organically grown and come in small and family sizes, so it's easy to order if you have kids in tow. The pizzas are the main attraction, but eat them here because they don't travel well. The chicken Bianca oreganato (topped with sautéed chicken breast, Gorgonzola, and mozzarella) is a big favorite; finicky little palates might prefer the Margarita, with tomatoes, garlic, basil, and mozzarella. The hefty calzones are also a good bet, as are the seafood dishes: New Zealand green mussels with garlic and lemon or the hearty cioppino. For dessert, the tiramisù is first rate. Kids get free gelato.

Pasta Vino

2391 Peachtree Rd. NE (in the Peachtree Battle Promenade at Peachtree Battle Ave.). ☎ **404/231-4946.** Reservations not accepted. Pizzas $10.75–$24, pastas $6.50–$8.25, main courses $7.95–$10.45, subs $5.50. No credit cards. Mon–Thurs 11am–3pm, 5–10pm; Fri–Sat 11am–3pm, 5pm–11pm; Sun 5–10pm. Free parking. ITALIAN.

This may not be the very best Italian restaurant in town, but the combination of high quality and low prices makes it a favorite neighborhood stop. Billy Petrucci runs this little trattoria, and his father, Nico, runs the chic, upscale Abruzzi in the same shopping center. It's a great choice when you want good food but don't want to dress up and go "out."

The pastas are all fresh and homemade, and the pizzas, most of which are available by the slice, are as good as anything to come out of Little Italy. Seafood and veal are done especially well. The very best traditional Italian dish on the menu is the lasagne; it's not the heavy, meat-laden kind usually served, but one with the tenderest of noodles, a little ground beef, delicate béchamel and tomato sauces, and lots of mozzarella. It's worth twice the price. The eggplant lasagne is even better. The house salad is made with boring iceberg lettuce, so choose the huge Caesar instead and split it. The wine is limited to the house variety, but it's not bad. This place is extremely kid-friendly and usually filled with families from the local, well-heeled neighborhood. The patio is a great spot in summer.

Rib Ranch

25 Irby Ave. NW (just west of Roswell Rd. between West Paces Ferry Rd. and East Andrews Dr.). ☎ **404/233-7644.** Reservations not accepted. Sandwiches and platters $3.95–$9.95; ribs $8.95–$25.95. MC, V. Mon 11am–10pm, Tues–Sat 11am–11pm, Sun noon–10pm. Free parking in a few spaces; paid parking in a nearby lot. TEXAS BARBECUE.

Fronted by a Texas flag awning shading a few picnic tables, the Rib Ranch is your archetypal Lone Star rib joint. The roadhouse interior, with dark-stained pine floors and cafe-curtained windows, is cluttered with longhorn skulls, neon beer signs, and license plates. Tables are covered with homey red-and-white checker cloths, and the jukebox is stocked with country tunes.

Come here for fork-tender Texas-style ribs that have been slow-cooked over hickory wood and basted with tangy sauce. The beef ribs are the most truly Texan, but the pork ribs are equally delicious. Be sure to bring a Texas-size appetite with you; portions are huge and it's a struggle to get to the bottom of the plate. Don't bother with the chicken; it's undistinguished. There are all kinds of side dishes, the best being spicy Brunswick stew—a Southern concoction of tomato, shredded pork and beef, okra, onions, and lima beans. Also noteworthy: all-beef chili; crisp, fresh-made onion rings; and creamy homemade coleslaw. Beer is the beverage of choice (good ol' domestic longnecks), and you can have a brownie or blackberry cobbler for dessert.

R. Thomas Deluxe Grill

1812 Peachtree Rd. NW (between Collier Rd. and Twenty-sixth St.). ☎ **404/881-0246.** Reservations not accepted. Most items $5.95–$11.95. AE, MC, V. Daily 24 hours. Free parking behind restaurant. AMERICAN.

This zany eatery is a popular stop after a late movie or a concert; the food isn't outstanding but neither are the prices. Thomas is an avid gardener, and there's a wild and wacky overstuffed display of potted flowers, roses, and other greenery on and around the tented patio. (Passersby have stopped, thinking it was a nursery.) It's a super-casual spot that's more like a garden party than a restaurant.

Nature-loving Thomas is health- and ecology-conscious, serving free-range chicken, steroid-free lean beef, and fresh fruit and vegetable juices (organic if possible). If you eat here, it's helpful to think of food as a fuel rather than an indulgence. Some of the dishes are downright bizarre (a breakfast stew of red potatoes, green peas, quinoa, garlic, nori, and dulse), but others, such as the chargrilled burger, aren't nearly as scary. Many of the listings are accompanied by reminders about their health benefits. There are pastas, salads, sandwiches, homemade soups, wraps, and quesadillas. Breakfast is served anytime.

Swan Coach House

3130 Slaton Dr. NW (at the Atlanta History Center). ☎ **404/261-0636.** Reservations not accepted. Main courses $7.25–$9.95. MC, V. Mon–Sat 11am–2:30pm. Closed Jan 1, Memorial Day, July 4, Thanksgiving, and Dec 25. AMERICAN.

If you visit the Atlanta History Center in Buckhead (see chapter 7, "What to See & Do in Atlanta"), this delightful restaurant is a great lunch option. It is a genteel spot with a "ladies' lunch" ambience, and the menu mirrors the setting, featuring fare such as salmon croquettes with cucumber relish and Dijon dill sauce. There's even a 1950s-style congealed salad on the list. The best choice is the chicken salad in pastry timbales served with cheese straws and creamy frozen fruit salad; it's a dependable favorite that's been on the menu for nearly 30 years. For dessert, order the French silk swan—a meringue base filled with chocolate mousse and covered with whipped cream and slivered almonds. There's a full bar.

Note: You don't have to be visiting the History Center to dine here; it has a separate entrance. A gift shop and art gallery adjoin the dining room.

6 Virginia-Highland/Little Five Points

Make a meal in this charming district the occasion to see a nontouristy part of Atlanta. Come a little early, so you can browse in the area's great little shops and galleries.(For a map with Virginia-Highland and Little Five Points restaurants, see "Dining in Midtown, Virginia-Highland & Little Five Points," on page 100.)

EXPENSIVE

✪ Babette's Cafe

471 N. Highland Ave. (at Cleburne Ave., 2 blocks south of North Ave.). ☎ **404/523-9121.** Reservations accepted only for special wine dinners held once a season. Main courses $10.25–$18.50; seasonal wine dinners $55–$75. AE, DC, DISC, MC, V. Tues–Thurs 6–10pm, Fri–Sat 6–11pm; Sun 10:30am–2:30pm, 5–9pm. Free parking in adjacent lot. EUROPEAN PROVINCIAL.

Owner-chef Marla Adams has put together a menu that's decidedly anti–haute cuisine—full of excellent interpretations of comfy, everyday provincial dishes. The rustic decor matches the fare. It's a cozy cross between a simple Left Bank bistro and a European farmhouse, and the crowd is full of knowledgeable locals.

Start off with the mussel appetizer, and don't let the offbeat combination of ingredients scare you off. Bivalves are Adams's specialty, and this unusual dish, steamed mussels with white wine, strawberries, and serrano peppers, is excellent. Also top-notch is the romaine and arugula salad with lemon thyme dressing, topped with shaved asiago cheese. A long-time favorite entree—grilled lamb loin chops with red-wine reduction and shoestring potatoes—is kept on the menu by popular demand. Ditto the thyme-roasted chicken and the cassoulet, a house specialty that's available fall, winter, and spring. The espresso flan is not to be missed. The one dish that is oddly lacking is the beef stroganoff, a frequent special.

All the selections from the reasonably priced wine list are available by the glass, part of Adams's strategy to encourage customers to sample different wines. There are special prix-fixe dinners held each season, the most famous of which is a re-creation of the food and wine from the book *Babette's Feast,* for which the restaurant is named. Babette's is a great place to stop after a visit to the Carter Center, just around the corner.

dish

870 N. Highland Ave. (at Drewry St.). ☎ **404/897-3463.** Reservations for 5 or more. Main courses $12–$17. AE, DC, MC, V. Sun–Thurs 5:30–10pm, Fri–Sat 5:30–11pm. Limited free parking; paid lot across the street. CONTEMPORARY AMERICAN.

This is the hottest restaurant in town (this week, anyway), and the 1- to 2-hour waiting list reflects its sizzling popularity. Is it worth the wait? You bet. Set in a converted gas station in the midst of other trendy restaurants, dish's decor is as whimsical and stylish as its menu. There are "tastes" at the top of the list—small appetizers such as crunchy shrimp spring rolls, and more substantial starters such as a spicy lobster gazpacho and an intriguing endive, grilled pear, and Gorgonzola salad. The excellent main dishes include hearty merlot-braised lamb shanks over beans and spinach, and roasted Arctic char in a lemony sauce over potato and artichoke hearts. The desserts are delectable—especially the chocolate trio—but *way* too tiny, so don't get yourself talked into sharing.

How to beat the hour-plus wait? Tables are most plentiful during warm weather when the patio is open. Arrive at 5:30 or put your name on the waiting list and stroll around the neighborhood. If you can grab a seat at the bar, do it. You can have drinks and appetizers while you wait for a table.

Harvest

853 N. Highland Ave. (at Briarcliff Place). ☎ **404/876-8244.** Reservations suggested; limited reservations accepted. Lunch items $7–$11; brunch items $6–$9; dinner main courses $10.50–$17.95. AE, DC, MC, V. Mon–Fri 11:30am–2:30pm, Sun 11am–2:30pm; Sun–Thurs 5:30–10pm, Fri–Sat 5:30–11pm. Limited valet parking; paid parking in nearby lots. REGIONAL AMERICAN.

A lovely restaurant set in an old two-story frame house with fireplaces and hardwood floors, Harvest is a favorite with the young professionals in a neighborhood filled with eateries. The menu reflects what's fresh and seasonal, so it changes frequently. There are a few favorites, however, that usually make the list. Try the sun-dried tomato Caesar for starters if you find it; if not, the arugula/leek salad with honey walnut dressing is a good bet. Fish is always nicely done, especially the sea bass with roasted vegetables and warm lentil vinaigrette. Light entrees and sandwiches are available at lunch, and brunch dishes include the excellent Low Country cheese grits with shrimp and sausage and the popular New England crab hash, topped with two eggs. There's a small bar upstairs if you arrive without reservations, but if the weather's nice, order a glass of wine and step out onto the front patio to watch the lively neighborhood scene.

✪ Terra Cotta

1044 Greenwood Ave. NE (at North Highland Ave.). ☎ **404/853-7888.** Reservations recommended. Main courses $14–$20.50. AE, CB, DC, DISC, MC, V. Mon–Thurs 6–10pm, Fri 6–10:30pm, Sat 5:30–10:30pm. Free but limited parking in front lot; try neighborhood streets or nearby paid parking. NEW AMERICAN.

A tiny 52-seat restaurant, Terra Cotta has been able to hold its own in the competitive Virginia-Highland neighborhood. The dining area, with its dark green walls and deep terra-cotta ceiling, is snappy yet cozy, and the clientele is serious about food. There's additional space on the patio for outdoor meals. The seasonal menu changes daily and has an international mix. Great starters include the goat cheese tart with caramelized onion and arugula, or the Thai crab cake with shrimp on a spicy red cabbage salad. Vegetarian dishes, such as the grilled vegetables and Fontina cheese in phyllo with red onion marmalade and salsa verde, are particularly inventive. The grilled pork tenderloin with garlic-roasted mashed potatoes, Southern greens, and sage shiitake jus is great Southern retro-comfort food.

MODERATE

Indigo Coastal Grill

1397 N. Highland Ave. NE (south of University Dr.). ☎ **404/876-0676.** Reservations recommended. Brunch $3.95–$10.50; main courses $13–$17. AE, DC, MC, V. Fri–Sat 5:30–11pm, Sun–Thurs 5:30–10pm; Sun 10:30am–2:30pm. Free parking in lot across the street. SEAFOOD.

Part restaurant and part funky island cottage, Indigo and its trendy coastal cuisine have been packing in the crowds for years. The ambience is both lively and laid-back (nobody will bat an eyelash if you're wearing flip-flops), and the tropical fish tank and witty decor add to the energy. The specialty is seafood, but there's always a chicken and a pork entree on the menu. Spicy conch fritters have been at the top of the appetizer list forever, but the creamy lobster corn chowder is a close second in popularity. There's always a seafood special in parchment, as well as a grilled and a steamed catch of the day. The mussel appetizer (in wine, garlic, herbs, and butter) is enough for a main course if you add a salad and crusty bread for dipping. Everything is so fresh you'll swear the bay is out back. Don't leave without at least a taste of the house dessert, authentic key lime pie, or the homemade brownie with coconut ice cream and hot fudge.

Besides the recently expanded main room, there's also a porch and a great deck for fair-weather dining. If you arrive without reservations, put your name on the list and wander into the neighboring shops or order a margarita (the best in town) and have a seat on the glider out front. Takeout is available next door at Indigo Out-To-Go. If you come for brunch, don't miss the cornmeal blueberry pancakes, the crab cake topped with poached egg, or the tender but substantial cream biscuits.

Note: Indigo changed hands at press time, but the new owners say that, except for the addition of a sushi bar, not too many changes are planned.

Murphy's

997 Virginia Ave. NE (at N. Highland Ave.). ☎ **404/872-0904.** Fax 404/872-9186. Reservations not accepted. Lunch, brunch, and breakfast items $6.75–$10.95; dinner main courses $7.95–$14.95. AE, DC, DISC, MC, V. Sun–Thurs 8am–10pm, Fri–Sat 8am–midnight. A few on-site parking spots, otherwise street only. Evenings you can pay to park at the gas station across the street. AMERICAN.

Murphy's, originally a wine-and-cheese shop that evolved into a restaurant and bakery, today comprises a cozy warren of rooms. Its interior is charming and inn-like, with the French doors flung open and the area cooled by ceiling fans in nice weather. Up front is the bakery/food shop with glass display cases overflowing with pastries, crusty fresh-baked breads, deli and salad items, and luscious desserts. You can sit at the counter here and have a snack and a cup of coffee. Murphy's is a popular destination for the surrounding neighborhood, which is full of young professionals who like casual dining. This is a good stop if you're exploring the Virginia-Highland area; if there's a wait, you can kill some time in the nearby shops.

Every so often, the food at Murphy's disappoints. For instance, a starch is served with the quiche, but a salad would be lots better. Still, there's plenty here to like. Worth a try are the Texas crab cakes or the shrimp and scallop risotto. The hefty sandwiches are always winners, and there's a selection of pastas and salads. Brunch includes quite a variety—egg dishes, breads, waffles, pancakes (try the honey wheats), and sandwiches.

Surin of Thailand

810 N. Highland Ave. (at Greenwood Ave.). ☎ **404/892-7789.** Reservations not accepted. Lunch items $5.95–$6.50; dinner main courses $6.95–$14.95. AE, DC, DISC, MC, V. Mon–Fri 11:30am–11:30pm, Sat noon–11:30pm, Sun noon–10:30pm. Free parking in lot behind restaurant. Paid lots close by. THAI.

This charming Thai restaurant opened in 1991 to big crowds, and it has continued to enjoy hearty acclaim. The place is full of neighborhood regulars and suburbanites looking for consistent Asian cooking in an upbeat, contemporary setting—bare oak floors, candlelit tables covered in royal blue linen cloths, cheerful yellow walls.

The same menu is offered throughout the day, with specials at both meals. The fresh basil rolls are some of the best around, but another appetizer favorite is chef Surin Techarukpong's exquisite deep-fried edible "baskets" filled with shrimp, chicken, and corn, served with a piquant vinegar-chili-peanut sauce. Entrees range from seafood dishes, such as soft-shell crabs with asparagus sauce, to traditional noodle and curry dishes. If it's on the specials menu, opt for *neur nam tok*–strips of grilled beef tenderloin seasoned with lime, hot serrano chili peppers, fresh basil, fish sauce, and green onion; it's eaten rolled in cabbage leaves. For a cool finale, try the creamy homemade coconut ice cream or one of the mango, green tea, or ginger versions.

On weekends, arrive early or late to avoid a wait, and try for a table in the window or along the wall. The tables in the middle of the room are uncomfortably close together. If you're offered a spot in one of the small back rooms, say no thanks. It's noisier but much more fun in the main dining area.

Tiburon Grille

1190B N. Highland Ave. (at Amsterdam Ave. behind the post office). ☎ **404/892-2393.** Reservations recommended. Main courses $9–$19.50. AE, DC, DISC, MC, V. Sun–Thurs 6–10pm, Fri–Sat 5:30–10:30pm. Free parking in lot or neighborhood. CONTEMPORARY AMERICAN.

This kicky little restaurant in the heart of Virginia-Highland looks like a bustling neighborhood bistro, but it attracts a crowd from all around town. Despite the fact that it opened late in 1994, the interior, with its distressed walls and old wood floors, looks as if this has been a favorite spot for decades. There's a full-service bar that's more than a pit stop before you're shown to your table, and a covered terrace that fills up fast on balmy evenings. It's a great place for a friendly gathering or a romantic dinner.

There's a little of everything on the menu, from Asian to Mediterranean to traditional Southern. The portions are large and the inventive dishes offer a variety of distinct but complementary flavors. The menu changes seasonally, but there are three outstanding specialties nearly always on the list: sesame-seared ahi tuna, ancho pepper filet mignon, and Asian spring rolls. The wine list is reasonably priced and well-chosen.

INEXPENSIVE

✪ Flying Biscuit Cafe

1655 McLendon Ave. (at Clifton Rd.). ☎ **404/687-8888.** Reservations not accepted. Breakfast $4.95–$8.50; main courses $4.95–$14.95 (most under $9). AE, MC, V. Tues–Sun 9am–10pm. CREATIVE AMERICAN.

This totally unpretentious neighborhood hangout has got the best biscuits in town, but that's not all that makes folks willing to wait up to an hour and a half for a table. A cozied-up storefront near the funky Little Five Points area, it's got an around-the-clock breakfast menu that will get you over the worst day-after-the-night-before and an assortment of dishes that are best described as comfort food for the granola crowd.

Orange-scented French toast with raspberry sauce and honey crème anglaise is hard to beat for breakfast or brunch, especially when accompanied by homemade turkey and sage sausage. But the aptly named Love Cakes, a mix of black bean and cornmeal, sautéed and topped with tomatillo salsa, sour cream, feta, and raw onion spears, will steal your heart away. Though there's a vegetarian slant to the menu, there's plenty to please carnivores, from turkey meat loaf, thick-sliced and grilled, to the ever-changing warm chicken salad atop organic field greens. There are nightly chicken, seafood, and pasta specials, too. You can get a cup of coffee while you wait outside for your table, but to avoid the serious crowds, come on a weekday or in the early afternoon. If you have any sullen teenagers in your party, they'll think you're really cool for bringing them here.

George's Restaurant and Bar

1040 North Highland Ave. NE (near Virginia Ave. intersection). ☎ **404/892-3648.** Main courses $3–$6.75. AE, MC, V. Mon–Sat 10:30am–midnight, Sun 12:30–9pm. Parking can be tight. Free parking on neighborhood streets or in the lot next to Highland Hardware after 6pm. AMERICAN.

Smack in the middle of trendy Virginia-Highland, surrounded by chic boutiques and cafes, is a comfy old neighborhood tavern—nearly a joint—that's managed so far to buck the gentrification sweep. This place, which has been operated by George Najour and his family for 38 years, is not trendy, so don't expect wild mushroom risotto or seared tuna. But its solid, anti-fern bar fare—burgers, sandwiches, fries, etc.—and unpretentious attitude can be a relief if you've overdosed on Yuppiedom.

Good bets are the substantial homemade black bean soup, the Greek salad (order it with oil and vinegar), and the crispy onion rings—even better than the Varsity's. When you order a burger, be sure to specify how you want it done or George will fix it the way he likes it. The charbroiled chicken salad, chunks of tender breast atop mixed greens, is a good alternative if you're watching your waistline. (If you're not, ask them to add some feta cheese.) The place is thick with neighborhood regulars and journalists from around town, and is home to a book discussion group, which meets there regularly. This is definitely the place to be if the Braves have a big game; George supplied champagne all around the night they won the World Series. On a sunny day, grab a table on the sidewalk out front.

7 Sweet Auburn

Beautiful Restaurant

397 Auburn Ave. (at Jackson St.). ☎ **404/223-0080.** Reservations not accepted. Everything, except steaks, under $6. No credit cards. Daily 7am–8:30pm. Free parking. MARTA: King Memorial. SOUTHERN/SOUL FOOD.

It's not really all that beautiful, but this tiny restaurant—one of a chain of soul-food cafeterias run by the Perfect Church—is a good place for a lunch break when you're touring the historic Sweet Auburn district (see chapter 8). There's seating in a few orange plastic booths and at long Formica tables; a few plants and shell hangings are the only decorations. You don't come here for ambience but for hearty home-made Southern fare. There's always a choice of meat dishes—baked pork chops, baked chicken in thick gravy, barbecued beef tips, meat loaf—plus a half dozen or so side dishes. These might include collard greens, candied yams, black-eyed peas, baked macaroni, lima beans, and spiced rice, all of them true to tradition. Fresh-baked corn bread is served with all entrees. And there are homemade desserts such as peach cobbler, sweet-potato pie, and banana pudding topped with vanilla wafers (yum), along with a Southern specialty called red velvet cake—a rich chocolate cake that is dyed red with food coloring. No alcoholic beverages are served. Good Southern-style breakfasts here, too.

8 East Atlanta

East Atlanta is a little bit out of the loop for most tourists, but the emerging commercial area around Flat Shoals and Glenwood avenues is worth a trip if you're looking for a nontouristy scene that's a little adventuresome. There are several shops, a coffeehouse, a couple of bars, a pizza parlor (great pies), and a handful of restaurants. Two of the best are listed here. East Atlanta is not hard to find, and it's not too far from Turner Field, the zoo, and the Cyclorama.

Burrito Art

1259 Glenwood Ave. (off Moreland Ave.). ☎ **404/627-4433.** Burritos $5.50–$7. MC, V. Mon–Sat 11:30am–10pm. Take I-20 east to Moreland Ave. exit. Go south on Moreland to Glenwood. Turn left on Glenwood. Restaurant is on the right in the middle of the block. Park out front. GOURMET BURRITOS.

This is not your ordinary beans-and-cheese burrito shop. It's gourmet dining burrito-style, if such a thing exists. Well, we're talking about the food here, not the ambience. The restaurant, in what was formerly Mr. Wizard's Appliance Store, is a simple space with a bar, vinyl booths, and a few tables out front. Order your wrap and a beer at the counter, then have a seat and await burrito nirvana. No kidding. Chef/owner Ryan Aiken has a pretty good local pedigree, including stints as chef at Indigo Coastal Grill and Terra Cotta. His ingredients are fresh and his creations are cross-cultural and refined. One of the best is the ginger- and chile-spiked Asian meat loaf, but the grilled pork tenderloin with collards and spicy mustard is a close second. If you can't decide, try the special of the day; it's always good. The burritos, made with 12-inch tortillas, are huge, more than enough to split, especially if you order a salad.

Heaping Bowl and Brew

469 Flat Shoals Ave. ☎ **404/523-8030.** Heaping Bowls $6.99–$13.99; brunch entrees $4.99–$7.25. AE, MC, V. Mon–Fri 5–11pm; Sat 10am–11pm, Sun 10am–10pm. Reservations not accepted. Take I-20 east to the Moreland Ave. exit. Go south on Moreland 1 block, turn left on McPherson Ave., then right on Flat Shoals. Parking on street out front. ECLECTIC.

When Todd Semrau moved into this transitional neighborhood a few years ago, he lamented the fact that there was no place to go for a good meal and a beer. Recognizing the potential, Semrau opened this modest but sassy little storefront restaurant with the hope of attracting neighborhood regulars. It quickly caught the attention of progressive in-town and suburban folks who don't mind venturing off the beaten track for simple but interesting fare at the right price. Semrau's restaurant was the first new venture to attract people from outside the neighborhood, and he gets a lot of the credit for beginning the East Atlanta commercial renaissance.

The big attractions here are the Heaping Bowls, hearty one-dish meals: a stew of greens and beans in an Italian herb broth; chicken and dumplings; comfy cheese-and-potato-filled pierogies with sausage, brown butter, sage, and mushrooms, to name three of the perennial favorites. Seasonal specials might include a summer pasta bowl (linguine sautéed in rosemary, lemon, and garlicky olive oil, with asparagus, tomatoes, eggplant, and feta cheese). There's a full bar, including Guinness on tap and a good selection of micro-brewed beers. For brunch, try the veggie scramble spiked with feta cheese or the multi-grain pancakes topped with fresh blueberries.

9 Vinings

✪ Canoe

4199 Paces Ferry Rd. NW (at the Chattahoochee River), in Vinings. ☎ **770/432-2663.**
www.canoe-atl.com. Reservations recommended. Lunch items $6.25–$15.95; brunch items
$8.25–$13.50; dinner main courses $15.50–$19.95. AE, DC, DISC, MC, V. Mon–Fri
11:30am–2:30pm; Sun 10:30am–2:30pm; Sun–Thurs 5:30–10pm, Fri–Sat 5:30–11pm.
Complimentary valet parking. CONTEMPORARY AMERICAN.

Superchef Gerry Klaskala, of Buckhead Diner fame, opened this stylish restaurant
to great fanfare in August 1995, and it has been wildly popular ever since. The
setting is divine—a picturesque spot on the Chattahoochee River surrounded by
heavenly gardens. The interior is ultra-upscale boathouse, polished wood, classy
fabrics, and fun but sophisticated metalwork. (Wrought-iron kudzu vines trail
through the dining room.) The canoe motif is everywhere; there's even a canoe-
shaped phone booth.

The menu is solidly American, but with Southern, Asian, and Mediterranean
accents. Dinner might start with the scallop salad with vegetable spring roll and
avocado-lime vinaigrette. The pastas and risottos are innovative, to say the least. If
it's available, try the slow-roasted rabbit with Swiss chard–country bacon ravioli and
balsamic glaze. Any of the fish is good, but for a regional dish with a twist, try the
seared Carolina trout with pecans and citrus brown butter sauce. The excellent wine
list is encyclopedic, even including organic wines. If the weather is good, ask for a
table on the large, canopied patio.

10 Decatur

EXPENSIVE

✪ Floataway Cafe

1123 Zonolite Rd., Suite 15 (west of the intersection of Johson and Briarcliff rds.). ☎ **404/
892-1414.** Reservations essential. Lunch items $8–$12; dinner main courses $8–$20.
AE, DC, MC, V. Wed, Thurs, Fri, Sun 11:30am–2:30pm; Tues–Sat 5–10pm. Free parking.
COUNTRY FRENCH AND ITALIAN.

Tucked away on a secluded industrial street in a renovated warehouse near Emory
University, the Floataway Cafe is not easy to find. But people have been flocking to
it since it opened in May 1998, the second venture by Anne Quatrano and Clifford
Harrison of the renowned Bacchanalia in Buckhead. This restaurant's decor is
hipper and more energetic than the first, and the menu is less formal and more
electric, too. The list changes daily, but the emphasis is on local organic produce
and other fresh and unusual ingredients. You'll find succulent wood-grilled or
roasted meats and seafood, homemade pastas, even two pizzas—all inventively
prepared. One favorite is a house specialty: grilled hanger steak with pommes frites
and red wine shallot butter. It's available on a baguette at lunch. You can make a
meal of the inventive starters; ricotta-stuffed sautéed squash blossoms and the
baby beet salad on spicy greens are two that shouldn't be passed up. Brunch is
outstanding and might include ricotta blintzes with raspberry preserves or a sautéed
turbot with cucumber relish. The wine list has an international slant and is chosen
to go well with food.

The only drawback to the place is that it's as loud as a working warehouse. Ask
for a table on the patio or at least away from the bar, which can be quite boisterous.

Outdoor Dining

Food always seems to taste better outdoors, and Atlanta's temperate climate makes alfresco dining possible 6 to 8 months out of the year. It's true that there are always some stifling midsummer days, but things usually cool off enough in the evening to make outdoor dining quite pleasant. And many of these places heat their patios during the winter, closing them only on the most frigid days. Here are a few prime spots.

Anis Cafe and Bistro: This tree-shaded spot outside a converted Buckhead bungalow is reminiscent of a terrace in the south of France. For just a little while, you can imagine you're in Provence. *(p. 118)*

Brasserie Le Coze: True, the patio of this authentic French restaurant overlooks the parking lot at Lenox Square, but there's also the glamour of Buckhead in the air, with the Swissôtel in the background and lots of Neiman-Marcus types going to and fro. *(p. 115)*

Canoe: Lovely gardens surround the covered terrace on the banks of the Chattahoochee River for a perfect setting. Wear your best Ralph Lauren outfit. *(p. 131)*

dish: In trendy Virginia-Highland, this is one of the most popular patios in town, even though it fronts on busy North Highland Avenue. *(p. 125)*

Fellini's Pizza: Have a beer or a slice of pizza, and watch the world sail down Peachtree Road. *(p. 121)*

George's Restaurant and Bar: There are only a few tables outside this plain-talking neighborhood tavern, but it's in the heart of trendy Virginia-Highland, prime people-watching territory. *(p. 129)*

Horseradish Grill: If you're looking for a place to propose, this is it. A candle-lit patio is set under ancient oaks and overlooks lovely Chastain Park. *(p. 116)*

Indigo Coastal Grill: There's a deck out back and a porch on the side for a trip back to the islands—with food to match. *(p. 126)*

Nava: Located at the busy intersection of Peachtree and West Paces Ferry roads, but comfortably away from the street, the lovely brick terrace is a great perch from which to watch all the Buckhead activity while sipping margaritas and nibbling totopos (the Southwestern answer to tapas). *(p. 117)*

South City Kitchen: There's limited seating outside this converted Midtown house, but it's a perfect spot to watch the comings and goings of all the beautiful young people who dine here. *(p. 102)*

Tiburon Grille: There's lots of competition for a place on the covered terrace of this neighborhood restaurant smack in the middle of Virginia-Highland, so arrive early. *(p. 128)*

Veni, Vidi, Vici: This patio has a prime view of the Atlanta skyline, and it overlooks a bocce ball lawn, besides. *(p. 102)*

MODERATE

✪ Thai Chilli

2169 Briarcliff Rd. NE (at LaVista Rd. in the BriarVista Shopping Center). ☎ **404/315-6750.**
Reservations recommended for dinner. Lunch items $5.25–$7.95; dinner main courses
$6.75–$14.95. AE, DISC, MC, V. Mon–Fri 11am–2:30pm, Sun–Thurs 5–10pm, Fri–Sat
5–11pm. Free parking. THAI.

This restaurant serves not only some of the best Thai food in town, but some of the
best food in town, period. Owner Robert Khankiew, who was a chef at several other
local Thai restaurants, has been packing people in since he and his family opened
the doors. The dishes are authentic, the flavoring bold, and the dining room casual
yet polished (tablecloths, soft lighting).

Start off with traditional basil rolls with plum sauce, or try the *namsod*—minced
pork with chilies, ginger, onion, and lime juice, which you roll up in a cabbage leaf.
The spicy basil lamb (charbroiled chops with mushroom and onions) is succulent
and exceptional, but make sure someone at the table orders the salmon in a
coconut-milk-based green curry sauce. It will tempt even those who think they
don't like curries. When in doubt, stick with the daily specials or the chef's special
section of the menu; all are good bets. The spicing in many dishes is fiery, so tell
your server if you'd like things toned down. There is a children's menu, and the
restaurant is very child-friendly. You can arrive without a reservation, but there's
likely to be quite a wait on the weekend.

INEXPENSIVE

✪ Athens Pizza

1341 Clairmont Rd. (at N. Decatur Rd.), Decatur. ☎ **404/636-1100.** Pizzas $4.70–$17.95;
main courses $3.70–$7.95. AE, DC, DISC, MC, V. Sun–Thurs 11am–11pm, Fri–Sat 11am–
midnight. Free parking. GREEK/PIZZA.

Who says pizza has to have an Italian pedigree? The Papadopoulos family migrated
here more than 20 years ago from Connecticut, and they've been serving up Greek
specialties and their interpretation of pizza ever since. Their restaurant draws a large
number of families and Emory University students from the surrounding area, but
plenty of folks make a special trip across town. The interior is ultra-casual, with
Naugahyde booths and Formica-topped tables, and you'll be welcome in shorts or
jeans.

There's quite a variety of excellent Greek dishes, from gyros to pastitsio to
rotisserie-cooked lamb. Portions are generous, prices are reasonable, and everything
is authentic. It's home-style rather than fancy—exactly what you would get if
the Papadopouloses invited you over for dinner. The signature creation is the
pizza, and if you've never had it Greek style, you're really missing something. To get
in the right frame of mind, start with a small Greek salad and a glass of Greek wine.
The salad (even though it's called small) is huge, so you'll want to split it. The pizzas
have thick, yeasty crusts and are loaded with toppings of your choice or come in
several varieties. The best, by far, is the vegetarian special, with fresh tomatoes,
onions, sweet green peppers, Kalamata olives, and a generous portion of feta
cheese. The pastries, if you have room, are quite good. Recommended are the
New York–style cheesecake, the chocolate eclairs, and, of course, the honey-
soaked baklava.

Note: There are several Athens Pizza restaurants and Athens Pizza Express takeout
stores around town. Check your phone book for other locations.

7

What to See & Do in Atlanta

People used to say Atlanta was a great place to live, but you wouldn't want to visit. Not anymore. A lot has happened here since Atlanta's humble beginnings as a railroad depot, and the city is rich in historic sites—Civil War sites, landmarks of the civil rights movement, and monuments (like the World of Coca-Cola) to the businesses that have energized the city's development. And all those elements that make Atlanta a great place to live are here for visitors, too. You can take a stroll through a world-class botanical garden, picnic in a scenic park, raft down a river, visit a major art museum, or enchant your children with a puppet show.

MARTA stops near attractions are listed where applicable. If you need bus-routing information, call ☎ **404/848-4711.**

SUGGESTED ITINERARIES

If You Have 1 Day

Head up to Buckhead and visit the Atlanta History Center. It will give you a good overview of the city's history and make the rest of your visit a richer experience. Especially noteworthy is a tour of the Tullie Smith Farm, once an authentic, antebellum working plantation (and decidedly unTara-like) that was moved here from outside Atlanta. Have lunch at one of the many upscale Buckhead restaurants, then take a drive or a leisurely walk through one of the lovely surrounding neighborhoods. In the afternoon, head downtown for a tour of the CNN studios, then walk across the street to Centennial Olympic Park, the gathering place during the Olympic Games. Early in the evening, visit the shops and galleries in the Virginia-Highland neighborhood, then have dinner at one of the many restaurants there. If you have the strength, have a nightcap in a cafe or bar along North Highland Avenue.

If You Have 2 Days

Follow the suggestions above on the first day. On the second day, get up early, go over to Auburn Avenue (see the walking tour in chapter 8) and visit the Martin Luther King, Jr., National Historic Site and surrounding neighborhood. In the afternoon, head over to Grant Park and see Cyclorama and/or Zoo Atlanta. If you're a shopper, you might prefer a stop at Lenox Square and Phipps Plaza instead.

If You Have 3 Days

On your first 2 days, see as many of the sights described above as a comfortable pace allows. If the weather is fine on the morning of your last day, nothing could be better than a day at Georgia's Stone Mountain Park. In summer, be sure to stay late and see the laser show.

If it's cold or rainy, plan a morning tour of the Carter Library and Museum, then take in the Margaret Mitchell House or the World of Coca-Cola. If you're traveling with kids, spend the day at SciTrek, the Center for Puppetry Arts, or the Fernbank Museum of Natural History.

If You Have 4 Days or More

Take it easy. Over the first 4 days, juggle the above suggestions as you see fit. On the fifth day, if you have children in tow, tour Turner Field, or visit Six Flags Over Georgia or the Yellow River Wildlife Game Ranch. Civil War buffs should take in the Kennesaw Civil War Museum and Kennesaw Mountain/National Battlefield Park (both can be done in one day). If none of the above interests you, take in the latest exhibition at the High Museum of Art, then stroll through Oakland Cemetery in the afternoon.

1 The Top Attractions

APEX Museum

135 Auburn Ave. (at Courtland St.). ☎ **404/521-2739.** www.apexmuseum.org. Admission $3 adults, $2 seniors and students, children under 4 free. Tues–Sat 10am–5pm; also Sun 1–5pm in Feb and June–Aug. Closed Thanksgiving, Christmas, and New Year's Day. Take bus no. 3 from the Five Points MARTA station.

The APEX (African-American Panoramic Experience) Museum both chronicles the history of Sweet Auburn, Atlanta's foremost black residential and business district, and serves as a national African-American museum and cultural center. In the museum's Trolley Car Theater, a replica of a turn-of-the-century tram that ran on Auburn Avenue, a 12-minute multimedia presentation, *Sweet Auburn: Street of Pride,* acquaints visitors with the area's history. Sweet Auburn history is also represented in tableaux such as a replica of an Auburn Avenue barbershop and a recreation of the Yates & Milton's Drugstore (Atlanta's first black pharmacy) in the 1920s, including some original furnishings. There are interactive displays for children as well.

A new three-story wing is under construction. It will include art and history galleries; a rotunda with a 360-degree screen used for live performances and multimedia presentations; a walk-through exhibit that traces African-American history from its African roots to contemporary times; galleries portraying the contributions of Africans and African-Americans in science, music, and other fields; and a vast gift shop. Inquire about special events and workshops taking place during your visit to Atlanta.

Across the street from the APEX Museum, at 100 Auburn Ave., is **Herndon Plaza,** where you can see a permanent exhibit on the Herndon family (former slave Alonzo F. Herndon founded the Atlanta Life Insurance Company) and changing shows of the works of African-American artists.

Atlanta Botanical Garden

1345 Piedmont Ave. NW (in Piedmont Park at Piedmont Ave. and the Prado). ☎ **404/ 876-5859.** www.atlantabotanicalgarden.org. Admission $6 adults, $5 seniors, $3 students with ID, free for children under 6. Free every Thurs 3pm–closing. A $2 taped audio tour is available in 5 languages. Tues–Sun 9am–6pm, until 7pm during daylight saving time. All areas accessible to visitors with disabilities. Free parking. MARTA: no. 36 bus from the Arts Center Station Tues–Sat; no. 31 bus from Five Points or Lindbergh stations on Sunday.

This delightful botanical garden, occupying 30 acres in Piedmont Park, consists of three main sections. The first highlights plants that flourish in North Georgia's extended growing season. Displays in this section include a carnivorous plant bog, a rock garden, a dwarf conifer garden, an English knot-designed herb garden, a tranquil moon-gated Japanese garden, a rose garden, and a fragrance garden built for the blind. Set to open in mid-1999 is a children's garden, which will focus on health and wellness for the body, mind, and spirit in a fun setting. These lovely gardens are complemented by fountains, stone statuary, benches, and pagodas. Lunch is served April through October, Tuesday to Sunday, on Lanier Terrace, overlooking the Rose Garden.

The second section consists of two wooded areas: The five-acre Upper Woodland, with a paved path, contains a fern glade, a camellia garden, gurgling streams, beautiful statuary, and a habitat designed to show visitors how to attract wildlife to their own backyards. Still more rustic is Storza Woods, 15 acres of natural woodlands and one of the few remaining hardwood forests in the city. Even though its path is unpaved, it makes for an easy and interesting walk.

Most exciting is the 16,000-square-foot, glass-walled Dorothy Chapman Fuqua Conservatory, housing rare and endangered tropical and desert plants—and a fascinating exhibit of poison dart frogs (more about them later). With acres of irreplaceable rain forest being bulldozed every minute, facilities such as this provide a much-needed haven for technology-threatened plant species. Approached via an arbored promenade and fronted by a water lily pond, the conservatory has a revolving globe outside its entrance showing the many regions worldwide where plant life is endangered.

The focal point of the conservatory is the misty Tropical Rotunda, housing fern collections, cycads (the most primitive seed-bearing plants known), epiphytes (plants that don't require soil to grow), gorgeous orchids, carnivorous plants, a wide variety of begonias, and towering tropical palms. It's a lush and humid jungle, with brightly hued tropical birds warbling overhead, a splashing waterfall, and winding pathways lined with fragrant hibiscus, African violets, and flowering jasmine vines. Of special interest is a double coconut palm seed from the Seychelles, the largest and heaviest seed in the plant kingdom. Its first 12-foot leaves have already begun to grow, but it will be 100 years before the tree reaches its full height.

In the midst of all this is an intriguing exhibit of Central and South American poison dart frogs—small, active ground dwellers in unbelievably bright colors (yellow, orange, lime green, cobalt blue) and vivid patterns. About 12 species are exhibited in three large terrariums filled with tropical rain-forest plants and designed to simulate the climates in the frogs' native lands. The exhibit is a big hit with visiting children.

The arid Desert House displays Madagascan succulents, such as a unique family of spiky plants called Didieriaceae. Here, too, are "living stones" (desert succulents that nature designed to look like pebbles to protect them from being eaten by animals), tree aloes, caudici-forms (with swollen stems and roots for storing water), and conifers from Africa and the Canary Islands. Adjoining is an area for special exhibits.

The building also houses an orangery of tropical mango, papaya, star fruit, lychee, coffee, and citrus trees. A 1996 addition was an "Olympic" olive tree presented by Greece in honor of the Centennial Olympic Games.

There are flower shows throughout the year, along with lectures and other activities. Call to find out what's on during your stay. A marvelous gift shop is on the premises; your purchases help support the garden.

✪ Atlanta History Center

130 W. Paces Ferry Rd. (at Slaton Dr.). ☎ **404/814-4000.** www.atlhist.org. Admission $7 adults, $5 seniors and students 18 or older, $4 children 6–17, under 6 free. General admission includes the museum and gardens. House tour tickets $1 additional for the Swan House, $2 additional for the Tullie Smith Farm, free for children under 6. Mon–Sat 10am–5:30pm, Sun and some holidays noon–5:30pm. Ticket sales stop at 4:30pm. Closed Thanksgiving, Christmas Eve, Christmas, and New Year's Day. Take MARTA rail to Lenox station; from there take bus no. 23 to Peachtree St. and West Paces Ferry Rd., then walk 3 blocks west on the latter.

The Atlanta History Center has, in recent years, expanded its concept to encompass Georgian and Southern history. The Center maintains a vast collection of photographs, maps, books, newspaper accounts, furnishings, Civil War artifacts, and decorative arts. It occupies 32 woodland acres, with self-guided walking trails and five gardens. Plan to spend the better part of a day here. And call ahead, or inquire on the premises, about lectures, films, festivals, and other events that take place here on a regular basis; activities range from sheep-shearing demonstrations to decorative arts forums. When you call, also check on house-tour times for the day of your visit. The Swan Coach House is a delightful restaurant on the premises (details in chapter 6).

Note: House-tour tickets are limited and can only be purchased on the day of your visit. Arrive early to avoid disappointment.

Begin your visit at the **Atlanta History Museum.** This is where you can buy tickets and get information about historic house tours (see below) and other activities. The museum's major permanent exhibit, "Metropolitan Frontiers: Atlanta, 1835–2000," traces Atlanta's history from the days of Native American and rural pioneer settlements to the present day. Displays, enhanced by hands-on discovery areas and informative videos, include hundreds of photographs, documents, and artifacts; an entire 1890s shotgun house; a fire engine that was used in Atlanta's great fire of 1917 (when 50 city blocks were ravaged by flames); a rare 1920 Hanson Six touring car; and a model of Atlanta's most complex interstate intersection, known locally as "Spaghetti Junction."

Also on the center's grounds is the **Swan House,** the 1928 estate of Edward Hamilton Inman, scion of an old Atlanta family. The house and gardens were designed by renowned architect Philip Trammell Shutze and are considered his finest residential work. The house is interesting not only architecturally but for its eclectic contents and furnishings, which comprise a veritable museum of decorative arts.

Swan House is fronted by a classical colonnaded porte cochére, leading to a circular entrance hall with Ionic columns and a dramatic floating stairway. The formal gardens include terraced lawns and waterfalls, retaining walls with recessed ivy arches, and fountain statuary. In the entrance hall, you'll notice that the fan light over the door centers on a swan, announcing the theme of the house. (In fact, there is supposed to be at least one swan emblem or decoration in each room—see if you can find them.)

Family china is displayed in the dining room. (Note the rococo marble-topped swan tables.) The Inmans took their morning meal in a charming octagonal breakfast room, with windows overlooking woodland scenery and a beautifully detailed vaulted ceiling.

---

❷ Did You Know?

- Atlanta has 32 streets named Peachtree.
- Georgia's major agricultural crop is peanuts, not peaches.
- Atlanta's earliest street lights burned whale oil.
- The world's largest bas-relief sculpture (Stone Mountain—90 feet by 190 feet) and the world's largest painting (Cyclorama, utilizing 20,000 square feet of canvas) are in Atlanta.
- Georgia Tech's Yellow Jackets set a world record football score in 1916: 222 to 0 (they were the zero).
- Because it has received over $250 million from Coca-Cola, Emory University is known as "Coca-Cola U."
- *Fortune* magazine consistently rates Atlanta one of the nation's best places to do business.
- Not a single scene from the movie *Gone With the Wind* was filmed in Georgia, though a few bushels of Georgia red clay were transported to the Hollywood set to add verisimilitude.
- Hartsfield is the country's second-busiest airport and is consistently ranked among the best airports in the world. Eighty percent of the U.S. population is within a three-hour flight of Atlanta.

Upstairs is Mrs. Inman's bedroom. Her adjoining faux-marble bathroom has a toilet hidden in a rattan chair (a Victorian holdover) and a huge-headed shower that must have provided heavenly cascades of water.

As you tour the house, you'll also see many museum-quality 17th- and 18th-century English paintings. And on the upstairs level is the Philip Trammell Shutze Collection of Decorative Arts—a marvelous array of china, silver, furnishings, textiles, and objets d'art. It can be seen only on tours weekdays at 11:15am and 3:15pm or by appointment. Half-hour tours of the house itself take place throughout the day on a continual basis.

Tullie Smith Farm depicts the life of Georgia's mid-19th-century farmers. A two-story "plantation-plain" house built in the early 1840s, it was brought here along with period outbuildings in 1972. This was no Tara-like colonnaded mansion—just an everyday farmhouse whose occupants lived in rustic simplicity.

A bedroom has a rope bed with a feather mattress and a crib that was always occupied by the youngest baby. Here a docent will demonstrate how to use a spinning wheel. The basket of pomander balls was typical—the 19th-century answer to today's air fresheners.

In a back room, there are weaving demonstrations. During cooler months, demonstrations of 19th-century hearth cookery take place in the whitewashed kitchen, where herbs hang from the rafters. Additional outbuildings are a barn, corncrib, root cellar, blacksmith shop, and smokehouse. The gardens and grounds are authentic to the period. Costumed docents give tours throughout the day, and there are frequent demonstrations of 19th-century farm activities.

Leave some time to stroll the gardens, most notably the forested mile-long **Swan Woods Trail.** It includes plants native to Georgia and the Garden for Peace, where you will see a sculpture by noted Soviet artist Georgi Dzhaparidze and Atlanta artist Hans Godo Frabel.

✪ Birth Home of Martin Luther King, Jr.

501 Auburn Ave. ☎ **404/331-3920**. www.nps.gov/malu. Free admission. Tickets are available from the National Park Service at Fire Station no. 6 (at Boulevard and Auburn Ave.). Tours depart from the ticket-purchase point about every 30 min. in summer, every hour the rest of the year. Daily 9am–5pm. Closed Thanksgiving, Christmas, and New Year's Day. From I-75/85 south, exit at Freedom Parkway/Carter Center. Turn right at first stoplight onto Boulevard. Follow signs to Martin Luther King National Historic Site. MARTA: King Memorial Station is about 8 blocks away. Or take bus no. 3 east from the Five Points Station.

Martin Luther King, Jr., was born in this two-story Queen Anne–style house on January 15, 1929, the oldest son of a Baptist minister and an elementary school music teacher. His childhood was a normal one. He preferred playing baseball to piano lessons, liked to play Monopoly, and got a kick out of tearing the heads off his older sister's dolls. (Nonviolence came later.) To quote his sister, Christine King Farris, "My brother was no saint ordained at birth, instead he was an average and ordinary man, called by ... God ... to perform extraordinary deeds."

King lived here through the age of 12, then moved with his family to a house a few blocks away. A visit provides many insights into the formative influences on one of the greatest leaders of our time. The Rev. A. D. Williams, King's maternal grandfather and pastor of Ebenezer Baptist Church, bought the house in 1909. Reverend Williams was active not only in the church, but in the community and early manifestations of the civil rights movement. He was a charter member of Atlanta's NAACP and led a series of black registration and voting drives as far back as 1917. He was instrumental in getting black officers on the Atlanta police force. Martin Luther King, Sr., moved in on Thanksgiving Day, 1926, when he married Williams's daughter Alberta. When Reverend Williams died in 1931, he became head of the household and also took over Williams's pulpit at Ebenezer Church.

The King family retained ownership of the house at 501 Auburn even after they moved away. King's younger brother, Alfred Daniel, lived here with his family from 1954 to 1963. In 1971, King's mother deeded the home to the Martin Luther King, Jr., Center. It has since been restored to its appearance during the years of King's boyhood. The furnishings are all originals or similar period reproductions, and some personal items belonging to the family are on display. Christine was actively involved in the restoration, providing a wealth of detail about its former appearance, as well as anecdotal material about life in the King family.

Tours of the house, conducted by National Park rangers, begin in the downstairs parlor, where you'll see family photographs showing Martin Luther King as a child. The parlor was used for choir practice, for the dreaded piano lessons, and as a rec room where the family gathered around the radio to listen to shows like "The Shadow." In the dining room, world events were regularly discussed over meals, and every Sunday, before dinner, each child was required to recite a newly learned Bible verse from memory. You'll also see the coal cellar (stoking coal was one of Martin's childhood chores); the children's play area; the upstairs bedroom of Martin's parents in which Christine, Martin, and Alfred Daniel were born; Reverend Williams's den, where the family gathered for nightly Bible study; the bedroom Martin shared with his brother ("always in disarray," says Christine); and Christine's bedroom.

Note: In summer, especially, tickets often run out early; for your best chance to tour the home, arrive at 9am.

✪ Centennial Olympic Park

285 International Blvd. NW (at Techwood Dr.). ☎ **404/222-PARK** (7275). Free admission. Daily 7am–11pm. MARTA: Omni or Peachtree Center. Centennial Olympic Park, one of the most enduring legacies of the 1996 Olympic Games, is a living monument to the city's

memories—both good and bad—of that seminal event. Conceived as a town square, it represents the heart of the Olympic effort, the site everyone flocked to celebrate the games. And when the games resumed after the tragic bombing in the park that claimed two lives, it was where people gathered to try to revive the Olympic spirit.

A 21-acre swath of green space and bricks, the park was carved out of a blighted downtown area. It was closed after the games, redesigned for permanent use, then reopened in 1998. Once again the universal gathering place it was intended to be, it's an oasis of rolling lawns crisscrossed by brick pathways and punctuated by artwork, rock gardens, pools, and fountains. Though there's not something going on all the time, there are usually a few free events each month—festivals, artists' markets, concerts, and other performances. Call the above number for a complete listing of happenings.

If you're visiting the park on your own, and not coming for a specific event, your first stop should be the visitor center on International Boulevard, in the southwest corner of the park, across from CNN Center. Here you'll find information about the park, and if you bought a $35 commemorative brick, someone will help you locate it among the nearly 500,000 engraved bricks that were used to pave the plaza and walkways. Even if you didn't buy a brick, it's fun to wander around and read the names and messages (some pretty intriguing) engraved on them. You'll find names from around the world.

The best part of the park—now and during the Olympics—is the fountain in the shape of five interlocking Olympic Rings. It's the central focus of a vast paved plaza bordered by 23 flags honoring all the host countries of the modern Games. If you're here in summer, you and the kids can frolic in the fountain (wear shirts and shoes, please), a good way to cool off in the sizzling Southern heat. (Don't be shy. Just about everybody in Atlanta has done this at one time or another.) If getting drenched is not your thing, you can still enjoy one of the concerts put on by the fountains. Seven songs are programmed to play during timed sequential water and light displays. The water jets, which normally shoot 12 feet into the air, can reach 35 feet during special effects.

New to the park are the Quilt Plazas, composed of light and dark color bricks. Located along the east border, the five plazas tell the story of the Centennial Olympic Games. The best "quilt" is also the most moving. Titled the Quilt of Remembrance, it pays homage to the bombing victims and contains colored marble from five continents. Be sure to read the inscriptions on its borders.

✪ CNN Studio Tour

CNN Center, Marietta St. (at Techwood Dr.). ☎ **404/827-2300.** www.cnn.com/studiotour. Admission $7 adults, $5 seniors, $4.50 children 12 and under. Children under 6 not permitted. A more in-depth, hour-long VIP tour costs $24.50. Note: Tickets are available on a first-come, first-served basis on the day of the tour and go on sale at 8:30 am. Arrive early for the tour you wish to take, since only 35 tickets are sold per tour. Best bet is to reserve in advance via American Express, MasterCard, or VISA. Tours are given daily every 15 minutes 9am–6pm. Closed Easter, Thanksgiving, and Christmas Day. Free tickets are available for "Talk-Back Live," a live interactive talk show on CNN. The show airs 3–4pm weekdays, and tickets can be reserved by calling ☎ **800/410-4266.** MARTA: Omni. Many parking lots around the building.

This tour of the world's largest news-gathering organization is lots of fun, and a uniquely Atlanta experience. The CNN Center is headquarters for media magnate Ted Turner's 24-hour cable news networks: CNN, CNN International, and Headline News. During 45-minute guided walking tours, visitors get a behind-the-scenes look at the high-tech world of 24-hour TV network news in action. You'll find the

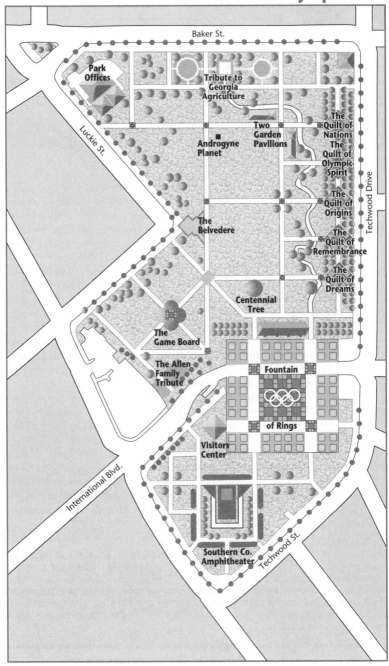

Baker St.

Park Offices

Tribute to Georgia Agriculture

Luckie St.

Androgyne Planet

Two Garden Pavilions

The Quilt of Nations

The Quilt of Olympic Spirit

The Quilt of Origins

The Belvedere

The Quilt of Remembrance

Techwood Drive

The Quilt of Dreams

Centennial Tree

The Game Board

The Allen Family Tribute

Fountain

of Rings

Visitors Center

International Blvd.

Southern Co. Amphitheater

Techwood St.

In the Spotlight

If you get to the CNN Center at the right time of day (3–4pm), you can get yourself on national television by being in the audience of "Talk Back Live," CNN's live talk show that encourages the audience to give opinions on a topic of the day. Be sure to call home and get someone to tape the show; the audience is in front of the camera much of the time.

Tour Desk in the main lobby near the base of an eight-story escalator. While you're waiting for the tour to begin, you can have a videotape made of yourself reading the day's top stories from behind a "retired" CNN anchor desk.

Tours start in an exhibit area where displays include MGM movie stills (Turner owns a portion of the MGM/RKO film library); an exhibit on TBS sports (Turner Broadcasting System owns the Atlanta Hawks and the Atlanta Braves, after all); an exhibit on the Goodwill Games; a 12-monitor video wall that continuously airs all TBS networks; a display on the 24-hour Cartoon Network; and items involved in CNN's much-lauded coverage of the Gulf War. A new theater shows a dramatic high-tech video on the history of Turner Broadcasting and CNN.

Next you'll enter a special effects studio and get a glimpse of the technology that goes into the production of global news. Here you'll see the magic of a high-tech Chroma Key system (it's what's used to broadcast that big map behind the weather folks), see how on-air graphics are made, and learn the secrets of the TelePrompTer.

On another level, visitors get a bird's-eye view of the main CNN newsroom from a glass-walled observation station. You'll see the hustle and bustle of the domestic desk and writers composing news scripts. If a live broadcast is in progress—and the chances are good that one will be—you can see CNN newscasters at work. Tour guides are knowledgeable and can answer virtually any question.

The longer, more extensive VIP tour allows visitors to actually step out on the main CNN newsroom floor and explore production areas not normally accessible to the public. You can even have a snack at the CNN commissary and rub elbows with the journalists.

After your visit, stop by the Turner Store, which carries network-logo clothing and gift items, along with MGM movie memorabilia. For sports fans, there's the Braves Clubhouse store, featuring anything you can imagine sporting the Atlanta Braves logo. There are several restaurants and fast-food outlets in the atrium of the CNN Center, as well as a few shops and a movie theater. The big attraction, though, is CNN.

Cyclorama

800 Cherokee Ave. (in Grant Park). ☎ **404/624-1071** or 404/658-7625. www. bcaatlanta.org. Admission $5 adults, $4 seniors, $3 children 6–12, under 6 free (not recommended for very young children). Daily June–Labor Day 9:20am–5:30pm; the day after Labor Day–May 31, 9:20am–4:30pm. Shows begin every half hour starting at 9:30am. Closed Thanksgiving, Christmas, New Year's Day, and Martin Luther King Day. Take Georgia Ave. bus no. 97 from Five Points Station or no. 105 from the West End station. By car, take I-20 East from downtown to Exit 26.

Though it sounds like something out of Disney World, this Cyclorama was created in the 1880s, and its concept—a huge, 360-degree three-dimensional cylindrical painting viewed from a rotating platform—dates back to a century earlier. Cycloramas were the rage of 18th- and 19th-century Europe, Russia, Japan, and later, the United States, depicting subject matter ranging from the splendors of Pompeii to

Napoleonic battles. Enhanced by multimedia effects and faux-terrain dioramas extending 30 feet from the painting into the foreground, they were the forerunners of newsreels, travelogues, and TV war coverage.

The one you'll see here—a 42-foot-high cylindrical oil painting, 358 feet in circumference (on about 16,000 square feet of canvas)—depicts in meticulous detail the events of the Battle of Atlanta, July 22, 1864. It took 11 eastern European artists, working in the United States in the studio of William Wehner, 22 months to complete.

For 20th-century tourists, the concept itself is as interesting as the action depicted, and the restoration is incredibly impressive. Though painted on fine Belgian linen in the painstaking methodology of the 19th-century academies, the work suffered in moves from city to city, and later (when motion-picture epics made cycloramas passé) from neglect. Well-intentioned but incompetent attempts at restoration caused further damage. In the 1970s, a severe storm waterlogged the painting, causing seemingly irreversible damage.

But Mayor Maynard Jackson recognized the historic and artistic importance of Cyclorama; under his auspices $11 million was raised for its restoration. It took 2½ years for renowned conservator Gustav Berger and his crew to repair the damaged work, a process that included mending more than 700 rips in the canvas. In the auditorium itself the Cyclorama viewing is preceded by a 14-minute film about the Battle of Atlanta.

The fascinating story of Cyclorama's development and restoration is related in a video format near the auditorium entrance. Cyclorama's central theme is Gen. John B. Hood's desperate attempt to halt Sherman's inexorable advance into the city. Comprehensively narrated, and complete with music and sound effects including galloping horses and cannon fire, it vividly depicts the troop movements and battles of the day in which the Confederates lost 8,000 men, the Federals 3,722. A figure highlighted far beyond his historic importance is Gen. John A. Logan of the Federal Army of Tennessee (who commissioned the painting at a cost of $42,000 as a campaign move in his bid for the vice presidency). He's shown gloriously galloping into the fray, bravely exposing himself and his men to enemy fire. The work was originally called *Logan's Great Battle.*

The building housing Cyclorama also comprises a museum of related artifacts, the most important being the steam locomotive *Texas* from the 1862 Great Locomotive Chase. Other exhibits include displays of Civil War arms and artillery, Civil War–themed paintings, portraits of Confederate and Union leaders, "life in camp" artifacts and photographs, and uniforms. A bookstore on the premises is a repository of Civil War literature, including a sizable black history section.

Ebenezer Baptist Church

407–413 Auburn Ave. NE. ☎ **404/688-7263.** www.ebenezer.org. Free admission (donations appreciated). Mon–Sat 9am–5pm. From I-75/85 south, exit at Freedom Parkway/Carter Center. Turn right at first stoplight onto Boulevard. Follow signs to Martin Luther King National Historic Site. MARTA: King Memorial Station is about 8 blocks away. You can also take a no. 3 bus from the Five Points Station.

Founded in 1886, Ebenezer was a spiritual center of the civil rights movement during the years 1960 to 1968, when Martin Luther King, Jr., served as co-pastor. His grandfather, the Rev. A. D. Williams, dedicated the church to "the advancement of black people and every righteous and social movement." Williams's activist example was followed by his son-in-law and successor, Martin Luther King, Sr., who worked for voting rights and other aspects of black civil and social

---

Factoid

For a different kind of action, check out Martinis & IMAX, a Friday night event for grownups. From 6:30 to 10pm during most of the year, enjoy a martini or other cocktail, watch the films and listen to a jazz group. Call the Martinis & IMAX hotline, ☎ **404/370-1833,** for continuously updated information on films, events and music.

---

advancement. Later, Martin Luther King, Jr., would join his forebears in pursuing justice for African-Americans. At press time, the congregation was due to open its new sanctuary directly across the street, but the older building where Martin Luther King, Jr., preached will continue to be open to the public. The new building is supposed to be called the Heritage Sanctuary, and it will be supervised by the parks department as a historic site. Here you can listen to a taped message on the history of the church and/or enter the sanctuary and watch a videotape.

One of the best things to do is attend a Sunday morning worship service in the new sanctuary. The public is welcome—and you'll realize just *how* welcome when the members of the congregation leave their seats at the beginning of the service to shake the hands of as many visitors as possible. It's a living testimonial to all that the church's most famous son stood for. Sunday services are at 7:45am and 10:45am. The sanctuary is usually packed, so it's a good idea to arrive well ahead of time. Groups of 6 or more should call the church office to make reservations. An ecumenical service also takes place here every year during King week.

Fernbank Museum of Natural History

767 Clifton Rd. NE (off Ponce de Leon Ave.). ☎ **404/370-0960.** www.fernbank.edu. Admission $8.95 adults ($13.95 includes an IMAX Theater ticket), $7.95 students and seniors ($11.95 includes an IMAX Theater ticket), $6.95 children 3–12 ($9.95 includes IMAX Theater ticket), 2 and under free. IMAX Theater admission alone $6.95 adults, $5.95 students and seniors, $4.95 children 3–12, under 3 free. Mon–Sat 10am–5pm, Sun noon–5pm. The IMAX Theater is open until 10pm on Friday night. Closed Thanksgiving and Christmas.

The largest museum of natural sciences in the Southeast, this architecturally stunning facility adjoins 65 acres of pristine forest. The building, which nearly eclipses the attractions inside, centers on a soaring three-story, skylit Great Hall—an Italianate brick atrium with spiral staircases, lofty columns, and windows embracing the woodlands beyond. Architect Graham Gund has achieved a marvelous integration of interior/exterior space. Look closely at the museum floors; embedded there are ancient fossil remains from the late Jurassic period.

The major permanent exhibit, "A Walk Through Time in Georgia," uses the state as a microcosm to tell the story of the earth's development through time and the chronology of life upon it. Eighteen galleries here re-create landform regions from the rolling pine-forested foothills of the Piedmont Plateau to the mossy Okefenokee Swamp, from the Cumberland Plateau (where you can walk through a typical "limestone cavern") to the marshy Coast and Barrier Islands. Exhibits are enhanced by creative films and videos, informational audiophones, interactive computers, sound effects, and old-fashioned field guides—not to mention more than 1,500 fabricated plants and mounted specimens of birds and animals. Visitors travel back 15 billion years—to experience the origins of the universe (the Big Bang) and the formation of galaxies and solar systems—and into the future to consider the fate of our planet. The highlight of it all, though, is the gallery of seven life-size dinosaurs and three massive murals of three prehistoric periods.

Another major permanent installation, "Spectrum of the Senses," comprises 51 participatory displays that tease the eyes and ears into understanding the concepts of light and sound. Here you can step into a life-size kaleidoscope, play with perspective, gaze into infinity, see physical evidence of sound waves, and mix colors on a computer. In Fantasy Forest, a colorful play area designed for preschoolers (ages 3 to 5), kids become bees and pollinate flowers, climb a treehouse, walk through a swamp, and play at being farmers. The state-shaped Georgia Adventure is a similar discovery room for ages 6 to 10.

If it's a weekend, see if there are any programs going on at the Harris Naturalist Center, a cluster of science laboratories where visitors often get to examine items under an electron microscope.

While you're here, be sure to catch a stunning IMAX film (buy tickets as soon as you enter the museum; they sometimes sell out). The immense IMAX screen—five stories high and 72 feet wide—puts you right in the middle of all the action.

Other museum attractions include a wetlands exhibit, a Caribbean coral reef aquarium, the Star Gallery (where 542 fiber-optic stars create a twinkling evening sky), the World of Shells, and the McClatchey Collection of jewelry and textiles from the old Silk Road countries. A museum store is stocked with entertaining and educational gifts and books, and there's a restaurant with arched windows overlooking Fernbank Forest, as well as outdoor patio seating.

Fox Theatre

660 Peachtree St. NE (at Ponce de Leon Ave.). ☎ **404/817-8700** for box office, 404/876-2041 for tours. Tours $5 adults, $4 seniors, $3 students. The Atlanta Preservation Center conducts walking tours of the Fox Theatre and the surrounding area Mon, Wed, and Thurs at 10am; Sat at 10 and 11am. Call to verify tour times before you go. MARTA: North Ave.

Originally conceived as a Shriners' temple in 1916, this lavish, block-long Moorish-Egyptian fantasyland ended up as a movie theater when the Shriners realized their grandiose plan had far exceeded their budget. In 1927, they sold the temple to movie magnate William Fox, who amended their plans and created a peerless pleasure palace. The building was designed by French architect Oliver J. Vinour, who used design motifs of the Middle East in his creation, including replicas of art and furnishings from King Tut's tomb.

Atlanta's new theater opened in 1929 as a masterpiece of Eastern splendor, its Moorish facade, onion domes, and minarets an exotic contrast to the surrounding Victorian boardinghouses. A brass-trimmed marble kiosk imported from Italy served as a ticket booth. The 140-foot entrance arcade led to a lushly carpeted lobby with blue-tiled goldfish pools. And the auditorium was an Arabian courtyard under a twinkling starlit sky that could, with state-of-the-art technology, be transformed to a sky at sunrise or sunset. A striped Bedouin canopy sheltered the balcony, and sequin- and rhinestone-studded stage curtains depicted mosques and Moorish horsemen.

As the show began, a gigantic gilded 3,610-pipe Möller organ rose majestically from its vault, its rich chords accompanied by a full orchestra. A medley of popular songs, cartoons, a follow-the-bouncing-ball sing-along, a stage-show extravaganza by a bevy of Rockette-like chorines called the Fanchon and Marco Sunkist Beauties, and a newsreel preceded every main feature. At night there were dances in the Egyptian Ballroom, designed to replicate Ramses' temple. And even the men's lounge was exotically appointed with hieroglyphic adornments, winged scarab-motif friezes, bas-reliefs of royal figures, and throne chairs.

Unfortunately, the Fox's opening coincided with the Great Depression, and it proved impossible to maintain its opulence. In 1932, the company declared bankruptcy and closed its doors. The theater reopened three years later for occasional concerts. By the 1940s, it was a successful concern once more, and in 1947, the Metropolitan Opera began a 20-year stint of week-long performances here. An oversize panoramic screen was installed in the 1950s, along with a 26-speaker stereo system. But like monumental movie palaces nationwide, the Fox inevitably declined in the age of television. In 1975 its doors were padlocked once again.

An organization of concerned citizens calling themselves Atlanta Landmarks raised $1.8 million and saved the Fox from the wrecking ball in 1978, foiling Southern Bell's plans to purchase and demolish it to make way for a regional headquarters building. Ever since, it's been a thriving entity, featuring Broadway shows, headliners, dance companies, and comedy stars. Best of all, the theater has been restored to its former glory, its fabulous furnishings and fixtures all refurbished or replaced with replicas.

✪ Georgia's Stone Mountain Park

6867 Memorial Dr., Stone Mountain, GA 30086 (16 miles east of downtown on U.S. 78). ☎ **770/498-5600.** www.stonemountainpark.org. Major attractions each $4.25 adults, $3.20 children 3–11, children under 3 free. A ticket for all 6 major attractions is $19.25 adults, $11.75 children. Year-round, gates open 6am–midnight. Major attractions open fall and winter 10am–5pm, spring and summer 10am–9pm. Parking charge $6 a day, $25 annually (one-time-only charge if you stay on the grounds). Attractions only are closed Christmas Day; park is open. Take a MARTA train to Indian Trail Station, where you can transfer to a bus to the park.

A monolithic gray granite outcropping (the world's largest), carved with a massive monument to the Confederacy, Stone Mountain is a distinctive landmark on Atlanta's horizon and the focal point of its major recreation area—3,200 acres of lakes and beautiful wooded parkland. It's Georgia's number-one tourist mecca and one of the 10 most visited paid attractions in the United States.

Stone Mountain itself was formed about 300 million years ago when intense heat and pressure caused molten material just below the earth's surface to push upward. That material cooled slowly (it took 100 million years) and formed compact, uniform crystals. Initially, a two-mile thick overlay of the earth's surface covered the hardened granite, but over the next two hundred million years, that eroded, exposing the mountain we see today. The dome-shaped rock rises 1,683 feet above sea level and covers 583 acres. Half of Georgia and part of North Carolina rest on the mountain's base.

The Face of a Mountain

Over half a century in the making, Stone Mountain's neoclassic carving—90 feet high and 190 feet wide—is the world's largest bas-relief sculpture. Originally conceived by Gutzon Borglum, it depicts Confederate leaders Jefferson Davis, Robert E. Lee, and Stonewall Jackson galloping on horseback throughout eternity. Borglum started work on the mountain sculpture in 1923; after 10 years he abandoned it, due to insurmountable technical problems and rifts with its sponsors. (He went on to South Dakota, where he gained fame carving Mount Rushmore.) No sign of his work remains at Stone Mountain, but it was his vision that inspired the project. Augustus Lukeman took over in 1925, but three years later, with the work still far from complete, the family that owned the mountain lost patience and reclaimed the property. It wasn't until 1963, after the state purchased the mountain and surrounding property for a park, that work resumed under Walter Kirtland Hancock and Roy Faulkner. It was completed in 1970.

Georgia's Stone Mountain Park

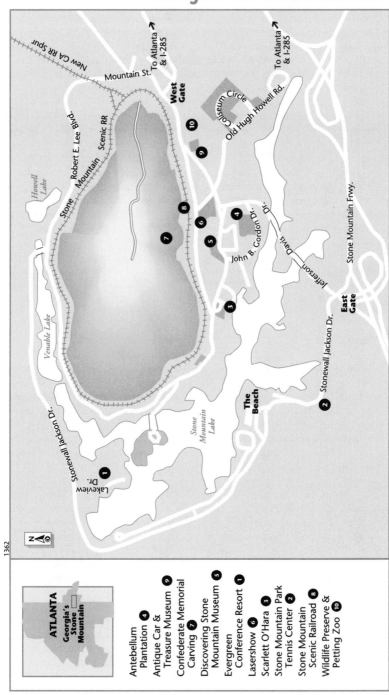

ATLANTA
Georgia's
Stone
Mountain

Antebellum
Plantation ④

Antique Car &
Treasure Museum ⑨

Confederate Memorial
Carving ⑦

Discovering Stone
Mountain Museum ⑤

Evergreen
Conference Resort ①

Lasershow ⑥

Scarlett O'Hara ③

Stone Mountain Park
Tennis Center ②

Stone Mountain
Scenic Railroad ⑧

Wildlife Preserve &
Petting Zoo ⑩

147

Although the best view of the mountain is from below, the vistas from the top are spectacular. Visitors who are part mountain goat can take a walking trail up and down its moss-covered slopes, especially lovely in spring when they're blanketed in wildflowers. From the top, which you can also reach by Swiss cable car, you have an incredible view of Atlanta and the Appalachian Mountains. (The best plan is to take the cable car up, then walk back down.)

A highlight at Stone Mountain is **Lasershow,** a spectacular display of laser lights and fireworks with animation and music. The brilliant laser beams are projected on the mountain's north face, a natural one million-square-foot screen. The show begins in April, Friday and Saturday at 9pm; it can be seen Friday to Sunday in early May; late May through Labor Day it can be seen nightly at 9:30pm; then it resumes its Friday-to-Saturday schedule through October. Bring a picnic supper and arrive early to get a good spot on the lawn at the base of the mountain.

New to the park is the **Discovering Stone Mountain Museum,** and it's a good idea to stop here first to get some perspective on the mountain's history. Exhibits take you through an intriguing chronological journey from the area's past into its present.

Other major park attractions include the **Stone Mountain Scenic Railroad,** which chugs around the 5-mile base of Stone Mountain. The ride takes 25 minutes. Trains depart from Railroad Depot, an old-fashioned train station. There's a restaurant at the depot with all the fixings for a fried chicken picnic, just in case you forgot to bring your own.

The *Scarlett O'Hara,* a paddlewheel riverboat, cruises the 363-acre Stone Mountain Lake.

The **Antique Car and Treasure Museum** is a jumble of old radios, jukeboxes, working nickelodeons, pianos, Lionel trains, carousel horses, and clocks along with classic cars.

Wildlife enthusiasts might enjoy the **Wildlife Preserve and Petting Zoo,** managed by Zoo Atlanta. Animals native to Georgia, such as cougar, otter, elk, bobcat, coyote, fox, and prairie dogs live in the 20-acre preserve. The petting zoo allows kids to get up close and personal with domesticated animals, including pigs and goats.

The 19-building **Antebellum Plantation** offers self-guided tours assisted by hosts in period dress at each structure. Highlights include an authentic 1830s country store; the 1845 Kingston House (it represents a typical overseer's house); the clapboard slave cabins; the 1790s Thornton House, elegant home of a large landowner; the smokehouse and well; a doctor's office; a barn, a coach house, and crop-storage cribs; a necessary; a cook house; and the 1850 neoclassical Tara-like Dickey House. The grounds also contain formal gardens and a kitchen garden. It takes at least an hour to tour the entire complex. Often (especially in summer), there are crafts and cooking demonstrations, medicine shows, storytellers, and balladeers on the premises. You can even take a 20-minute horse-drawn carriage ride around the area ($5 for adults, $3 for children 3 to 11; free for children under 3).

Additional activities: golf (on a top-rated 36-hole course designed by Robert Trent Jones and John LaFoy), miniature golf, 15 tennis courts, a sizable stretch of sandy lakefront beach with wonderful water slides, carillon concerts, boating (rowboats, canoes, sailboats, and paddleboats), bicycle rental, fishing, hiking, picnicking, and more.

Stone Mountain is one of the most beautiful parks in the nation. Consider spending a few days of your trip here; it's a great place for a romantic getaway or a family vacation. On-site accommodations are detailed in chapter 5,

"Accommodations." If you can only spare a day, it's an easy drive (about 30 minutes) from downtown.

✪ High Museum of Art

1280 Peachtree St. NE (at Sixteenth St.). ☎ **404/733-HIGH.** www.high.org. Admission $6 adults, $4 seniors and students with ID, $2 children 6–17, children under 6 free. Free to all on Thurs 1–5pm. Fees subject to change for special exhibitions. Open Tues–Sat 10am–5pm, Sun noon–5pm, and until 9pm the fourth Friday of each month. Closed July 4, Thanksgiving, Christmas, and New Year's Day. MARTA: Arts Center. (A covered walkway links the station to the museum.) A parking garage is located behind the museum on Lombardy Way between Fifteenth and Sixteenth sts.

Designed by architect Richard Meier, this facility—part of the Woodruff Arts Center complex—is itself a work of art. A dazzling white porcelain-tiled building with an equally pristine white interior (The *New York Times* jokingly cautioned that visitors risk snow blindness on a sunny day), it houses four floors of galleries connected by semicircular pedestrian ramps girding a spacious, sun-filled, four-story atrium. It's a lovely building and a favorable setting in which to view art. The north wall of this atrium is enhanced by a 62-foot-high jewel-toned ink drawing by Sol Le Witt, and there's a giant mobile by Alexander Calder on the front lawn.

The permanent collection includes more than 10,000 pieces, among them a significant group of 19th- and 20th-century American paintings. It features Hudson River School artists such as Thomas Cole and Frederic Church, as well as works by Thomas Sully, John Singer Sargent, and William Harnett. The Virginia Carroll Crawford Collection of American Decorative Arts comprehensively documents styles from 1825 to 1917. The Samuel H. Kress Foundation collection comprises Italian paintings and sculpture from the 14th through the 18th century. The Uhry Print Collection contains important works by French impressionists and post-impressionists, German expressionists, and American 20th-century artists. Also notable are collections of sub-Saharan African art, a folk art collection, and works by noted 19th- and 20th-century American and European photographers.

In addition to its permanent collection—which is shown on a rotating basis—the museum hosts a number of major traveling exhibitions each year, complemented by films, lectures, workshops, gallery talks, concerts, and other cultural events. Inquire at the desk about happenings during your stay, and call in advance to find out when you can take a free gallery tour.

The museum also has a wonderful gift shop with an impressive stock of art books, prints, and interesting art-oriented objects. There's also an excellent cafe run by Alon's, which has two other locations in town. It's a delightful space, accented with the same colors as the Calder mobile, which is just outside its big glass windows. The cafe serves up sandwiches, soups, pastries, and desserts, fresh juice, tea, and specialty coffees. It's open Monday 8:30am to 3pm, Tuesday through Friday 8:30am to 5pm, Saturday and Sunday 10am to 5pm. You don't have to enter the museum to get to the cafe.

Jimmy Carter Library and Museum

441 Freedom Pkwy (Exit 96 off I-75/85). ☎ **404/331-0296** or 404/331-3942. www.cartercenter.org Admission $5 adults, $4 seniors, children 16 and under free. Mon–Sat 9am–4:45pm, Sun noon–4:45pm. Closed New Year's Day, Thanksgiving, Christmas.

Set on 30 acres of gardens, lakes, and waterfalls, this impressive presidential library houses some 27 million pages of documents, memoranda, and correspondence from Jimmy Carter's White House years. There are also 1½ million photographs and hundreds of hours of audio- and videotapes. The library's hilltop site is a historic one; it was from this spot that Sherman watched the Battle of Atlanta.

Searching for Margaret Mitchell

Six decades after Margaret Mitchell published *Gone With the Wind,* the novel continues to attract new fans and fascinate people around the world. And thousands of them come to Atlanta each year, looking for some trace of Tara or the woman who wrote about it.

Well, Tara doesn't exist, no matter how much the book and subsequent movie brought it to life for us. And searching for it is as hopeless as combing downtown Atlanta for women in hoop skirts. In fact, the white-columned mansion we equate with Tara was more the product of Hollywood's fancy than of Mitchell's imagination. She begged filmmakers to represent the house as she envisioned it— a plain structure without columns—which was far closer to the reality of a working plantation than the image that's been perpetuated.

Until the Margaret Mitchell House and Museum opened in 1997, evidence of Mitchell herself was nearly as elusive as the fictional Tara. An extremely private person, she left a will stipulating that her papers and manuscripts be burned upon her death. Only a portion of the manuscript of *Gone With the Wind* was spared, enough to prove that Mitchell was its author. It was also her wish that her parents' home on Peachtree Street be torn down after she died, a request that was honored. Several other places she lived fell victim to development or were destroyed in 1917, when a second great fire swept the city.

Still, it's possible to walk the streets of Atlanta and find traces of the famous author, either by viewing exhibits honoring her or by retracing some of her steps.

- **1401 Peachtree St.** The house is gone, but a plaque commemorates the site of the home where Mitchell spent her adolescence. She ordered that it be torn down after her death, possibly because she wasn't happy there. Her mother's dream house, it was a white, two-story Colonial Revival with Doric columns.
- **Margaret Mitchell House and Museum,** 990 Peachtree St. (at Tenth Street; ☎ **404/249-7012**). In 1925, newlywed Mitchell and her husband, John Marsh, moved into Apt. 1 on the bottom floor of this building, and it's where they lived until 1932. It was in "The Dump," as she called it, that Mitchell wrote much of her novel. A group of dedicated preservationists recently rescued the building from the wrecking ball, renovated it, and opened it to the public. MARTA: Midtown.
- **Georgian Terrace,** 659 Peachtree St. It was in this former hotel in 1921 that debutante Mitchell shocked polite society by performing an Apache dance— all the rage in Paris—with her partner at a charity ball. As a result, she was blackballed from the Junior League. Years later, when the Junior League held a costume ball the night before the world premiere of *Gone With the Wind,* Mitchell declined their invitation to be guest of honor. It was also here that Mitchell handed over her manuscript to Harold Latham, an editor for Macmillan. MARTA: North Avenue.
- **Margaret Mitchell Square,** intersection of Peachtree and Forsyth streets and Carnegie Way. It's possible to walk right by this spot and not even know that you've just passed one of the few public memorials to Atlanta's most famous author, which is probably just the way Mitchell would have preferred it. (Friends and acquaintances say she would have disliked the idea of a monument to her life.) The understated square contains a fountain, an inscription,

and a sculpture symbolizing the columns of Tara. One block away is the famous intersection known as Five Points, which Mitchell referred to in her book. MARTA: Peachtree Center.

Across the street from the square is the **Atlanta-Fulton Public Library** (☎ **404/730-1700**), which has on display on its main floor a permanent Margaret Mitchell exhibit. Among the interesting memorabilia, you'll find numerous photographs, a facsimile copy of one of the pages of the original manuscript, her library card, and the coat, scarf, veil, and armband she wore when she worked for the Red Cross. The library also possesses Mitchell's personal literary collection, including the books she used to research *Gone With the Wind.* If you sign the guest book at the exhibit, take a look back through its previous pages. You'll be astounded at the number of people from foreign countries who have visited the display. This is also the site of an earlier building, the Carnegie Library, where Mitchell did much of her research. It was there that she rummaged around in the musty basement among bound copies of Civil War–era newspapers. Her father was one of the founders of the library, and in the years after his death, Mitchell made many contributions in his name. The Carnegie Library was razed in 1977 to make way for the new building. Open Monday to Thursday from 9am to 9pm, Friday and Saturday from 9am to 6pm, and Sunday from 2 to 6pm. MARTA: Peachtree Center.

Across Peachtree Street is the rose granite **Georgia-Pacific Building,** built on the site of the Loew's Grand Theatre, where *Gone With the Wind* had its premiere on December 15, 1939. The theater burned in 1979, but there's an inscription to the right of the main entrance to the current building. See if you can find the misspelling. MARTA: Peachtree Center.

- **Accident scene,** Peachtree and Thirteenth streets. On August 11, 1949, Mitchell and her husband were crossing the street to attend a play. She darted into the path of a taxi rounding the curve, was struck, and died five days later.
- **Gravesite,** 240 Oakland Ave. SE. Mitchell was laid to rest in Oakland Cemetery on August 17, 1949. Only 300 guests were allowed to attend, but after the service fans invaded the cemetery, many taking funeral flowers as souvenirs. The cemetery (☎ 404/688-2107), which is an interesting place in and of itself, is open daily 8am to 6pm (until 7pm during daylight saving time). Admission is free, and a map of famous graves is available for a small fee at the cemetery office Monday to Friday from 9am to 5pm. MARTA: King Memorial.
- **Atlanta History Center,** 730 W. Paces Ferry Rd. (☎ 404/814-4000). For a look at what plantation life was really like, visit the Tullie Smith Farm on the grounds of the history center. The house itself, built in 1845 and moved here in 1972, is a plain, columnless two-story building, typical of an antebellum working plantation in North Georgia. In addition, a popular exhibit, "Disputed Territories: *Gone With the Wind* and Southern Myths," contrasts images from the famous book and movie with historical evidence.

For more information, read *Looking for Tara,* a small but informative guidebook to Margaret Mitchell's Atlanta. It's written by Don O'Briant, a staff writer for the *Atlanta-Journal Constitution,* and is available in local bookstores.

In the facility's extensive museum, you'll see an exact replica of the Oval Office during Carter's presidency, an exhibit enhanced by a recording of Carter speaking about his experiences in that office. A large display of "gifts of state" runs the gamut from a Dresden figurine of George and Martha Washington (a gift from Ireland) to a carpet from the Shah of Iran. You'll see the table setting used when the Carters entertained Chinese Vice Premier Deng Xiaoping and his wife in the State Dining Room; a video of artists such as the late pianist Vladimir Horowitz performing in the East Room; campaign memorabilia; and a large display devoted to the activities of Rosalynn Carter.

Other exhibits focus on Carter's support of human rights (there's a letter from Soviet dissident Andrei Sakharov and Carter's reply); his boyhood days (his sixth-grade report card and a photo of the Plains High basketball team are two of the items on display); and his pre-presidential life as a peanut farmer, governor, and state senator.

There are informative videos throughout, including an interactive "town meeting" format in which visitors can ask Carter questions on subjects ranging from world affairs to his personal life. And a most interesting participatory video lets you choose your response to a terrorist crisis and learn the probable consequences of your choice. The whole tour is self-guided so you can go at your own pace.

Consider having lunch here. There's an excellent cafeteria —run by one of the city's top catering companies—with patio seating overlooking a Japanese garden and pond. Or if you're still in a political mode, stop by nearby **Manuel's Tavern,** a local pub at 602 N. Highland Ave. that's popular with journalists and politicians. President Carter stops in occasionally, too.

Margaret Mitchell House and Museum
(Birthplace of *Gone With the Wind*)
990 Peachtree St. (at Tenth St.). ☎ **404/249-7012.** www.gwtw.org. Admission $6 adults; $5 seniors, students and children ages 7–17; children under 7 free. Open daily 9am–4:30pm. Closed Thanksgiving, Christmas, and New Year's Day. Free parking. MARTA: Midtown.

Six decades after it was first published, *Gone With the Wind* continues to fascinate people around the world. But until this attraction opened in 1997, after a 10-year effort to preserve the house from demolition, disappointed pilgrims found precious little evidence here of the famous book or its author. Now the house and museum are a must-see for visiting *GWTW* fans.

It's rather surprising that it took so long for restoration efforts to get under way on the dilapidated Tudor-revival apartment house where Margaret Mitchell wrote most of her epic novel and lived with her husband, John Marsh, from 1925 to 1932. The structure was built as a single-family dwelling in 1899, then moved to the back of the lot in 1913 and converted into a 10-unit apartment building six years later. It remained an apartment building until 1979, when it was abandoned and eventually boarded up. When the newlyweds moved in, they called it "The Dump"; it was not an affectionate nickname. According to a friend of Mitchell's, she disliked living there (finances left few alternatives) and would probably be offended by the notion of its restoration. But the house has been attracting its share of visitors—37,000 in its first year from all 50 states and 70 foreign countries.

The building includes a re-creation of Mitchell's first-floor apartment and exhibits telling the complex story of the famous novelist. Tours, which last about an hour, begin in the visitors center, where guests see a 17-minute film titled "It May Not Be Tara," featuring an overview of Mitchell's life and interviews with some of her friends and family members. Also in the theater is an exhibition of photos taken of Mitchell in her teens and 20s. The guided tour of the house includes a visit to the Mitchell-Marsh apartment, which is furnished much as it was during their stay there. Mitchell wrote much of her novel in the front room, seated at a typewriter and desk below the beveled glass windows in the small corner alcove. Like most writers, she preferred to keep her literary efforts private and would throw a towel over her typewriter when friends dropped in—which was often.

Beyond the apartment is an exhibit that celebrated Mitchell's life, explores her civic work, and examines the impact of her book and the subsequent movie. Here you'll see her typewriter, which she used to write her novel, and the Pulitzer Prize she won for her efforts. The tour concludes in the museum shop, which includes a variety of *GWTW* collectibles and memorabilia.

If you finish your tour around mealtime, walk one block north on Peachtree to Pasta da Pulcinella, an excellent little hole-in-the-wall pasta place that is open for lunch and dinner. (Details on page 105 in chapter 6.)

✪ **Martin Luther King, Jr., Center for Nonviolent Social Change**
449 Auburn Ave. (between Boulevard and Jackson sts.). ☎ **404/524-1956.** Free admission. Daily 9am–6pm. Closed Thanksgiving, Christmas, New Year's Day. From I-75/85 south, exit at Freedom Parkway/Carter Center. Turn right at first stoplight onto Boulevard. Follow signs to Martin Luther King National Historic Site. MARTA: King Memorial Station is about 8 blocks away; or take bus no. 3 east from the Five Points Station.

Martin Luther King, Jr.'s commitment to nonviolent social change lives on at this memorial and educational center under the direction of his son, Dexter Scott King. A nongovernmental member of the United Nations, the center works with government agencies and the private sector to reduce violence within the community and among nations. Its library and archives house the world's largest collection of books and other materials documenting the civil rights movement, including Dr. King's personal papers and a rare 87-volume edition of *The Collected Works of Mahatma Gandhi,* a gift from the government of India. The library is open by appointment only for scholarly research. Equally important, the center is Martin Luther King's final resting place, a living memorial to an inspiring leader, which is visited by tens of thousands each year, including heads of foreign governments.

The tour, which is self-guided, begins in Freedom Hall, where memorabilia of King and the civil rights movement are displayed. Here you can see his Bible and clerical robe, a hand-written sermon, a photographic essay on his life and work, and, on a grim note, the suit he was wearing when a deranged woman stabbed him in New York City. Also on display is the key to his room at the Lorraine Motel in Memphis, Tennessee, where King was assassinated. In an alcove off the main exhibit area is a video display on Martin Luther King's life and works. Additional exhibits include a room honoring Rosa Parks (whose refusal to give up her seat on a city bus led to the Montgomery bus boycott) and another honoring Gandhi.

Outside is Freedom Plaza, where Dr. King's white marble crypt rests, surrounded by a beautiful five-tiered Reflecting Pool, a symbol of the life-giving nature of water. The tomb is inscribed with his words: "Free at Last. Free at Last. Thank God Almighty I'm Free at Last." An eternal flame burns in a small circular pavilion directly in front of the crypt.

The Freedom Walkway, a vaulted colonnade paralleling the pool, will eventually be painted with murals depicting the civil rights struggle. Located at the end of Freedom Walkway is the Chapel of All Faiths, symbolizing the ecumenical nature of Dr. King's work and the universality of the basic tenets of all the world's great religions.

Martin Luther King, Jr., National Historic Site

Under the auspices of the National Park Service is an area of about 2 blocks around Auburn Avenue, designated as a National Historic Site and established to preserve the birthplace and boyhood surroundings of the nation's foremost civil rights leader. It includes King's boyhood home and the Ebenezer Baptist Church, of which King, his father, and his grandfather were ministers. Tours of the Birth Home originate at Fire Station No. 6, which was recently restored by the NPS. Other Auburn Avenue attractions, not under NPS auspices, include the Martin Luther King, Jr., Center for Nonviolent Social Change (where King is buried) and the APEX Museum. Several more surrounding blocks have been designated as a preservation district.

The area is known as Sweet Auburn. John Wesley Dobbs, maternal grandfather of former Atlanta mayor Maynard Jackson, is the person who first called it such, after Oliver Goldsmith's *The Deserted Village,* the first line of which reads, "Sweet Auburn! loveliest village of the plains." Mayor Jackson says his grandfather called the area "sweet" because the keys to black liberation existed here in the form of "the three b's—bucks, ballots, and books."

(See chapter 8, "A Walking Tour of Sweet Auburn," for tips on how to explore the area.)

There is a visitors center at 450 Auburn Ave., across from the King Center. It provides a complete orientation to area attractions and includes a theater for audiovisual and interpretive programs, exhibits, and a bookstore. The visitors center is fronted by a beautifully landscaped plaza with a reflecting pool and outdoor amphitheater for National Park Service programs.

A store on the premises offers King memorabilia and a wide selection of books and cassettes. Ranger talks focusing on the community and the civil rights movement take place frequently on Freedom Plaza.

Michael C. Carlos Museum of Emory University

571 S. Kilgo St. (near the intersection of Oxford and North Decatur rds. on the Main Quadrangle of the Emory campus). ☎ **404/727-4282.** www.cc.emory.edu/CARLOS/carlos.html. $3 donation suggested. Mon–Sat 10am–5pm, Sun noon–5pm. Closed major holidays. Parking can be difficult on the Emory campus. Paid visitor parking is available in the Boisfeuillet Jones Center lot and in Fishburne Parking Deck; free parking is allowed anywhere on campus except in 24-hour restricted areas or reserved spaces. MARTA bus: 6 or 36.

Emory University's antiquities collection dates to 1875 and this intriguing museum to 1919, when it was founded to display the art and artifacts collected by Emory faculty in Egypt, Cyprus, Greece, Sicily, the Sea of Galilee, and the sites of ancient Babylon and Palestine. Today, the museum also maintains collections of ancient art and archaeology of Rome, Central and South America, the Near East, and Mesoamerica; works of the native cultures of North America; art of Asia and Oceania; and some 1,000 objects from sub-Saharan Africa. Additionally, a sizable collection of works on paper encompasses illuminated manuscript pages, drawings, and prints from the Middle Ages and the Renaissance to the 20th century. It's all housed partly in a 1916 beaux-arts building that is on the National Register of Historic Places, its interior redesigned in 1985 by postmodernist architect Michael Graves. The remainder is in a 35,000-square-foot exhibition space (also designed by Graves) that opened in 1993.

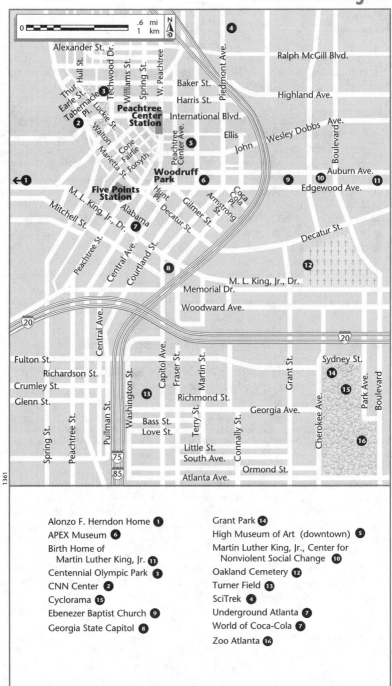

Alonzo F. Herndon Home **1**

APEX Museum **6**

Birth Home of
  Martin Luther King, Jr. **11**

Centennial Olympic Park **3**

CNN Center **2**

Cyclorama **15**

Ebenezer Baptist Church **9**

Georgia State Capitol **8**

Grant Park **14**

High Museum of Art (downtown) **5**

Martin Luther King, Jr., Center for
  Nonviolent Social Change **10**

Oakland Cemetery **12**

Turner Field **13**

SciTrek **4**

Underground Atlanta **7**

World of Coca-Cola **7**

Zoo Atlanta **16**

Factoid

The annual Kingfest, held mid-May and mid-June, features music, theatrical performances, a kids' day, and many other events. Every October 2, Gandhi's birthday
is celebrated with Indian food, music, and entertainment. Inquire about events
taking place during your stay.

The first-floor galleries feature exhibits from the extensive permanent
collection—objects that were part of the daily life of people from five continents as
early as the seventh millennium B.C. They include Bronze and Iron Age clay pots,
jugs, loom weights, and oil lamps from Palestine; Egyptian mummies, pottery, cosmetic containers, and headrests; Greek and Cypriot pottery, flasks, and statuary;
and Mesopotamian pottery, coins, tools, sculpture, and cuneiform tablets inscribed
with ancient writing. Also on this level: the Thibadeau Pre-Columbian collection,
comprising over 1,300 objects spanning 2,000 years of creativity—gold jewelry,
pottery, and statues, including many ceramic, volcanic stone, greenstone, and gold
sculptures from ancient Costa Rica.

The upper floor is used for changing exhibits ranging in subject matter from
Pueblo Indian pottery to impressionist art. Throughout the museum, 210 plaster
casts of ancient architectural elements—reliefs, friezes, column capitals, and decorative elements from temples and monuments—adorn hallway and lobby walls.
Allow about at least an hour to see the collections.

There are many interesting workshops, lectures, films, and gallery tours here; call
to find out what's on during your stay. There's also a nice museum shop with a
variety of educational books and gifts, as well as jewelry inspired by the collections.
The museum's cafe, on the third floor, serves continental breakfast, lunch, coffee,
and tea, and is open during regular museum hours.

✪ Oakland Cemetery

248 Oakland Ave. SE (main entrance at Oakland Ave. and Martin Luther King Dr.).
☎ **404/658-6019.** Free admission. Daily sunrise to 7pm (6pm in winter); visitors center
Mon–Fri 9am–5pm. Purchase an informative, self-guided walking-tour map brochure at the
visitors center for $1. Free parking inside the cemetery, near the visitors center. MARTA: King
Memorial.

On the National Register of Historic Places, this outstanding 88-acre Victorian
cemetery was founded in 1850. It survived the Civil War and remained the only
cemetery in Atlanta for 34 years. Among the more than 48,000 people buried here
are Confederate and Union soldiers (including five Southern generals), prominent
families and paupers, governors and mayors, golfing great Bobby Jones, and *Gone
With the Wind* author Margaret Mitchell. There's a Jewish section (consecrated by
a temple), a black section (dating from segregation days), and a potter's field. Two
monuments honor the Confederate war dead. And standing at the marker that
commemorates the Great Locomotive Chase, you can see the trees from which the
Yankee raiders were hanged (Confederate conductor Captain William Fuller is
buried here).

Almost every grave has a story. Real-estate tycoon Jasper Newton Smith had a
life-size statue of himself erected on his grave so he could watch the city's goings-on
into eternity. (The sculptor originally gave Smith a tie, but Smith, who never wore
one, refused to pay for the piece until the tie was chiseled off.) Dr. James Nissen,

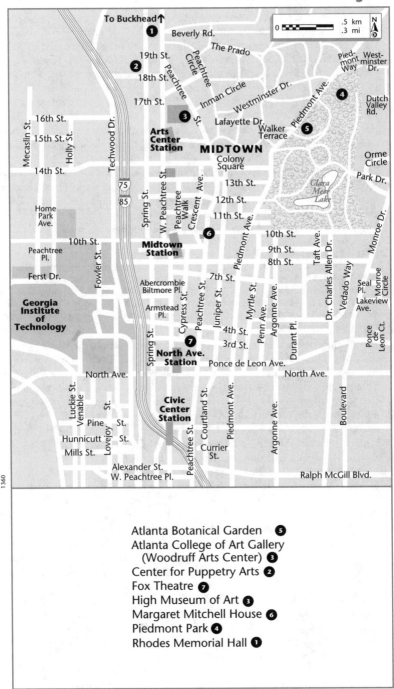

Atlanta Botanical Garden ⑤
Atlanta College of Art Gallery
 (Woodruff Arts Center) ③
Center for Puppetry Arts ②
Fox Theatre ⑦
High Museum of Art ③
Margaret Mitchell House ⑥
Piedmont Park ④
Rhodes Memorial Hall ①

Oakland's first burial, feared being buried alive; his will stated that his jugular vein be severed prior to interment. And John Morgan Dye was a baby who died during the siege of Atlanta; his mother walked through the raging battle to the cemetery carrying the small corpse. The smallest grave, however, is that of "Tweet," a pet mockingbird buried in his family's lot. You'll also learn about graveyard symbolism on the tour: a lopped-tree-trunk marker indicates a life cut short or goals unachieved, rocks on a grave denote a life built on a solid foundation, and a shell means resurrection.

The cemetery is renowned not only for historical reasons, but as an outdoor "museum" of Gothic and classical-revival mausolea, bronze urns, stained glass, and Victorian statuary.

Atlanta residents also view Oakland's rolling terrain as parkland; dozens of people actually jog here every day, and picnickers are a common sight. Every October, there's a celebration to commemorate the cemetery's founding, with turn-of-the-century music, food, and storytelling. Though you can visit whenever the cemetery is open, try to come when you can take a guided tour. It's fascinating.

✪ The World of Coca-Cola

55 Martin Luther King, Jr., Dr. SW (at Central Ave., adjacent to Underground Atlanta). ☎ **404/676-5151.** Admission $6 adults, $4 seniors 55 and over, $4 students, $3 children 6–12, under 6 free. Sept–May, Mon–Sat 9am–5pm, Sun noon–6pm; June–Aug, Mon–Sat 9am–6pm, Sun 11am–6pm. Closed New Year's Day, the second Sun in Jan, Easter, Thanksgiving, Christmas Eve, and Christmas Day. Parking garage on Central Ave. off Martin Luther King Dr. MARTA: Five Points.

An exposition showcasing the world's most popular soft drink, the World of Coca-Cola sounds like a huge Coke commercial. And it is. But it's also one of the biggest attractions in the city and a must-see for anybody who's ever had a taste of the Real Thing. (And who hasn't?) Its vast three-story pavilion houses a massive collection of Coca-Cola memorabilia, along with numerous interactive displays, high-tech exhibits, and video presentations. A self-guided tour begins on the third level, where visitors are greeted by a Rube Goldberg–like kinetic sculpture called a "Bottling Fantasy." Exhibits throughout trace the history of Coca-Cola from its 1886 debut at Jacob's Pharmacy in downtown Atlanta to its current worldwide fame.

Highlights include: a re-creation of a 1930s soda fountain (a jukebox on the premises plays Coke-themed pop songs of yesteryear, like "Sweet Coca-Cola Bush" sung by Shirley Temple); diverse advertising campaigns over the years (Did you know that Maxwell House's "good to the last drop" was originally a Coke slogan?); a video on the making of the "Hilltop Reunion" Coke commercial (it kicked off the "I'd Like to Teach the World to Sing" campaign); print ads featuring screen stars such as Jean Harlow, Claudette Colbert, Clark Gable, and Cary Grant; and an interactive audio exhibit that lets you listen to Coke commercials sung by pop stars.

And, in case you've worked up a thirst by this time, you can sample unlimited amounts of 38 Coca-Cola Company beverages at Club Coca-Cola, including 18 international drinks that are not sold in the United States (for example, a pineapple/orange/banana beverage marketed only in Kenya). The kids will go wild, but the drinks are on the house, so what the heck. The tour ends in the first-floor gift shop, which sells a mind-boggling array of Coca-Cola logo items; everything from T-shirts to Coke polar bears. There's much, much more; this experience is a total immersion in Coca-Cola. Allow about 90 minutes to drink it all in; come on weekdays to avoid long lines.

2 More Attractions

Alonzo F. Herndon Home

587 University Place (between Vine and Walnut sts.). ☎ **404/581-9813.** Free admission (donations requested). Tues–Sat 10am–4pm, with tours on the hour. Closed New Year's Day, July 4, Thanksgiving, and Christmas. MARTA: Vine City.

Alonzo Herndon was born into the last decade of slavery in 1858. After emancipation, he worked as a field hand and sharecropper, supplementing his meager income by selling peanuts, homemade molasses, and axle grease. He arrived in Atlanta in the early 1880s, where he worked as a barber and eventually owned several barbershops of his own. He acquired real estate with earnings from these shops. By 1900, with only a year of formal education and less than 40 years out of slavery, Herndon was the richest black man in Atlanta. In 1905, he purchased a church burial association, which, with other small companies, became the nucleus of the Atlanta Life Insurance Company, today the nation's second-largest black-owned insurance company.

In 1910, Herndon built this elegant 15-room house in the beaux-arts neoclassical style with a stately colonnaded entrance. The tour begins in a receiving room with a 10-minute introductory video called *The Herndon Legacy.* Herndon and his wife, Adrienne McNeil, a drama teacher at Atlanta University, were the primary architects of the house, and construction was accomplished almost completely by African-American artisans. Because the home was occupied until 1977 by their son Norris, much of the original furniture remains, and there are family photographs throughout. Adrienne died about a week after the house was completed.

The tour takes you through the reception hall; the music room, with rococo gilt-trim walls and Louis XV–style furnishings; the living room, with a frieze on its walls depicting the accomplishments of Herndon's life; the dining room, furnished in late Renaissance style with family china and Venetian glass displayed in a mahogany cabinet; the butler's pantry; and the sunny breakfast room. Upstairs, you'll see the bedroom used by his second wife, Jessie, with its Jacobean suite and Louis XV–style furnishings; Herndon's Empire-furnished bedroom, where a book from a Republican National Convention displayed on a table lets you know his political bent; the collection room (Norris collected ancient Greek and Roman vases and funerary objects); Norris's bedroom; a sitting room; and a guest bedroom.

Atlanta College of Art Gallery

1280 Peachtree St. NE (in the Memorial Arts Building of the Woodruff Arts Center). ☎ **404/733-5050.** Free admission. Tues–Sat 10am–5pm, Sun noon–5pm.

The Atlanta College of Art, housed in the Woodruff Arts Center complex, features an ongoing series of gallery shows. A recent example: "Light Over Ancient Angkor," a photo exhibition of Cambodian Angkor ruins. There are also faculty exhibitions, juried student shows, lectures, and concerts here. Call for details.

Callanwolde Fine Arts Center

980 Briarcliff Rd. NE (north of Ponce de Leon Ave.). ☎ **404/872-5338.** Free admission, except for some special events. Guided tours, by special appointment only, $1.50 adults, 50¢ children under 12. If you're interested in a tour, call to arrange it as far in advance as possible. Mon–Fri 9am–9pm, Sat 10am–4pm.

A magnificent Gothic/Tudor–style mansion, built for Coca-Cola heir Charles Howard Candler in 1920, Callanwolde today serves as a fine-arts center for in-town residents. Classes are given in pottery, painting, photography, drawing, and more, and there are numerous workshops for adults and children. While touring the

Regional Atlanta Sights

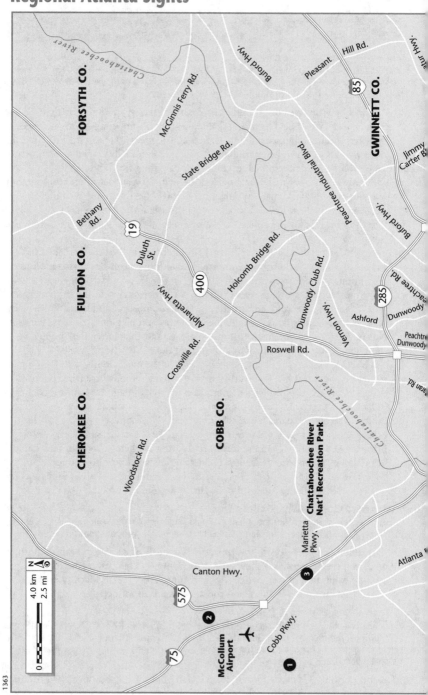

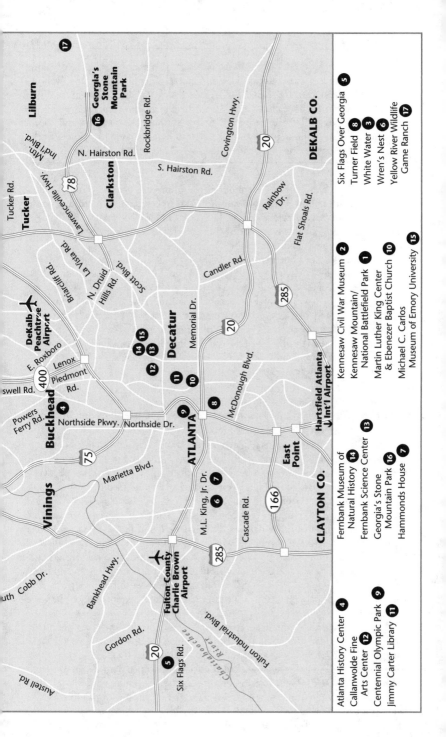

Atlanta History Center **4**
Callanwolde Fine
Arts Center **12**
Centennial Olympic Park **9**
Jimmy Carter Library **11**

Fernbank Museum of
Natural History **14**
Fernbank Science Center **13**
Georgia's Stone
Mountain Park **16**
Hammonds House **7**

Kennesaw Civil War Museum **2**
Kennesaw Mountain/
National Battlefield Park **1**
Martin Luther King Center
& Ebenezer Baptist Church **10**
Michael C. Carlos
Museum of Emory University **15**

Six Flags Over Georgia **5**
Turner Field **8**
White Water **3**
Wren's Nest **6**
Yellow River Wildlife
Game Ranch **17**

Factoid

In addition to its interior attractions, Château Élan has nature trails along St. Emilion Creek and by Romanée–Conti pond. On select Saturday evenings between Memorial Day and Labor Day there's dancing to live beach music in an adjoining outdoor facility called Le Pavillion. There is an admission charge; you can order a picnic box (call ahead for prices). Shag (jitterbug) lessons begin at 7:30pm. In addition, there are numerous events at Château Élan, ranging from harvest celebrations to concerts to equestrian shows; call to find out what's on during your visit.

house, you may be surprised that most of the rooms are bare, and only Callanwolde's exquisite walnut paneling, beautifully carved ceilings and moldings, grand staircase, magnificent marble and stone fireplaces, and leaded-glass windows evoke its luxurious past. But this is a working arts center, not a museum, and the rooms are used for the classes and workshops.

The estate occupies 12 acres (originally 27) in the Druid Hills section of Atlanta, an area planned by Frederick Law Olmsted, designer of New York's Central Park. Visitors are welcome to peruse shows of local artists in the Petite Hall gallery upstairs; enjoy the lawns, formal gardens, and nature trails, which are maintained by the county; and participate in the many events here—concerts, storytelling evenings, and dance performances. Especially memorable is Christmas at Callanwolde (see the "Atlanta Calendar of Events" in chapter 2), when the entire house is decorated for the season and shops are set up in different rooms. Attending a function here is the best way to experience the estate.

Château Élan Winery & Resort

100 Tour de France, Braselton, GA (30 miles north of Atlanta at Exit 48 off I-85). ☎ **800/ 233-WINE** or 770/932-0900 in Atlanta. www.chateauelan.com. Free admission. Open daily at 10am. Closing hours vary.

Château Élan is a hilltop winery that replicates a 16th-century French estate surrounded by verdant countryside. Its first wines were produced in 1985, and already they have garnered more than 200 awards. Guided tours are given daily between 11am and 4pm (call ahead for hours; you can also take self-guided tours after 5pm).

On view are the crushing and pressing machines, oak barrels used to age and flavor wines, the cask room, and the bottling area. The tours conclude with a wine tasting. Grapes ripen in July/August, so if you're here during harvesting in August and September, you'll actually see the wine-making procedure. More than 300 tons of grapes are harvested and processed each year. The interior of the château, a stageset version of a Paris street, has a quarry-stone floor, wrought-iron fences, and street lamps. The building houses an art gallery offering monthly exhibits by regional and national artists, displays of antique European wine-making equipment, and a wine market.

There are also three on-premises restaurants, so plan to eat lunch or dinner here. **Café Élan,** open daily from 11am to 10pm, features sandwiches, salads, and light entrees for $7 to $12.95 at lunch; $12.95 to $20 at dinner. It's a charming setting, with seating under a green awning. **Paddy's Irish Pub,** open Saturday at 3pm and the rest of the week at 5pm (closing hours vary), serves traditional Irish fare and spirits. Entrees range from $8 to $14. The fancier **Le Clos**—with pale pink walls, lace-curtained French doors, and tables covered with crisp white linen—is open for dinner only Wednesday through Saturday evenings, with seatings from 6:30 to

9:30pm. A seven- or eight-course prix-fixe meal beginning at $76 features haute-cuisine entrees; appropriate Château Élan wines with each course are included. Reservations are imperative. Men are required to wear a coat and tie.

There are also several restaurants at the adjoining Château Élan resort. And there are picnic areas on the lovely grounds; custom picnic baskets can be purchased here.

You might also consider an overnight or longer stay at the 274-room **Inn at Château Élan,** a luxurious resort where facilities include four golf courses (three 18-hole and one par-3, 9-hole) and seven tennis courts (both offering pro shops and instruction), a full-service European-style health spa and salon (days of pampering are an option), an outdoor Olympic-size pool and an indoor heated pool, a fitness center, and lawn games; boating and fishing can be arranged nearby. Room rates are reasonable, beginning at $149 double; call the above numbers for details and inquire about golf, tennis, spa, and other packages.

Georgia State Capitol

Capitol Ave. (at Washington St.). ☎ **404/656-2844.** www.sos.state.ga.us. Free admission. Mon–Fri 8am–5pm. Tours given weekdays only at 10 and 11am and 1 and 2pm, but self-guided tours are possible at any time the capitol is open. Closed major holidays, including state holidays. Parking lot behind the capitol building on Capitol Ave. is closed to the public during legislative sessions; other lots are on M. L. King Dr. at Central Ave. and on Courtland St. between M. L. King Dr. and Central Ave. MARTA: Georgia State.

It wasn't until after the Civil War (1868) that Atlanta became, once and for all, the state capital; its present capitol building, completed July 4, 1889, was hailed as a testament to the city's recovery.

Modeled after the nation's Capitol, another neoclassical edifice atop a "crowning hill," its 75-foot dome, covered in gold leaf and topped by a Statue of Freedom, is a major Atlanta landmark. The building is fronted by a massive four-story portico with a pediment supported by six Corinthian columns set on large stone piers. In the rotunda, with its soaring 237-foot ceiling, are busts of famous Georgians, including signers of the Declaration of Independence and the Constitution. The capitol building's public spaces were recently restored to their 1889 grandeur.

Tours begin in the entrance hallway of the main floor, and this level also serves as an information center for city and state attractions. The governor's office is off the main hall. The tours take 45 minutes; allow at least another 30 minutes to browse around on your own after the tour. Highlights of the grounds are detailed in a brochure available at the tour desk. *Note:* For security reasons, your bag will be searched when you enter.

Grand staircases in both wings rise to the third floor, where you'll enter the House of Representatives, and, across the hall, the Senate chambers. The legislature meets for 40 days, beginning the second Monday in January (it can also be called into special sessions); all of its sessions are open to the public. The fourth floor houses legislative galleries and the State Museum of Science & Industry, with exhibits on cotton, peach, and peanut growing; cases of mounted birds, fish, deer, insects, and other species native to Georgia; rocks and minerals; Indian artifacts; and more. Note, too, museum displays on the first floor.

Some events of note: The week before Thanksgiving is Indian Heritage Week at the capitol. A wattle-and-daub Indian dwelling is constructed in the rotunda, and there are Native American lecturers, music, and arts-and-crafts demonstrations. At Christmas, a beautifully decorated 40-foot tree adorns the rotunda. And on January 15, Dr. Martin Luther King, Jr's. birthday, there's an annual memorial program; local dignitaries, including the governor, give speeches, and King's family attends.

Hammonds House Galleries & Resource Center of African-American Art

503 Peeples St. (at Lucile St., 2 blocks north of Ralph David Abernathy Blvd.). ☎ **404/752-8730.** Admission $2 adults, $1 seniors and students. Tues–Fri 10am–6pm, Sat–Sun 1–5pm. MARTA bus: no. 71 from the West End station.

Occupying the 1857 Eastlake Victorian-style former home of Dr. Otis T. Hammonds, a black anesthesiologist and art patron, Hammonds House is a national center for the exhibition, preservation, research, and documentation of African-American art and artists. The house was purchased with these aims in mind by the Fulton County Commission after Hammonds's death in 1985.

Hammonds's extensive collection included works by African-American and Haitian artists, as well as African masks and carvings. Along with later acquisitions—including works by Romare Bearden, William H. Johnson, Robert S. Duncanson, and Elizabeth Catlett—the permanent collection is shown on a rotating basis and is supplemented by exhibitions of renowned black artists from all over the world. The Resource Center on the premises, housing documents on African-American art and artists, is open to the public by appointment.

The house is located in the thriving West End neighborhood, declared a historic district in 1991. While you're in the area, take a look at the other lovingly restored Victorian bungalows and houses. A short walk away is the Atlanta University Center, the largest historically African-American education complex in the world, which includes Morehouse College. Dr. Martin Luther King, Jr., is its most famous alumnus, and a chapel there was built to honor his memory.

High Museum of Art, Folk Art, and Photography Galleries

30 John Wesley Dobbs Ave. (at Peachtree St. NE), Atlanta, GA 30303. ☎ **404/577-6940.** www.high.org. Free admission. Mon–Sat 10am–5pm. MARTA: Peachtree Center.

Inside the impressive Georgia-Pacific Building near Five Points, this downtown branch of the High Museum of Art displays folk art and photography. Allow about an hour for your visit. Visitors can enter through an elegantly landscaped courtyard on John Wesley Dobbs Avenue, or from Peachtree Street via the imposing Georgia-Pacific lobby, itself the setting for Louise Nevelson's vast indoor environmental sculpture in white wood, *Dawn's Forest.* Spanning three levels, the museum has beautiful walls paneled in an African wood called angré, and pedestrian ramps affording visitors a view of the downtown skyline as they descend to the galleries.

The two levels of galleries provide approximately 5,000 square feet of exhibition space. The upper gallery has a barrel-vaulted ceiling with Plexiglas inserts allowing daylight to flood the space. In addition to exhibitions, the museum offers films, lectures, concerts, and gallery talks (call for details). The Georgia-Pacific Building, by the way, is built on the site of the Loew's Grand Theatre, where *Gone With the Wind* premiered in 1939.

Kennesaw Civil War Museum

2829 Cherokee St., Kennesaw, GA 30152. ☎ **800/742-6897** or 770/427-2117. Admission $3 adults; $2.50 seniors, service people, and AAA members; $1.50 children 7–15; children 6 and under free. Families pay a maximum of $12. Mar 15–Oct 15 Mon–Sat 9:30am–5:30pm, Sun noon–5:30pm; Oct 16–Mar 14 Mon–Sat 10am–4pm, Sun noon–4pm. Free parking. Take Exit 117 off I-75N and follow the signs.

On this site began the wild adventure known as the "Great Locomotive Chase." The Civil War had been under way for a year on April 12, 1862, when Union spy James J. Andrews and a group of 21 Northern soldiers disguised as civilians boarded a locomotive called the *General* in Marietta, buying tickets for diverse destinations to avert suspicion. When the train made a breakfast stop at the Lacy Hotel in Big

Shanty, they seized the locomotive and several boxcars and fled northward to Chattanooga. The goal of these daring raiders was to destroy tracks, telegraph wires, and bridges behind them, thus cutting off the Confederate supply route between Virginia and Mississippi.

Conductor William A. Fuller, his breakfast interrupted by the sound of the *General* chugging out of the station, gave chase on foot, then grabbed a platform car and poled along the tracks. With him were a railroad superintendent and the *General's* engineer. At the Etowah River, Fuller and crew commandeered a small locomotive called the *Yonah* and made better progress. Meanwhile, the raiders tore up track behind them, and when the pursuers got close, the raiders slowed them down by throwing ties and firewood onto the tracks. Andrews, a very smooth talker, managed to convince station attendants en route that he was on an emergency mission running ammunition to Confederate general Beauregard in Mississippi.

Fuller's chances of catching the *General* improved when he seized the southbound *Texas* and began running it backward toward the raiders, picking up reinforcements along the way and eventually managing to get a telegraph message through to Gen. Danville Leadbetter, commander at Chattanooga. The chase went on, with Andrews sending uncoupled boxcars careening back toward Fuller as obstructions. Fuller, however, who was running in reverse, merely attached the rolling boxcars to his engine and kept on. At the covered Oostanaula Bridge, the raiders detached a boxcar and set it on fire in hopes of finally creating an impassable obstacle—a burning bridge behind them. But the *Texas* was able to push the flaming car off the bridge; it soon burned out, and Fuller tossed it off the track and continued.

By this time the *General* was running low on fuel and water, the *Texas* was hot on its heels, and the raiders realized that all was lost. Andrews gave his final command: "Jump off and scatter! Every man for himself!" All were captured and imprisoned within a few days. Some escaped, others were exchanged for Confederate prisoners of war, and the rest were hanged in Atlanta, most of them at a site near Oakland Cemetery. Though the mission failed, the raiders, some of them posthumously, received the newly created Medal of Honor for their valor.

The museum, occupying a building that was once the Frey cotton gin, houses the *General* (still in running condition, but don't get any ideas), a walk-through caboose, exhibits of Civil War artifacts, memorabilia, and photographs relating to the chase and its participants. You can view a 20-minute narrated video about the chase, but if you really want the full story, rent the Disney movie, *The Great Locomotive Chase*, starring Fess Parker as the dashing Andrews. (You can also buy a copy in the museum gift shop.)

The museum is 3 miles from Kennesaw Mountain/National Battlefield Park (details below), so consider visiting both of these Civil War–related sights the same day.

Kennesaw Mountain/National Battlefield Park

Old Hwy. 41 and Stilesboro Rd., Kennesaw, GA. ☎ **770/427-4686.** www.nps.gov/kemo. Free admission. Visitors center open daily 8:30am–5pm, until 6pm weekends June–Aug; front gate closes at around 8pm June–Aug, around 6pm the rest of the year. Closing hours can vary; please check the sign before you enter a gated area. Closed Christmas. Take I-75 north to Barrett Pkwy. (Exit 116), then follow the signs.

This 2,882-acre park was established in 1917 on the site of a crucial Civil War battle in the Atlanta campaign of 1864. A very popular attraction, it draws some 2 million visitors annually.

The action began in June 1864. A month earlier, Gen. Ulysses S. Grant had ordered Sherman to attack the Confederate army in Georgia, "break it up, and go into the interior of the enemy's country as far as you can, inflicting all the damage you can upon their war resources." In response to this order, Sherman's army, 100,000 strong, had been pushing back Confederate forces composed of 65,000 men under Gen. Joseph E. Johnston. By June 19, Union troops had driven Johnston's men back to a well-prepared defensive position on Kennesaw Mountain. Southern engineers had built a line of entrenchments in its rocky slopes, allowing the Confederates to cover every approach with rifle or cannon. An Ohio officer later commented that if the mountain had been constructed for the sole purpose of repelling an invading army, "it could not have been better made or placed."

On June 27, following a few weeks of skirmishing, Sherman, underestimating the strength and still-feisty morale of the rebels, attempted to break through Confederate lines and annihilate them in a grand no-holds-barred assault from two directions. Confederate Gen. Samuel French described the onset of the attack: "As if by magic, there sprang from the earth a host of men, and in one long, waving line of blue the infantry advanced and the battle of Kennesaw Mountain began."

Sherman's men were repelled by massive bursts of firepower and huge rocks rolling down the mountain at them. Federal casualties far outnumbered Confederate losses. Meanwhile, 8,000 Union infantrymen in five brigades attacked from another angle; in this battle the Union lost 3,000 men, the Confederates 500. Weeks of torrential rain, which had turned these battlegrounds into a muddy mire, added significantly to the misery on both sides. There was no rain the day of the battle, but the day was swelteringly hot and muggy.

Allow at least two hours for exploring. Start your tour at the **visitors center,** where you can pick up a map, watch an 18-minute film about the battle, and view exhibits of Civil War artifacts and memorabilia. A new visitors center is scheduled to open by June 1999 and will include many excellent new exhibits, including ones on the Signal Corps, Civil War medicine, and how the war affected civilians. On weekdays you can drive or hike up the mountain to see the actual Confederate entrenchments and earthworks, some of them equipped with Civil War artillery. (On weekends it may be too crowded to drive, but you can take a shuttle bus.) The steep trail is about 2 miles round-trip, so wear comfortable shoes. You'll find interpretive signs at key spots, and, weekends and holidays Memorial Day through Labor Day, interpretive programs give further information about the battle. You'll also want to drive to **Cheatham Hill,** site of some of the fiercest fighting. There are 16 miles of hiking trails for those who want a more extensive tour (trail maps are available at the visitors center), and picnicking is permitted in designated areas, some with barbecue grills. The scenery is gorgeous, so even if Civil War battles are not your thing (that is, if you're reluctantly accompanying an enthusiastic spouse), it makes for beautiful hiking or driving.

Rhodes Memorial Hall

1516 Peachtree St. NW (at Peachtree Circle). ☎ **404/885-7800.** Admission for self-guided tour $3 adults, $2 seniors and children under 12; $5 adults, $4 seniors and children under 12 for guided tour. Mon–Fri 11am–4pm, Sun noon–3pm. Free parking in designated lot behind building on Spring St. MARTA: Arts Center.

Rhodes Hall is one of a few remaining pre–World War I Peachtree Street mansions and is significant as a reminder that Peachtree was once a fashionable residential street. The house was designed shortly after the turn of the century by Willis Franklin Denny (at the time Atlanta's leading residential architect) as a home for affluent Atlanta businessman Amos Giles Rhodes and his family.

Its medieval baronial-cum-high Victorian Romanesque style was inspired by Rhineland castles. The Stone Mountain granite exterior is replete with arched

Romanesque windows, battlements and buttresses, parapets, towers, and turrets. A large Syrian-arched veranda wraps the east and north facades. And the interior is grandiose, with maple- and mahogany-bordered oak parquet floors, mosaics surrounding the fireplaces, and a gracefully winding hand-carved Honduran mahogany staircase with nine stained-glass stairwell panels depicting "The Rise and Fall of the Confederacy." The house and stables originally occupied 150 acres of land and included servants' quarters, a carriage house, and other outbuildings. When it was built, this site was in suburbia, an afternoon's drive from downtown.

Upon Rhodes's death in 1929, his residence was deeded to the state of Georgia in keeping with his desire to preserve it. The house was entered on the National Register of Historic Places in 1974. Today, it is headquarters for the Georgia Trust for Historic Preservation and is in an ongoing process of restoration. To date, the original dining-room suite and some other furnishings are in place, and all the mahogany woodwork and decorated ceilings on the first floor have been restored. Original landscaping—with white and red cedars, dogwoods, banana trees, and a circular flower bed—has been re-created in the front yard.

Underground Atlanta

50 Upper Alabama St. (bounded by Wall St., Central Ave., Martin Luther King, Jr., Dr., and Peachtree St.). ☎ **404/523-2311.** Free admission. There is a charge for parking in the garages off Martin Luther King Dr., but it's reduced if you get your ticket validated at a store or restaurant. Mon–Sat 10am–9pm, Sun noon–6pm. Some restaurants and clubs stay open until midnight (or later) nightly. MARTA: Five Points Station has a short pedestrian tunnel that connects directly with Underground Atlanta.

The site of Underground Atlanta is the historic hub of the city, centered on the Zero Milepost that marked the terminus of the Western & Atlantic Railroad in the 1800s. For many years a flourishing locale, the area became so congested in the early 1900s that permanent concrete viaducts were constructed over it, elevating the street system and routing traffic over a maze of railroad tracks. Merchants moved their operations up to the new level, using the lower level for storage space. For most of the 20th century, it remained a deserted catacomb.

In 1969, a group of Atlanta businesspeople decided to create an underground entertainment complex of restaurants, shops, and bars in a setting that retained the historic feel of the area. The idea was great, but the complex declined and closed after a little over a decade. In 1989—after a public–private infusion of $142 million—a larger, livelier Underground reopened to much fanfare and for several years was once again an entertainment mecca and urban marketplace. Local civic leaders pinned their hopes for downtown revival on the complex, and for some time it looked as if the concept would work. But, beset by lease disputes, financial problems, and changes of management, Underground has failed to sustain its early promise. The complex is still worth a look if you're in the downtown area, but keep in mind that it's mostly a tourist attraction at this point. It's still struggling to find its place in the urban mix, perhaps because locals prefer the shopping and entertainment areas in Buckhead and Virginia-Highland. When you visit Underground, here's what you'll find:

Occupying 12 acres in the center of downtown, the complex is heralded by a beacon of oscillating searchlights emanating from a 138-foot light tower, an outdoor staging area used for performances and concerts, and the cascading waters of Peachtree Fountain Plaza. Underground offers nearly 100 retail operations, restaurants, and nightclubs, many of them national chains. Humbug Square—where street vendors and con artists flourished in the early 1900s—has a colorful street market with turn-of-the-century pushcarts and wagons displaying offbeat wares. Clustered around a section called **Kenny's Alley,** there are several restaurants and nightclubs. There's also a food court purveying everything from egg rolls to stuffed baked potatoes.

Markers throughout the complex indicate historic sites. Their origins are fascinating, so be sure to pick up an information sheet at the visitors booth and take your own self-guided tour. The **Atlanta Convention and Visitors Bureau** (☎ **404/222-6688**) operates its most comprehensive center at 65 Upper Alabama St. Open Monday to Saturday 10am to 6pm, and Sunday noon to 6pm, it includes displays and interactive exhibits depicting the city's rich history. There's also **AtlantTIX!,** a ticket booth where visitors can purchase day-of-show half-price tickets to theater, dance events, and other live performances throughout the metro area.

PARKS

Refer to section 1, "The Top Attractions," earlier in this chapter, for full details on Georgia's Stone Mountain Park.

Piedmont Park, the city's most popular and centrally located recreation area (with its main entrance on Piedmont Avenue at Fourteenth Street), was once a farm and a Civil War encampment. Its first public usage was by the elite Gentlemen's Driving Club, which bought the property as a site for horseback riding and racing. It soon became a venue for state fairs, culminating with the spectacular Cotton States and International Exposition of 1895. In 1904, the property's 180-plus acres of woodsy meadow and farm acreage were transformed into a city park with a varied terrain of rolling hillsides, verdant lawns, and lush forest around Lake Clara Meer.

Today, Piedmont Park is the setting for many popular regional attractions: jazz and symphony concerts, art and music festivals, marathons, etc. It contains two softball fields, two soccer fields, public tennis courts, a public swimming pool, and paths for jogging, skating, and cycling. The Atlanta Botanical Garden (see section 1, "The Top Attractions," above) is next door.

The park gets a lot of use, and in some spots it can be downright scruffy-looking, but the Piedmont Park Conservancy and the City of Atlanta continue to upgrade the park's landscaping. A visitors center, where you can find information on the park and the surrounding area, opened recently in the Boathouse Building at the Piedmont Avenue and Twelfth Street entrance. When you're in the center, check out the domed ceiling with its mural of park activities.

The park is closed to auto traffic, so it's a good spot to let the kids run around, throw a Frisbee, or have a picnic. The people-watching is superb, and the Midtown skyline beyond is magnificent. Don't let the kids miss PlayScape at the Twelfth Street entrance. Created by well-known sculptor Isamu Noguchi, it's a climbable series of brightly colored geometric shapes complete with ladders and slides.

Parking can be impossible, especially during special events, and authorities are quick to tow cars illegally parked. (All the activity in the park is a constant source of irritation to residents in surrounding neighborhoods.) It's easiest to take MARTA to the Arts Center station and walk the few blocks down 14th Street. During festivals it's usually possible to take a shuttle to and from the station.

A pleasant way to see the park is on an Atlanta Preservation Center **walking tour.** Tours depart at 10:30am from the Twelfth Street gate 1 day each month, April to October. Tours alternate between Saturday and Sunday, so call ☎ **404/876-2041** for the schedule and further details. Tour charges are $5 for adults, $4 for seniors, $3 for students.

Named for Confederate captain Lemuel P. Grant, who helped build Atlanta's defense line, **Grant Park** (bordered by Sydney Street and Atlanta Avenue, Boulevard and Cherokee avenues) still contains vestiges of his fortifications. Grant also donated its 100 acres to the city for a park on this site. Near the intersection of Boulevard and Atlanta avenues, you can see the remaining earthwork slopes of Fort Walker, a commanding artillery bastion with its original gun emplacements. Its cannons and caissons can be seen in the museum area of Cyclorama (see section 1, "The Top Attractions," above), one of Grant Park's two major attractions. The other is Zoo Atlanta (see "Especially for Kids," below). The park is open daily from 6am to 11pm; it's best to visit during daylight hours.

3 Especially for Kids

Though the following attractions are great choices if you're traveling with kids, don't pass them up if you're not. Especially worthwhile are the Center for Puppetry Arts, SciTrek, Wren's Nest, and Zoo Atlanta (visit in conjunction with Cyclorama and Oakland Cemetery). In addition, be sure to take the kids to the Fernbank Museum of Natural History and to the Birth Home of Martin Luther King, Jr., and Center for Nonviolent Social Change (all described above).

✪ Center for Puppetry Arts

1404 Spring St. NW (at Eighteenth St.). ☎ **404/873-3089,** box office 404/873-3391. www.puppet.org. E-mail: puppet@mindspring.com. Museum $5 adults; $4 children 13 and under, students, and seniors; or $2 if you see a show or take a workshop. Show prices $7.50 adults, $6.50 children 2–13, students, and seniors. Workshop $5; $2 when you see a show or visit the museum. Mon–Sat 9am–5pm. Closed New Year's Day, Memorial Day, July 4, Labor Day, Thanksgiving, and Christmas. Limited free parking. MARTA: Arts Center.

Don't miss this place if you're traveling with the kids. In fact, you might not want to miss it even without kids in tow. The center is dedicated to expanding public awareness of puppetry as a fine art and to presenting all its international and historic forms. Opened in 1978, with Kermit the Frog cutting the official ribbon (he had a little help from the late Jim Henson), it contains a 300-seat theater, two smaller theaters, gallery space, and a permanent museum. The puppet shows are marvelous—sophisticated, riveting, full-stage productions with elaborate scenery. Some are family oriented; others, with nighttime showings, are geared to adults. Call ahead to find out what's on; reservations are essential. You can also call a week or so in advance to enroll yourself or your kids in a puppet-making workshop.

In its permanent exhibit, "Puppets, The Power of Wonder," visitors can use joysticks to manipulate interactive puppets on their own. A video with the late Jim Henson as host provides an overview of puppetry and takes visitors around the world to meet masters of the art. There's also a huge display of puppets ranging from ritualistic African figures to Punch and Judy to Henson's Pigs in Space. It's an excellent collection, one of the largest in North America, and it includes turn-of-the-century Thai shadow puppets, Indonesian *wayang golek* puppets used to tell classic stories (a centuries-old tradition), Chinese hand puppets, rod-operated marionettes from all over Europe, original Muppets, pre-Colombian clay puppets that were used in religious ceremonies circa A.D. 1200, and Turkish shadow figures made of dried animal skins. Reservations are required for guided tours of "Puppets, The Power of Wonder"; the tour lasts about an hour. Another gallery features visiting exhibits from all over the world.

The gift shop is like no other, with oodles of marionettes, one-of-a-kind handmade puppets, masks, videos, and other related items.

Fernbank Science Center

156 Heaton Park Dr. NE (at Artwood Rd. off Ponce de Leon Ave.). ☎ **404/378-4311.** www.fernbank.edu. Admission free. Planetarium shows $2 adults, $1 students, free for senior citizens. Note: Children under 5 not admitted to the planetarium. Mon 8:30am–5pm, Tues–Fri 8:30am–10pm, Sat 10am–5pm, Sun 1–5pm. Planetarium shows at 8pm Tues–Fri and 3:30pm Wed and Fri–Sun. The Observatory open Thurs–Fri 8 (or whenever it gets dark)–10:30pm, weather permitting. Forest trails open Sun–Fri 2–5pm, Sat 10am–5pm. The Greenhouse open Sun only 1–5pm. Closed all school holidays.

Owned and funded by the DeKalb County School System, this museum/planetarium/observatory, located adjacent to the 65-acre Fernbank Forest, is an educational partner of the Fernbank Museum of Natural History (details above in "The Top Attractions"). Plan to visit the entire complex the same day. There's a 1½-mile forest trail here, with trees, shrubs, ferns, wildflowers, mosses, and other plants marked for identification, and an extensive rose garden next door to the museum.

The indoor facility houses museum exhibits such as a video display on geological phenomena (volcanoes, earthquakes, mountain formation); a gem collection; development of life in Georgia from 500 million years ago to a million years ago; a complete weather station; fossil trees; the original *Apollo 6* space capsule and space suit (on loan from the Smithsonian); computer games; a replica of the Okefenokee Swamp, complete with sound effects; and replicas of dinosaurs that roamed Atlanta in prehistoric times. There are planetarium shows, and, at the Observatory, which contains the largest telescope in the world dedicated to public education, an astronomer gives a talk and lets visitors use the telescope.

If you're here on a Sunday, allow time to visit the nearby **Greenhouse,** about 2½ miles from the center. A horticulturist gives a talk to visitors, and children can take a plant home. There are many workshops, lectures, tours, and films for adults and children on subjects ranging from nature photography to astronomy to weather forecasting.

✪ SciTrek (Science and Technology Museum of Atlanta)

395 Piedmont Ave. (between Ralph McGill Blvd. and Pine St.). ☎ **404/522-5500.** www.scitrek.org. Admission $7.50 adults; $5 seniors, students, and children 3–17; free for children under 3. Parking $4. Mon–Sat 10am–5pm, Sun noon–5pm. Closed Easter, Thanksgiving, Christmas, New Year's Day. MARTA: Civic Center.

This museum offers hands-on adventures for adults and kids in science and technology. It houses over 150 interactive exhibits.

Here you can create a magnetic field to hurl a disc upward, change light into electricity, produce electric current using your own hand as a "battery," see how much electricity you can generate pedaling a bicycle (How many bulbs can you light up?), and test various metals for electrical conductivity.

A kinetic light sculpture lets you vary frequency, intensity, and revolutions to create an infinite variety of designs. You can also examine the range of your peripheral vision, step inside a kaleidoscope, watch yourself on video while walking through a distorted room (demonstrating how the brain visually perceives things based on past experience), mix over 16 million colors (time permitting) on a computer, bend light beams, and look into infinity. An especially intriguing exhibit for kids of all ages is the frozen shadow room, in which you can "freeze" your shadow on a wall of light-sensitive phosphorous vinyl film; a bright flash causes the panel to glow except in the area your body shields from the light. It's lots of fun dancing and jumping to create shadow art on the wall.

KIDSPACE has simple exhibits geared to the 2- to 7-year-old set. Here the kids can paint their faces in a mirror, explore a crystal cave, squirt water to float toys downstream, play electronic instruments, make images on heat-sensitive liquid crystal with their hands, and use furnished play environments including an office, puppet theater, and a TV news/weather station. There are also very easy computer games. A new exhibit, "I Can Discover Nature," includes a huge (really) ant farm and an aquarium that demonstrates the river system in simple terms.

Pulleys, levers, wheels, axles, and such are explored in another area. You can lift billiard balls with a screw auger, become a human gyroscope, and suspend a ball in the air using a Bernoulli blower.

In Mathematica, a history wall portrays the achievements of major mathematicians from the 12th century to the present. Other hands-on displays here demonstrate various aspects of mathematics, from the laws of planetary motion to probability theory.

Exhibits are supplemented by an ongoing series of lectures, demonstrations, workshops, and temporary shows. You can take some science home with you from the Science Store, which has a wonderful array of games, books, and activities. There's no snack bar on the premises, unless you count the vending area, but you can take your lunch and park it in a locker for a nominal fee until you finish the exhibits. There's a picnic area inside.

Six Flags Over Georgia

7561 Six Flags Pkwy. SW (at the Six Flags exit off I-20W), Austell, GA. ☎ **770/948-9290.** www.sixflags.com. Admission $35 adults, $25 for children ages 3–9 and for seniors (55 and over), under 3 free. A 2-day adult pass $41, 2-day child/senior pass $31. A nominal fee ($3–$6) is charged for amphitheater concerts. Weekends only Mar to mid-May, Sept, and Oct; daily Memorial Day–Labor Day. Gates open 10am daily; closing hours vary. Pet kennels are available on a first-come, first-served basis for $2. Parking $6.

One of the state's major family attractions, Six Flags offers a great day's entertainment. Arrive early (at least 30 minutes before opening), note where you've parked in the vast lot, and take 10 minutes or so to plan out your show and ride schedule.

The park's 10 themed areas reflect the historical heritage of the region, both Southern (Cotton States, Confederate, Georgia, Lickskillet, and Promenade) and European (France, Britain, Spain, and U.S.A.). The Promenade section, which showcases the heritage and charm of the South, includes a variety of dining and retail options, including a gazebo where guests can meet Bugs Bunny. The wascally wabbit is just one of many costumed Looney Tune characters (Sylvester, Daffy Duck, and others) that roam the park greeting kids. Bugs even has a signature restaurant, The Carrot Club, where Warner Brothers cartoons are aired on a video wall and Looney Tunes characters make appearances.

Thrill rides include several wet ones such as Ragin' Rivers (two-person inflatable boats that careen down contoured water channels), a log flume, and Thunder River (a simulated whitewater rafting adventure). White-knuckle coasters include The Viper (which goes from 0 to 60 mph in less than 6 seconds and has a 360-degree loop), Ninja (the "black belt" of roller coasters that turns riders upside down five times and offers thrilling loops, dives, and corkscrew turns), the Georgia Cyclone (a classic wooden roller coaster with 11 dramatic drops, patterned after Coney Island's), the Great American Scream Machine (another classic wooden coaster), and Mind Bender, a triple-looper. Other highlights are the Batman, The Ride, Great Gasp (a 20-story parachute jump), Splashwater Falls (plummet down a soaring 50-foot waterfall), and Free Fall (ever wonder what it would be like to fall off a 10-story building?). A less dizzying adventure is Monster Plantation, a

Impressions

Joel Chandler Harris, former owner of Wren's Nest, died at the age of 62 on July 3, 1908. He wrote these words, which later appeared on his gravestone:

I seem to see before me the smiling faces of thousands of children—some young and fresh—and some wearing the friendly marks of age, but all children at heart, and not an unfriendly face among them. And while I am trying hard to speak the right word, I seem to hear a voice lifted above the rest saying, "You have made some of us happy." And so I feel my heart fluttering and my lips trembling and I have to bow silently and turn away and hurry into the obscurity that fits me best.

Disneyesque boat ride through an antebellum mansion haunted by over 100 animated monsters. There's much, much more.

Shows vary from year to year, but they usually include a major musical revue, a country music show, a golden-oldies show, thrill cinema adventures on a 180-degree screen, a Don Rickles–style comic (much modified, of course) in the form of a sharp-tongued bird named Buford Buzzard, a Batman stunt spectacular show, and an animated character show. In addition, headliners such as Ray Charles, Tanya Tucker, Willie Nelson, Pam Tillis, and Tracy Lawrence play the 8,072-seat (with lawn seating for 4,000) Southern Star Amphitheatre.

There are restaurants and snack bars throughout the park, though you might consider bringing a picnic.

White Water

250 N. Cobb Pkwy NE (Exit 113 off I-75), Marietta, GA. ☎ **770/424-9283.** www.whitewaterpark.com. Admission $21.99 adults; $12.99 children from age 3 and up to 48 inches tall; children under 3 and senior citizens free. Weekends only in May, daily Memorial Day–late summer and Labor Day weekend 10am–late evening (closing hours vary). Closed mid-Sept–Apr.

Forty acres of wet, splashy fun await you at White Water, one of the largest water-theme parks in the south. Its star attraction is the $1-million Tree House Island, a four-story fantasy treehouse with over 100 different activities—curvy slides, net bridges, water cannons, chutes, etc. A giant 1,000-gallon bucket of water empties over the whole attraction every few minutes. Other park highlights include: Cliffhanger, a 990-foot freefall, one of the tallest such attractions in the world; the 735-foot Run-A-Way River, an enclosed tunnel raft ride; the "Atlanta Ocean," a 750,000-gallon wave pool; and a host of different slide and splash experiences. There's much more, including a special section for children 48 inches and under called Little Squirt's Island, offering 25 tot-size water attractions. Captain Kid's Cove, adjacent to it, has dozens of additional activities for kids 12 and under. Restaurants and snack bars are on the premises, as are rental lockers and shower facilities. Swimsuits are essential.

Next to White Water is **American Adventures** (☎ **770/424-9283**), an indoor/outdoor family amusement park featuring 15 children's rides in Fun Forest (bumper cars, a small roller coaster, a tilt-a-whirl, and others); a classic carousel; a penny arcade with over 130 games; Professor Plinker's Laboratory—a large children's play area with ball crawls and nets to climb; 18-hole miniature golf; and the Foam Factory, a huge, multilevel interactive play area featuring scads of foam ball activities. It's all geared to children 12 and under. A 180-seat family-style restaurant is on the grounds. Admission to American Adventures is $13.99 for children 4 to 17, $4.99 for children 3 and under. Adults pay $2.99 There's a separate charge for laser tag. To visit just the Foam Factory, admission is $2.99 for parents, $4.99 for children 3 and under, $7.99 for children 4 to 17. The park is open year-round; hours vary seasonally.

Wren's Nest

1050 Ralph David Abernathy Blvd. (2 blocks from Ashby St.). ☎ **404/753-7735.** Admission $6 adults, $4 seniors and students 13–19, $3 children 4–12, under 4 free; storytelling $2 per person additional. Tues–Sat 10am–4pm, Sun 1–4pm, with tours departing every 30 minutes on the hour and half hour. Closed on major holidays. Take I-20 West to Ashby St., turn left on Ashby, then right on Ralph David Abernathy Blvd.; Wren's Nest is 2 long blocks down on the left. MARTA bus: no. 71 from West End rail station.

Named for a family of wrens that once nested in the mailbox, Wren's Nest is the former home of Joel Chandler Harris, who chronicled the wily deeds of Br'er Rabbit and Br'er Fox. It's been open to the public since 1913, when his widow sold it to the Uncle Remus Memorial Association.

Harris's literary career began at the age of 13, when he apprenticed on the *Countryman,* a quarterly plantation newspaper. In four years spent learning journalism there, young Harris spent many an evening hanging about the slave quarters, drinking in African folk tales and fables spun by George Terrell, a plantation patriarch who became the prototype for Uncle Remus. Sherman's army put the *Countryman* out of business, and Harris went on to other newspapers, working his way up to editorial writer at the *Atlanta Journal-Constitution* by age 28. There, plagued by writer's block one gloomy winter afternoon, he remembered the plantation stories of his youth and evoked Uncle Remus to fill his column. Enthralled readers clamored for more, and the rest is history.

The house itself is an 1870s farmhouse with a Queen Anne–style Victorian facade added in 1884. Harris lived here from 1881 until his death in 1908, doing most of his writing in a rocking chair on the wraparound front porch. On a 30-minute tour, including a slide presentation about Harris's life, you'll see much Uncle Remus memorabilia. The stuffed great horned owl over the study door was a gift from Theodore Roosevelt, whose White House Harris visited; the original wren's nest mailbox reposes on the study mantel; and all of Harris's books, along with signed first editions of major authors of his day (Mark Twain and others) are displayed in a bookcase.

The house is interesting, but the best part is the **storytelling.** Call ahead to find out when storyteller-in-residence Akbar Imhotep will be telling stories culled from African and African-American folklore; it's a real treat. Mid-June through mid-August, Akbar and storytellers perform daily at 11:30am and 12:30 and 1:30pm. There are other storytelling programs year-round; call for details.

Yellow River Wildlife Game Ranch

4525 Hwy. 78, Lilburn, GA. ☎ **770/972-6643.** Admission $6 adults, $5 children 3–11, 1 child under 3 admitted free. Memorial Day–Labor Day daily 9:30am–dusk; until 6pm the rest of the year. Closed Thanksgiving and Christmas. Take I-85N to I-285E. Exit to State Hwy. 78 (30B), and follow it east for 10 miles.

This 24-acre animal preserve bordering the Yellow River offers close encounters of the four-legged kind—a chance to view, pet, feed, and generally mingle with some 600 animals (always including quite a few babies) living in open enclosures, or right out in the open, along a 1-mile oak- and hickory-shaded forest trail. Owner Art Rilling knows every animal on the ranch by name and can give you chapter and verse on each one's personality, preferences, and in some cases, romantic history. You'll feel like you're in a Disney movie when the deer (there are over 100 white-tailed deer) sidle up and nuzzle you. The animals know they're among friends here and are highly socialized, so you have a unique chance to study them up close. Inhabitants include donkeys named Rhett and Scarlett, Georgia black bears that stand up and beg for marshmallows, the goats at Billy Goat Gruff Memorial Bridge (they climb it to get food at the top), dozens of rabbits in Bunny Burrows (kids can walk right into this enclosure and pet the bunnies), a wide assortment of interesting-looking chickens, a herd of buffalo, sheep, burros, ponies, a skunk named General Sherman (we are in Atlanta, after all), and a groundhog named General Beauregard Lee who lives in a white colonnaded Southern mansion complete with miniature satellite dish. As if that's not enough, there will soon be a beaver exhibit. You can get animal food in the gift shop at the entrance or buy it along the trail.

Bring your camera and consider packing a picnic lunch; there are tables throughout the property, and one especially nice picnic area overlooks the river. An exciting time to visit is Sheep-Shearing Saturday in mid-May; in the fall there are after-hours "wilderness hayrides."

Zoo Atlanta

800 Cherokee Ave. (in Grant Park). ☎ **404/624-5600.** www.zooatlanta.org. Admission $9 adults, $6.50 seniors, $5.50 children 3–11, children 2 and under free. Strollers can be rented. Daily 9:30am–4:30pm, until 5:30pm on weekends during daylight saving time. The admission booth closes an hour before zoo closing. Closed New Year's Day, Thanksgiving, Christmas. Free parking. Take I-75 south to I-20 east. Get off at the Boulevard exit and follow the signs to Grant Park; or take a no. 105 bus from the West End rail station.

This delightful 40-acre zoo dates from 1889, when George W. Hall (a.k.a. "Popcorn George") brought his traveling circus to town. Employee claims against Hall for back wages forced him to relinquish his menagerie, and the animal entourage was purchased by a prominent Atlanta businessman who donated the collection to the city as the basis for a zoological garden in Grant Park. It's grown considerably since then, but the real turnaround came in 1985, when the zoo began a still-ongoing multimillion-dollar renovation.

Today, Zoo Atlanta is an innovative and creatively run facility, with animals housed in large open enclosures that simulate their natural geographical habitats. The zoo participates in breeding programs, many of them focusing on endangered species, and is home to many of those animals, including: Sumatran orangutans, 19 western lowland gorillas, two black rhinos, three African elephants, two Komodo monitors, and big-mouthed African dwarf crocodiles.

Flamingo Plaza is the first habitat you'll see when you enter the zoo. Farther on, Mzima Springs and Masai Mara house elephants, rhinos, lions, zebras, giraffes, gazelles, and other African animals and birds. The landscape resembles the plains of East Africa, with honey locust trees and yuccas; and the lion enclosure replicates an East African *kopje* (rocky outcropping). Frequent animal demonstrations, African storytelling, and educational programs take place under the Elder's Tree in Masai Mara.

The lushly landscaped Ford African Rain Forest—one of the most popular sections—centers on four vast gorilla habitats separated by moats. Studies on gorilla behavior take place here, and there are usually quite a few adorable babies. They're hard to spot sometimes, so be sure to ask if there are any to be seen. The zoo's mascot, Willie B. (named for former Atlanta mayor William B. Hartsfield), and his daughters Kudzoo and Olympia live in the forest and usually put on a pretty good show. Kudzoo is often seen practicing her mother skills by carrying her little sister on her back. A good time to visit is around 2pm, when the gorillas are fed. Also in the section: a walk-through aviary of West African birds, small African primates, and the Gorillas of Cameroon Museum. Landscaping includes burned-out areas of forest and deadfall trees—gorillas do not live in manicured gardens.

In the Ketambe section, three families of high-climbing orangutans show off their skills among the trees and bamboo clusters of an Indonesian tropical rain forest. If you're lucky enough to be there at feeding time—around 2:30pm—you might see them swinging on ropes from tree to tree. In the Sumatran Tiger Forest, rare Sumatran tigers prowl a lush forest, sometimes dipping into a stream or water-fall. Nearby is a superb Reptile House—the zoo is home to one of the finest reptile collections in the country—and a special exhibit area, often used to house visiting animals.

Plan to catch entertaining and informative free animal shows in the Wildlife Theater, presented daily at 11:30am and 1:30 and 3:30pm, May through September. Ditto the African Elephant Demonstration given daily year-round at 11am and 2pm.

A new zoo train travels through the Children's Zoo area, where you'll find a playground and petting zoo where kids can get friendly with llamas, sheep, pot-bellied pigs, and goats. There are aviaries here, too.

There are snack bars (including a McDonald's) throughout the zoo. Or you can picnic in tree-shaded areas in Grant Park. At the Zoo Atlanta Trading Company, which features zoo memorabilia and gifts, you can pick up a watercolor painted by Starlet O'Hara, one of the zoo's African elephants. Don't laugh; some of her works have fetched as much as $1,800.

4 Special-Interest Tours

The **Atlanta Preservation Center,** a private, nonprofit organization headquartered at 156 Seventh St. NE, Suite 3 (☎ **404/876-2040**), offers ten 1½- to 2-hour guided walking tours in the city. Cost of each tour is $5 for adults, $4 for seniors, $3 for students, free for children under 5. Tours of the Fox Theatre District are given year-round; the remaining tours are offered as noted. Call for days, hours, and tour departure points.

During the **Fox Theatre District Tour** you'll explore in depth this restored 1920s Moorish movie palace, a theater whose auditorium resembles the courtyard of a Cairo mosque and whose architecture and interior were influenced by the discoveries at King Tut's tomb. The tour also includes turn-of-the-century buildings in the area.

The **Historic Downtown Tour** (March–November) is an architectural survey of Atlanta's downtown from Victorian buildings to modern high-rises. You'll learn about the architects, the businesspeople, and the prominent families who created the city's early commercial center. It includes six historic interiors.

The **Inman Park Tour** (March–November) visits Atlanta's first trolley suburb, where you'll see preserved and restored Victorian mansions (exterior views only). Highlights include the homes of Coca-Cola magnates Asa Candler and Ernest Woodruff.

The **Historic Underground/Birth of Atlanta Tour** (March–November) explores the city's historic hub—today a complex of shops, restaurants, and night-clubs. It also includes information on the state Capitol, City Hall, and three inner-city churches with pre-Civil War roots.

The **Sweet Auburn/MLK District Tour** (March–November) focuses on the area that 20th-century African-American entrepreneurs developed into a prosperous commercial hub. You'll also visit the boyhood home of Martin Luther King, Jr., as well as the church where he preached.

Run the Peachtree

The Peachtree Road Race is more than just the world's largest 10K road race. It's a social event in Atlanta, as thousands of spectators line Peachtree Street, Atlanta's main drag, to cheer the runners.

If you're lucky enough to be in town on July 4th, you can do the same. Pack a breakfast and station yourself just about anyplace along Peachtree from Lenox Square to Fourteenth Street. Or go straight to the finish in Piedmont Park and take part in the chaos of the finale. Be sure to arrive early. The wheelchair division of the race begins at 7am, and the official footrace begins at 7:30am. Peachtree is closed to traffic that morning, and you'll have difficulty crossing the street—even on foot—after 7am.

The race is quite a sight to behold, as 55,000 runners surge down Peachtree, a far cry from the 110 runners who gathered to run the first race July 4, 1970. (The only spectators then were a few surprised pedestrians walking their dogs.) The race is so large now that it takes 500 volunteers to coordinate the start, and 50 minutes for the final group to pass the starting line. By then, the winner has already covered the 6.2-mile distance and rested for a at least a quarter of an hour.

Don't even think about entering the race at the last minute. Many more applicants than can be accommodated vie for the available spots, and the event always closes out in a few days. You can, however, run the course other days of the year. There are sidewalks all the way down Peachtree, so it's a fairly safe course. Here's the route you should follow:

Start at the corner of Peachtree and Lenox roads, right across from Lenox Square. Proceed down Peachtree through Buckhead. Along the way you'll pass by some of Atlanta's most elegant neighborhoods, and just after West Wesley Road you'll have a magnificent view of the downtown skyline. Don't let the easy, downward trend of the first few miles fool you. This is a tough run, and just about halfway through the course there's a fairly steep incline—appropriately dubbed Heartbreak (or Heart Attack) Hill. (Fortunately, the top of the hill is right in front of Piedmont Hospital.) In Midtown, turn left at fourteenth Street and proceed through the entrance to Piedmont Park. Once inside the park, turn to the left and follow the pavement around a small lake and toward Park Drive, which is approximately at the 6-mile mark. Continue on another two-tenths of a mile, and you've completed the course. The finish will be marked by peaches painted on the pavement. To return to Lenox Square, backtrack to the Arts Center station and take MARTA back to the Buckhead or Lenox station.

For more information, call the Atlanta Track Club at ☎ **404/231-9064.**

Walking Miss Daisy's Druid Hills (March–October) explores the neighborhood that was the setting for the play and film *Driving Miss Daisy.* The gracious parklike area was laid out by noted landscapist Frederick Law Olmsted and contains many architecturally important homes.

West End, Hammonds House, and Wren's Nest Tour (March–November) focuses on the home of Joel Chandler Harris (author of the Uncle Remus stories) and Hammonds House (a museum of African-American and Haitian art), while also noting Victorian homes and churches in the West End area, Atlanta's oldest neighborhood.

The **Ansley Park Tour** (March–November) explores one of Atlanta's first garden suburbs (today a charming Midtown neighborhood), partly designed by Frederick

Law Olmsted. Its broad lawns, majestic trees, parks, and beautiful houses make for a lovely tour. It's easy to get lost in Ansley Park, so if you want to explore the area, this tour is a good idea.

The **Piedmont Park Tour** (March–October) focuses on the history of this central Atlanta park. In previous incarnations, it was a farm, a Civil War encampment, a driving club, and the grounds for the 1895 Cotton States and International Exposition.

The **Atlanta University Center Tour** focuses on the Vine City area, home to the largest concentration of African-American colleges in the United States, including Spelman, Morehouse, Morris Brown, and Clark Atlanta University. This area was the birthplace of many civil rights leaders—Julian Bond and Hosea Williams, among others. You'll also tour the home of Alonzo Herndon, a former slave who founded the Atlanta Life Insurance Co.

5 Outdoor Pursuits

See also section 1, "The Top Attractions," earlier in this chapter, for a full description of **Georgia's Stone Mountain Park,** one of the best places in the region for all kinds of outdoor activities: picnicking, boating (rowboats, canoes, and sailboats), biking (rentals are available), fishing, hiking, golf, tennis, and swimming. Admission to the park (which includes parking) is $6 per car per day; an annual pass is $25.

FISHING

There's good trout fishing on the Chattahoochee River, in the North Georgia Mountains, about 1½ hours from downtown. Many lakes in the area are good for bass and striper, including **Lake Lanier,** a 38,000-acre reservoir about 45 minutes away. Fishing licenses, which can be bought at most sporting-goods stores, are $3.50 for 1 day, $7 for 7 days, and $24 for a season. A trout-fishing stamp, valid for 1 year, is $13.

The **Fish Hawk,** 279 Buckhead Ave. NE, between Peachtree and Piedmont roads (☎ 404/237-3473), is an excellent and convenient supplier in Atlanta for quality tackle. It carries all kinds of fishing gear and outdoor clothing and can also supply the requisite license. The staff is extremely knowledgeable and can tell you where to find the fish you seek and anything you need to know about applicable state regulations. They're open Monday through Friday from 9am to 6pm, Saturday from 9am to 5pm.

For additional information, serious anglers can write or call the **Georgia Department of Natural Resources,** Wildlife Resources Division, 2123 U.S. Hwy. 278 SE, Social Circle, GA 30025 (☎ 770/918-6406).

GOLF

Georgia's Stone Mountain Park Golf Course (☎ 770/498-5715) is nationally ranked. Robert Trent Jones designed 18 of the 36 holes. It's a beautiful facility, some parts of it adjacent to the park's lake. A pro shop is on the premises, and lessons are available. For weekends and holidays, reserve the Tuesday prior to the day you want to play; other times, reserve a week in advance. A restaurant/clubhouse has a large deck overlooking the lake. Greens fees, which include a cart, are $45 Monday through Thursday, $48 Friday through Sunday. There is a fee of $6 per car to enter the park. The course is open Monday to Friday from 8am to dark, from 7am until dark weekends and holidays.

IN-LINE SKATING

Piedmont Park is the place. **Skate Escape,** 1086 Piedmont Ave. NE, at Twelfth Street (☎ **404/892-1292**), is located close by. It offers all kinds of bicycles and skates for rent or sale, as well as helmets, bicycle locks, and accessories. You can also buy skateboards here. Conventional or in-line skates can be rented for $5 per hour, $20 per day; it's $5 per hour for a single-speed or children's bike. If you have an out-of-state driver's license, a major credit card is required for ID; or you can leave a deposit of $100 for skates, $200 for bikes. Skate Escape is open every day 10am to 7pm, and the folks here will give you good advice about routes through the park. MARTA: Midtown.

NATURE WALKS & SCENIC STROLLS

In addition to city strolls, Atlanta offers many wonderful places for quiet nature walks and easy day hikes.

The **Atlanta History Center,** 130 W. Paces Ferry Rd. (☎ **404/814-4000**), described fully in section 1 of this chapter, stands on 32 woodland acres and offers self-guided walking trails and five gardens. You'll discover many plants native to the region along the forested mile-long Swan Woods Trail.

The **Chattahoochee River National Recreation Area** is a series of "units" or parklands that punctuate the 48 miles along the Chattahoochee River—from Buford Dam at Lake Lanier north of the city to Paces Mill at Vinings just outside Atlanta's northwestern limits. Along the way are trails that range from flat, easy walks, to more strenuous ridge and valley hikes. It's an excellent way to enjoy some of the unspoiled parts of the scenic Chattahoochee River. For maps and more information, contact the **National Park Service** (☎ 770/399-8070 or www.nps.gov.chat).

Georgia's Stone Mountain Park, 16 miles east of downtown on U.S. 78, is also covered in section 1 of this chapter. It offers thousands of acres of beautiful wooded parkland and lakes. There's a walking trail that goes up and down the moss-covered slopes of the mountain; you'll be delighted by the wildflowers that bloom here each spring. There are also 20 acres of wildlife trails in the park with natural animal habitats and a petting zoo, as well as more challenging hiking trails.

There are 16 miles of extensive hiking trails at **Kennesaw Mountain/National Battlefield Park,** Old Highway 41 and Stilesboro Road, Kennesaw (☎ 770/427-4686). The scenery is beautiful, and trail maps are available at the visitors center. See section 2.

Piedmont Park, centrally located with its main entrance on Piedmont Avenue at Fourteenth Street, offers a glorious setting for strolls, jogging, and biking. The wonderful **Atlanta Botanical Garden** is next door. See section 2 of this chapter for a full description of the park, section 1 for coverage of the botanical garden.

Château Élan, 30 miles north of Atlanta at Exit 48 off I-85 in Braselton (☎ 770/932-0900), has nature trails along St. Emilion Creek (forested with tulip poplar, oak, hickory, and beech trees) and by Romanée–Conti Pond. And there are picnic areas on the lovely grounds; custom picnics can be purchased at Café Élan. See section 2 of this chapter for a complete description of its other attractions.

Also described in section 3 is the **Fernbank Science Center,** 156 Heaton Park Dr. NE (☎ **404/378-4311**), which has a 1½-mile nature trail with trees, wildflowers, and plants labeled for identification. This unspoiled natural environment is home to many animals and birds, and a small pond teems with aquatic life.

The nonprofit **PATH Foundation** (☎ 404/355-6438), which is dedicated to creating and maintaining a network of trails in metro Atlanta for pedestrians and bicycles, has so far completed 18 miles of greenway trails. The most accessible is around **Chastain Park** in the northern part of the city. It's an easy, paved 2.6-mile loop around the rolling hills of the park and golf course. The **Atlanta-Stone Mountain trail,** which goes from the Carter Center to Stone Mountain Park, is another popular trek. Maps are available at most bicycle and sporting good stores. Call the above phone number for more information and advice about where to begin your journey.

RIVER RAFTING/CANOEING/KAYAKING

The **Nantahala Outdoor Center** (☎ 800/232-7238) offers white-water rafting adventures on the scenic Chattooga River in North Georgia (it's the one you saw in the movie *Deliverance*) and the Ocoee in Tennessee (which was an Olympic venue). Put-in points for both rivers are about a 2-hour drive from Atlanta. Trips vary in length (from a few hours to a few days) and difficulty.

The Chattooga offers Class II and III rapids in Section III and Class III, IV, and V in Section IV. The roller-coaster Ocoee has Class III and IV rapids only. Kids must be at least 10 for easy trips, 12 or 13 for more difficult rapids. The company also offers canoeing and kayaking, and trips of varying difficulty on other rivers. All of the expeditions are immensely popular, so make reservations as far in advance as possible.

Prices vary depending on length and difficulty of the trip. Weekends are more expensive than weekdays. Half-day trips begin at about $35, full-day trips at about $62; both rates include equipment, a guide, and transportation from the outpost to the river. Rafting season is April 1 to October 31, with occasional trips in March and November.

The **Chattahoochee National Recreation Area** (see "Nature Walks & Scenic Strolls," above) has several spots where canoers, kayakers, and rafters have access to the cold, slow-moving Chattahoochee River. Call the **National Park Service** (☎ 770/399-8070) for more information. Watercraft can be rented from the **Chattahoochee Outdoor Center** (☎ 770/395-6851) at the Johnson Ferry and Powers Island units in the recreation area.

SWIMMING

Almost every Atlanta hotel features a swimming pool. In addition, there is a sandy lakefront beach (complete with water slides) in Stone Mountain Park.

If you're *really* serious about getting wet, there's also **White Water,** Exit 113 off I-75 on North Cobb Parkway, in Marietta (☎ 770/424-9283), a water theme park described in detail in section 3, "Especially for Kids," of this chapter.

TENNIS

The City of Atlanta Parks and Recreation Department operates 12 outdoor hard courts at **Piedmont Park,** all of them lighted for night play (☎ 404/853-3461). No reservations are taken; it's first-come, first-served. There's free parking at the courts, and showers, lockers, and a pro shop are on the premises. Hours are weekdays from 10am to 9pm, Saturday and Sunday from 9am to 6pm. Fees are $1.50 per person per hour during the day, $1.75 per person per hour when courts are lighted.

The city also has 13 outdoor clay courts and 10 outdoor hard courts (16 are lighted) at the **Bitsy Grant Tennis Center,** 2125 Northside Dr., between I-75N and Peachtree Battle Avenue (☎ 404/609-7193). Courts are available on a first-come, first-served basis. No reservations. There are showers, lockers, and a pro shop on the premises. The courts are open Monday to Friday from 9am to 9pm, Saturday and Sunday from 9am to 6pm. It's $2.50 per person per hour for clay courts, $1.50

per person per hour for hard courts. Rates go up 25¢ after 6pm when the lights come on. There's a lot of team tennis played here; call ahead to check court availability. For information about other city courts, call the **Bureau of Recreation** (☎ **404/817-6766**).

The **International Tennis Center,** 5525 Bermuda Rd., Stone Mountain, GA 30087 (☎ **770/469-0108**), was built as the tennis venue for the Centennial Olympic Games and has some of the finest public courts in the state. There are 15 lighted hard-surface courts, located near Georgia's Stone Mountain Park, 18 miles east of downtown. Hours are daily 9am to 10pm. Cost is $3 per person per hour. Take U.S. 78 to Bermuda Road, one exit past the entrance of Stone Mountain Park.

6 Spectator Sports

Atlanta has four professional major league teams: the Braves, the Hawks, the Falcons, and the Thrashers (a new NHL team). Good tickets can be extremely hard to come by during a winning season. Tickets can be obtained from the individual teams, or you can charge tickets by phone by calling **TicketMaster** (☎ **800/ 326-4000** or 404/249-6400), but a fee will be added to each ticket.

AUTO RACING

Situated on 700 scenic wooded acres about 45 minutes north of downtown Atlanta, **Road Atlanta** is one of the Southeast's premier road-racing motor-sports facilities. Its 2.5-mile Grand Prix racecourse offers a challenging combination of turns, elevation changes, and high-speed straightaways. A year-round season includes sports car, motorcycle, truck, and vintage/historic racing, among others. Call ☎ **800/ 849-RACE** or 770/967-6143, or visit the Web site at www.roadatlanta.com, for information and a schedule of events. Tickets usually run $10 to $55, with higher prices for the Petit Le Mans, a 1,000-mile race.

Road Atlanta is located in Braselton on Georgia Highway 53 between I-85 and I-985 (take I-85N to Exit 49, make a left, and follow the signs). If you're attending an event, you can rent a campsite for $5 a night; during special events campsite prices can range up to $50. If you prefer a room to a tent, try The Lodge, a new limited-service hotel owned by Château Élan, a nearby resort. Prices are $65 to $105 double. Call **800/329-7466** or 770/867-8100 for information.

BASEBALL

The **Atlanta Braves** are perpetual playoff contenders. With one of the best pitching rotations ever assembled in baseball, they've been "the team of the '90s," consistently posting a terrific record, though they've only won the Series once in recent memory, in 1995. In 1997 the team moved to **Turner Field,** a new stadium that had been built to host the Centennial Olympic Games and was later modified to become a world-class ballpark. (See "Stadiums" below for details.) The regular season runs from the first week of April until the first week of October; post-season play is over by the end of October.

Advance-purchase seats run from $5 (Upper Pavilion) to $25 (Club Level), and ticket availability is inversely proportional to the team's success. Call customer service (☎ **404/522-7630**) for more information, or visit the Web site at www.atlantabraves.com. You can charge by phone through TicketMaster or buy directly from the stadium box office, which is located at the northwest corner of the ballpark. It's open 8:30am to 6pm Monday through Friday, 9am to 5pm Saturday, and 1pm to 5pm Sunday. Even if you can't get tickets in advance, it's sometimes possible to get $1 Skyline tickets (bleacher seats) and $5 standing-room-only tickets. Skyline tickets are available only on game day and go on sale 3 hours before game time. Fans are limited to one ticket per customer, and immediate entry to the ballpark is required. Standing-room-only tickets are sold on game day only and are available 1 hour before the first pitch, but only when all other tickets for the game have been sold. Check the designated ticket window in the main ticket area.

BASKETBALL

The **Atlanta Hawks** are the local NBA franchise, and their season runs from November to April. The Hawks, who used to play in the recently demolished Omni Coliseum, will play in the Georgia Dome and the Alexander Memorial Coliseum on the Georgia Tech campus through April 1999. In November 1999, they're scheduled to move into a new arena, which is being built downtown on the site of the old Omni, adjacent to CNN Center. Tickets range from $10 for a nosebleed seat in the rafters to $45 for something up close and personal. Call ☎ **404/827-3865** for information.

On the college front, the **Georgia Tech Yellow Jackets** play in the highly competitive ACC. The season runs from mid-November through early March. Their home games are played in Alexander Memorial Coliseum, on campus at Tenth and Fowler streets (see "Stadiums," below, for details). Tickets are usually $18, but they are difficult to come by. Available tickets go on sale at the Coliseum the day of the game. Call ☎ **404/894-5400** for information.

FOOTBALL

Vastly improved in the 1998–99 season, the **Atlanta Falcons** are the city's NFL franchise, playing eight games (plus exhibition games) each season in the Georgia Dome (see "Stadiums," below, for details). Watching a game in the Dome is an interesting, noisy experience. The regular season begins in September and runs through December, with post-season games played in January. Pre-season games begin in August. Ticket prices are $20–$36. Call ☎ **404/223-8000** for information.

As for college football, the "Ramblin' Wrecks from Georgia Tech" have played their home games at 43,000-seat Bobby Dodd Stadium/Grant Field, on campus at North Avenue and Techwood Drive (MARTA: North Avenue) since 1913. The season runs from September through November. Call ☎ **404/894-5447** for information. Tickets run $22 and are usually available. Games are played on Thursday nights and Saturday afternoons. Parking is limited; MARTA is the best option. Go early and stop at the Varsity for a hamburger or a hot dog; it's on North Avenue between the MARTA station and the stadium.

HOCKEY

The **Atlanta Thrashers,** a new NHL team, take to the ice in October 1999 at the new arena being built downtown on the site of the old Omni Coliseum. The season extends through May, and tickets run from $24 to $70. Call ☎ **404/584-PUCK** for information.

STADIUMS

Atlanta Arena
100 Techwood Dr. NW. (at Marietta St.). ☎ **404/681-2100.** MARTA: Omni.

The Omni Coliseum was razed in 1997 to make way for a new arena, to be the home of the Atlanta Hawks and the Atlanta Thrashers (see above). The arena, unnamed at press time, is being called the Atlanta Arena for the time being. It is scheduled to be completed in the fall of 1999.

Georgia Dome

1 Georgia Dome Dr. (at International Blvd. and Northside Dr.). ☎ **404/223-9200** for information. MARTA: Omni/GWCC/Georgia Dome.

Atlanta's $214-million, 71,500-seat domed mega-stadium, which hosted Super Bowl XXVIII in 1994 and several Olympic events in 1996, is also the home of the Atlanta Falcons. Its oval shape provides a good view of stadium action from every seat. It is the site of the annual Peach Bowl each January, and will host Super Bowl XXXIV in 2000 and the NCAA Men's Basketball Final Four in 2002. The Dome also hosts tennis matches, tractor pulls, college basketball, track and field events, and Supercross events. Check the papers or call the above number to find out what's on during your stay. Parking is extremely limited and expensive; take MARTA and walk to the Dome.

Forty-five-minute tours of the Georgia Dome (including the visitors' locker and dressing rooms, press box, executive suites, sports lounge, and other areas of interest) are offered on the hour Wednesday to Friday between 10am and 4pm. Call ☎ **404/223-8687** for reservations and details. Adults pay $4; seniors, students, and children 3 to 12 pay $3. Tours, which are not recommended for children under 3, are sometimes postponed or cancelled when events are taking place.

Turner Field

755 Hank Aaron Dr. SW. ☎ **404/522-7630.** Parking $7, but extremely limited, in official lots. Handicapped parking is in the South lot, east of I-75/85 on a first-come, first-served basis. MARTA: Park free at a MARTA rail station, ride the train ($1.50) and then take the free shuttle from the Five Points station to the stadium. Shuttle service begins 90 minutes before game time and continues until the ballpark is empty; or take MARTA to the Georgia State University station and walk several blocks to the stadium. Call MARTA at ☎ **404/848-4711** for more information.

This spectacular 50,000-seat ballpark started life as an 80,000-seat stadium built to host the Centennial Olympic Games in 1996. It was the site of the opening and closing ceremonies and numerous track and field events. After the Olympics, the north end of the stadium (with approximately 35,000 seats) was demolished and the stadium was modified to accommodate baseball. It's built in the style of old-time ballparks, but also includes a number of attractions besides the baseball game itself. The folks who run the stadium like to call it a baseball theme park, and it's not a bad idea to come to the game early and take in the various attractions, especially if you have children along. They include:

- **Braves Museum and Hall of Fame,** which features memorabilia commemorating legends and key moments in Braves history. (Take a gander at the bat Hank Aaron used to hit his 715th home run.) The museum is open to ticket holders on game days 3 hours before game time and 1 hour after the completion of the game.
- **Scouts Alley,** designed to teach fans about the fine art of scouting. Fans can also test their hitting and throwing skills, call up scouting reports on former and current Braves, play a trivia game, call a play-by-play inning of a game, learn about Hank Aaron's "hot" spot, and much more.
- **The Cartoon Network's Tooner Field,** where the kids can hang out with Cartoon Network characters or play interactive games in the Digital Dugout.
- **The East Pavilion,** where fans can have their images inserted into a baseball card or a great moment in Braves history.

- **The West Pavilion,** where fans can nosh on famous food items from other ballparks.
- **The Braves Chop House,** a casual dining restaurant that overlooks the Braves' bullpen.
- **The Braves Clubhouse Store,** which is full of Braves-themed merchandise.

It's possible, and fun, to tour Turner Field. Tours depart every half hour Tuesday through Saturday 9:30am to 4pm and Sunday 1pm to 4pm on non-game days, and Tuesday through Saturday 9:30am to noon on game days. Prices are $7 adults; $4 children 3 to 12; children under 3 free. Call ☎ **404/614-2311** for information. Tours include the museum, the dugout, the press box and broadcast booth, the clubhouse, and more. On non-game days, there's ample free parking in the north lot.

Museum-only tickets are $3; the museum is open Monday through Saturday 9am to 5pm, Sunday 1 to 5pm.

Alexander Memorial Coliseum
Georgia Institute of Technology, Tenth and Fowler sts. ☎ **404/894-5400** for information. MARTA: North Avenue.

This 10,000-seat stadium—newly renovated for the Olympics—is home to Georgia Tech's Yellow Jackets college basketball team. Parking is limited around the stadium; it's easiest to take MARTA.

8

A Walking Tour of Sweet Auburn

You never really understand a city unless you walk around it a bit. Atlanta's climate makes walking tours an option just about year-round.

In addition to the tour below, consider the guided walking tours listed in chapter 7, "What to See & Do in Atlanta." Also, note that the following attractions detailed in that chapter are walking tours in and of themselves: Georgia's Stone Mountain Park, Kennesaw Mountain/National Battlefield Park, Oakland Cemetery, and the Atlanta Historical Society in Buckhead. Auburn Avenue is specially set up for a walking tour.

Start: The corner of Howell and Irwin streets. To get to this inter-section, take I-75/85 south, then exit at Freedom Parkway/Carter Center. Turn right at the first stoplight onto Boulevard. Follow signs to Martin Luther King National Historic Site: You can park in a lot on the north side of Irwin Street between Boulevard and Jackson Street. By MARTA: King Memorial Station is about 8 blocks away; or take bus no. 3 east from the Five Points Station.

Finish: Auburn Avenue and Courtland Street.

Time: Allow about half a day to explore this area thoroughly. If you want to include a tour of Martin Luther King, Jr.'s, Birth Home (stop no. 3)—and a visit to this area would not be complete without it—start out early in the day and obtain your tickets at Fire Station no. 6 at Boulevard and Auburn Avenue. Only a limited number are available each day.

Sweet Auburn includes the Martin Luther King, Jr., National Historic Site, which comprises about 2 blocks along Auburn Avenue, and the surrounding preservation district, about 10 more blocks. A neighborhood that nurtured scores of 20th-century black businesspeople and professionals, it contains the birthplace, church, and gravesite of Martin Luther King, Jr. The area was a vibrant commercial and entertainment district for black Atlantans from the late 1800s until the 1930s, when it went into a steep decline.

In the 1980s, the area where Martin Luther King, Jr., was born and raised was declared a National Historic Site, and now, under the auspices of the National Park Service, portions of Auburn Avenue are in an ongoing process of restoration. The street has been beauti-fied by much new landscaping, and about 75% of the homes on the

"Birth Home" block have been restored to their 1920s appearance. (For more information about the National Historic Site, contact the **National Park Service** at ☎ **404/331-3920** or visit the Web site at www.nps.gov.malu.) This walking tour provides insight into black history, the civil rights movement, and black urban culture in the South. If you're traveling with children, it's a wonderful opportunity to teach them about a great American. The major attractions are covered in detail in chapter 7.

Begin your stroll at:

1. Howell and Irwin Streets. Walk south along Howell Street where renovated historic homes and recently built housing, designed to harmonize with the architecture of the neighborhood, provide testimony to the area's renaissance. Note no. 102 Howell, built between 1890 and 1895, which was the home of Alexander Hamilton, Jr., Atlanta's leading turn-of-the-century black contractor. Its architectural details include Corinthian columns and a Palladian window.

Turn right on Auburn Avenue, and as you proceed look for interpretive markers indicating historic homes (mostly Victorian and Queen Anne) and other points of interest en route to:

2. Martin Luther King, Jr., Center for Nonviolent Social Change, 449 Auburn Ave. (☎ **404/524-1956**). This organization continues the work to which King was dedicated—reducing violence within the community and among nations. Freedom Plaza, on the premises, is his final resting place. The center is open every day from 9am to 6pm. Here you can take a self-guided tour of exhibits on King's life and the civil rights movement. Admission is free.

Now double back a few blocks east to:

3. The Birth Home of Martin Luther King, Jr., 501 Auburn Ave., where free half-hour guided tours are given on a continual basis from 9am to 5pm. On weekends, especially, arrive early, since demand for tickets often exceeds supply. Tickets are obtained at Fire Station no. 6 at Boulevard and Auburn Avenue.

After you leave and walk back toward stop 2, note some turn-of-the-century homes in the area such as:

4. The Double "Shotgun" Row Houses, 472–488 Auburn Ave., two-family dwellings with separate hip roofs that were built in 1905 to house workers for the Empire Textile Company. They were so named because rooms were lined up in a row; if you so desired, you could fire a shotgun right through them.

At the corner of Auburn and Boulevard is:

5. Fire Station no. 6, one of Atlanta's eight original firehouses, completed in 1894. The two-story Romanesque-revival building was situated to protect the eastern section of the city. The station houses a museum, open daily from 9am to 5pm, where exhibits include restored fire engines and vintage fire-fighting paraphernalia. Admission is free. Note the Italianate arched windows on the second story.

Continuing west, a notable stop on your tour is:

6. Ebenezer Baptist Church, 407 Auburn Ave. (☎ **404/688-7263**), founded in 1886, where Martin Luther King, Jr., served as co-pastor from 1960 to 1968. The church is open Monday through Saturday 9am to 5pm. Here you can listen to a taped message on the history of the church and/or enter the sanctuary and watch a videotape. The church is building a new sanctuary across the street; when it is completed, the original building will remain as a historic site under The State Department of Parks & Recreation auspices.

Walking Tour—Sweet Auburn

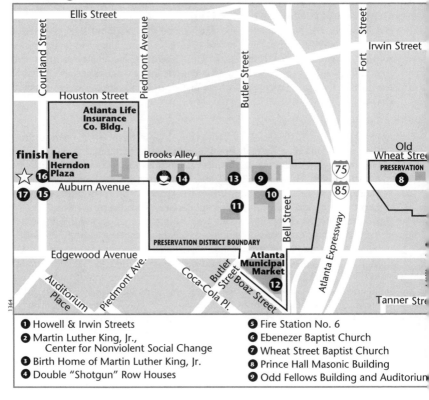

① Howell & Irwin Streets
② Martin Luther King, Jr.,
    Center for Nonviolent Social Change
③ Birth Home of Martin Luther King, Jr.
④ Double "Shotgun" Row Houses
⑤ Fire Station No. 6
⑥ Ebenezer Baptist Church
⑦ Wheat Street Baptist Church
⑧ Prince Hall Masonic Building
⑨ Odd Fellows Building and Auditorium

☕ **TAKE A BREAK** At the corner of Auburn Avenue and Jackson Street is a good, and very inexpensive, Southern/soul food cafeteria, the **Beautiful Restaurant** (☎ 404/223-0080). It's open daily from 7am to 8:30pm. See chapter 6 for details.

One block west is the:

7. Wheat Street Baptist Church, 365 Auburn Ave., built in the 1920s, but serving a congregation since the late 1800s. Auburn Avenue was originally called Wheat Street in honor of Augustus W. Wheat, one of Atlanta's early merchants. The name was changed in 1893.

Further west, on Auburn between Hilliard and Fort streets, is:

8. The Prince Hall Masonic Building, an influential black lodge led for several decades by John Wesley Dobbs. Today, it houses the national headquarters of the Southern Christian Leadership Conference.

On the other side of the expressway, note:

9. The Odd Fellows Building and Auditorium, 228–250 Auburn Ave., another black fraternal lodge, which originated in Atlanta in 1870. Completed in 1914, the building later became headquarters for an insurance company.

Across the street is:

10. The Herndon Building, 231–245 Auburn Ave., named for Alonzo Herndon, an ex-slave who went on to found the Atlanta Life Insurance Company. It was

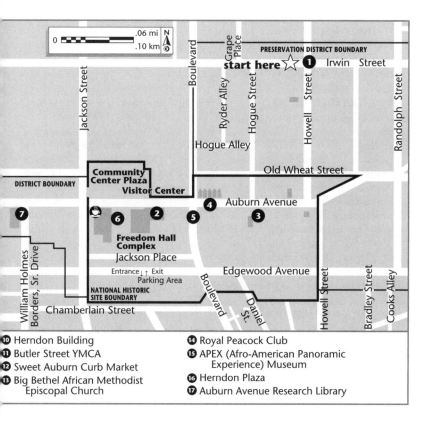

erected in 1924. By 1930, the Auburn business district supported 121 black-owned businesses and 39 black professionals.

Make a left on Butler Street and you'll see:

11. The Butler Street YMCA, built in the early 1900s, and a popular meeting place of civil rights leaders. Today, it's augmented by a new YMCA across the street.

Continue south along Butler Street to the:

12. Sweet Auburn Curb Market, just below Edgewood Avenue. Formerly called the Municipal Market, this historic spot dates to 1924 when Atlanta was still a seg-regated city. Whites shopped within, but blacks were only permitted to patronize stalls lining the curb. The market's current name reflects that era. Today, it's filled with displays of groceries and fresh produce—including many regional and ethnic items such as ham hocks and chitlins ("We sell every part of the pig here but the oink," says the owner). There are also collard, mustard, and turnip greens, boiled peanuts, red velvet cake (one of many fresh-baked items), and home remedies such as yellowroot tea (for arthritis). Sometimes there are pro-duce and flea market stalls out front, and there's a food court on the premises with covered outdoor seating. Open Monday through Thursday from 8am to 6pm, Friday and Saturday from 8am to 7pm.

Walk back to Auburn Avenue on Butler Street, turn left, and to your right is:

13. The Big Bethel African Methodist Episcopal Church, at 220 Auburn Ave., originally built in the 1890s and then rebuilt in 1924 after a fire. In the 1920s, John Wesley Dobbs called the Bethel "a towering edifice to black freedom."

Farther along is:

14. The Royal Peacock Club, 186 Auburn Ave., with walls painted from floor to ceiling with peacocks. It presented top black entertainers such as Ray Charles, Aretha Franklin, and Dizzy Gillespie in its heyday.

☕ **TAKE A BREAK** The **Caribbean Restaurant,** 180 Auburn Ave., between Piedmont Avenue and Butler Street (☎ **404/658-9829**), has a plain but pleasant interior. Walls are hung with posters of Caribbean destinations and musicians, diners are seated on glossy white wooden benches at big picnic-style tables, and reggae and calypso music plays in the background. The low-priced menu lists authentic Caribbean foods such as oxtail stew, curried goat, spicy jerk chicken, red snapper stew, fried plantains (served with blue cheese dressing), and rôti skin (a pancakelike bread). All entrees come with rice and two vegetables. For dessert, try the homemade carrot cake or the red velvet cake. Drink options range from beer and stout to fresh-squeezed lemonade and Ting (a Jamaican grapefruit soda). Major credit cards are accepted. Open Monday to Thursday from 11:30am to 9pm, Friday and Saturday from 11:30am to 10pm.

At Auburn Avenue and Courtland Street is:

15. The APEX (African-American Panoramic Experience) Museum, 135 Auburn Ave. (☎ **404/521-2739**), featuring exhibits on the history of Sweet Auburn and the African-American experience, including a children's gallery with interactive displays. See chapter 7 for further details.

Cross the street to:

16. Herndon Plaza, where you can see exhibits on the Herndon family.

If you'd like to do further research on the history of Auburn Avenue—or on any aspect of African-American history and culture—continue on to:

17. The Auburn Avenue Research Library on African-American Culture and History, 101 Auburn Ave. (☎ **404/730-4001**). This is the place to go for answers on African-American history. Operated by the Atlanta-Fulton County Library System, the library's collection includes literature, documents, rare records, and more. A Heritage Center on the premises features special exhibits, workshops, seminars, lectures, and events. Open Monday and Wednesday 10am to 8pm, Tuesday and Thursday noon to 8pm, Friday 1 to 5pm, and Saturday and Sunday 2 to 6pm.

9

Atlanta Shopping

Atlanta is the shopping mecca of the Southeast. Period. Visitors might *say* they come to Atlanta to steep themselves in Southern history, take in a play or two, or contemplate the masterpieces in a museum. But what they really want to do is trot on over to Buckhead for a little retail therapy.

It's not just that there's a lot of shopping here; it's that it's so varied. There are chic boutiques that can hold their own with the best of Los Angeles or New York, flea markets bursting at the seams with collectibles, giant department stores, and interesting little browsable areas such as Virginia-Highland. It's a great town for antiquing, and there are plenty of art galleries worth a look. And even if you don't want to buy anything, it's great fun to wander around the shopping areas, where you can check out the locals and take the pulse of the city.

1 Great Shopping Areas

BUCKHEAD

The stomping ground of well-to-do Atlanta, Buckhead is the ultimate shopping area, with two major malls and lots of little boutiques, antique shops, and galleries. If you're serious about shopping, this is the place to start. Even though the area has an upscale reputation, don't let that stop you. There's lots of variety, and the fierce competition can make for some excellent bargains.

Ground zero for the best of Buckhead is at the corner of Peachtree and Lenox roads, where two major malls—**Phipps Plaza** and **Lenox Square**—face off against each other (see section 2 of this chapter). If your time is limited, pick one of these malls and spend the morning.

If you have more time and are interested in art, antiques, or decorative accessories, head straight to **Bennett Street,** where you'll find a healthy concentration of stores in a 2-block strip. There are also many shops in the **Buckhead West Village,** near the intersection of Peachtree and West Paces Ferry Roads, but there are many more establishments up and down Peachtree and scattered along smaller side streets.

BENNETT STREET

Located just off Peachtree, on the south edge of Buckhead, is a quaint little avenue that's become one of the most interesting shopping destinations in the city. Once a rude supply path that linked Atlanta to the surrounding countryside during the Civil War, Bennett Street evolved into a thriving warehouse district around the turn of the century. Several years ago those same warehouses were transformed into a handy concentration of shops and galleries specializing in art, decorative accessories, and antiques. There are also two recommended restaurants (Fratelli di Napoli and Mick's, detailed in chapter 6) and two small but excellent cafes.

It all makes for a pleasant afternoon ramble, but if you don't have time to wander the whole street, check out The Stalls and the Interiors Market, both of which house many dealers in one location. Most shops are open Monday through Saturday from 10am to 5pm, and a few are open on Sunday. Bennett Street—little more than a dead-end alley—is only a couple of blocks long, but it's built on a hill, so wear comfortable shoes. It's just off Peachtree Road between Collier Road and Peachtree Battle Avenue. To get there, take bus no. 23 from the Arts Center MARTA station. Here's some of what you'll find; stores are arranged in the order you'll find them if you start at the top of the street near Peachtree.

Bennett Street Gallery

22 Bennett St. NW. ☎ **404/352-8775.** www.bennett gallery.com.

Contemporary fine art, glass, ceramics, and jewelry. Paintings in oil, acrylic, casein, and watercolor.

Bittersweet Ltd.

45 Bennett St. NW. ☎ **404/351-6594.**

Direct importers of English antiques and gifts, including a large collection of Blue Willow china, plus a special corner holds sporting antiques.

Interiors Market

55 Bennett St. NW. ☎ **404/352-0055.**

A large consortium of absentee antique and art dealers all under one roof. Locals looking for just the right home accessory know to start here or at The Stalls rather than schlepping around to all the different shops in town. There's an ever-changing variety, with myriad booths featuring everything from fine antiques to old books.

The Eclectia is a tiny cafe amid all the plunder, and it's a perfect spot to stop for a light but elegant lunch.

Jeff Jones Antiques

25A–1 Bennett St. NW. ☎ **404/350-0711.**

Fine antiques, primitive pieces, architectural ornaments rescued from the wrecking ball, antique garden pieces, including one-of-a-kind planters and pots.

Kilim Collection

22 Bennett St. NW. ☎ **404/351-1110.**

An excellent source for old and new hand-woven flat-weave wool rugs and pillows. Also vests, handbags, and upholstered pieces.

Nottingham Antiques

45 Bennett St. NW. ☎ **404/352-1890.**

Direct importers of European antique pine furniture. Some custom furniture, too.

Out of the Woods

22 Bennett St. NW. ☎ **404/351-0446.**

Unusual wooden gifts, accessories, and artwork from ancient and contemporary cultures.

Provence
95 Bennett St. NW. ☎ **404/350-0750.**

Continental antiques and accessories, including statuary and garden furniture.

The Stalls
116 Bennett St. NW. ☎ **404/352-4430.**

Just like the Interiors Market, this is a large assortment of dealers under one roof, which increases the odds that you'll find that special piece you've been searching for. Tuohy's Cafe, a small restaurant on the premises, serves an interesting array of gourmet salads and sandwiches.

Tula
75 Bennett St. NW. ☎ **404/351-3551.**

One large building near the end of the street housing about 10 to 12 galleries and artists' studios. There's an assortment of pottery, paintings, sculptures, textiles, and photographs.

MIAMI CIRCLE

Most design centers are open to the trade only, and this street of showrooms and warehouses started out that way. But now the majority of the nearly 100 merchants on Miami Circle in Buckhead are open to the public. It's a virtual smorgasbord of furnishings and accessories—from fine European and American antiques to country and primitive pieces. There are three showrooms that specialize in antique and reproduction pine, but there's also painted furniture, antique statuary, heirloom wicker, fine artwork, majolica, custom and antique rugs, antique books and bookcases, clocks, antique chandeliers, and at least one warehouse of designer fabrics.

This is not a quaint street suitable for a pleasant stroll, but it is a great place to browse for serious merchandise. Most establishments are open Monday to Saturday from 10am to 5pm, and some are open on Sunday. If you need something shipped home, it's not a problem. Also, those establishments that sell to the trade only are happy to let you look around and will refer you to a local designer if you wish to make a purchase. Miami Circle is off Piedmont Road, just a half mile south of Peachtree and about a third of a mile north of the Lindbergh MARTA station. If you're here around lunchtime, stop in at Eclipse di Luna (details in chapter 6), located all the way at the end of the street. It's a great little spot for a casual lunch.

WEST VILLAGE OF BUCKHEAD

The intersection of Peachtree and West Paces Ferry Road is the heart of the original Buckhead community. On the east side of Peachtree is the center of Buckhead nightlife, with loads of bars and clubs, most of which don't tune up until after dark. The retail shops are on the west side of Peachtree, where you'll find everything from art and antiques to women's apparel. The West Village, as it is called, is bounded by West Paces Ferry Road, Roswell Road, and East Andrews Drive.

There are a couple of places to stop for a snack or lunch as you wander through the neighborhood. Try **La Madeleine French Bakery & Cafe,** a cozy, upscale, cafeteria-style restaurant at 35 W. Paces Ferry Rd. NW (☎ **404/812-9304**). Or you can cross the **Peachtree to fado'** at 3035 Peachtree Rd. (☎ **404/841-0066**), an authentic Irish pub that serves very good Gaelic fare; especially good is the boxty (filled Irish potato pancake) and the corned beef and cabbage.

Here's some of what you'll see in the West Village:

Antiques & Decorative Accessories

Boxwoods
100 E. Andrews Dr. NW. ☎ **404/233-3400.**

It's hard to see everything in this delightful shop in one visit. There are intriguing gifts and serious gardening accessories, as well as numerous antiques, lamps, fresh flowers, and greenery. The handmade objets d'art are unlike any you will find in the city—and all are fashioned by local artists. Open Monday to Saturday from 10am to 6pm.

C'est Moi
3198 Paces Ferry Place NW. ☎ **404/467-0095.**

This is probably one of the best shops in the West Village. Like many of the others, it has a French slant, but the stock is so well-chosen there's always something interesting to see, including tableware, fine linens, custom furniture, unusual picture frames, bath items, and jewelry. There's also a corner devoted to children's gifts and accessories. Open Monday to Saturday from 10am to 5pm.

Lush Life Home
3240 Roswell Rd. NW. ☎ **404/233-6882.**

This is the home decor offshoot of the popular Lush Life specialty nursery, located at 146 East Andrews Dr. It's stocked with sophisticated and witty Parisian-style decor, antiques, linens, fine milled soaps, and fragrances. The nursery is worth a visit, too. Open Monday to Saturday from 10am to 5pm.

Art

Ann Jacob Gallery
3261 Roswell Rd. NW. ☎ **404/262-3399.**

This whimsical gallery features regional folk art and contemporary regional paintings, sculpture, and glass. Open Monday to Saturday 10am to 5:30pm.

Lagerquist Gallery
3235 Paces Ferry Place NW. ☎ **404/261-8273.**

The contemporary fine art in this gallery includes sculpture, paintings, watercolors, and works on paper by regional, national, and international artists. Open Tuesday to Saturday from 10am to 5:30pm.

Macon & Co.
3215 Cains Hill Place NW. ☎ **404/364-0828.**

This large gallery has quite a variety under one roof—from sculpture to paintings to unique art furniture. The emphasis is on late-career artists, with a great percentage from the Southeast. Open Tuesday to Saturday from 10am to 5pm.

Signature Shop & Gallery
3267 Roswell Rd. NW. ☎ **404/237-4426.**

Everything here is handcrafted by contemporary American artists: dinnerware, decorative and functional clay, metal, fiber, art glass, jewelry, and handbound books. Open Tuesday to Saturday from 10am to 5:30pm.

Fashion Boutiques

CP Shades
3106 Roswell Rd. NW. ☎ **404/816-0872.**

This California-based company specializes in loose, comfortable clothing made of all-natural fibers. The apparel, for women of all ages (some men shop here, too), is reasonably priced and quite stylish, and most of the pieces can be machine washed and dried. Open Monday to Saturday from 10am to 6pm and Sunday from noon to 5pm.

Peoples
3236 Roswell Rd. NW. ☎ **404/816-7292.**

The women's clothing in this friendly shop—suits, tops, skirts, dresses, jackets, swimwear—is contemporary, but with clean, classic lines. The mother–daughter proprietors are knowledgeable and attentive and have put together a sleek, well-chosen collection you will not find in department stores. Open Monday to Friday from 10am to 7pm and Saturday from 10am to 5pm.

Potpourri
56 E. Andrews Dr. NW. ☎ **404/365-0880.**

If you're in search of upscale traditional women's apparel, Potpourri will fit the bill. There are lots of lovely sportswear separates, as well as dinner dresses, belts, costume jewelry, and other accessories. Open Monday to Saturday from 10am to 6pm.

Razzle Dazzle
49 Irby Ave. NW. ☎ **404/233-6940.**

Razzle Dazzle has been on the Buckhead scene for more than two decades. Sportswear is the main staple here (great pants, sweaters, jackets, etc.), but there are also stunning little dresses, some eveningwear, hats, and a wonderful assortment of jewelry, some of it handmade. You'll find lines by Max Studio, Johnny Was, Michael Stars, and more. A big draw for the younger crowd is the supply of vintage Levi's. Open Monday to Saturday from 10:30am to 5:30pm.

White Dove
18 E. Andrews Dr. NW. ☎ **404/814-1994.**

White Dove is full of feminine, sexy, upscale clothing for day and evening. Many of the fabrics are delicate and antiquey—silky rayons, linens, chiffons, and gauzy cottons—and the hats are festooned with silk flowers. Open Tuesday to Saturday from 11am to 6pm.

Home Brewing Equipment
Brew Your Own Beverages
20 E. Andrews Dr. NW. ☎ **404/365-0420.**

If you're interested in brewing at home, this is a good place to start. There's lots of beer gear, as well as supplies and instructions for making your own wine. There are even extracts for concocting liqueurs and sodas. Open Monday to Friday 11am to 8pm, Saturday 10am to 6pm, and Sunday noon to 5pm.

Sporting Goods
Patagonia
34 E. Andrews Dr. NW. ☎ **404/266-8182.**

You've probably seen the Patagonia catalog, but this is the first Atlanta store. It's huge and jammed full of top-notch merchandise. There's lots here for outdoor enthusiasts, no matter what sport you enjoy—canoeing, paddling, skiing, cycling, climbing, surfing, etc. There's equipment, as well as boots, outerwear, and organic cotton clothing for men, women, and children. Open Monday to Friday 10am to 7pm, Saturday 10am to 6pm, and Sunday noon to 6pm.

CHAMBLEE'S ANTIQUE ROW

Antique Row, on New Peachtree Road at Broad Street and North Peachtree Road (☎ 770/458-6316), is a quaint complex of more than 30 shops located in historic homes, churches, and other buildings. Some of them date as far back as the 1800s. There are dealers of antique American and European furniture, glassware, pottery, Victoriana, Orientalia, wicker, collector toys, quilts, sports equipment, Coke memorabilia, jewelry, architectural antiques, Olympic collectibles, and crafts items. It's a great little excursion. Hours vary with each store. Almost all are open Monday through Saturday from 10:30am to 5pm; most are open Sunday from 1 to 5pm as well. You can take a MARTA train to the Chamblee station; it's about three-fourths of a mile from the shops. On weekdays you can get the no. 132 Tilly Mill bus from there; on weekends walk or take a taxi.

VIRGINIA-HIGHLAND

This charming area of town, centered on North Highland Avenue between University Drive and Ponce de Leon Avenue, boasts antique shops, junk stores, trendy boutiques, and art galleries. Since you'll want to browse through all its shops in one excursion, they're grouped together here in the order in which you will find them while walking south through the neighborhood. There are three major concentrations: on North Highland just south of University Drive; at the intersection of North Highland and Virginia avenues; and just north of Ponce de Leon around St. Charles Place. From one end to the other, it's about a mile and a half, but it's a nice walk and there are cafes where you can stop and take a break. If you have just a short time, go to North Highland and Virginia and take in the stores there. For lunch, try Murphy's (see chapter 6, "Dining").

Affairs

1401 N. Highland Ave. (just below University Dr.). ☎ **404/876-3342.**

This shop offers many exquisite giftware items, an extensive collection of picture frames, dinnerware, and gourmet foods. There are even doo-dads for your favorite baby or pet. Affairs also carries French and Italian kitchenware and a full line of Crabtree & Evelyn products. Delightful browsing. Open Monday to Thursday from 10am to 9:30pm, Friday and Saturday from 10am to 10pm, Sunday from 11am to 6pm.

Aliya Gallery

1402 N. Highland Ave. NE (in the Highland Walk Center between University and Morningside drives). ☎ **404/892-2835.**

This contemporary gallery showcases North American artists in many different media. Open Tuesday to Thursday from 2 to 9pm, Friday from 2 to 10pm, Saturday from noon to 10pm, and Sunday from 11:30am to 9pm.

Marcia Wood Gallery

1198 N. Highland Ave. (at Amsterdam Ave.). ☎ **404/885-1808.**

There's always an excellent exhibition at this intimate gallery, which specializes in contemporary paintings, drawings, sculptures, and prints. Open Tuesday to Saturday 11am to 7pm.

Metropolitan Deluxe

1034 N. Highland Ave. NE (just north of Virginia Ave.). ☎ **404/892-9337.**

At first glance, this looks like nothing more than an interesting gift shop with lots of cards, candles, and unusual cut flowers. But not too long ago, it added a fabulous assortment of linens (sheets, towels, comforters, etc.) and other home furnishings, including pillows, wooden tables, armoires, lamps, and upholstered pieces. (Be sure you go downstairs, where the largest display is housed.) There are also vases, glassware, lots of fragrant products for bath and body, picture frames, dried flowers, wrapping paper, and many lovely gift items. Open Monday to Thursday from 10am to 10pm, Friday and Saturday from 10am to 11pm, and Sunday from 11am to 7pm.

Mitzi & Romano

1038 N. Highland Ave. (between Virginia and Los Angeles aves.). ☎ **404/876-7228.**

Mitzi Ugolini buys designer women's clothes in New York and California. Her contemporary clothing is fashion-forward—the kind that makes a statement instead of blending in with the crowd. Great jewelry and accessories, too, including Kate Spade handbags. Most prices are affordable. Don't miss the great sale section at the back of the store. Open Monday to Thursday from 10am to 9pm, Friday and Saturday from 10am to 10pm, and Sunday from noon to 7pm.

Modern Primitive Gallery

1393 N. Highland Ave. NE (between University and Morningside drives). ☎ **404/892-0556.**

There's lots of the unexpected in this gallery, which specializes in folk, outsider, and visionary art from nationally known artists. Shows change every 6 weeks. Open Tuesday to Saturday from noon to 9pm, and Sunday from noon to 5pm.

Mooncake

1019 Virginia Ave. NE (just off North Highland Ave.). ☎ **404/892-8043.**

The ever-changing inventory of whimsical wearables for women might include cloche and straw hats, cotton dresses, and ethnic and handcrafted jewelry. The retro-style clothing looks vintage, but it's all new. You'll also find body and bath items, hair accessories, diaries, and greeting cards. Open Monday to Saturday from 11:30am to 9pm, and Sunday from noon to 6pm. Winter hours may be shorter.

Natural Body

1403 N. Highland Ave. (just below University Dr.). ☎ **404/876-9642.**

This appealing shop invites you to pamper yourself with all manner of skin treatments, bubble baths, massage and body oils, potpourris, soaps, lotions, and cosmetics. There's also an extensive line of aromatherapy products. All of their products are natural and animal- and environment-friendly. They carry, among other lines, Kiehl, Aveda, Ahava (made in Israel with minerals from the Dead Sea), and Bindi/Oja (products made from ayurvedic herbs, roots, and flowers). Natural Body also runs a day spa across the street (☎ **404/872-1039**) offering massages, facials, manicures, pedicures, body wraps, aromatherapy, and other beauty aid treatments. Open Monday 10am to 6pm, Tuesday to Saturday from 10am to 9pm, Sunday from 1 to 6pm.

Planetarian

784 N. Highland Ave. NE (north of Ponce de Leon Ave.). ☎ **404/607-7694.**

This shop is full of colorful women's apparel and accessories with an international connection. For example, there are patchwork jackets of Indonesian batik, dresses made of fabric-inspired aboriginal artwork, and vests cross-stitched by hill tribes of northern Thailand. There's also a collection of furniture from around the world, with an emphasis on Asia. Open Sunday and Monday from 11am to 7pm, Tuesday and Wednesday from 11am to 8pm, and Thursday to Saturday from 11am to 9pm. Hours are shorter in winter.

Rapture
1039 N. Highland Ave. (between Los Angeles and Virginia aves.). ☎ **404/873-0444.**

This New York-style boutique sells cutting-edge women's clothing, featuring contemporary designers such as Leon Max and BCBG, as well as great shoes. There's also interesting jewelry, hats, and handbags. Open Monday and Tuesday from noon to 8pm, Wednesday and Thursday from noon to 9pm, Friday and Saturday from 11am to 10pm, and Sunday from noon to 6pm.

Reader's Loft
1402 N. Highland Ave. (between University and Morningside drives). ☎ **404/881-6511.**

Billing itself as a "metaphysical resource center," Reader's Loft sells books, audiotapes, and CDs relating to meditation, self-help and recovery, Eastern philosophy, spirituality, astrology, and angels. It also carries related items, such as crystals and incense, as well as New Age greeting cards and Native American and contemporary jewelry. Open Monday from 11am to 6pm, Tuesday to Thursday from 11am to 9pm, Friday and Saturday from 11am to 10pm, and Sunday from noon to 5pm.

20th Century
1044 N. Highland Ave. (between Los Angeles and Virginia aves.). ☎ **404/892-2065.**

As its name implies, this shop specializes in international antiques and reproductions made during this century. The inventory is wide-ranging, including some terrific jewelry, Limoges porcelain boxes, whimsical clocks, art deco items, Belgian tapestries, and furnishings running the gamut from 19th-century reproductions to '50s Heywood-Wakefield blond-wood pieces. Also in the mix: campy nostalgia items such as back issues of *Life* magazine, Elvis trading cards, and antique radios and telephones. Great browsing. Open Monday to Thursday 11am to 9:30pm, Friday and Saturday 11am to 10pm, and Sunday 11:30am to 7pm.

V. Reed Fine Art & Craft Gallery
780 N. Highland Ave. NE (north of Ponce de Leon Ave.). ☎ **404/897-1389.**

This is an energetic space with colorful, contemporary art and funky collectibles. The emphasis is on American artists, the majority from Georgia. You'll find interesting and affordable silver jewelry, ceramics, paintings, and unique metal sculptures and lamps. Especially fun are the works by Susan Sisk; the cat paintings look like something from "Through the Looking Glass." Open Tuesday to Saturday from noon to 8pm, and Sunday from noon to 6pm.

LITTLE FIVE POINTS

An area similar to Virginia-Highland (see above)—though a lot funkier and much rougher around the edges—Little Five Points is as much a happening as an offbeat shopping area. There are still authentic hippies here and enough young people with wildly colored hair and pierced body parts to give you a '60s flashback. In addition to the shops, there are a number of taverns and cafes, as well as Sevananda, an excellent health-food store and grocery. It is also close to Virginia-Highland, so if you crave additional boutique browsing, both areas are easily covered in a few hours.

While you're shopping here, plan to have lunch at the Bridgetown Grill, or at the Flying Biscuit Cafe, which is about a mile up McLendon Avenue (details in chapter 6).

Begin your stroll on Moreland just north of Euclid, then proceed southwest along Euclid. Because shopping here is more of a browsing experience than a search for specific merchandise, stores in this area are listed in geographic order rather than by type of store. Most shops are open Monday to Saturday from 11am to 7 or 8pm, and Sunday from noon to 7 or 8pm. Be sure to call ahead. This is a very laid-back shopping district, and hours can change on a whim.

Abbadabbas's
421–B Moreland Ave. NE (between Euclid and North aves.). ☎ **404/588-9577.**

If you're searching for truly comfortable shoes and don't care if they're a little off-beat, step into Abbadabba's, a wild little shoe store that's been a fixture in the neighborhood for years. There are Birkenstocks, Doc Martens, Clark's, Converse, and Simple Tennis Shoes, to name a few of the better-known brands, as well as a great assortment of socks.

Abbadabba's has four other locations around town, including one in Buckhead at 322 E. Paces Ferry Rd. NE (☎ **404/262-3356**).

A Cappella Books
1133 Euclid Ave. (at Colquitt Ave.). ☎ **404/681-5128.**

This is the kind of offbeat bookstore that makes for great browsing. They carry new, used, and out-of-print books, many of them relating to counterculture, literature, history, and the arts. Signed editions here, too. Open Friday and Saturday until 10pm.

African Connections
1107 Euclid Ave. (between Colquitt and Washita aves.). ☎ **404/589-1834.**

This interesting shop carries soapstone carvings from Kenya; textiles, such as *asooke* cloth from Nigeria and *kente* cloth from Ghana; and hand-crafted jewelry from Africa, India, and Indonesia, as well as pieces made by African-American jewelers using African materials. You'll also find traditional and contemporary clothing from the Ivory Coast, Ghana, and Nigeria; traditional West African masks; Nigerian Fulani wedding bead necklaces; and African ceremonial combs and medicine bowls. Open Thursday to Saturday 11am to 6pm; other days by appointment only.

The Clothing Warehouse
1146 Euclid Ave. (between Moreland and Colquitt aves.) ☎ **404/524-5070.**

Vintage Levis are the main attraction here, but there's also a good selection of other casual used clothing—corduroys, overalls, Hawaiian shirts, dresses, blouses, and leather jackets.

Crystal Blue
1168 Euclid Ave. NE (between Moreland and Colquitt aves.). ☎ **404/522-4605.**

This esoteric emporium specializes in crystals and minerals touted for healing and other purposes. For example, black tourmaline supposedly promotes balance to the endocrine system, and meteorite helps reveal past lives from other planets and galaxies. Other items here include New Age books and cassettes, chakra oils, and Acusphere exercise balls to stimulate acupuncture points.

Identified Flying Objects
1164 Euclid Ave. NE (between Moreland and Colquitt aves.). ☎ **404/524-4628.**

Just about everything in here is designed to be airborne—kites, Frisbees, golf discs, windsocks, boomerangs, darts, and juggling paraphernalia. There are also glow-in-the-dark stars for your bedroom ceiling and other nifty items suggesting that up is the best direction. Open until 6:30pm Monday to Saturday and until 6pm Sunday.

Junkman's Daughter
464 Moreland Ave. NE (between Euclid and North aves.). ☎ **404/577-3188.**

This funky 10,000-square-foot store looks like a transplant from New York's East Village. The merchandise includes inexpensive club clothing for men and women,

T-shirts, shoes (from fetish footwear to Doc Marten's), and other bizarre and totally tasteless wares. The staircase leading to the mezzanine is in the shape of a 20-foot red high-heeled shoe. A tattoo parlor, smoking-accessories room, and body-piercing operation are also on the premises.

René René
1142 Euclid Ave. (between Moreland and Colquitt aves.). ☎ **404/522-RENE.**

Atlanta magazine, in a "best and worst" awards issue, once named René René the city's "best women's clothing" shop in the "funky club scene" category. It's true, but some of owner René Sanning's designs are more sophisticated—possibly wearable for business. There's an early Hollywood-inspired evening line and even high-fashion menswear ("not for the IBM man," says René). Interesting accessories here, too, such as black gloves adorned with silk roses.

Stefan's
1160 Euclid Ave. NE (between Moreland and Colquitt aves.). ☎ **404/688-4929.**

Most of Stefan's merchandise is vintage clothing for men and women from the early 1900s through the early 1960s, plus accessories like cigarette cases, cuff links, evening bags, hats, and glitzy period costume jewelry. There are cashmere overcoats, 1950s net-skirt prom dresses, lingerie, cocktail and evening gowns, tuxedos, wedding gowns, Hawaiian shirts, bowling shirts, and suits. Prices are low and merchandise is usually in impeccable condition. Some classy vintage stuff here; definitely a cut above the other neighborhood shops.

Throb
1140 Euclid Ave. (between Moreland and Colquitt aves.). ☎ **404/522-0355.**

Throb specializes in unconventional (to put it mildly) club wear for men and women. You can shop here for see-through vinyl minis, hot pants, bondage-look clothing, black fishnet and silver vinyl dresses, intergalactic plastic jewelry, the latex look, leather lingerie, lingerie meant to be worn as outerwear, chartreuse wigs, and, to complete the look, wild hair dye and makeup colors.

Wax n Facts
431 Moreland Ave. NE (between Euclid and North aves.). ☎ **404/525-2275.**

Looking for that ancient Bob Dylan album that your college girlfriend got custody of when you broke up? It's probably here, along with all the other old vinyl everybody misses. Plenty of nostalgia for sale here.

STONE MOUNTAIN
Stone Mountain Village, just outside the West Gate of Georgia's Stone Mountain Park (bounded by Second and Main Streets north and south, Lucille Street and Memorial Drive east and west; ☎ **770/879-4971**), is worth a visit. It has been developing since the 1800s, and many of the shops are housed in historic buildings. Merchants here keep to a high standard, and their wares are tasteful and of good quality. A lot of the stores specialize in antiques, crafts, and collectibles. Some examples: country furniture, canning jars, dried-flower wreaths, imported toys, handmade candles, jewelers, dolls, baskets, homemade jams, potpourri, handmade patchwork quilts and quilting fabrics, handcrafted dulcimers, Civil War memorabilia, and out-of-print books.

It's great fun to wander about this quaint village, and there's usually some festive event going on—perhaps an arts-and-crafts fair or live entertainment. During Christmas season, the streets are candlelit and the village becomes a magical place populated by St. Nick, elves, carolers, and harpists. Hours for most shops are

Monday through Saturday from 10am to 6pm; many are also open Sunday from 1 to 5pm.

Be sure to stop by the **Village Visitor Center,** housed in a restored 1915 caboose at the corner of Main and Poole streets, to find out about special sales and events. It's open Monday to Saturday from 10am to 4pm, Sunday from 1 to 4pm. Parking is free at several lots in town.

Stop for a meal at the nearby **Village Corner Bakery, Tavern and German Restaurant** at 6655 Memorial Dr., at Main Street (☎ **770/498-0329**). For breakfast there are croissants, German apple pancakes, or ham-and-egg platters with homemade biscuits. Later, you can opt for sandwiches on fresh-baked breads, homemade salads, quiche, soups, and home-baked desserts. And the dinner menu highlights European fare, especially German specialties such as Wiener schnitzel and sauerbraten. There are also 30 German-style beers available. Open Tuesday to Thursday 8am to 11pm, Friday 8am to midnight, Saturday 7am to midnight, and Sunday 10am to 3:30pm and 5 to 9pm. Major credit cards (AE, DC, DISC, MC, V) accepted.

2 Department Stores & Malls

Lenox Square
3393 Peachtree Rd. NE (at Lenox Rd.). ☎ **800/344-5222** or 404/233-6767. MARTA: Lenox.

The vast upscale Lenox Square mall was built in 1959 and has since undergone four major expansions, the latest of which was completed in late 1995. It included a facelift and a new level, which brought square footage up to 1.5 million and added 40 new shops for a grand total of 240. Lenox is the largest mall in the Southeast, and its interesting mix of stores makes it immensely popular with locals and visitors alike. You can buy just about anything here, from hiking boots to an engagement ring, and even if you're not in the mood to buy, there's great people-watching.

Anchors include Neiman-Marcus, Macy's, and Rich's department stores, and the J. W. Marriott hotel. There are six movie theaters in the complex, 30 fast food and fine dining restaurants (including Prime, Brasserie Le Coze, and Mick's, detailed in chapter 6, "Dining"), and 250 specialty shops. Among the best known are Ann Taylor, Britches of Georgetown, Burberrys, J. Crew, Warner Bros. Studio Store, a Metropolitan Museum of Art store, BCBG, Cartier, Disney Store, Sharper Image, Laura Ashley, Nature Company, Crate & Barrel, Brooks Brothers, Polo/Ralph Lauren, Bally of Switzerland, F. A. O. Schwarz, Speedo, and Louis Vuitton.

There are also many stores that you will not find elsewhere in the city. They include Snooty Hooty & Co., with upscale, contemporary women's apparel; Crane & Co., known for fine stationery and paper products; Pella, a large selection of the latest in women's shoes; Oilily, with colorful and creative clothing from the Netherlands for women and children; Blue Ridge Mountain Sports, for equipment and apparel for the serious outdoor enthusiast; and Pottery Barn, carrying a selection of home furnishings and accessories, including many items usually available only by catalog. Other exclusives include Nicole Miller, Max Mara, Joan & David, Mondi, and St. John's Boutique.

A full complement of service shops are here as well—shoe repair, optician, locksmith, post office, airline offices, you name it. There's even a concierge where you and the others in your party can get complimentary pagers so that you can shop independently and still stay in touch. Open Monday to Saturday from 10am to 9pm, Sunday from noon to 6pm, with extended hours during the Christmas season. Some stores close at 7pm on Saturday night. Valet parking is complimentary. There's also a free shuttle to Phipps Plaza at the main entrance.

Macy's Peachtree

180 Peachtree St. (between International Blvd. and Ellis St.). ☎ **404/221-7221.** MARTA: Peachtree Center.

Opened in 1927, this downtown branch of Macy's is a department store in the grand tradition, its main floor featuring 30 lofty Corinthian columns, marble floors, and glittering crystal chandeliers. However, it's perfectly up-to-date when it comes to merchandise. Like most branches of Macy's nowadays, it has a Cellar—a street market with tiled brick floors and shops specializing in housewares. The mezzanine houses a shop selling Atlanta sports team merchandise, other Atlanta-themed merchandise, and shops based on current fads. Open Monday to Saturday from 10am to 6pm, Sunday from noon to 6pm.

Mall at Peachtree Center

Peachtree St. at International Blvd. ☎ **404/654-1296.** MARTA: Peachtree Center.

Part of the vast Portman-designed Peachtree Center complex, this downtown mall offers around 70 shops, restaurants, and services on three levels. It's not exactly a shopping destination, but its location near major hotels makes it a convenient place to stop in if you're staying downtown and are in need of goods or services. There are several apparel shops, including Brooks Brothers, and other stores offering gifts, jewelry, books, candy, and computer hardware and software. Services include florists, hairstylists, a travel agency, Federal Express, UPS, a dry cleaner, an optician, and several dentists. As for dining, a food court dishes up everything from gyros to Mrs. Field's cookies, and full-service restaurants include some great choices: Mick's (see chapter 6, "Dining") and Azio Pizza and Pasta. Most stores are open Monday to Friday from 10am to 6pm, and Saturday from 10am to 5pm.

Phipps Plaza

3500 Peachtree Rd. NE (at the Buckhead Loop). ☎ **800/810-7700** or 404/262-0992. MARTA: Lenox.

Just across the street from Lenox Square is Atlanta's most exclusive shopping venue, Phipps Plaza. In 1992, it underwent a vast multimillion-dollar renovation/expansion, adding new shops, spacious promenades, and grand interior courts. Phipp's 100-plus shops and restaurants are anchored by Lord & Taylor, Parisian (a Birmingham, Alabama-based department store with a fantastic women's shoe department), and Saks Fifth Avenue. The exclusive Ritz-Carlton Buckhead hotel is just a few steps away.

Phipps Plaza's posh emporia (many of them area exclusives) include Gucci, Tiffany & Co., Jaeger, Jil Sander, Gianni Versace, Niketown, Dolce & Gabbana, The Original Levi's Store (with computerized fitting), A/X Armani Exchange, Ross-Simons (upscale jewelry, china, and silver), and Cole Haan and Kenneth Cole for shoes. You'll also find chic boutiques selling ladies' and men's apparel, luggage, jewelry, home furnishings, shoes, and specialty gifts.

The ambience is sedate and elegant, and there's usually something special going on—perhaps an art or fashion show. Services include complimentary personal shoppers, gift locators, valet parking, and a concierge, and among the mall's restaurants is the Peasant Uptown. Also on the premises: a restaurant complex called the Veranda Food Court and a 14-screen movie theater. Stores are open Monday to Saturday from 10am to 9pm, Sunday from noon to 5:30pm. There's also a free shuttle to Lenox Square.

Underground Atlanta

Alabama Street (between Peachtree St. and Central Ave.). ☎ **404/523-2311**. MARTA: Five Points.

This 12-acre mix of shops, nightclubs, and restaurants is not as vibrant as it was a couple of years ago, but it still can be fun to browse. There are dozens of shops, plus vendors in Humbug Square selling merchandise off antique pushcarts. Shopping options include clothing shops for men, women, and children, running the gamut from upscale T-shirts at Dallas Alice to Victoria's Secret's sexy lingerie to sportswear at the Gap. Other interesting emporia include Art by God (fossils and rare mineral specimens), African Pride (gifts and apparel with an African-American theme), Kandlestix (where candle-makers display their craft), Papier D'Couleur (papier-mâché birds, fruit, and animals), and Georgia Grande General (Georgia-related gifts and crafts). There are also novelty stores such as the bargain mecca, Just a Dollar.

Of course, there's a food court and several good restaurants, including Mick's (see details in chapter 6). For lunch you might try Johnny Rockets, an entertaining 1950s-style hamburger joint the whole family will enjoy. If you're driving, there's parking in two garages off Martin Luther King Drive. Be sure to get your ticket validated inside for discounted parking. Open Monday to Saturday from 10am to 9:30pm, Sunday from noon to 6pm.

3 More Shopping Around Town

ANTIQUE/FLEA MARKETS

Atlanta is home to several permanent flea markets selling everything from custom furniture to antique toys, but the most exciting markets are those that set up shop once a month. The lineup of dealers—from all parts of the country—is ever-changing, so no matter how often you go, you'll always see something new and fresh.

If you're in search of real finds, shop on the first day as soon as the market opens—that's when local dealers swoop in to snatch up the very best merchandise. Serious bargaining often takes place in the closing hours of the last day, when many dealers are anxious to avoid lugging their wares home with them. Be sure to keep your admission ticket; it's good for the whole weekend.

Lakewood Antiques Market

At the Lakewood Fairgrounds, between downtown Atlanta and the airport. Take I-75/I-85 south to Exit 88. Go east to the fairgrounds. ☎ **404/622-4488**. Free parking.

Held at the historic Lakewood Fairgrounds, this huge market has 1,500 dealer spaces, most of them in the huge old fair buildings. You'll find thousands of rare antiques and collectibles, old architectural treasures, books, glassware, tools, cookware, linens, jewelry, and so on. There's also some new merchandise, such as cut-rate (but excellent) garden pottery, wrought-iron sculpture, and custom wood furniture, as well as fruits and vegetables in summer and fall. There are several food stands throughout, some of them selling homemade baked goods. Because many of the stalls are outside, it's fun to browse this one when the weather is pleasant. The place is huge and fascinating, so plan to spend much of the day.

Open the second weekend of each month, Thursday to Saturday from 10am to 6pm, Sunday from 10am to 5pm. Admission is $3, except for Thursday, which is "early buyer day" and costs $5. Some dealers will still be setting up their booths on Thursday, but you have the advantage of getting the first peek at all the merchandise.

Pride of Dixie Antique Market

At the North Atlanta Trade Center, north of Atlanta. Take I-85 north to the Indian Trail exit (about 25 min. from downtown), then follow the signs. ☎ **770/279-9853.** Free parking.

This is the newest of the markets, and it is more of a true antique market than a flea market. There are spaces for 600 dealers, who have searched the countryside for fabulous finds, combing through attics and old barns, and arriving at estate sales at the crack of dawn. You'll find fine antique furniture as well as interesting primitive painted pieces, heirloom jewelry and silver, antique books, baskets, ancient sewing machines, roll-top desks, and much more. This entire market is held inside an air-conditioned building, so weather is not a factor. The market is not as big as Lakewood, but it's a good bet if you're looking for serious antiques. Open the fourth weekend of each month, Friday and Saturday from 9am to 6pm, and Sunday from 11am to 5pm. Admission is $4.

Scott Antique Market

At the Atlanta Exposition Center south of the city. Take I-75 south to I-285. Go east on I-285 to Exit 40 (Jonesboro Rd.) and follow the signs. ☎ **404/366-0833** or 404/361-2000. Free parking.

Scott is an immense and immensely popular market that has had so much success it's had to open another location across the interstate from the original spot. There are spaces for 2,400 booths, all indoors, and the antiques and collectibles are some of the finest you'll see anywhere. This market is similar in atmosphere to Pride of Dixie, but much bigger, with loads of heirloom furniture, jewelry, silver, and so on, as well as a huge assortment of collectibles.

There's a free shuttle between the two Scott facilities, so it's easy to visit both locations if you have the energy. The market is held the second weekend of every month. (If you're really ambitious, you can do Scott's and Lakewood—see above—in one day.) Open Friday and Saturday 9am to 6pm and Sunday 10am to 5pm. Although the market's not officially open for business, you can come as early as 5am on Thursday, as many retailers do, and shop while the vendors are setting up their booths. Admission (good for both locations) is $3.

BOOKSTORES

In addition to the independent bookstores in Atlanta, the nationwide chain stores of B. Dalton, Waldenbooks, Borders, Doubleday, and Barnes & Noble are represented locally. Barnes and Noble's major store can be found in Buckhead, at 2900 Peachtree Rd., just a few minutes south of Lennox Square (☎ **404/261-7747**). The main Border's store is also in Buckhead. They are located 3 blocks north of Lennox Square, at 3637 Peachtree Rd., (☎ **404/237-0707**).

Books & Cases & Prints Etc.

800 Miami Circle NE, Suite 100 (just off Piedmont Rd.). ☎ **800/788-9107** or 404/231-9107.

There are some used books here, but the big attraction is the vast collection of antique books, especially the complete leatherbound sets. There are also old Bibles, children's books, scholarly books, and magnificent antique and reproduction bookcases. You'll find rare prints of all kinds, and original artwork by well-known children's illustrators such as Arthur Rackham. It's wonderful browsing for bibliophiles and convenient to many fine antique stores on Miami Circle. Open Monday to Saturday 10am to 5pm.

Chapter 11—The Discount Bookstore
1544 Piedmont Rd. (in the Ansley Mall at the corner of Monroe Dr.). ☎ **404/872-7986.**

These large, first-class bookstores, in distinctive yellow and black, make up the largest bookstore chain in Atlanta. They are also the least expensive. They take 30% off the cover price for the top 15 hardcover *New York Times* bestsellers, and all other books in the store are at an everyday discount of 11%. Their service also sets them apart. The staff, all serious readers themselves, excel at answering questions and finding particular titles. Chapter 11 will also special order books at no additional cost. Open Monday to Saturday from 10am to 9pm, Sunday from noon to 6pm.

Besides the Ansley Mall store, there are several suburban locations and three other in-town stores: 3509 Northside Pkwy. (☎ **404/841-6338**), 1 block north of West Paces Ferry Road; 2091 North Decatur Rd. (☎ **404/325-1505**), near Emory University; and 2345–A Peachtree Rd. (☎ **404/237-7199**), in the Peachtree Battle Shopping Center at Peachtree Battle Avenue. Hours vary, but the Emory and Peachtree stores are open later than the others.

Engineer's Bookstore
748 Marietta St. NW (at the corner of Means St., just off Tech Pkwy. and approximately 1 mile from Georgia World Congress Center). ☎ **800/635-5919** or 404/221-1669.

The largest technical bookstore in Atlanta, Engineer's has an incredible selection of computer and engineering titles as well as the graduate and undergraduate texts for Georgia Tech. Relocated in 1993 to make way for the Olympic Village Dormitories, Engineer's Bookstore has been in business since 1954. The 10,000-square-foot store, a rehabbed 1930s brick building, is located in a historic district of Marietta Street, near art galleries, restaurants, and Georgia Tech. Open Monday to Friday from 9am to 5:30pm and Saturday from 10am to 2pm.

Tall Tales Book Shop, Inc.
2999 N. Druid Hills Rd. ☎ **404/636-2498.**

This general bookstore in the Emory University area offers a large selection of mainstream titles with an emphasis on literary selections. All large publishers are represented as well as university and small presses. There's a coffeehouse in the store, and a friendly atmosphere prevails. The staff is knowledgeable and will be happy to process special orders. Open Monday to Thursday from 9:30am to 9:30pm, Friday and Saturday from 9:30am to 10pm, and Sunday from 12:30 to 6:30pm.

FACTORY & DISCOUNT OUTLETS

North Georgia Premium Outlets
800 Hwy. 400 (35 min. north of Atlanta on Georgia 400), Dawsonville, GA 30534. ☎ **706/216-3609.**

This 100-store center is a cut above most outlets, with names such as Anne Klein, Donna Karan, Tahari, Emanuel Ungaro, and Calvin Klein, to name a few. There are also outlets for Saks Fifth Avenue, Brooks Brothers, Crate & Barrel, Joan & David, Timberland, Bose, Williams-Sonoma, Stone Mountain Handbags, Nine West, and The Gap. It's a bargain-hunter's paradise, and the mix of stores is excellent, with everything from toys to vitamins to leather goods. Definitely worth the trip. Open Monday to Saturday 10am to 9pm and Sunday noon to 6pm.

Tanger Factory Outlet Centers
198 Tanger Dr. and 800 Steven B. Tanger Blvd. (at Exit 53 off I-85N), Commerce, GA. ☎ **706/335-4537.**

Tanger has oodles of factory-outlet stores (75 in the complex north of the city, 55 in the one on the south side). Included are the likes of Oneida, Liz Claiborne,

Corning Revere, American Tourister, Farberware, Levi's, Reebok, Mikasa, L'Eggs/Hanes/Bali, Maidenform, and Van Heusen, among others.

The Commerce center is about 50 minutes north of downtown Atlanta. There's another location at 1000 Tanger Dr. (at Exit 68 off I-85S), in Locust Grove (☎ **770/957-0238**); that one is about 45 minutes to the south. Both are open Monday to Saturday from 9am to 9pm, Sunday from noon to 6pm.

FARMERS MARKETS

Atlanta State Farmers Market
16 Forest Pkwy., Forest Park, GA. ☎ **404/366-6910.** Take I-75 south to Exit 78; the market is on your left.

The State Farmers Market is a vast 146-acre outdoor facility where stall after stall is piled high with produce. There are also vendors of home-canned pickles, jams, and relishes; plants and flowers; and seasonal items such as pumpkins in October, holly and Christmas trees in December. It's a colorful spectacle. You can have a good meal at a restaurant on the premises. Open 24 hours daily except Christmas.

DeKalb Farmers Market
3000 E. Ponce de Leon Ave., Decatur, GA. ☎ **404/377-6400.**

Even if you have no intention of purchasing, this incredible market, started in 1977 by Robert Blazer, merits a visit. A mind-boggling array of international food items is temptingly displayed in a 140,000-square-foot building. Tables are laden with mountains of produce from broccoli to bok choy, not to mention winter melons and water chestnuts, lily root, curry leaves, breadfruit, Jamaican jerk marinade, Korean daikon, a multiplicity of mushrooms, chick-pea miso, a vast beer and wine section, dried fruits, plants and flowers, seafood, meat, poultry, every imaginable variety of fresh herbs and hot peppers, fresh-baked breads and pastries, stalks of sugarcane, many varieties of cheese, frogs' legs, conch meat, quail, and so on. As you shop, you can nibble sections of grapefruit or whatever else is offered at sample tables throughout the facility. There's also a small cafeteria on the premises. It's about a 20-minute drive from downtown. Open daily from 9am to 9pm.

Harry's Farmers Markets
1180 Upper Hembree Rd., Alpharetta, GA. ☎ **770/664-6300.**

Harry Blazer (brother of Robert Blazer of DeKalb Farmers Market) left that market and started his own establishment in 1988. There are now three metro locations, and several smaller Harry's in Hurry stores around town.

Like the DeKalb Farmers Market, this megamarket must be seen to be believed. It is generally the same in concept—mountains of fresh produce, incredible selections of cheese, seafood, meats, gourmet items, wines, beers, and more exotica than you can imagine. The cut flowers are exceptional.

There is a difference between the two, though. DeKalb attracts a more international clientele, although the selection of goods is not necessarily more international in scope. Harry's is a bit more upscale and polished, and attracts many suburbanites, probably because of its locations. DeKalb has a wider variety of organic foods and produce, while Harry's does better at baked goods, prepared foods, and cheese. Saturday and Sunday are extremely crowded at all markets, but it seems to add to the fun if you don't have to do serious shopping. Don't eat lunch before you go; instead snack on the many samples or buy a baguette sandwich or gourmet salad to take with you. Open Monday to Thursday from 9am to 8pm, Friday from 9am to 9pm, Saturday from 9am to 8pm, and Sunday from 9:30am to 7pm.

There are two other Harry's locations: 2025 Satellite Blvd., Duluth (☎ **770/416-6900**), and 70 Powers Ferry Rd., Marietta (☎ **770/578-4400**). The Duluth store is open Monday to Saturday from 9am to 9pm, Sunday from 9:30am to 7:30pm; Marietta's hours are the same as Alpharetta's. The Marietta store is closest to downtown, about 20 minutes away. Take I-75 north to Exit 112, bear right, and go east to the first traffic light. Turn left onto Powers Ferry Road; Harry's is about a mile down the road on the left.

FASHION

See also sections 1 and 2 of this chapter for more stores.

The Bilthouse

511 E. Paces Ferry Rd. NE (5 blocks west of Peachtree Rd., on the corner of Maple Ave.). ☎ **404/816-7702.**

Set in an old cottage in Buckhead, this little store is the place to go if you're looking for something casual that's a little out of the ordinary. Most of the clothing is designed for comfort—which is not to say that it doesn't also look great—and much of it is of natural fabrics. There are linen shifts and separates, cotton sweaters, lots of one-of-a-kind dresses, tights, flowing skirts, and more—for women of all ages. There's also unique furniture, jewelry, children's clothing, artwork by local artists, and little goodies for body and bath. Open Monday to Saturday from 9:30am to 6pm; hours may be longer in spring and summer.

Cornelia Powell Antiques Inc.

271–B E. Paces Ferry Rd. NE (1 block east of Peachtree Rd.). ☎ **404/365-8511.**

The name is a little misleading. This is not a place for antique furniture and collectibles, but a dreamy little shop brimming with impeccably restored antique clothing and new designs made of antique laces and new silks. There are exquisite Victorian tea dresses, frilly little christening gowns and bonnets, romantic antique bridal gowns and accessories, unique hats, ribbons, vintage linens, and antique jewelry. Everything in the shop—new and old—is one-of-a-kind and quite hard to resist if you have any romance in your soul at all. Custom work is also available. Open Monday to Saturday from 10am to 6pm.

A Pea in the Pod

In the Phipps Plaza mall, 3500 Peachtree Rd. (at Lenox Rd.). ☎ **404/261-0808.** MARTA: Lenox.

This cleverly named shop features maternity clothes, but we're not talking T-shirts with an arrow pointing to your stomach and the word *baby*. These are gorgeous clothes—the kind you wore when you weren't pregnant—including designer lines by Adrienne Vittadini, Carol Little, Laundry, and Joan Vass. They run the gamut from really elegant business garb (perfect for board meetings) to evening wear and chic sports clothing. In fact, the clothes are so beautiful that women who are not pregnant shop here as well. Open Monday to Saturday from 10am to 9pm, Sunday from noon to 5:30pm.

Rexer-Parkes

2140 Peachtree Rd. NE (in the Brookwood Square shopping center). ☎ **404/351-3080.**

This sophisticated shop offers cutting-edge American and European clothing for women who are looking for apparel with clean, classic lines that will not blend in with the crowd. You'll find sportswear, suits, dresses, and lingerie from names like Nicole Miller, Gruppo Americano, and Cynthia Rowley. A good selection of the latest in jewelry, too. Open Monday to Wednesday and Friday from 10am to 7 pm, Thursday from 10am to 9pm, and Saturday from 10am to 6pm.

GIFTS, ART & COLLECTIBLES

City Art Works

2140 Peachtree Rd. NW (in the Brookwood Square shopping center). ☎ **404/605-0786.**

Tucked away in a strip shopping center, this place is pretty overwhelming. You'll find a huge array of one-of-a-kind quality gift items and artwork by local and national artists—jewelry, sculpture, pottery, lamps, frames, glassware, and so on. The mix is eclectic, ever-changing, and hard to resist. Open Monday to Wednesday, Friday, and Saturday from 10am to 6:30pm, Thursday from 10am to 8pm, and Sunday from 1 to 5pm.

Erika Reade

3732 Roswell Rd. (in the Powers Square shopping center, about 1½ miles from Peachtree Rd.). ☎ **404/233-3857.**

The emphasis here is on interesting home-related accessories and furnishings— paintings, antique and primitive furniture, mirrors, exquisite bed linens (Palais Royal and Peacock Alley), and tabletop items. You'll find French soaps and candles, hand-blown glass from Vermont, crystal from Scotland, adorable gift items for adults and children, and much more. It's all absolutely up-to-date and extremely tasteful. Open Monday to Thursday from 10am to 6pm, Friday and Saturday from 10am to 5pm.

SPORTING GOODS

Recreational Equipment Inc.

1800 Northeast Expressway (on the I-85 access road; take the Clairmont Rd. exit and go south). ☎ **404/633-6508.**

This Seattle-based company, more commonly known as REI, has everything imaginable for the outdoor enthusiast: clothing, shoes, outerwear and accessories for biking, hiking, camping, rock climbing, canoeing, kayaking, and so on. The staff is extremely knowledgeable, and the sales are frequent and fabulous. If you don't find what you need in this store, REI will search its other stores and its distribution center for the merchandise you're looking for. Open Monday to Saturday 10am to 9pm, Saturday 10am to 7pm, and Sunday 11am to 6pm.

There's another REI just north of the city at 1165 Perimeter Center West NE (☎ **770/901-9200**).

Atlanta After Dark

10

This is a city that sizzles after dark, with numerous music clubs featuring jazz, rock, country, and blues. It also offers a comprehensive cultural scene, including symphony, ballet, opera, and theater productions. And major artists headline regularly at Atlanta's many large-scale performance facilities.

Nightlife tunes up all over Atlanta, but the biggest concentration of clubs and bars is in Buckhead (near the intersection of Peachtree Road and East Paces Ferry Road); in Virginia-Highland (at the intersection of Virginia and North Highland Avenues, and on North Highland just north of Ponce de Leon Avenue); in Little Five Points (near the intersection of Moreland and Euclid avenues); and downtown near Peachtree Center.

The Buckhead scene, for the most part, is like a huge fraternity party, especially on the weekends. Virginia-Highland is full of older young adults and professionals. Little Five Points is an eclectic mix of wildly, weirdly dressed folks and neighborhood regulars; downtown has a large proportion of out-of-town visitors and convention goers.

To find out what's on during your stay, consult the *Atlanta Journal-Constitution.* Its "Preview" section, published every Friday, highlights movies, plays, festivals, gallery openings, and other happenings for the upcoming weekend. There's also an extensive listing of live music. The newspaper's Saturday "Leisure" section offers a calendar of extensive listings of events for the weekend and the week ahead. Or pick up a copy of *Creative Loafing,* a free publication you'll see in stores, restaurants, and other places around town (to obtain a free copy prior to your visit call ☎ **800/950-5623**).

Tickets to many performances are handled by TicketMaster. Call ☎ **404/249-6400** (for popular performances) or ☎ **404/817-8700** (for cultural events) to charge by phone. TicketMaster also has 110 locations throughout Georgia, including all Publix Supermarkets, where customers can purchase tickets in person, though they must be paid for in cash. To avoid the TicketMaster surcharge, it's often possible to purchase tickets at the box office. If you are staying in a large hotel, the concierge service often is able to obtain tickets to even the most popular events.

Day-of-show half-price tickets are available at AtlanTIX! ticket booth at the Atlanta Convention and Visitors Bureau in Underground Atlanta. Customers can look over the showboard to see what plays and other live performances have tickets available that day, purchase a voucher for the show, and pick up the ticket at the show's box office before curtain time. Vouchers must be paid for in person; phone sales are not available. Call ☎ **404/222-6688** for more information.

1 The Performing Arts

BALLET

The Atlanta Ballet

Performing in the Fox Theatre, 660 Peachtree St. NE, at Ponce de Leon Ave., and at the Robert Ferst Center for the Arts, 349 Ferst Dr. NW on the Georgia Tech campus. ☎ **404/892-3303** or www.atlantaballet.com for information. Tickets $10–$45.

The oldest continuously operating ballet company in the United States, the Atlanta Ballet presents six productions each fall-through-spring season. Performances range from classics to new works and include *The Nutcracker* every December. Tickets are available through TicketMaster (☎ **404/817-8700**), at the Fox Theatre box office (☎ **404/881-2100**) and the Ferst Center box office (☎ **404/894-9600**).

CLASSICAL MUSIC

In addition to the city's symphony, listed below, the **Atlanta Chamber Players** (☎ **770/242-2227**) perform a wide spectrum of classical and contemporary masterpieces, and each year they commission works by leading composers. Their season runs from November through spring, and most tickets are $12. Call to find out where they'll be playing during your stay.

Atlanta Symphony Orchestra. Performing in the Woodruff Arts Center, 1280 Peachtree St. NE (at Fifteenth St.). ☎ **404/733-5000** (box office) for information and tickets. www.atlantasymphony.org. Most tickets $19–$55. Box office is open Mon–Fri 10am–8pm, Sat noon–8pm. Parking available in the Arts Center Garage on Lombardy Way between Fifteenth and Sixteenth sts. MARTA: Arts Center.

The Atlanta Symphony Orchestra, which celebrated its 50th anniversary during the 1994–95 season, performs under music director Yoel Levi. Complementing it is the 200-voice Atlanta Symphony Orchestra Chorus, enabling performances of large-scale symphonic/choral works. The season runs from September through May in the Woodruff Arts Center, plus there are summer concerts in Chastain Park Amphitheatre and in various parks and churches.

The ASO's annual schedule is extensive. The main offering is the **Master Season Series.** Master Season concerts, held on selected Thursday, Friday, and Saturday evenings in the plush 1,762-seat Atlanta Symphony Hall, feature renowned guest artists such as violinists Robert McDuffie, cellist Lynn Harrell, pianists Jon Kimura Parker and Marcus Roberts, and mezzo-sopranos Denyce Graves and Frederica von Stade. The **Vocal Gems** series gives voice to some of today's leading interpreters of vocal and choral works, including the ASO Chorus. Also held during the season is a series of four Sunday afternoon **Family Concerts** geared to children, **Casual Classics** on selected Saturday afternoons, **Holiday Hurrahs** at Christmas, and a tribute to Martin Luther King, Jr., in mid-January.

The ASO's **Classic Chastain Series** concerts are held in the 6,000-seat Chastain Park Amphitheatre on Wednesday, Friday, and Saturday evenings from June to August. All except lawn seating is reserved. It's customary to bring elaborate picnics and wine to these events. The series features headliner performers such as Wynton Marsalis, Art Garfunkel, Mary Chapin Carpenter, and Gladys Knight performing with the ASO. There are also free concerts in parks throughout the Atlanta area on summer evenings. These run the gamut from full symphony performances to light classical repertoires.

OPERA

Atlanta Opera
Performing in the Fox Theatre, 660 Peachtree St. NE (at Ponce de Leon Ave). ☎ **800/ 35-OPERA** or 404/355-3311 for information. www.atlantaopera.org. Single tickets available through the Fox box office (☎ **404/881-2100**) and TicketMaster (☎ **404/817-8700**). Tickets $16–$115. MARTA: North Avenue.

Under the artistic direction of William Fred Scott, the Atlanta Opera offers four fully staged productions between April and October at the Fox Theatre. Principal performers are drawn from top opera companies from across the United States and Europe. Three performances are given of each opera. Recent productions included Verdi's *La Traviata,* Massenet's *Manon,* and Mozart's *Don Giovanni.* Tickets can be difficult to obtain; charge them in advance if possible.

THEATER

The **Alliance Theatre Company** is the major theater company in Atlanta, but there are a many other excellent companies with performances ranging from experimental to classic. Most are located near downtown and Midtown, but there are a number in the suburbs. Some of the notables include **Actor's Express** (☎ 404/ 607-7469), **Dad's Garage** (☎ 404/523-3141), **Horizon Theatre Company** (☎ 404/584-7450), **Jomandi Productions** (☎ 404/873-1099), **Neighborhood Playhouse** (☎ 404/373-5311), **7 Stages Theatre** (☎ 404/523-7647), **Shakespeare Tavern** (☎ 404/874-5299), **Theatrical Outfit** (☎ 404/872-0665), **Theatre Gael** (☎ 404/876-9762), and **Theatre in the Square** (☎ 770/ 872-0665). Check the *Atlanta Journal-Constitution* on Friday and Saturday to see what's on during your visit. There are also performances by the **Georgia Shakespeare Festival** (☎ 404/264-0020) each summer.

Alliance Theatre Company
Performing in the Woodruff Arts Center, 1280 Peachtree St. NE (at Fifteenth St.). ☎ **404/ 433-5000** for information or to charge tickets. www.alliancetheatre.org. Tickets $17–$36. "Rush tickets" often available for $15 on the day of a performance; they must be purchased in person at the box office after 5pm. Box office is open Mon–Fri 10am–8pm, Sat noon–8pm. Parking in the Arts Center Garage on Lombardy Way between Fifteenth and Sixteenth sts. MARTA: Arts Center.

The Alliance Theatre Company, under the artistic direction of Kenny Leon, is the largest regional theater in the Southeast. On two stages, it produces about 10 plays a year (the season runs from September through June, with occasional productions during the summer). Many well-known actors have played these stages, among them Jane Alexander, Richard Dreyfuss, Esther Rolle, and Morgan Freeman. Recent seasons have included Dickens's *A Christmas Carol* (performed annually), *Medea,* starring Phylicia Rashad, and the world premiere of Elton John and Tim Rice's musical, *Elaborate Lives: The Legend of Aida.* The Alliance Children's Theatre presents plays geared to youngsters from January through May (tickets are $8).

MAJOR VENUES

In addition to the special places listed below, many of the stadiums listed in section 6, "Spectator Sports," in chapter 7, host major concerts from time to time. These include the Alexander Memorial Coliseum and Bobby Dodd Stadium/Grant Field at Georgia Tech, Road Atlanta, and the Georgia Dome.

Atlanta Civic Center

395 Piedmont Ave. NE (between Ralph McGill Blvd. and Pine St.). ☎ **404/523-6275** for general information. MARTA: Civic Center (about 5 blocks away); buses go to the door.

The Civic Center offers a wealth of entertainment options in its 4,600-seat auditorium. It hosts headliners, touring Broadway shows, traveling symphonies and opera companies, and fashion shows.

Chastain Park Amphitheatre

449 Stella Dr. NW (in Chastain Park at Powers Ferry Rd.). ☎ **404/249-6400** or 404/817-8700 for information.

This delightful 7,000-seat outdoor facility offers concerts under the stars from May to October. Everyone brings food; a picnic on the grass or at your amphitheater seat is a tradition (people bring gourmet feasts and even candelabra). Big-name performers are featured. It's hard to get tickets, so order as far in advance as possible (months ahead if you can). See for the Atlanta Symphony Orchestra on page 208, which offers a summer series here.

Coca-Cola Lakewood Amphitheatre

202 Lakewood Way (at the Lakewood exit of I-75/85, 3½ miles south of downtown). ☎ **404/627-9704** or 404/627-5700. www.lakewoodamp.com. Take I-75 or I-85 south to Lakewood Freeway exit (88E or 88W) and follow the signs. Free parking. MARTA: Lakewood/Fort McPherson (shuttle buses take patrons to and from the station).

The $15-million Lakewood Amphitheatre accommodates 19,000—7,000 reserved seats plus a sloping lawn that holds an additional 12,000. Needless to say, this is a vast facility used for major shows. Eric Clapton, Elton John, Pearl Jam, and Aerosmith have all performed here. There are umbrellaed picnic tables on the grounds, and though you can't bring in food or drink, a wide variety of refreshments is available, including beer, champagne, fruit and cheese, sandwiches, pizza—and of course Coca-Cola.

Fox Theatre

660 Peachtree St. NE (at Ponce de Leon Ave.). ☎ **404/881-2100** for information or 404/817-8700 to charge tickets. Many paid parking lots nearby. MARTA: North Avenue.

Built in 1927, when movie theaters were conceived along lavish lines, the Fox is a Moorish-Egyptian extravaganza complete with arabesque arches, onion domes, and minarets. Its exotic interior reflects the Egytomania of that decade—a phenomenon resulting from archaeologist Henry Carter's discovery of the treasure-laden tomb of King Tut. Throne chairs, scarab motifs, and hieroglyphics are seen throughout the theater, and the auditorium evokes a Middle Eastern courtyard under an azure sky. See chapter 7 for details on the Fox's history and architecture, as well as information on tours. The Fox is home to the **Atlanta Opera** and the **Atlanta Ballet** (see above). In addition, a wide spectrum of headliners plays the Fox, along with diverse entertainment ranging from Broadway musicals to rock 'n' roll.

Variety Playhouse

1099 Euclid Ave. (near Washita St.). ☎ **404/521-1786** for information. Paid parking lot on Euclid Ave. near Colquitt Ave.

Built in Little Five Points in the 1930s as a neighborhood movie theater, the Variety today is an intimate concert hall offering an eclectic array of performances, from folk rock to jazz. There are also frequent album-release parties here. It's definitely worth checking out.

2 The Club & Music Scene

Nightclubs come and go, so it's always a good idea to call ahead. Most clubs are open until 2, 3, or even 4am.

DANCE CLUBS

Cotton Club

1021 Peachtree St. NE (between Tenth and Eleventh sts.). ☎ **404/874-1993.** www. atlantaconcerts.com. Cover $6–$10. Parking $2 in the lot behind the club on Juniper St. MARTA: Midtown.

With a dance floor stretching across the front of the stage, this rock 'n' roll club is the place for people who like to be close to the action. A full bar is located on each side of the sprawling stage, and seating is available on a second tier that surrounds the dance floor. The Cotton Club hosts a variety of popular bands, including Fastball, Dishwalla, Cowboy Mouth, Seven Mary Three, and even '80s favorite, The Outfield. Tickets are available at TicketMaster (☎) 404/249-6400 and at the door, but tickets go fast for big name bands.

Johnny's Hideaway

3771 Roswell Rd. (2 blocks north of Piedmont Rd.). ☎ **404/233-8026.** www. johnnyshideaway.com. No cover, but there's a 2-drink minimum after 8pm. Free self and valet parking.

"Atlanta's Only Nightclub for Big Kids" has been one of Atlanta's top nightspots for nearly 20 years. Ebullient host Johnny Esposito, always on hand to greet his guests, is a well-known Atlanta character. The music sweeps through the decades, from the big-band era to the '80s, attracting a crowd of all ages. The music gets "younger" as the night wears on, and the patrons do too. This is a place for serious dancing, and though it's unpretentious, there are celebrities who drop by when in town (George Clooney and Robert Duvall). Check out the Frank Sinatra Room, filled with over 100 pieces of memorabilia. A reasonably priced menu lists items ranging from deli sandwiches to prime-rib main courses. Attire is dressy-casual.

Masquerade

695 North Ave. NE (just east of Boulevard). ☎ **404/577-8178.** www.masq.com. Cover $5 in Hell and Purgatory ($8 for ages 18–20); $2–$20 (depending on the performer) in Heaven; Music Park tickets vary with the performer. Parking $3–$5.

Housed in a century-old stone-walled Romanesque building—a former excelsior factory—Masquerade looks like the Bastille. Its interior, divided into three main areas: Heaven, Hell, and Purgatory, are all appropriately decorated. Up in Heaven, live local and national acts perform (the latter have included Crystal Method, Anthrax, Jesus and Mary Chain, and Judas Priest). Call the hotline at **404/577-2007** for information. Sunday is Swing Night, when young and old groove to the tunes of the Big Band Era. Lessons begin at 8pm.

✪ Otto's

265 E. Paces Ferry Rd. NE (1 block off Peachtree Rd.). ☎ **404/233-1133.** Cover $10 for men, no cover for women Thurs–Sat; $20 per person on Sun. Paid parking in 2 lots on East Paces Ferry; have your ticket validated for a discount.

This elegant, upscale Buckhead club attracts a sophisticated, well-dressed older crowd (mostly singles in their late 20s, 30s, and 40s) looking for dancing and easy-listening music. There are six separate bar areas, all with different themes, on two floors. Upstairs, where a deejay plays dance music Friday through Sunday, there are three sleek bars with either tables or comfortable couches; downstairs there's a scotch and cigar room. The main bar (with a dance floor) features a live band Thursday through Saturday—blues, jazz, soft pop, or a cabaret-type show. The dress code frowns on T-shirts, tennis shoes, and baseball caps.

Tongue & Groove

3055 Peachtree Rd. (between East Paces Ferry Rd. and Buckhead Ave.). ☎ **404/261-2325.** www.tongueandgroove-atl.com. Cover $10 for women, $10 for men Wed–Sat; $5 cover for men, no cover for women on Tuesday; no cover on Sunday. Paid parking across Peachtree Rd.

Really more of an elegant cocktail lounge than a dance club, Tongue & Groove attracts a chic upscale crowd—an older group than at many Buckhead establishments. The spacious interior is on the plush side, with glossy oak floors and lofty ceilings. The deejayed dance music has a different theme every night—everything from swing to disco to Latin dances. The bar food is out of the ordinary (sushi, yakitori skewers, wontons, etc.), and there's also a wide selection of fine wines and champagnes. T & G enforces a strict dress code, so lose the jeans, caps, and sport shoes. You must be 23 to get in.

Note: On Friday and Saturday nights, the Buckhead streets surrounding T & G and Otto's are mobbed with revelers, and numerous nightspots in the area make this an ideal base for club-hopping.

Yin Yang Café

64 Third St. NE (between Spring St. and I-75/I-85 at Georgia Tech). ☎ **404/607-0682.** E-mail: reidluster@mindspring.com. Cover $5–$7 Tues–Sat.

This hip and happening live music venue is comfortable, casual, and candlelit, with exposed brick walls used to display funky exhibitions by local artists. There's a pool table and dance floor, and some couches in the back room provide a conversation area. The crowd that gathers here is an eclectic mix of all ages. Every evening features a musical showcase, ranging from live on Mondays to straight-ahead classical jazz on Saturday. Sunday is ladies' night, no cover, with deejays mixing the dance tunes. The cafe has a full bar and menu.

JAZZ CLUBS

A Point of View at Nikolai's Roof

255 Courtland St. (in the Atlanta Hilton and Towers hotel). ☎ **404/659-2000.** Complimentary valet parking. MARTA: Peachtree Center.

For a spectacular view of the city, take a ride to the 30th floor of the Atlanta Hilton and have a drink at this upscale lounge. The bar specializes in scotch, cigars, and infused vodkas. There's a jazz ensemble on Wednesday nights, very laid-back and mellow. You'll find a sophisticated group—business types, convention goers, and downtown diners who've come to take a gander at the skyline after dark.

Dante's Down the Hatch

3380 Peachtree Rd. NE (across the street from the Lenox Square mall). ☎ **404/266-1600.** Cover $6 for seating on the jazz ship, free on the wharf. MARTA: Buckhead.

This jazz supper club is the realm of Dante Stephensen, who mans the decks of this well-rigged schooner, a fantasy 18th-century ship (actually afloat in murky waters) in a colorful seaport village. It's a mix of antiques and nautical kitsch. There are many intimate seating areas, but the most romantic spot is in semi-enclosed private "cabins" on the lower deck where the Paul Mitchell Trio plays traditional jazz. Earlier in the evening, classical folk guitarists perform on the "wharf," and weekend nights a solo pianist plays on the ship prior to the show. If you wish to have dinner during the show, the specialty is fondue, available by special reservation only.

Sambuca Jazz Cafe

3102 Piedmont Road NE (between Peachtree and East Paces Ferry rds.). ☎ **404/237-5299.** Free valet parking.

Part restaurant, part jazz club, Sambuca is the third in a new string of jazz cafes; the first two were in Texas. The bar is chic and large, and there's almost always a wait to get in, especially as the evening wears on. The big attraction here is the bar, not the restaurant, where there's a combo on the bandstand each night and a crowd on the dance floor. There are upscale couples and singles, often four-deep at the bar, and everyone is sharply dressed. The bar opens daily at 4:30pm.

A COMEDY CLUB

Punchline Comedy Club

280 Hildebrand Dr. NE (off Roswell Rd. in the Balconies Shopping Center), Sandy Springs. ☎ **404/252-5233.** Cover $8–$15 Tues–Thurs and Sun, $10–$15 Fri, $12–$15 Sat. Free parking.

This popular suburban comedy club, about a 40-minute drive from downtown, features pros on the national comedy-club circuit—the comedians you see on Leno and Letterman, like the Amazing Jonathan or Judy Tenuta. Doors open an hour before showtime. Reasonably priced food is offered, along with a full bar. Thursday and early Friday shows are smoke-free. Though you can buy tickets at the club, they often sell out, so it's best to reserve by phone. You must be 21 and have a valid ID to get in.

ACOUSTIC/FOLK

Eddie's Attic

515–B N. McDonough St., Decatur (next to the old courthouse on the square). ☎ **404/ 377-4976.** www.eddiesattic.com. E-mail: eddiesattic@mindspring.com. Cover $3–$10. Parking available on the square or at the lot on Church St., directly behind Eddie's. MARTA: Decatur.

Eddie's Attic is the city's most popular venue for acoustic singer/songwriters. The Indigo Girls, Billy Pilgrim, and Shawn Mullins started their careers here. The tavern is divided into three main sections. The attic's main bar is perfect for music lovers with its small stage, intimate arrangement of seats, and excellent acoustics. Rowdier folks are invited into the pool room or onto the covered patio, where there's a full bar and TV monitors playing the live performance from the main stage. The entire family is welcome for a 7pm nonsmoking show on Friday and Saturday. There is a full menu, mostly typical bar fare.

KENNY'S ALLEY IN UNDERGROUND ATLANTA

Since so many nightclubs offering varying entertainment formats are grouped conveniently at Underground Atlanta, Kenny's Alley club-hopping is very popular.

Dante's Down the Hatch

60 Upper Alabama St. SW (Kenny's Alley). ☎ **404/577-1800.** Cover $2 for acoustic guitar on the wharf, $6 for weekend jazz on the ship. MARTA: Five Points.

This is the original Dante's, the prototype for the Buckhead branch described, under Jazz Clubs above. The most interesting features of this club, though, are the historic sites highlighted inside. A sign informs visitors, for instance, that an exposed wall of the hatchway staircase is from the 1850s Planter Hotel and is the actual site of the hospital depicted in *Gone With the Wind.* An 1810 well on the premises was the water source for Atlanta's first fire department, and a steam engine on view powered the Frank E. Block Candy Company from 1868 to 1888. Like the Buckhead club, this is a fantasy ship moored in crocodile-infested waters, and there's plenty of nautical ambience. A singer and guitar player entertain on the "wharf," while on weekends there's jazz on the "ship." Fondue dinners are featured (see details, under Jazz Clubs, above Buckhead listing).

Fat Tuesday

50 Upper Alabama St. SW (Kenny's Alley). ☎ **404/523-7404.** No cover. MARTA: Five Points.

This New Orleans–concept club has a bar similar to a Mardi Gras float, but adorned with busts of Rhett and Scarlett. Special machines behind the bar mix over 20 flavors of frozen daiquiris—margarita, peach colada (that's mixed with peaches, rum, ice cream, and coconut cream), white Russian, and more—and you can sample an ounce of any flavor on the house. Po'boy sandwiches are also available. Rock and top-40 tapes are played at an ear-splitting level. IDs are checked at the door: You have to be 21.

Note: Fat Tuesday has another location in Buckhead at 3167 Peachtree Rd. NE (☎ **404/233-9584**).

3 The Bar Scene

Atkins Park

794 N. Highland Ave. NE (at St. Charles Place, 1 block north of Ponce de Leon Ave.). ☎ **404/876-7249.** Some free parking in lot off St. Charles; paid parking in nearby lots.

There's a mix here of casually dressed neighborhood regulars and young adults from other parts of town. The atmosphere is friendly and the ambience mellow and comfortable. Atkins Park began as a deli in 1922 (it holds the oldest existing tavern license in the city) and now includes a full-scale restaurant that stays open until 11pm on weeknights and midnight on Friday and Saturday. After that, better-than-average bar food is available. Atkins Park is known as the place to go for Jagermeister; it sells more than almost any other bar in Atlanta. Things get louder when the restaurant closes and the music (rock, blues, and jazz) is turned up.

Champions

At the Marriott Marquis, 265 Peachtree Center Ave. (between Baker and Harris sts.). ☎ **404/586-6017.** MARTA: Peachtree Center.

Champions is the quintessential sports bar. The circular oak bar is plastered with thousands of baseball cards under a laminated surface, and 27 TVs and two large screens air nonstop sporting events. If all the testosterone is too much for you, there's a patio with a full bar. Sports celebrities tend to stop in when in town. There's a serious Braves collection where you can buy autographed balls, bats, and more.

Dark Horse Tavern

816 N. Highland Ave. NE (2 blocks north of Ponce de Leon Ave.). ☎ **404/873-3607.** Cover $3–$5 for entertainment downstairs. Free parking in lot around back; paid lot across the street.

This tavern is primarily a neighborhood hangout during the week, but it attracts a mix of young professionals and college students on the weekend. There's live entertainment downstairs Tuesday through Saturday, featuring everything from swing music to alternative rock. Upstairs there's a dining area serving solid American fare, where you can eat, drink, and socialize into the wee hours. For major sporting events, there's a big-screen TV.

✪ Fado'

3035 Peachtree Rd. NE (at the corner of Buckhead Ave., just south of East Paces Ferry Rd.).
☎ **404/841-0066.** E-mail: fadoatlanta@mindspring.com. Limited parking on neighboring streets; $5 valet parking out back.

If you haven't had a good glass of Guinness since your last trip to Dublin, Fado' (Gaelic for "long ago") is the place to pause for a pint or two. The interior is divided into five pub areas, each one distinct from the next: a cottage pub with a peat-burning fireplace, a Victorian pub with dark wood and stained glass, and so on. It's a pleasant, unhurried atmosphere, but only in the early evening before the serious revelers invade. After that it's loud and crowded. There's a traditional Irish session Monday night, and Celtic music on Wednesday, Saturday, and Sunday afternoons. A full menu is served until 11pm, until 9pm on Thursday, Friday, and Saturday. The Irish fare is good, especially the boxty (the Irish version of potato pancake) and the fish and chips in Guinness batter.

John Harvard's Brew House

3041 Peachtree Rd. NE (at Buckhead Ave.). ☎ **404/816-2739.** www.johnharvards.com. Limited free parking on neighboring streets; paid parking nearby.

The first of Atlanta's brewhouses, John Harvard's is still one of the best—appropriately dim and pubby with the exception of the gleaming brewery itself. It's right in the middle of Buckhead nightclub territory, and it really packs in the crowds on Thursday, Friday, and Saturday nights. If you prefer a quieter time, come in early evening or during the day, when the pub caters to a business lunch crowd. The food's good, but most folks come here for the beer. The Scotch Ale was voted the best in the country at the '97 Great American Beer Festival. Out back is a large, pleasant patio.

✪ Manuel's Tavern

602 N. Highland Ave. NE (at North Ave.). ☎ **404/525-3447.** Free parking.

Not far from the yuppieness of Virginia-Highland and the funkiness of Little Five Points is an authentic neighborhood bar that's been a gathering spot for over 40 years. Owned by former DeKalb County chief executive officer Manuel Maloof, it's a regular watering hole for journalists, politicos, cops, students, and writers. Former President Jimmy Carter often drops by with the Secret Service in tow. The main bar, with its dark wood and large booths, is the best spot in the building, but there are two larger rooms with tables to accommodate the considerable crowds. It's lots of fun to watch the Braves here if you can't get tickets to the game. There's a full bar with 16 beers on tap, and at least 25 more bottled beers. The food is good, but it is bar food (wings, burgers, sandwiches, salads).

Mumbo Jumbo

89 Park Place NE (at Woodruff Park). ☎ **404/523-0330.** Paid parking in nearby garages. MARTA: Peachtree Center.

If you're looking for a place to see and be seen, this is the ticket. Downtown's hottest nightspot since it opened just before the Olympics, it's full of beautiful people, old and young—professionals, high-rollers, and creative types dressed in the very latest. Be sure to wear black or you'll stick out like a sore thumb. There's a 50-foot bar downstairs and a luxurious cigar lounge upstairs. The crowd becomes louder and more avant-garde as the night rolls on, but it's high-energy posturing all evening. Consider having dinner here before you repair to the lounge; the food is good.

Star Community Bar

437 Moreland Ave. NE (between Euclid and Mansfield aves.). ☎ **404/681-9018.** Cover $5–$10. Free parking in a lot behind the club.

Housed in a former bank, this funky and cavernous club features the "Grace-Vault"—a small shrine filled with Elvis posters, an all-Elvis jukebox, Elvis clocks, and other memorabilia. Primarily a Little Five Points neighborhood hangout, it's very low-key and offbeat. Live music Wednesday through Sunday nights runs the gamut from rockabilly to rock 'n' roll and R&B. Most of the performers are local and regional, but occasionally bigger names play here as well.

Treehouse Restaurant and Pub

7 King's Circle (just off Peachtree Hills Ave.). ☎ **404/266-2732.** Free parking.

Nestled among the towering trees and quaint houses of this Peachtree Hills neighborhood, the Treehouse features a wrap-around wooden deck, spotted with umbrella-covered tables and potted plants. The crowd is mostly locals, but its European charm sometimes attracts international visitors. Inside you'll find the rustic decor of a cabin in the woods; there's even a fireplace downstairs. The Treehouse offers over 80 microbrews and 40 imports and a menu that ranges from basic appetizers to full entrees.

A GAY & LESBIAN BAR

Otherside

1924 Piedmont Rd. (just north of Cheshire Bridge Rd.). ☎ **404/875-5238.** E-mail: otherside@mindspring.com. Cover $5 Wed and Fri–Sat; free Mon, Tues, Thurs, and Sun. Limited free parking; valet parking $3.

Otherside is a relaxed, slightly unhinged place to hang out and dance, where conversation is provocatively unpredictable. The clientele is described as "gay and straight, black and white, bi and tri, pre- and post-op." There's a full bar (specializing in martinis), billiards, video games, and a large-screen TV that airs videos appropriate to the evening's entertainment—for instance, rodeo footage on country music night. There's a deejay most nights except Friday and Saturday, when there's live entertainment. Sunday features female impersonation. Otherside has the unfortunate distinction of being the target of a terrorist bomb in recent years. The bomb was disabled and no one was injured, but authorities believe that the person who planted the bomb was also responsible for the Olympic Park bombing in 1996.

4 Coffeehouses, Cafés & Late-Night Bites

Cafe Diem

640 North Highland Ave. (just south of Ponce de Leon Ave.). ☎ **404/607-7008.** www.cafediem.com. Free but limited parking.

Cafe Diem likes to call itself a "local international cafe," and the description is right on the money. You can linger here undisturbed over an espresso or glass of wine. It attracts a large number of neighborhood regulars of all ages, but it's also a magnet for foreign residents, especially students. There are poetry readings the first Tuesday of every month; Classical Day is all day Sunday, with soft music played by a local musician; and Monday night features live Brazilian music. There's a full menu and a variety of French-style coffee drinks and teas. If the weather's nice, grab a table on the patio.

Majestic Food Shop
1031 Ponce de Leon Ave. NE (west of North Highland Ave.) ☎ **404/875-0276.** Free parking.

Known simply as "the Majestic" to the locals, this 24-hour restaurant has been serving up diner food and a slice of life since 1935. You'll find obnoxious drunks, middle-class regulars, working girls, cops, street people, couples on dates, you name it. Sooner or later just about everybody comes to the Majestic for a late-night breakfast, a cup of coffee, or just to take in the scene. The late Nick Bitzis, a long-time owner who used to keep an aluminum baseball bat behind the register, once chased a group of customers with a butcher knife for smoking pot in one of the booths. The Majestic is open 24 hours, and things invariably get more interesting as the night wears on.

Red Light Cafe
553 W. Amsterdam Ave. (between Monroe Dr. and Piedmont Park). ☎ **404/874-7828.** www.redlightcafe.com. E-mail: redlight@mindspring.com. Cover $3–$5. Plenty of free parking.

As one of the first cyber cafes in the nation, this classic San Francisco–style coffeehouse with a funky red-walled, high-ceilinged interior decked with a mix of tables and comfy sofas, offers a mix of art, music, conversation, and beverages. After surfing the Web, you can view changing art exhibitions displayed on a gallery-white wall, sip port or beer (microbrewery, imported or draft) on the patio, and order from the menu that lists salads, fresh pastas, and sandwiches.

Virginia's
1243 Virginia Ave. (between Briarcliff and Rosedale rds.). ☎ **404/875-4453.** Free parking.

If you're having dinner in Virginia-Highland, Virginia's is a perfect, candlelit spot to continue your after-dinner conversation—especially if you're not up for one of the more energetic nightspots. The place to be is the patio, a secret garden with seating under a bamboo-twig awning. No liquor is served, but there are dozens of varieties of coffee and tea to choose from, not to mention ice cream sodas, hot chocolate with marshmallows, and Thai iced tea. Dessert, too. Open daily until 11pm.

Appendix: Useful Toll-Free Numbers & Web Sites

AIRLINES

Air Canada
☎ 800/776-3000
www.aircanada.ca

Alaska Airlines
☎ 800/426-0333
www.alaskaair.com

American Airlines
☎ 800/433-7300
www.americanair.com

America West Airlines
☎ 800/235-9292
www.americawest.com

British Airways
☎ 800/247-9297
☎ 0345/222-111 in Britain
www.british-airways.com

Canadian Airlines International
☎ 800/426-7000
www.cdnair.ca

Continental Airlines
☎ 800/525-0280
www.flycontinental.com

Delta Air Lines
☎ 800/221-1212
www.delta-air.com

Hawaiian Airlines
☎ 800/367-5320
www.hawaiianair.com

Kiwi International Air Lines
☎ 800/538-5494
www.jetkiwi.com

Midway Airlines
☎ 800/446-4392

Northwest Airlines
☎ 800/225-2525
www.nwa.com

Southwest Airlines
☎ 800/435-9792
www.iflyswa.com

Tower Air
☎ 800/34-TOWER
  (800/348-6937)
www.towerair.com

Trans World Airlines (TWA)
☎ 800/221-2000
www.twa.com

United Airlines
☎ 800/241-6522
www.ual.com

US Airways
☎ 800/428-4322
www.usairways.com

Virgin Atlantic Airways
☎ 800/862-8621 in the
  Continental U.S.
☎ 0293/747-747 in Britain
www.fly.virgin.com

CAR RENTAL AGENCIES

Advantage
☎ 800/777-5500
www.arac.com

Alamo
☎ 800/327-9633
www.goalamo.com

Auto Europe
☎ 800/223-5555
www.autoeurope.com

Avis
☎ 800/331-1212 in the Continental U.S.
☎ 800/TRY-AVIS in Canada
www.avis.com

Budget
☎ 800/527-0700
www.budgetrentacar.com

Dollar
☎ 800/800-4000
www.dollarcar.com

Enterprise
☎ 800/325-8007
www.pickenterprise.com

Hertz
☎ 800/654-3131
www.hertz.com

Kemwel Holiday Auto
☎ 800/678-0678
www.kemwel.com

National
☎ 800/CAR-RENT
www.nationalcar.com

Payless
☎ 800/PAYLESS
www.paylesscar.com

Rent-A-Wreck
☎ 800/535-1391
rent-a-wreck.com

Thrifty
☎ 800/367-2277
www.thrifty.com

Value
☎ 800/327-2501
www.go-value.com

MAJOR HOTEL & MOTEL CHAINS

Best Western International
☎ 800/528-1234
www.bestwestern.com

Clarion Hotels
☎ 800/CLARION
www.hotelchoice.com/
    cgi-bin/res/webres?clarion.html

Comfort Inns
☎ 800/228-5150
www.hotelchoice.com/
    cgi-bin/res/webres?comfort.html

Courtyard by Marriott
☎ 800/321-2211
www.courtyard.com

Days Inn
☎ 800/325-2525
www.daysinn.com

Doubletree Hotels
☎ 800/222-TREE
www.doubletreehotels.com

Econo Lodges
☎ 800/55-ECONO
www.hotelchoice.com/
    cgi-bin/res/webres?econo.html

Fairfield Inn by Marriott
☎800/228-2800
www.fairfieldinn.com

Hampton Inn
☎ 800/HAMPTON
www.hampton-inn.com

Hilton Hotels
☎ 800/HILTONS
www.hilton.com

Holiday Inn
☎ 800/HOLIDAY
www.holiday-inn.com

Howard Johnson
☎ 800/654-2000
www.hojo.com/hojo.html

Hyatt Hotels & Resorts
☎ 800/228-9000
www.hyatt.com

ITT Sheraton
☎ 800/325-3535
www.sheraton.com

La Quinta Motor Inns
☎ 800/531-5900
www.laquinta.com

Marriott Hotels
☎ 800/228-9290
www.marriott.com

Motel 6
☎ 800/4-MOTEL6 (800/466-8536)

Quality Inns
☎ 800/228-5151
www.hotelchoice.com/
    cgi-bin/res/webres?quality.html

Radisson Hotels International
☎ 800/333-3333
www.radisson.com

Ramada Inns
☎ 800/2-RAMADA
www.ramada.com

Red Carpet Inns
☎ 800/251-1962

Red Lion Hotels & Inns
☎ 800/547-8010
www.travelweb.com

Red Roof Inns
☎ 800/843-7663
www.redroof.com

Residence Inn by Marriott
☎ 800/331-3131
www.residenceinn.com

Rodeway Inns
☎ 800/228-2000
www.hotelchoice.com/
    cgi-bin/res/webres?rodeway.html

Super 8 Motels
☎ 800/800-8000
www.super8motels.com

Travelodge
☎ 800/255-3050

Vagabond Inns
☎ 800/522-1555
www.vagabondinns.com

Wyndham Hotels and Resorts
☎ 800/822-4200 in Continental U.S.
    and Canada
www.wyndham.com

Index

FROMMER'S® COMPLETE TRAVEL GUIDES

Alaska
Amsterdam
Arizona
Atlanta
Australia
Austria
Bahamas
Barcelona, Madrid & Seville
Belgium, Holland &
  Luxembourg
Bermuda
Boston
Budapest & the Best of
  Hungary
California
Canada
Cancún, Cozumel &
  the Yucatán
Cape Cod, Nantucket &
  Martha's Vineyard
Caribbean
Caribbean Cruises & Ports
  of Call
Caribbean Ports of Call
Carolinas & Georgia
Chicago
China
Colorado
Costa Rica
Denver, Boulder &
  Colorado Springs
England
Europe
Florida

France
Germany
Greece
Greek Islands
Hawaii
Hong Kong
Honolulu, Waikiki & Oahu
Ireland
Israel
Italy
Jamaica & Barbados
Japan
Las Vegas
London
Los Angeles
Maryland & Delaware
Maui
Mexico
Miami & the Keys
Montana & Wyoming
Montréal & Québec City
Munich & the Bavarian Alps
Nashville & Memphis
Nepal
New England
New Mexico
New Orleans
New York City
Nova Scotia, New Brunswick
  & Prince Edward Island
Oregon
Paris
Philadelphia & the
  Amish Country

Portugal
Prague & the Best of the
  Czech Republic
Provence & the Riviera
Puerto Rico
Rome
San Antonio & Austin
San Diego
San Francisco
Santa Fe, Taos &
  Albuquerque
Scandinavia
Scotland
Seattle & Portland
Singapore & Malaysia
South Pacific
Spain
Switzerland
Thailand
Tokyo
Toronto
Tuscany & Umbria
USA
Utah
Vancouver & Victoria
Vermont, New Hampshire
  & Maine
Vienna & the Danube Valley
Virgin Islands
Virginia
Walt Disney World &
  Orlando
Washington, D.C.
Washington State

FROMMER'S® DOLLAR-A-DAY GUIDES

Australia from $50 a Day
California from $60 a Day
Caribbean from $60 a Day
England from $60 a Day
Europe from $50 a Day
Florida from $60 a Day

Greece from $50 a Day
Hawaii from $60 a Day
Ireland from $50 a Day
Israel from $45 a Day
Italy from $50 a Day
London from $75 a Day

New York from $75 a Day
New Zealand from $50 a Day
Paris from $70 a Day
San Francisco from $60 a Day
Washington, D.C.,
  from $60 a Day

FROMMER'S® PORTABLE GUIDES

Acapulco, Ixtapa &
  Zihuatanejo
Alaska Cruises & Ports of Call
Bahamas
California Wine Country
Charleston & Savannah
Chicago

Dublin
Las Vegas
London
Maine Coast
New Orleans
New York City
Paris

Puerto Vallarta, Manzanillo
  & Guadalajara
San Francisco
Sydney
Tampa & St. Petersburg
Venice
Washington, D.C.

FROMMER'S® NATIONAL PARK GUIDES

Family Vacations in the
   National Parks
Grand Canyon

National Parks of the
   American West
Yellowstone & Grand Teton

Yosemite & Sequoia/
   Kings Canyon
Zion & Bryce Canyon

FROMMER'S® GREAT OUTDOOR GUIDES

New England
Northern California

Southern California & Baja
Pacific Northwest

FROMMER'S® MEMORABLE WALKS

Chicago
London

New York
Paris

San Francisco
Washington D.C.

FROMMER'S® IRREVERENT GUIDES

Amsterdam
Boston
Chicago

London
Manhattan

New Orleans
Paris

San Francisco
Walt Disney World
Washington, D.C.

FROMMER'S® BEST-LOVED DRIVING TOURS

America
Britain
California

Florida
France
Germany

Ireland
Italy
New England

Scotland
Spain
Western Europe

THE COMPLETE IDIOT'S TRAVEL GUIDES

Boston
Cruise Vacations
Planning Your Trip to Europe
Hawaii

Las Vegas
London
Mexico's Beach Resorts
New Orleans

New York City
San Francisco
Walt Disney World
Washington D.C.

THE UNOFFICIAL GUIDES®

Branson, Missouri
California with Kids
Chicago
Cruises
Disney Companion

Florida with Kids
The Great Smoky &
   Blue Ridge
   Mountains

Las Vegas
Miami & the Keys
Mini-Mickey
New Orleans

New York City
San Francisco
Skiing in the West
Walt Disney World
Washington, D.C.

SPECIAL-INTEREST TITLES

Born to Shop: Caribbean Ports of Call
Born to Shop: France
Born to Shop: Hong Kong
Born to Shop: Italy
Born to Shop: New York
Born to Shop: Paris
Frommer's Britain's Best Bike Rides
The Civil War Trust's Official Guide
   to the Civil War Discovery Trail
Frommer's Caribbean Hideaways
Frommer's Europe's Greatest Driving Tours
Frommer's Food Lover's Companion to France
Frommer's Food Lover's Companion to Italy
Frommer's Gay & Lesbian Europe

Israel Past & Present
Monks' Guide to California
Monks' Guide to New York City
New York City with Kids
New York Times Weekends
Outside Magazine's Guide
   to Family Vacations
Places Rated Almanac
Retirement Places Rated
Washington, D.C., with Kids
Wonderful Weekends from Boston
Wonderful Weekends from New York City
Wonderful Weekends from San Francisco
Wonderful Weekends from Los Angeles